The Siege of Atlanta, 1864

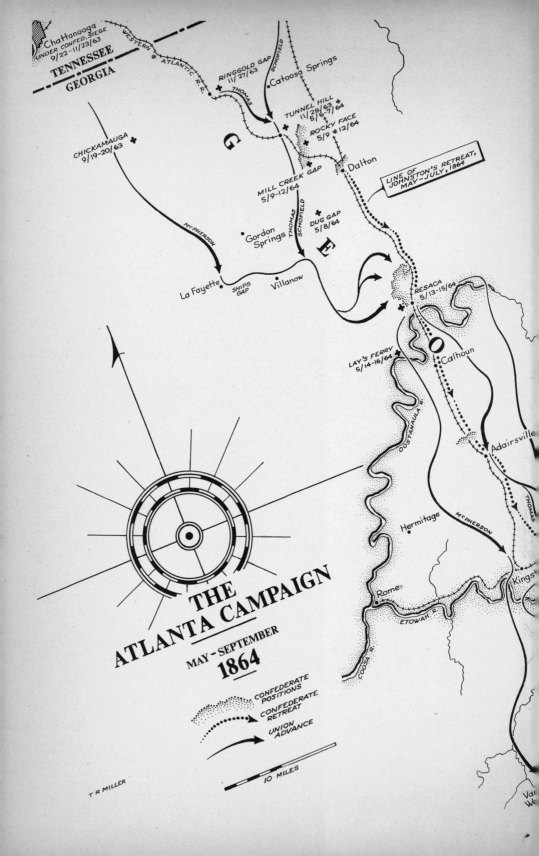

THE ATLANTA CAMPAIGN

MAY - SEPTEMBER
1864

CONFEDERATE
POSITIONS

CONFEDERATE
RETREAT

UNION
ADVANCE

10 MILES

T R MILLER

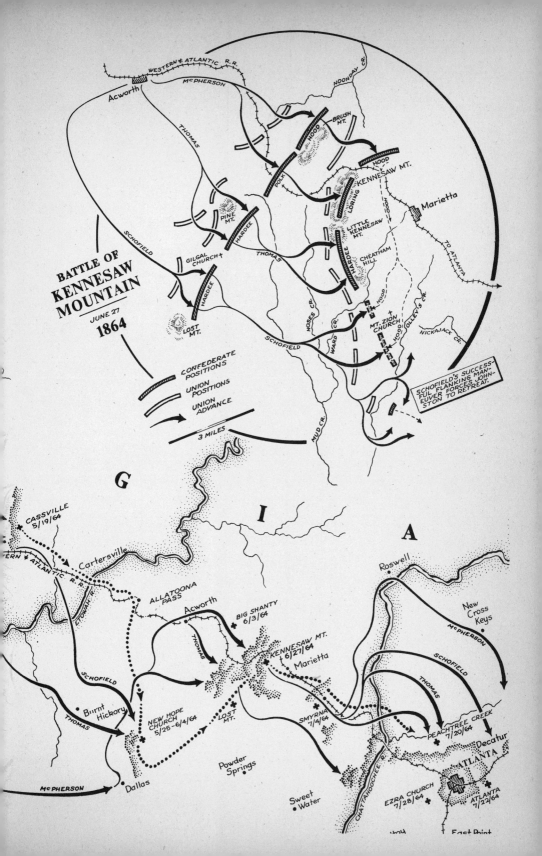

BATTLE OF KENNESAW MOUNTAIN

—— JUNE 27 ——
1864

CONFEDERATE
POSITIONS

UNION
POSITIONS

UNION
ADVANCE

3 MILES

SCHOFIELD'S SUCCESS-
FUL FLANKING MAN-
EUVER FORCES JOHN-
STON TO RETREAT.

WESTERN & ATLANTIC R.R.

McPHERSON

Acworth

NOONDAY CR.

THOMAS

BRUSH MT.

HOOD

HOOD

KENNESAW MT.

SCHOFIELD

PINE MT.

POLK

LORING

LITTLE KENNESAW MT.

Marietta

GILGAL CHURCH

HARDEE

THOMAS

HARDEE

CHEATHAM HILL

TO ATLANTA

HARDEE

HOOD

LOST MT.

NOSES CR.

WARD CR.

SCHOFIELD

MT. ZION CHURCH

HOG JOLLEY'S CR.

NICKAJACK CR.

MUD CR.

G

I

A

CASSVILLE 5/19/64

ERN & ATLANTIC R.R.

Cartersville

ALLATOONA PASS

ETOWAH R.

Acworth

BIG SHANTY 6/3/64

THOMAS

Roswell

New Cross Keys

McPHERSON

KENNESAW MT. 6/27/64

Marietta

SCHOFIELD

SCHOFIELD

THOMAS

PEACHTREE CREEK 7/20/64

THOMAS

Burnt Hickory

NEW HOPE CHURCH 5/25-6/4/64

LOST MT.

SMYRNA 7/4/64

Decatur

McPHERSON

Dallas

Powder Springs

CHATTAHOOCHEE R.R.

ATLANTA

Sweet Water

EZRA CHURCH 7/28/64

ATLANTA 7/22/64

East Point

The Siege

of Atlanta, 1864

SAMUEL CARTER III

Bonanza Books · New York

For Helen
because she was always there, and cared.

Contents

Maps

Designed and executed by Theodore R. Miller

Acknowledgments

Wars and battles long past have a way of sliding back into contemporary focus, bridging both time and generation gaps. More than half a century ago, 1919 to be exact, veteran journalist Edward Lowry returned from Europe, brooding over the devastated towns of France and Belgium and the mammoth task of reconstruction facing the ravaged countries of the Great War. He had been to Arras, Cambrai, Ypres, St. Quentin, Lens, and Amiens, and had been "stunned and dazed" by the destruction.

So had many others, both the curious and the concerned. But the difference, applying to Lowry's case, was this. As a child in nineteenth century Georgia he had seen also the swath that Sherman had cut through his native state, and had heard at first hand of the devastation of Atlanta in the autumn of that year. Now, comparing the two in his mind—Europe and the South —he concluded that if Atlanta could come back so resolutely and so quickly, as indeed it had, then any city on earth could do the same. Others, he found, agreed. In the wake of the First World War, the most destructive man had known, Atlanta stood as a beacon of hope to a generation tempted to abandon hope.

The same may be true today, when reconstruction in the

wake of war is the primary task of a world recovering its sanity. No city in America, before or since, has been more thoroughly destroyed than was Atlanta in the last full year of Civil War. And no city in the past one hundred years has moved ahead so far, so fast, and with so little doubt about its glowing future. If the old Atlanta is gone forever, the new Atlanta is a veritable Camelot of marble, glass, and steel.

Yet the city, in striving for progress, has never yielded to the human tendency to overlook the dark days in its past. Perhaps that is the source of its vitality—the awareness that it has built upon the ruins of another Troy—that has pulled it out of the ashes with little more than human sweat and perseverance. A fact as big as a monument. Atlanta does not choose to forget; it cares to remember.

Not far from the site of one of the first great battles for the city, in the vicinity of Peachtree Creek, is the gracious Buckhead home of the Atlanta Historical Society, a treasury of private papers and collections, unpublished manuscripts, maps, genealogies, and records pertaining to Atlanta's past unmatched by any other institution in the South. This wealth of material was made available through the kind cooperation of the Society's director, Franklin M. Garrett, who surely must know more about Atlanta's past and present than any living human being.

Also to the Society's archivist, Richard T. Eltzroth, my thanks are due for direction and counsel in exploring this material. While many documents and papers used in this work, and sometimes quoted, are mentioned in the bibliography, it would be impossible to list every item that slipped into the story in the course of writing.

From the Robert W. Woodruff Library, at Emory University, came the letters of Andrew Jackson Neal and other Confederate letters and diaries cited in these pages. For the opportunity to review these papers and for his permission to quote therefrom, my thanks to David B. Estes, who heads the Special Collections Department of the Library. Records of individual Confederate soldiers were also obtained from the Georgia Department of Archives and History, and from its six-volume roster of men who served with Georgia volunteer units between 1861 and 1865.

At Georgia State University in downtown Atlanta, much is owed to Miss Marie Tedesco of the Department of History, and to her untiring diligence in tracking down hard-to-find material and data. Without her research aid, the story of Atlanta's days of peril would be left with many gaps. Would there were more whose native curiosity and perseverance were available to the historian.

The excellent Atlanta Public Library with its Margaret Mitchell Room, the files of the Georgia Historical Society, and the University of Georgia Libraries all contributed much of value to this work. From the University's list of Confederate Reprints came an item of personal as well as historical interest: the original words and music for the Southern ballad *Lorena*, whose lyrics are, in part, reprinted in pages following.

A special word of gratitude should go to Norman Shavin of Atlanta, creator of *The Atlanta Century*, a monumental work which won the National Civil War Centennial Commission's First and Highest Award for Excellence. Mr. Shavin's cooperation and his permission to use this compilation of contemporary news and comments as a chronological guide and as a source of invaluable material is greatly appreciated.

Since the campaign for Atlanta was a two-way affair, with the North as vitally concerned as the South, much material regarding the Federal armies, their officers and personnel, was obtained from New England sources, notably Yale University, Trinity College, Dartmouth's Baker Library, Fairfield University, and the Connecticut State Library at Hartford which contains the massive 128-volume set of the *War of the Rebellion: The Official Records of the Union and Confederate Armies*, compiled by the United States War Department over a twenty-one-year period.

At the National Archives in Washington, ever a substantial source of Civil War material, my thanks extend especially to Mr. Elmer Parker for his research guidance; while at the Library of Congress the kind advice of Mr. Milton Kaplan, author of the Civil War history, *Divided We Fought*, led to the obtaining of much material and many of the illustrations for this volume.

Closer to home in Connecticut, the ably staffed Ridgefield Library and the Wilton Library Association offered invaluable help in obtaining books from sources not otherwise accessible, and my thanks go to Miss Phyllis Paccadolmi of the former, and Mrs. Robert W. Given of Wilton, for their kind cooperation in this effort. And to Sibyl Martin my gratitude for her typing expertise in the preparation of the manuscript.

With an appended bibliography listing primary sources and reference material, footnotes are deliberately omitted from the text, as well as numbered references—in the writer's often expressed belief that a reader should not have to look elsewhere for information essential to the story.

If memory serves correctly, it was Arnold Toynbee who said, in effect, that no piece of historical evidence would stand up in a court of law. Perhaps General Sherman, confounded by the reports of his commanders, said it better in stating that no three honest witnesses could agree on the details of a simple brawl, much less a climactic battle of a major war.

Since this story is told, wherever possible, from the standpoint of eyewitnesses or those who were close to the events (and often reportorial amateurs, at that) it would be extraordinary if any two agreed precisely. Their impressions are real and human and immediate—and rarely altogether accurate. Yet they often give a truer feeling of what transpired than do professional histories compiled years later with the benefit of hindsight. As to the clashing discrepancies, one can do no more than select whatever account or version seems to fit the picture best, aware that others may not agree with the selection or interpretation.

Differences in nomenclature can be bothersome to the unwary. The South and North often gave different names to the same battles. What the Confederates referred to in 1861 as "First Manassas" was the "Battle of Bull Run" to the Union armies. Since this book is oriented on Atlanta, the Southern choice of names is generally observed throughout. Conversely, similarities can be confusing. The South's Army of Tennessee, named for the state, may be incautiously confused with the Union's Army of *the* Tennessee, named for the river. Since these two forces were often juxtaposed, one has to be on guard.

Military statistics are a necessary, generally desirable facet of a story such as this. But again, caution! When it comes to the size of armies, or units within armies, battle casualties, desertions, and the like, the North and South followed different measures and procedures. Joseph Johnston numbered his Confederates according to such arbitrary standards as those "present" (one figure) and those "effective" (another figure), while men wounded in battle were not listed as "casualties" if it was deemed possible for them later to return to service.

So unless one regards Civil War statistics as approximate, strict comparisons between the Federal and Union armies can be tricky. Sticking to round figures, however, one can feel on reasonably safe ground—remembering always that reporting commanders tended to minimize their battle losses and exaggerate the losses of the enemy. Also, compilation methods differed even at the highest levels. Thus the Surgeon General's reports of war casualties (and thus indirectly of survivors) are often at variance with those of the War Departments of both sides.

In view of such opportunities for error, and the many other construction hazards in the wide-screen story of Atlanta, abundant thanks are due to Franklin M. Garrett, dean of Atlanta historians, for consenting to review the manuscript before its publication, and for making invaluable suggestions and corrections. If at any point the text fails to measure up to his high standards, the author (probably from obstinacy) is to blame.

Finally, my gratitude to Thomas J. McCormack of St. Martin's Press for breathing life into this book with his initial suggestion; to Thomas Dunne for guiding the work through its step-by-step development; and to Malcolm Reiss, as always, for services beyond the call of duty.

The Siege of Atlanta, 1864

Warpath to Atlanta

Rocking south through Georgia at a dizzy nineteen miles an hour, the train from Charleston arrived at Fernandina around noon of Wednesday, November 7, 1860. There the stationmaster gave the news to the conductor, and it passed among the passengers. Abraham Lincoln had been elected. Mary Boykin Chesnut of Charleston heard a woman passenger exclaim: "That settles the hash!"

No somber, well-chosen words to announce the greatest crisis in the nation's history. But being from South Carolina, Mrs. Chesnut got the message, and agreed. More than any other single factor, the election of a "Black Republican" made the Civil War inevitable. For slavery was the issue, however much it might be clouded by such phrases as "states' rights" and Northern "tyranny." Before eight weeks had passed, Mary's home state would have pulled the first plug from the Union and Mary's husband, James Chesnut, Jr., would lead the exodus from Washington of senators and statesmen who had represented Southern seniority in the government since 1776.

There were those, even in 1860, who advocated caution, prudence, reason over hasty rupture. The so-called "Georgia Bloc" headed by Howell Cobb, Robert Toombs, and Alexander Stephens worked at first for compromise, but once the die was cast were militantly loyal to the Southern cause. Saying farewell to the United States Senate in which he had represented Georgia for eight years, Robert Toombs warned his Northern colleagues: "You see the glittering bayonets and you hear the tramp of armed men from your capitol to the Rio Grande. Keep us in the Union by force? Come and do it! Georgia is on the warpath! We are ready to fight now."

Ready, too, was South Carolina where the palmetto flag flew over the state the day after Lincoln's election, and where the Charleston *Mercury* declared, "The tea has been thrown overboard, the revolution of 1860 has been initiated." A hundred years later Charles Beard would call the war that was to follow "the Second American Revolution." Others would call it the War for Southern Independence, the War for Constitutional Liberty, and the War Between the States. But it was a conflict between civilian factions within the Republic and warranted no other title than the Civil War.

On December 20, 1860, in convention in Charleston, delegates declared "that the Union now subsisting between South Carolina and other states under the name of 'The United States of America' is hereby dissolved." Georgia offered to rush troops to the seceding state, as did Alabama; while South Carolina took possession of Federal property, arsenals, and forts except Fort Sumter in Charleston harbor. During January 1861, Mississippi, Florida, Alabama, Georgia, and Louisiana followed suit, with Texas making a seven-state bloc the first of February.

Even before South Carolina seceded, Georgia had advocated a convention to consider a Southern confederacy. Now, the first week in February, the convention was held, not in Georgia but in Montgomery, Alabama, with Georgian planter-politician Howell Cobb presiding. A constitution was adopted, based on that of the United States. Although Robert Toombs of Georgia was considered for the presidency of the new Confederated States of America, the final choice went to West Point graduate and former Secretary of War, Jefferson Davis—a man so much like Abraham Lincoln that they were rumored to be related.

Georgia, however—largest of the Confederated states, and largest of any state east of the Mississippi—was strongly represented in the government. Alexander H. Stephens of Talliaferro County, east of Atlanta, was elected Vice President, with ex-senator from Georgia, Robert Toombs, appointed Secretary of State. Though both would later become captious critics of the government, Toombs bitter at being passed by for the presidency, they agreed for now with the selection for the presidency of Kentucky-born Jefferson Davis.

The next two months comprised a time of apprehensive waiting, while the Southern states appropriated almost all the Federal arms and arsenals and forts within their borders. When Lincoln refused to abandon Fort Sumter, General Pierre Gustave Toutant Beauregard, in command at Charleston, ordered a battery to fire on the fort—in which a garrison lieutenant named, ironically, Jefferson Davis, would later make a reputation in the campaign for Atlanta.

The bombardment of Sumter in April, 1861, marked the point of no return. Lincoln promptly called for 75,000 troops to suppress what he branded as "rebellion," and ordered the blockading of all Southern ports. Regarding this as a declaration of war, Virginia seceded from the United States, a dissident area across the Blue Ridge Mountains forming the state of West Virginia in June of 1863. Arkansas and Tennessee followed Virginia's example. Kentucky and Missouri wavered, but arms and persuasion kept them in the Northern family, although the Bonnie Blue Flag of the South showed two stars in their honor. Reflecting another shattered hope, "Maryland, My Maryland," became a wishful Southern ballad during the war—long after Maryland had been impressed into the Union.

Somehow the rupture, brewing for twenty years, seemed suddenly unexpected, and it caught the nation unprepared. Statistically the weight was all in favor of the North. The agricultural South with a population of 8,000,000 (3,700,00 of them Negro slaves), had little going for it but King Cotton. The twenty-three states of the North contained 20,000,000 people, with a 10-to-1 superiority in manufacturing, a 30-to-1 superiority in arms production, and double the railroad mileage and telegraph facilities of the eleven Southern states—these latter assets important in a conflict that would prove to be, in large measure, dependent upon railroads and communication.

There were factors, however, which modified these bare statistics. The average Southerner, "equal to five Yankees" in Atlanta's popular opinion, was dedicated to outdoor pursuits, well adapted to campaigning, trained from infancy to hunt and ride and shoot. And the South at the start had better military leaders, more West Point graduates among its officers, despite the population gap. The vast reservoir of blacks was an asset in that slaves could be conscripted for such essential labor as building and maintaining roads and railways, bridges and fortifications, thus releasing all potential fighting men for service in the field.

There were other hidden assets in the South's position. "All we want is to be left alone," said Jefferson Davis—which meant that the Confederates had only to stand firm along their borders, and force the Federals to move from their Northern bases into unfamiliar territory against a well-positioned foe. Georgians fought with the winds of Georgia at their backs. The average Southerner was battling on native soil for home and family and for a way of life he cherished, in which bravery and chivalry played major roles. These were secret weapons capable of working miracles.

And the South believed it was protected by a cotton curtain. Three quarters of Southern cotton had been going to the textile mills of Europe which relied heavily on this supply. Sooner or later, it was felt, the need for cotton would bring England and possibly France to the defense of Southern independence. Unfortunately, recent years had yielded a bumper crop of cotton; foreign mills were well stocked; and it might take time for this support to be forthcoming.

The Confederacy, despite its somewhat cavalier attitude toward the war, moved more quickly and more surely toward preparedness. Jefferson Davis called for 100,000 twelve-month volunteers in March and, as in the Northern states, the response was gratifying; only time and the realities of combat would erode that patriotic fervor. True, on both sides these were green and untrained troops, amateurs led by officers of their own election. Most of them were under twenty years of age, some even in their early teens. This, throughout, was to be a young man's war. Even the states' militias were inexperienced, ill-equipped, and little trained beyond the demands of ceremonial parades.

In May 1861, the Confederate capital was moved from Montgomery to Richmond, partly to confirm Virginia's loyalty, and the military lines were drawn. From the gates of West Point, and from the ranks of its alumni, officers chose sides as at a ball game. Classmates Robert E. Lee and Joseph Eggleston Johnston, both of Virginia, resigned from the United States Army virtually on the same day, to become Generals in the Confederate forces. Former fellow cadets Sherman and Grant, holding civilian jobs when war broke out, accepted low ranks in the Union forces, later to rise to generals of the army. Curiously, both the latter had been misnamed. Tecumseh Sherman had been arbitrarily baptized "William" by a minister who rejected his "pagan" given name; while Hiram Grant had been registered "Ulysses S." by the admissions officer at West Point, and he let it stand, the initial "S" accepted by his classmates as denoting "Sam."

For Georgia-born William Joseph Hardee, another West Pointer, the decision as to where one's loyalty belonged was easy. Once a Georgian always a Georgian. He became almost at once a brigadier general in the Confederate army. When his native Kentucky refused to leave the Union, John Bell Hood, left the Union himself by enlisting in a Texas brigade as a lieutenant. All six, Johnston and Lee, Sherman and Grant, Hood and Hardee, would rise to the rank of generals, and confront each other on the battlefield before the war was over.

More by geographical exigencies than by decision, three theaters of the war emerged: the East, between the seacoast and the Appalachians; the West, between the Appalachians and the Mississippi, with a line extending from northeastern Georgia to the Gulf; and the Trans-Mississippi stretching to the Rio Grande. Key to the Trans-Mississippi was New Orleans, gateway for supplies from overseas. Center of the Western theater and the Southern heartland was Atlanta, workshop of the Confederacy, boiling with arms and armament production. And in the East stood Richmond, symbol and capitol of the fledgling nation, precariously vulnerable, by proximity, to invasion from the North.

On both sides so-called military districts and departments were created, each with its own general in command. Often exclusive in nature, they were commensurately uncoordinated to the extent that the commander of one could not draw reinforcements and provisions from another. Sometimes these districts and departments overlapped; often they shifted names and boundaries and commanders, creating the inefficiencies they were established to avoid.

Even the titles were confusing, an army and department often bearing the same designation though becoming geographically divided. Northern armies were generally named for rivers: the Army of the Cumberland, the Army of the Ohio, the Army of the Potomac. Southern armies were named for states or regions such as the Army of Northern Virginia and the Army of Tennessee. The terminology became, and still becomes, especially confusing when two similarly designated armies met in the same engagement or campaign. In 1864 before Atlanta, for example, the Confederate Army of Tennessee opposed the Union Army of *the* Tennessee.

At the outbreak of hostilities, the Northern battle-cry, bannered in Horace Greeley's *Tribune,* was "On to Richmond!" Major General Benjamin Butler ran into trouble trying to respond to that demand. Driving up the peninsula between the York and James rivers in the first of six campaigns for the Confederate capital, he was stopped on June 6 at Big Bethel by a makeshift Confederate force in the initial "formal" battle of the war. In that engagement a young lieutenant named Oliver Otis Howard performed with distinguished gallantry. He also lost an arm, an injury which did not halt his rise to fame in the later campaign for Atlanta.

Meanwhile, Major General Irvin McDowell with 32,000 troops pressed down on Richmond from the north, confident of victory over 23,000 Confederates under General Beauregard at Manassas Junction south of Bull Run Creek. McDowell pushed across the creek in a confused and scrambling charge that almost routed the Confederates. Beauregard called for help from Johnston guarding the neck of the Shenandoah Valley with 15,000 Southern troops. Ignoring a Union army sent to hold him in place, Johnston responded; and the vanguard of his forces turned the tide, with the pivotal resistance of Thomas Jonathan Jackson's brigade earning that general the sobriquet of "Stonewall."

First Manassas, known in the North as the Battle of Bull Run, was, with 55,000 men involved, the curtain raiser of the war. The South rejoiced at this demonstration of superiority, and throughout the Southern soldiery the news was heady wine. "I have never seen anything to equal the enthusiasm created," wrote Lieutenant Andrew Neal of Atlanta, from his Confederate encampment.

For the North it was "One bitter, bitter hour," wrote Walt Whitman. Gone were all hopes for a short war and an easy victory. Lincoln replaced McDowell with General George B. McClellan. Promoted shortly afterward to commander in chief of all the Union armies, McClellan was authorized to raise a force of 100,000 for an advance on Richmond. McClellan did better than that. He brought under arms 190,000 men, the mightiest army in the hemisphere, and started training them in camps on the Potomac.

In the West an obscure and misjudged dipsomaniac was on his erratic way to glory. Colonel Sam Grant, commanding an "unruly regiment," had won an unscheduled battle at Belmont, Missouri, toward the close of 1861. As a result, he was made a brigadier general over his own protest that he had not earned it, did not deserve it, and was incapable of handling the responsibility. He also renewed his West Point friendship with "Cump" Sherman who was back in service after recovering from a nervous breakdown. Both were under the command of Henry W. Halleck in charge of Union operations in the West.

Halleck had his eye on Tennessee where, in early 1862, General Albert Sidney Johnston commanded the overextended Confederate forces in the West. Grant proposed an inventive type of river war to divide and conquer the western section of that state. With specially built, troop-carrying barges, he captured Fort Henry on the Tennessee River, then sailed up the Cumberland and forced the submission of Fort Donelson with 17,000 men and 65 guns, on terms that won him the nickname of "Unconditional Surrender Grant."

Pushing south with 40,000 Federals in a drive to cut the vital Confederate Memphis-to-Chattanooga railway line, Grant was confronted by Johnston's 40,000 troops at Shiloh Church near Pittsburg Landing. In a two-day battle, April 6–7, 1862, Albert

Sidney Johnston was killed; but Grant, though reinforced by 20,000 men under General Don Carlos Buell, was hurled back with frightful casualties amounting to almost a quarter of his army.

Grant's losses at Shiloh led to a cry for his removal, to which Lincoln replied, "I can't spare this man—he fights!" There was some consolation to the North in the capture of New Orleans by Rear Admiral David Farragut in April of 1862. But in the East the aspirations of Lincoln and his new commander, George McClellan, were withering on the Potomac. Cautioned by reports from the detective Allan Pinkerton that Joseph Johnston had 250,000 Confederates defending Richmond, McClellan drilled his troops for six exhausting months—until an exasperated President growled, "If he doesn't intend to use his army, I would like to *borrow* it!"

McClellan finally got going. But not by land as planned. In 400 vessels he carried 121,000 troops, 15,000 horses, 1,200 wagons, and 44 batteries of artillery down the Potomac and Chesapeake to the tip of the Virginia Peninsula. Luckily the naval clash of the U.S.S. *Monitor* and the C.S.S. *Virginia* (formerly the Union *Merrimack*) had forced the *Virginia* to retire up the James, clearing a landing for McClellan's unwieldy forces. "In ten days I shall be in Richmond," "Little Mac" told the nation.

It was an empty boast. Marching up the Peninsula, he was stopped at Yorktown by a meager Confederate garrison, and took time out to bring up guns for a prolonged siege of the place. Again an exasperated Lincoln urged him: "Act! The enemy can use time as advantageously as you can!"

The President was right. Joseph Johnston had been waiting along the Rappahannock River for the expected Federal advance on Richmond. Now he raced south with 50,000 troops, one division commanded by fellow Virginian Robert Edward Lee, and deployed his veterans across the tongue of land between the York and James below the Southern capital. Johnston's Fabian tactics of hit and run, retreat and ambush, baffled the ponderous McClellan. The Union general could not force a decisive battle on his elusive foe. By the end of May, 1862, the "ten days" in which McClellan had promised to take Richmond had expanded to eight weeks.

It was Johnston who finally forced a showdown. Turning furiously on McClellan at Fair Oaks, the Confederate General was seriously wounded in the chest and shoulder in a battle that checked but failed to rout the Union forces. Johnston, taken to Richmond to recuperate, was replaced by General Robert E. Lee, son of "Light-Horse Harry" Lee of Revolutionary War fame.

Stalled before Richmond, McClellan called repeatedly on Washington for reinforcements. That they were never forthcoming was due to Confederate pressure in the Shenandoah Valley where Stonewall Jackson was carving a niche for himself in the hall of the immortals. With less than 17,000 men he kept 100,000 Federal troops so occupied that none could be released to join McClellan's siege of Richmond. Kept them more than occupied, in fact. In a series of notable victories along the Shenandoah River he sent the Union forces stumbling back to Harpers Ferry. By June 21, with the Valley secure, Jackson was ready to join Lee on the Peninsula.

His arrival was tardy. Lee had already launched a Confederate offensive that, in seven days of fighting, sent McClellan reeling back to Harrison's Landing on the James. The Peninsula campaign was over, Richmond saved—but at a cost of 20,600 men which Lee could ill afford to lose. Lincoln appointed Henry Halleck commander in chief of the armies of the United States, and Halleck called McClellan back to Washington, his "invincible army" smaller by almost 16,000 men lost in the long Peninsula campaign.

The South, in the fall of 1862, was picking up momentum. In the Western theater, Braxton Bragg commanded the Confederate forces in Tennessee. As Bragg invaded Kentucky, two Confederate cavalry leaders, Nathan Bedford Forrest and John Hunt Morgan began rampaging through Kentucky and through Tennessee, destroying Federal outposts, depots, and supplies.

Robert E. Lee had been riding on the rising tide. Before McClellan's diminished army could recover from the Peninsula campaign, Lee and Jackson, with 57,000 men, headed north to intercept John Pope's 62,000 troops advancing south toward Richmond. Nearing Bull Run Creek, Lee sent Jackson on a wide sweep to the left, and both wings of his army closed on Pope at the blood-soaked battlefield of Bull Run or Manassas. Second Manassas, August 29–30, was another stunning triumph; and Lee, who up to now had fought no major battles, was being compared with Joseph Johnston as one of the outstanding generals in the South.

Never had the Confederacy seemed so close to victory. Both England and France considered recognizing Southern independence, each waiting on the other; and some days later William E. Gladstone, Chancellor of the Exchequer, made his celebrated observation that "the leaders of the South have made a nation" and those of the North "have not yet drunk of the cup which the rest of the world sees they nevertheless must drink."

Lee's troops were weary, battle-scarred, but nonetheless inspired. He decided to carry the war to enemy territory, invade Maryland, and possibly force Washington to sue for peace. Lincoln reinstated McClellan as commander of the Union forces defending Washington, and the "Young Napoleon," with his reorganized army of 80,000, set out to intercept Lee and Jackson —if he could discover where they were. He found out at Antietam where by nightfall of September 17 the most savage fighting of the war concluded. So concluded, also, Lee's hope of invading Maryland. Though McClellan suffered heavy casualties, Lee and Jackson lost almost 13,000 men, a third of the Confederate troops engaged.

Both sides claimed victory at Antietam. Actually, neither won. One man, however, helped to sustain the Southern hope for victory in 1862. He was not a Southerner, but a Union major general. Irked by McClellan's failure to follow up the Battle of Antietam by pursuing Lee across the Potomac, Lincoln replaced McClellan with Ambrose Everett Burnside, of the luxuriant side whiskers, who protested with astute self-knowledge, "I do not want the command. I am not competent to command so large an army."

Burnside proved his incompetence in mid-December, 1862, when he crossed the Rappanhannock for another advance on Richmond, and ran into Lee, entrenched and strongly armed, at Fredericksburg. In six successive, senseless charges, Burnside hurled 113,00 troops against Lee's fortifications, in the face of withering fire from 300 Confederate cannon and 75,000 muskets, each time leaving heaps of dead and wounded on the field. "It is well that war is so terrible," said Lee as he watched the slaughter, "or we should grow too fond of it."

That night, as news of Fredericksburg reached Washington, Lincoln confided to Senator Orville Browning, "We are now on the brink of destruction. It appears to me the Almighty is against us, and I can hardly see a ray of hope."

In the West, however, Braxton Bragg was running into trouble. Driving deep into Kentucky, hoping to swing that state into the Confederacy, he collided with Don Carlos Buell at Perryville and retreated, badly mauled, across the border into Tennessee. General William S. "Rosey" Rosecrans, replacing Buell, gave him another mauling in four days of furious fighting at Murfreesboro in central Tennessee. Bragg delivered as much in the way of damage to his foe as he received, and even more, but finally tottered back, exhausted, to Tullahoma, near the Alabama border.

Against his personal bias, but influenced by increasing distrust of Braxton Bragg, Jefferson Davis named Joseph Johnston chief commander in the West. At about the same time in late November the three corps of William Joseph Hardee, Edmund Kirby Smith, and Leonidas Polk were united under Braxton Bragg to form the Confederate Army of Tennessee—a name to match in glory Robert E. Lee's Army of Northern Virginia.

Things moved fast in 1863 as the war appeared to near a climax. "Fighting Joe" Hooker replaced Burnside as commander of what the Union still referred to as "the finest army on the planet." Hooker contrived to hold Lee at Fredericksburg while the bulk of his 134,000 troops crossed the Rappahannock to advance on Richmond. Lee sideslipped to the Wilderness, near Chancellorsville, to meet him, sending Stonewall Jackson to flank Hooker's army from the west.

In the resultant clash, in early May, Lee scored a stunning victory over Hooker, hurling the Union army, minus 17,300 killed and wounded, back across the Rappahannock. The South, however, lost one of its great leaders in the battle. Charging from the Wilderness in his flank attack on Hooker, Stonewall Jackson was mistakenly shot by his own men.

Inspired by his success at Chancellorsville, Lee planned a

second, fateful invasion of the North—up the broad avenue of the Shenandoah Valley into Maryland and Pennsylvania. An alarmed President in Washington replaced the punch-drunk Hooker with corps commander George G. Meade. While the cavalry of both sides sparred with one another in Virginia, Meade moved to meet Lee at the northern threshold of the Shenandoah Valley.

In the West, General Grant, after being disciplined by Halleck for the catastrophe at Shiloh, was back in command of the Federal armies in Tennessee and Mississippi (Halleck having gone to Washington as Union Chief of Staff) and was teamed again with Sherman with one goal in mind: batter down Vicksburg and control the Mississippi River. By water and land, Grant's gunboats and "Cump" Sherman's troops closed in upon the citadel while civilians took to their cellars or dug caves for shelter in the riverbank, living off mules, dogs, and even rats.

With his 30,000 defenders, General John Pemberton clung to the city from mid-May till the first week in July, through six weeks of merciless bombardment from the Federal artillery. With Braxton Bragg pinned down by Union General Rosecrans at Tullahoma, Joe Johnston, a man with authority but no army of his own, was powerless to help. He advised Pemberton to evacuate the besieged city, but Pemberton saw no way of getting out alive. On July 3, with troops and civilians on the border of starvation, Pemberton raised the white flag over Vicksburg and conferred with Grant on terms for its surrender.

"The Father of Waters again goes unvexed to the sea!" proclaimed a joyous Lincoln. The Confederacy had been split in two and the Trans-Mississippi, though never a major department of the war, was on its own.

The siege and fall of Vicksburg had severe repercussions in Atlanta, center of the Confederacy's railway network, just as Vicksburg was a key point in its river transportation system. Could it happen here? The city raised two more militia companies and Georgia Governor Joseph Brown called for 8,000 additional volunteers. Atlanta's *Daily Intelligencer* assured its readers that "when the boastful enemy attempts to venture upon a raid in Georgia from Tennessee or Alabama it will meet with a resistance it little expects."

In the little town of Gettysburg, Pennsylania, that first week in July, a seemingly insignificant skirmish between the vanguard of Lee's army and some Union cavalry of George Meade's forces erupted into what was called "the greatest battle fought in the Western Hemisphere." Both Meade and Lee, responding to the rifle fire, swung full force into Gettysburg. In their initial clash, the Federal troops were driven back to a defensive line on hook-shaped Cemetery Ridge, while Lee's men occupied positions on the paralleling Seminary Ridge.

The three-day battle, July 1–3, climaxed by George E. Pickett's famous charge, became the bloodiest conflict of the war. Of 163,000 men engaged, a third had fallen. Meade suffered casualties of 23,000; Lee lost almost half his army, 28,000 veterans he would sorely miss. Though undefeated, he was prompted to withdraw to the Potomac where the rain-swollen river kept his troops immobilized for several days. Meade, equally shaken, made no attempt to pursue the stalled Confederates, and Lee retreated in good order to Virginia.

"Our Army held the war in the hollow of their hand," Lincoln complained, "and would not close it."

All eyes turned to the West which seemed to hold the key now to the future of the war.

While Lee and Meade remained mired in a virtual stalemate in Virginia, skirmishing from time to time around the Rapidan and Rappahannock, these clashes seemed little more than exercises to keep the troops in shape. Jefferson Davis and Joseph Johnston were more concerned with the deteriorating situation in the West, especially in Tennessee where Braxton Bragg and "Rosey" Rosecrans, the one at Tullahoma and the other at Murfreesboro, spent six months in prayer and meditation and in filing complaints to their superiors.

A week before Gettysburg, Rosecrans finally moved to push Bragg out of Tennessee. There was some skirmishing between the two as Rosecrans approached Tullahoma the last week in June, but Bragg offered no real opposition. He thought it safer to shift his base to Chattanooga, key point in the vital railroad link between Virginia and the West.

Chattanooga was, in fact, more than a key railway junction. It was the potential jumping off place for a Union invasion of

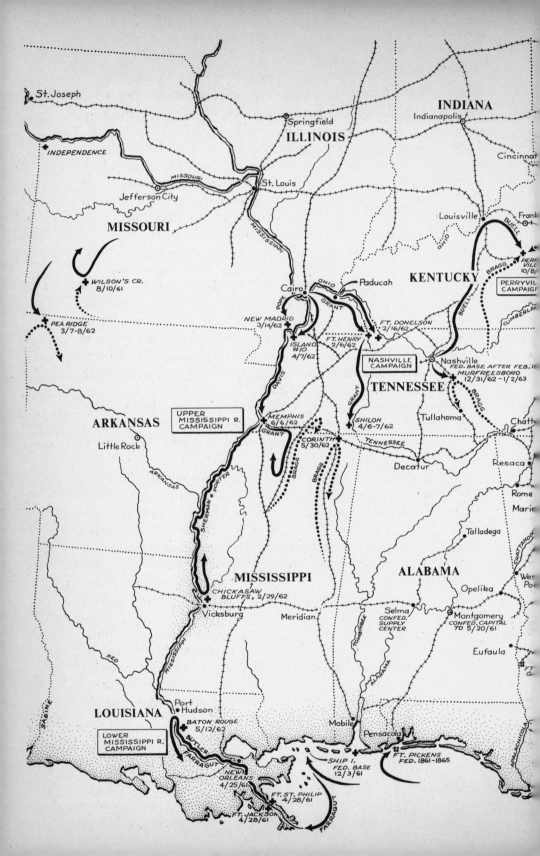

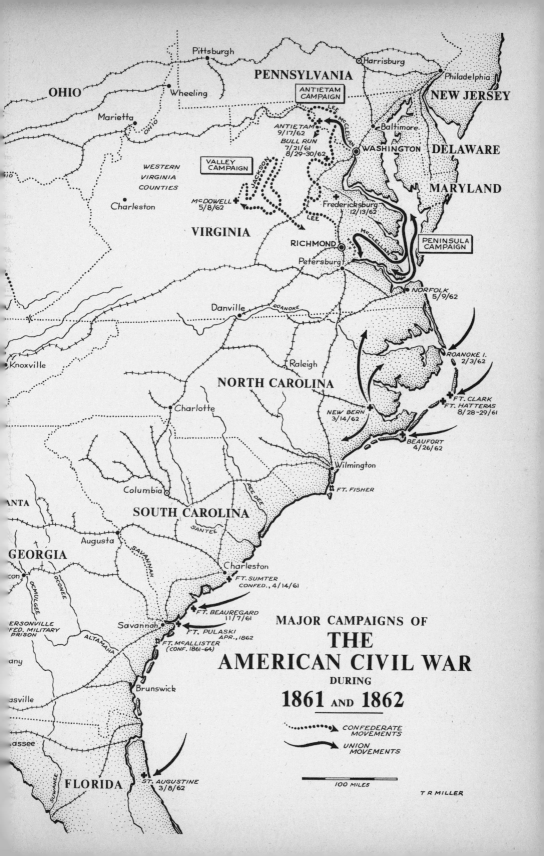

OHIO

Pittsburgh

Wheeling

Marietta

OHIO

PENNSYLVANIA

Harrisburg

Philadelphia

NEW JERSEY

ANTIETAM CAMPAIGN

Baltimore

LEE *McCLELLN*

WASHINGTON

DELAWARE

ANTIETAM 9/17/62

BULL RUN 7/21/61 8/29-30/62

JACKSON

MARYLAND

WESTERN VIRGINIA COUNTIES

VALLEY CAMPAIGN

Charleston

McDOWELL 5/8/62

LEE

Fredericksburg 12/13/62

VIRGINIA

RICHMOND

McCLELLAN

PENINSULA CAMPAIGN

Petersburg

NORFOLK 5/9/62

Danville

ROANOKE

Knoxville

Raleigh

ROANOKE I. 2/3/62

NORTH CAROLINA

Charlotte

NEW BERN 3/14/62

FT. CLARK FT. HATTERAS 8/28-29/61

BEAUFORT 4/26/62

Wilmington

Columbia

PEE DEE

FT. FISHER

SOUTH CAROLINA

SANTEE

ANTA

GEORGIA

Augusta

SAVANNAH

Charleston

FT. SUMTER CONFED., 4/14/61

con

OCMULGEE

OCONEE

FT. BEAUREGARD 11/7/61

ERSONVILLE FED. MILITARY PRISON

Savannah

FT. PULASKI APR., 1862

FT. McALLISTER (CONF. 1861-64)

any

ALTAMAHA

MAJOR CAMPAIGNS OF

THE

AMERICAN CIVIL WAR

DURING

1861 AND 1862

asville

Brunswick

SUWANEE

assee

FLORIDA

ST. AUGUSTINE 3/8/62

∙∙∙∙▶ *CONFEDERATE MOVEMENTS*

───▶ *UNION MOVEMENTS*

─────── *100 MILES*

T R MILLER

Georgia—a thrust into the very heart of the South where Atlant's mills and factories and foundries were pumping life into the faltering Confederacy, and Atlanta's asterisk of railway lines comprised the most important transportation center in the South. Atlanta was, as well, a gateway to the sea. A strike from that city to Charleston or Savannah or Mobile would more completely, and more mortally, divide the South than had the fall of Vicksburg.

For the first time Atlanta felt a tremor of alarm. The important Western & Atlantic Railroad running up to Chattanooga was the city's lifeline in the north. Governor Brown ordered the state reserves to be ready for action at a moment's notice. Lee released James Longstreet's corps to reinforce Bragg, but by the time Longstreet got under way, Bragg had evacuated Chattanooga for fear of being cut off by Rosecrans' cunningly divided army crossing the Tennessee River from Alabama and the north.

The war had moved into Georgia, heartland of the Confederacy.

Urged by Johnston, Lee, and Davis to take the offensive, Bragg moved to meet the approaching Rosecrans at Chickamauga Creek, an Indian name appropriately meaning "River of Death." Here on September 19–20 he hurled his 57,000 troops against the Union line. The Federal defenses crumbled, all except those of George H. Thomas whose strong resistance earned that general the title of "the Rock of Chickamauga."

Though both sides lost heavily—more than a quarter of their respective armies—Chickamauga was a victory of sorts for Bragg, though not what the South had hoped for. Not the sort that Bragg had hoped for, either ("one more like this and I am ruined"). Rosecrans, battered but not destroyed, withdrew into Chattanooga. It would take a siege of several weeks to drive him out, "a battle on which," the Atlanta *Intelligencer* warned, "hangs the issue of the war."

It came on November 23–25, by which time the balance of power had shifted in the Union's favor. Sam Grant, now in command of the armies of the West, replaced Rosecrans with the redoubtable George Thomas. Sherman, succeeding Grant as head of the Army of the Tennessee, arrived from Vicksburg to support the Federal forces at Chattanooga. Braxton Bragg deliberately weakened his army by sending James Longstreet to chase Burnside out of Knoxville, and was himself reduced to a feeble shelling of Chattanooga from the heights of Missionary Ridge, southeast of the city.

Five days after Lincoln had vowed at Gettysburg that the government of the Union "shall not perish from the earth," "Fighting Joe" Hooker took possession of Lookout Mountain west of Missionary Ridge in what was known as "the Battle above the Clouds," so named because of the heavy fog enveloping the mountain. In the two days following, Hooker, Thomas, and Sherman stormed the heights of Missionary Ridge—the Army of the Cumberland taking the initiative without orders, its men climbing like mountain goats over peaks and precipices, muskets in hand, in the face of sixty thundering cannon and two lines of rebel trenches. They dug the Confederates out like stubborn moles from their entrenchments and sent them stumbling back to Ringgold Gap and finally to Dalton.

To complete the Federal triumph, Longstreet was repelled at Knoxville, virtually all of Tennessee was in Grant's hands, and a deep wedge had been driven into the northern boundary of the Confederated states.

Bragg offered to resign as a result of the debacle. Davis accepted, temporarily put Hardee in his place, then assigned Joseph Johnston to command the Army of Tennessee. He had never liked Johnston, nor had Johnston ever trusted or accepted Davis as his chief commander. Some said it dated back to West Point days and a quarrel over a girl. But each had followed his own star in this war, and their stars were not in the same orbit.

Georgia, long secure behind its northern mountains, with its land routes open to the sea—Georgia, the heart of the Confederacy—was suddenly a battle zone. Three years after Robert Toombs had told the United States Senate, "Georgia is on the warpath!" Georgia had become the warpath—and for General Sherman's armies that projected warpath led directly to Atlanta.

This Was Their Georgia

Those who were here first, the enlightened and civilized Cherokees, called it "The Enchanted Land" and referred to a spot northeast of the site of Atlanta as "The Center of the Universe."

But their universe, though bright, was small. What was first known as Georgia in the New World stretched in a wide band clear to the Pacific, an area larger than Great Britain, Holland, Belgium, Spain, France, Austria and Switzerland combined. This immensity, however, was a parchment dream of King George II who granted Georgia, named in his honor and extending "in a direct line to the South Seas," to James Edward Oglethorpe in 1732—partly as a repository for the poor of overcrowded London, partly as a buffer zone between South Carolina and hostile Spanish Florida.

It was not the first attempt to colonize the area. Sir Robert Montgomery, a visionary Scot, obtained in 1717 dubious permission from South Carolina (which laid claim to this land below its borders) to establish a private domain "between the Altamaha and Savannah rivers extending west to the Pacific Ocean." Naming the tract Azilia for reasons of his own, Montgomery promoted this future Eden in a pamphlet which represented one of the earlier impressions Europeans gained of this "most amiable country in the Universe." One section which noted that Azilia lay in the same latitude as the promised land of Canaan, went on to say:

> It abounds with Rivers, Woods, and Meadows. Its gentle Hills are full of Mines, Lead, Copper, Iron, and even some of Silver. . . . Vines, naturally flourishing upon the Hills, bear Grapes in most luxuriant Plenty. They have every Growth which we possess in England, and almost every Thing that England wants besides. The Orange and the Limon thrive in the same common Orchard with the Apple, and the Pear-Tree, Plumbs, Peaches, Apricots, and Nectarins bear from Stones in three years growing. The Planters raise large Orchards . . . to feed their hogs with.

Montgomery's dream blew up with the bursting of the South Seas Company bubble three years later. But an even more quixotic Scot, Sir Alexander Cumming, conceived an even more fantastic project. He would persuade the Cherokee Indians to cede their lands in northern Georgia for the founding of an eighteenth century Zion to be settled by 300,000 European Jews. To promote the venture, Sir Alexander visited the Cherokees, persuaded a number of warriors to return with him to London, naming them kings, admirals, and generals on the way. The Indians were a great success in the Empire's capital, especially when displayed in local theaters. The sole result of their visit, however, was that the delegates returned to Cherokee country impressed with the might of the English King—which tended to keep the Cherokees neutral in the War of 1812.

The Georgia which Oglethorpe invested on his arrival was little more than a hummock on the Eastern seaboard, on which he planted a town he called Savannah. As to the western stretches of his domain—some of it claimed, anyway, by France and Spain—he could never have reached it in a hundred years, and never tried. He extended his settlement as far as Augusta, then went back to England. In time the disillusioned trustees of the colony returned it to the Crown.

Georgia's first settlers, those whom Oglethorpe brought and those who followed, were anything but riffraff. Though generally impoverished, they were screened for character, ability, and hardiness. Even so, the colonists had trouble getting started. Expected to raise silkworms and grow grapes for wine, they finally eked out a living planting cotton and tobacco, with some help from neighboring South Carolina. Henceforth, cotton and tobacco would be Georgian staples. In its first two decades the colony shrank in size to a total population of 2,000 whites and 1,000 blacks. But the Treaty of Paris in 1763 eased the pressure from the Spanish, French, and Indians that had constricted Georgia's growth, and the colony began to flourish. Prior to the Revolutionary War, settlers from overseas, mainly Germans and Scotch-Irish, helped to swell the population to approximately 50,000, half of them African slaves.

Georgia at first took no great interest in the Revolution. Signs of its sovereign and independent posture were already evident. What applied to the northern colonies, matters of controlling trade with Europe, for example, did not apply in the same degree to Georgia which traded mostly with the Caribbean. Also, as youngest of the thirteen colonies, Georgia's ties with England were still warm. English money and aid had helped the colony survive and grow. English troops had protected the settlers from the Indians.

When the First Continental Congress met in Philadelphia in 1774, no Georgia delegates were present. Instead, Georgia held its own Provincial Congress to debate the matter of independence, and was consequently ostracized by the other twelve colonies. The Continental Congress placed a non-intercourse ban on Georgia; South Carolina threatened to execute any merchant trading with her wayward neighbor.

To say that Georgia fought her own War of the Revolution would be hardly accurate, but she early showed an inclination to handle things her own way in her own good time. Three Georgians finally signed the Declaration of Independence, Button Gwinnett among them.

Since, at first, there were no English troops around to fight, Georgians engaged in frequent scraps among themselves, Whigs versus Tories, with Button Gwinnett killed in a duel defending his radical opinions. Late in 1778, however, the British, getting nowhere in the North, invaded Georgia by land and sea from

Florida. It took the combined efforts of Generals Nathanael Greene and "Mad Anthony" Wayne to repossess the state, both being awarded plantations in southern Georgia for their trouble.

During this actual fight for its survival, Georgia did contribute substantial numbers of militia to the Continental Army and was hailed by John Adams as "a spirited, powerful addition to our phalanx." But perhaps the best known warrior in Georgia was a woman. Nancy Hart, a red-haired, fiery mother of eight, set a tradition of female fortitude that would endure throughout the Civil War. When six Tories tried to drive her from her home, she at first resisted, then finally agreed to serve them dinner before leaving. Once they were seated at the table, Nancy reached for a musket on the wall shot one of them dead and held the rest at bay until neighbors alerted by the shot arrived to hang them.

When the war ended, Georgia welcomed back as many Loyalists as cared to come back. She needed manpower and had no national prejudices. Great Britain and the United States were one and the same to Georgia; politically, she could get along without them. Georgia was Georgia, sufficient unto herself, and with the aid of her polyglot population she began to build an almost sovereign state. Embarrassed, however, by scandalous land frauds, Georgia was forced to sell much of her western territory to the United States in exchange for the government's promise to rid the state of Indians.

The first of these aims was achieved in the War of 1812 when most of the hostile Creeks were driven down to Florida. There remained the Cherokees in the north, with their highly developed parliamentary government, their own alphabet and language, printing press, newspaper, schools and hospitals; but they would be eliminated in due time.

Georgia had now shrunk to its present roughly oblong size of 60,000 square miles, still the largest state of the Union, with its population quadrupling in the first three decades of the nineteenth century, from 162,000 in 1800 to 691,000 in 1830. By 1838, through the efforts of Andrew Jackson and General Winfield Scott, the Cherokees were finally driven out of northern Georgia, over the long Trail of Tears to Oklahoma Territory, and Georgia was as homogeneous in land and people as it would ever be.

It was a varied land of three geographic regions. The north was furrowed by the ridges of the southern Appalachian range, among the oldest mountains in the world. Here were deep valleys and forbidding peaks, secluded hardwood forests, with a rugged independent type of mountain people, grubbing a living from the soil.

Central or Middle Georgia was Piedmont country, a plateau of red clay, long leaf pine, and good land irrigated by innumerable streams. A farmer could make a handy living here from cotton, corn, potatoes, and tobacco, and eventually peanuts.

To the south, along and inward from the seaboard, was the rich savannah country, perfect for growing rice and cotton; here the great plantations of the state were born and flourished.

There was some gold around Dahlonega in the north, and good lumbering both north and south. And peaches of course, though nary a tree would grow on Peachtree Street which Atlantans would, in time, believe ran clear around the world. In short, a fair abundance of resources. Adequate transportation was the needed catalyst to bring them all together.

At first Georgia depended on its rivers and its privately supported turnpikes for transporting goods to market and to Charleston and Savannah for transshipment overseas. But when South Carolina built a railway line from Charleston to the Georgian border, Georgia responded with a line extending to the prosperous central farmlands of the state. Then another railroad from Chattanooga to the Chattahoochee River; and another to Macon; and another from the junction of these three to West Point near the Alabama border. The asterisk formed by the confluence of these four railway lines was named, in 1845, Atlanta—almost at birth a boisterous upstart of a city to which all roads led.

By 1860 Georgia had 1404 miles of tracks, more than any other Southern state except Virginia, and its future as well as its conduct of the coming war rested to a large degree on rails of steel.

Going back to the turn of the century and to Nathanael Greene's plantation, Mulberry Bend, outside Savannah,

Georgia had reason to celebrate the visit of young Eli Whitney from Connecticut. General Greene himself had died a few years after chasing the British out of Georgia, and mechanical-minded Eli made himself useful inventing small household gadgets for the general's widow. Mrs. Greene suggested he talk with the local planters of their difficulty separating cotton from the seeds. Whitney did; and came up with a drumlike device that got rid of the seeds but did not properly extract the lint. Mrs. Greene allegedly handed him her hairbrush, which perfected the machine.

Whitney's cotton engine, "gin" for short, made a tremendous difference to southern planters, especially to Georgians who soon led the world in cotton production with 150,000 bales a year by 1825. Whitney spent a small fortune in Georgia trying to protect his patent, was thoroughly squelched, and returned to Connecticut to perfect a method of mass-producing guns, especially for the Federal army. He had not intended the guns to be used against Georgians, but through the mysterious workings of justice, they eventually were.

As more and more Georgia land was planted with cotton, and the plantations grew in size and productivity, the importance of slave labor grew proportionately. Considered essential to survival, slavery became a sacred institution. Even in Liberty County on the southern coast, settled by devout New Englanders such as the Reverend Charles Alcock Jones, the system was considered beneficial to both blacks and whites, the former profiting from the blessings bestowed upon them by the latter. The Reverend Jones devoted a large part of his life to the education and advancement of his slaves.

Yet it was on the not-too-distant plantation of Pierce Butler, husband of the English actress Fanny Kemble, that Fanny wrote in 1838–1839 her bitter diatribe, *Journal of a Residence on a Georgia Plantation*, which had almost as much effect in arousing antislavery sentiment as *Uncle Tom's Cabin*. Fanny herself, however, found something irresistible in the grace and luxury of plantation life. In surroundings of beauty such as this, she wrote, she would choose to die "breaking my neck off the back of a good horse at a full gallop on a fine day."

While there was no "Tara" as in Margaret Mitchell's Georgia, there were many counterparts. They stood like Greek Temples in groves of oak and long leaf pine, with magnolia-bordered avenues leading to white-columned mansions. The manors themselves were graced with imported French and English furnishings, mahogany and rosewood heirlooms, crystal chandeliers, marble mantels and gold-framed mirrors reflecting spacious halls and chambers. And life within was seemingly as gracious as the legends of the South maintain. Sir Charles Lyell, visiting Georgia in the mid-1850s, noted:

> There is a warm and generous openness of character in the Southerners which mere wealth and retinue of servants cannot give and they have often a dignity of manner without stiffness which is most agreeable. The landed proprietors here visit each other in the style of the English country gentlemen, sometimes dining out with their families and returning at night or, if the distance be great, remaining to sleep and coming home the next morning.

One of the stronger ties cementing this landed aristocracy was its dependence upon slaves. The institution of slavery had to be protected at all costs. Without slave labor the planters were doomed, as surely as a manufacturer without machines. Of Georgia's population of 1,057,286 before the Civil War, approximately half were slaves, with a mere one percent of freemen. (There was an attempt, under pressure of demand for labor, to reinstate this fraction into servitude.) In the plantation belt the ratio of blacks to whites might be as high as forty or fifty to one.

Though the importation of slaves had been banned by the United States in 1808, and even earlier by Georgia, the domestic slave trade flourished, and the smuggling of "Black Gold" from the Caribbean islands via Florida and Savannah was a booming business. In 1858 a profitable load of Africans was landed on Jekyll Island by a slaver flying the colors of the New York Yacht Club! On Thomas Spalding's 4,000-acre plantation on the Georgian island of Sapelo, Spalding undertook the breeding of slaves for sale to neighboring planters—a project which failed through the spread of a strange disease among the blacks.

In short, during the first half of the century and up until the Civil War, the slave-oriented plantation system came into full flower in the state of Georgia. In its comfortable framework the planter could rightfully share the feeling of Clay Wingate, as described by Stephen Vincent Benét, that "This was his Georgia, this his share of pine and river and sleepy air." By the end of the period there were nearly a thousand plantations of more than a thousand acres—greater in number than in any other state—plus 2,700 plantations of 100 to 500 acres. Some 6,400 Georgia planters owned twenty slaves or more, which was considered the dividing line between the aristocratic planters and the produce farmers who comprised a different and more humble class.

While most of the larger establishments were in the savannah area, many flourished in the environs of Atlanta. The Covington plantation of Dolly Lunt Burge comprised a Doric-columned mansion surrounded for miles by red clay fields worked by a hundred slaves—the gardens still scented, when Julian Street visited the postwar Burge descendants, with "pine trees, tulip trees, Balm-of-Gilead trees, blossoming Judas trees, Georgia crabapple, dogwood, peach blossom, wisteria, sweet shrub, violets, pansies, Cherokee roses, wild honeysuckle, azaleas and the evanescent green of new treetops, all carried in solution in the sunlight. . . ."

Near Stone Mountain east of Atlanta was the Promised Land Plantation of Thomas Maguire who, like a number of Georgia landowners, had originally come from Ireland early in the century. Close to a thousand acres, it was worked by a modest corps of twenty-six slaves. Unlike the leisurely savannah planters, Maguire exerted himself in making the shoes for his family and supervising such recorded activities as "Cotton, corn, wheat, garden vegetables, fruit grown on plantation; cattle, sheep, hogs raised; additionally—carpentry, blacksmithing, ginning, tanning, milling flour, grinding cane, making brick."

Dean of the Georgian planters, Howell Cobb, was all over the map, with ten plantations worked by a thousand slaves. An ardent advocate of slavery, Cobb left the supervision of his land to overseers, to engage in law and politics and service to the state —becoming successively Georgia representative in Congress, governor from 1851 to 1853, and Secretary of the Treasury in President Buchanan's cabinet. For good reason, Cobb main-

tained one plantation southeast of Atlanta and close to Milledgeville which had become state capital in 1806.

The railroads built in part to serve the cotton kingdom, providing faster transportation to the North and to the shipping
points of trade with Europe, did much to change the economic
face of Georgia with the growth of mills and manufactures. The
state remained predominantly agricultural, with King Cotton as
its staple product. But the cotton gin fathered the textile mills.
By 1850 there were forty such mills in Georgia, one of them the
leading cotton textile producer in the South. With machinery
more easily transported by rail from the North, other industries
began to sprout: tanneries, shoe factories, machine shops, flour
mills, brick and lumber works.

Because the principal railway lines converged upon Atlanta,
much of this new activity developed there—iron foundries, rolling mills, sawmills, leather works, wholesale distributors, food
merchants, carriage and wheelwright shops, and railroad maintenance barns. Not all of them were major industries perhaps,
but large enough to bring to Georgia a new breed of citizen
comprising engineers, mechanics, artisans, salesmen, realtors,
and opportunists, agressive in thought and action in contrast to
the *dolce vita* of the great plantations.

The landed gentry, however, still remained in power during
this mid-century period of rapid growth. It was still their
Georgia during the critical decade which began in 1850.

At the beginning of the period 1850–1860, Georgia rounded
the corner which led inexorably to the Civil War. The Compromise of 1850 which, among other things, left the question of
slavery in the Western territories up to popular election and
established a more stringent Fugitive Slave Act, was merely a
temporizing salve to mounting frictions between North and
South. It was pushed through Congress largely through the
efforts of the "Georgia Bloc" headed by three men destined to
guide the future of the state and to a large degree the future of
the Confederate States: Howell Cobb, Robert Augustus
Toombs, and Alexander Hamilton Stephens.

They were a strong triumvirate; and on them, to a large extent, Georgia's immediate future rested. All three had been born

in the state between 1810 and 1815, of similar education, wealth, and background. Stephens and Toombs had been close friends since boyhood days; their careers in law had been intertwined. But as a wealthy landowner of distinguished Georgian lineage, Howell Cobb stood perhaps a little taller than the other two, a little more representative of Southern aims, traditions, aspirations.

Cobb, Toombs, and Stephens at this point were proslavery and pro-Union both, defenders of the status quo as represented by the Constitution. All three had held public office at one time or another, as senators or representatives in Congress, with Cobb, of course, governor of Georgia until 1853. He had been succeeded for two terms by Herschel V. Johnson, a moderate who could do little to stem the mounting North-South tension over slavery, and who was eclipsed in 1857 by his successor, a new star on the state's horizon.

Joseph Emerson Brown, defined as "a homespun mountaineer, hero of the ploughing bull . . . with his cool sense and iron nerve," had been cutting wheat on his farm thirty miles north of Atlanta when told of his nomination as a dark horse candidate for governor. He was as surprised as was Robert Toombs who asked the prevalent question, "Who's Joe Brown?" Yet the tall, cadaverous, awkward yeoman farmer—who had gone without shoes to afford to study for a law degree—would so exercise his gubernatorial powers that the question would never be asked again. Plainspoken, intransigent, and a strong states' rightist, he would be hailed as "the genius of a great commonwealth in its fiery ordeal."

By the time John Brown was hanged for his raid at Harpers Ferry in October, 1859 ("That new saint . . . will make the gallows glorious like the cross," wrote Emerson), the nation was spinning inexorably toward civil war. Had Georgia's favored John C. Breckinridge won the nomination over Stephen Douglas the year following, and then won the presidential election over Lincoln, the conflict might have been postponed but not resolved. Alexander Stephens, for one, was all for seeing how Lincoln worked out as President; perhaps some understanding could be reached with his administration. But there were few who shared this hope.

The Georgia legislature, in session at Milledgeville, reacted to news of Lincoln's election with cold fury. On Governor Brown's recommendation, the legislators voted a million dollar budget for the state's defense and authorized the raising of 10,-000 state militia. Witnessing this feverish mobilization for war, former Governor Herschel V. Johnson noted, "I felt that the State of Georgia would soon be launched upon a dark, uncertain and dangerous sea. I never felt so sad before."

Even from the quiet distance of south Georgia's placid shores this sadness was reflected. The Reverend Charles Alcock Jones expressed the attitude of the educated, churchgoing aristocracy: "The final issues are with Him who rules among the nations. A nation to be born in a day, without a struggle, would be a wonder on earth. If the Southern states resolve on a separate confederacy, they must be prepared for any emergency, even that of war . . . although I do not fear it if the Southern states are united."

Addressing an assembly in Atlanta to debate South Carolina's parting from the Union, Georgia-born Francis Bartow cried to the crowd, "Shall this noble, gallant little state of South Carolina stand alone?" Atlantans responded with an unanimous, resounding "No!" The cry was echoed in January by the Georgia legislature which voted 208 for secession, 89 opposed, a count that was later made unanimous by popular consent. As a curious consequence, the fiery Francis Bartow, one of the first to call for war, was also the first Confederate officer to fall in battle, killed at First Manassas six months later.

Howell Cobb's brother, Thomas R. R. Cobb, was a principal author of the Confederate Constitution created at the Montgomery convention in January, 1861. And, as noted, the Confederate government, voted into office at that time, was strongly Georgian in flavor, with Alexander Stephens made Vice President and Robert Toombs becoming Secretary of State. Even the elected President, Jefferson Davis, boasted of his Georgian parentage. On leaving Washington and the Senate, the dour, didactic Davis told his colleagues, "Gentlemen of the North, a war is to be inaugurated, the like of which men have not seen."

With two Georgians in key positions in the government, and a militantly independent governor at Milledgeville, Georgia was not only a highly influential state in the Confederacy, but something of a maverick as well. Governor Brown was not only adamant on states' rights, he was also adamant on Georgia's rights. Almost from the start, he pitted himself against Jefferson Davis in defense of Georgia's sovereignty to the point that it was fair to say, as one historian did in fact state, Brown as a wartime governor "saw everything from the Georgia viewpoint regardless of the needs of the Confederacy."

There was some criticism of Brown's dictatorial attitude, but he had strong support from the soon-to-be-disillusioned Alexander Stephens, the embittered Robert Toombs, and former Governor Herschel Johnson. With this backing, Brown fought Davis and Davis's surrogates, on almost every major issue. He opposed conscription and Confederate impressment of needed war supplies; argued with Davis over the manner of appointing officers and the disposition of Georgian troops; quibbled over state versus Confederate ownership of arms and munitions; quarreled with Confederate leader Joseph Johnston on the military use of Georgia's railroads.

This was not to say that Georgia under Governor Brown failed to give more than its share of men and arms to the Confederacy. A final tally would show that Georgia contributed more men under arms that any other Southern state (120,000), and lost more in combat in proportion to its population. With the first call for troops, the rush to volunteer was overwhelming, taxing the state's ability to supply the necessary arms and equipment. By mid-May, 1861, a month after the firing on Sumter, Georgia newspapers reported that 263 companies were "ready for the field—a force of not less than 18,000 vigorous men." Governor Brown, who himself had organized six regiments and two battalions, made it known to the Richmond government that "These have all been fully armed and accoutered and equipped *by the state*" [italics his]. By early fall of 1861, 25,000 Georgia troops were in Confederate service.

The state also contributed some of the South's outstanding officers, many of whom would fight on Georgia's soil against a powerful invader. Among them were Brigadier General, later Major General, William J. Hardee of Camden County; and diminutive, five-foot-five Cavalry General Joseph Wheeler

whose troops were so fond of "living off the land" that Robert
Toombs later observed that Georgia would be better off if
Wheeler left the state. Toombs himself quickly grew impatient
with his passive role in Davis' cabinet, and resigned after First
Manassas to become a brigadier general serving with the army
in Virginia. At about the same time, Howell Cobb at his request,
was commissioned Colonel of the 16th Georgia Volunteers. He,
too, would later be raised to brigadier general.

The matter of arms and equipment was a pressing one in this
primarily agricultural state. Almost 23,000 stands of arms were
seized from United States arsenals in Georgia and given by
Brown to the Confederate government. The shortage of arms,
resulting in part from this generosity, prompted a burst of individual enterprise in the state, with small family-operated factories devoted to the manufacture of sidearms, muskets, and ammunition.

Erstwhile local inventors produced a special bayonet to be
used on double-barreled shotguns; an adaptation of the Colt
six-shooter by which "red hot shot might be thrown thrice the
range of heretofore": and a four-barreled cannon hurling 16
shots a minute fabricated in Atlanta (but never, so far as is
known, put to use). When there was difficulty finding rifles for
the flood of Georgia volunteers, Brown supplied them with the
famous "Georgia Pike" similar to the seventeenth-century
crook-and-spear, far easier and quicker to produce than guns.

While Georgia's principal cities, led by Atlanta and including,
among others, Macon, Rome, Augusta, and Savannah, turned to
wartime production, the farms and plantations had to be relied
upon to feed the civilian population and Confederate forces in
the region. For once, Governor Brown concurred with Jefferson
Davis in urging the planters to substitute wheat, corn, barley,
potatoes, and other edible crops for the traditional cotton. Most
of them did; but not Howell Cobb, whose fervor for the Southern cause did not extend that far. Cotton, in Cobb's mind, was
as sacred as the new Confederate flag. What was Georgia
fighting for, if not its plantation economy and way of life?

The shooting war began within seventy-five miles of Georgia's eastern border when the first shell exploded over Sumter.
The mercurial Robert Toombs who had earlier boasted that "we

can lick the Yankees with cornstalks," had cautioned against firing upon the fort, warning, "It will loose on us a storm of hornets that would sting us to death." Apparently the artillerist, Edmund Ruffin, who fired the first shot on Sumter, also was concerned about the consequences. When the ensuing war turned sour for the South, he shot himself rather than "live under Yankee rule."

The sound of guns over Sumter reminded Georgia that its most vulnerable border was its seacoast. Robert E. Lee's first assignment as a Confederate general was to direct the defenses of Georgia's coastline from South Carolina to Florida. A brigade of state troops under General William H. T. Walker was rushed to Savannah in November, 1861, to fortify the city and the mouth of the Savannah River. The move effectively discouraged an invasion of the state by sea, though United States troops occupied many of the islands off the coast, forced the evacuation of Fort Pulaski, and attempted to blockade Savannah with a fleet of forty-one armed vessels.

Commodore Josiah Tattnall organized Georgia's small "Mosquito Fleet" composed of four tugs and a river steamer which, with hit-and-run tactics, kept the Federal fleet a mile off shore. A woman of Savannah who signed herself only "P.M.L." wrote to Governor Brown suggesting that a thousand barrels of turpentine be poured into the Savannah River and, allowing time for the current to carry it to the Union anchorage, the fuel to be set on fire "and it will do much damage if not entirely rout them." The ingenious plan was not, however, executed; the enemy vessels generally kept their distance, remaining only a worrisome threat for the first two years of the war.

The *"Trent* affair" of this same November, 1861, coming so soon after First Manassas, was regarded in Georgia and elsewhere in the South as another defeat of sorts for the United States. Two Confederate emissaries on their way to Paris and London were removed from the British ship *Trent* by the U.S.S. *San Jacinto* and taken to Boston as prisoners—a blatant violation of international law. While the North rejoiced at this show of Federal power on the high seas, England protested violently, threatening war with the United States if the men who had been in their custody were not released.

The South was delighted with this Northern blunder. Charles

C. Jones, Jr. of Liberty County, at the time lieutenant of Confederate forces in Savannah, wrote to his father of this clash between Northern arrogance and Britain's demand for release of the prisoners, "If a compliance with the demand be refused, then our war is practically at an end. The English and French navies will sweep their blockading squadrons from the coast, our ports will be again open, our staples will go forward, and practical peace and plenty again lie down at every door."

The affair was settled when the two Confederate emissaries were "cheerfully released," President Lincoln confessing "It was the bitterest pill I ever swallowed." But it emphasized to both sides that, at this point of the war, European sympathies were with the South, a factor important to Georgia with that state's reliance on the waning and restricted cotton trade.

Though Georgia, in the early war years, seemed remote from the land fighting in the West, two incidents brought the conflict close to home. One was the celebrated Andrews raid which aimed at severing the vital Western & Atlantic Railroad between Chattanooga and Atlanta. Led by the self-styled "Captain" James J. Andrews, a score of Federal soldiers dressed as civilians, seized a locomotive near Marietta in April, 1862, and raced north to destroy the tracks and bridges which they left behind them. Too hotly pursued to do much damage, they were captured at Ringgold, with the leaders later hanged in Atlanta as saboteurs.

A year later a second thrust into northern Georgia was led by Colonel Abel D. Streight and a detachment of Federal cavalry which attempted to cut the railroad south of Dalton. They were intercepted by General Nathan Bedford Forrest, advocate of the policy of being "firstest with the mostest," who was guided through part of the Georgia wilderness by a teen-aged heroine sharing his saddle. Forrest was neither the firstest nor had he the mostest in this running battle, but he ultimately captured Streight's entire division of 1600 men with his own force of one third that number.

Otherwise the state of Georgia was free, until the end of 1863, of fighting on its native soil. There was, however, plenty of conflict within the state on matters politic and military, none greater than the question of conscription. While Governor

Brown went along protestingly with the first conscription act of April, 1862, even though it ate up most of his state militia, he balked at the second conscription act the following September which raised the age limit from 35 to 45 (with a bottom age of 18). Brown immediately and arbitrarily exempted his own militia officers, thereafter known as "Brown's pets." Through other exemptions and recruitments below and above the Confederate age limits, he organized another state militia which he regarded as his private army. It would fight for Georgia, but only over Brown's dead body would it serve outside the state.

There was dissension, too, over the curbing of the cotton crop to allow planting of food crops. Besides Howell Cobb, who flatly refused to go along with it, one Georgia planter argued that "One week's supply of cotton for England estimated at 40,000 bales is worth two and a half million dollars—a sum sufficient to clothe and arm 50,000 men." There were others who insisted that in King Cotton lay the strength of the Confederacy.

In this instance, Governor Brown wisely went along with Richmond. Food was the immediate need; and the reduction of Georgia's cotton crop from an annual average of 700,000 bales to 60,000 in 1862 spelled the doom of the old plantation system. Only overseers on plantations having more than twenty slaves were exempted from conscription. The planters themselves were obliged to assume the roles of overseers—all right, possibly, for the men but hard on the women whose husbands were away at war.

In other areas, and to an extraordinary degree, the women of Georgia responded to war's demands and, probably more than elsewhere in the South, devoted themselves to war-oriented work. Tending the wounded or assisting army surgeons was considered too rough for female sensitivities (although many young girls volunteered, insisting that they were "unengaged"). But through "Soldiers Relief Societies" and "Hospital Relief Societies" women assembled to make bandages, sheets, and blankets, to sew or knit underwear, socks, shirts, and coats; to weave and dye the cloth for soldiers' uniforms; to make cartridges and collect "lead pipes to mould bullets."

These groups, according to one participant, were "anything but a mere pastime assembly of talkative women." Wrote another, "From 1861 to the close of the War. . .our busy hands were never idle." Through tableaux, musicals, and amateur dramatics, money was raised for medicines and hospital supplies, food for the men at the front, ammunition, and even, in one case, gunboats. In a quiet unprotesting way the women of Georgia went without everything that they had been accustomed to; household help, male companionship, decent clothing, food and drink, substituting a brew of chickory and okra seed for coffee, and making the homespun dress a badge of honor.

And above all, uncomplainingly. "We have plenty to eat and know that it's only you that is having a hard time," wrote a Georgia woman to her husband at the front.

These behind-the-scenes activities continued, at an accelerating pace, until the end of 1863. Perhaps it was just as well that there was time to grow accustomed to the pressure, to the flow of wounded to the cities, to the mounting casualty lists including family or friends, to the harsh realities of war. Georgia women were being toughened for an even greater ordeal in the months to come.

Those who could not physically serve in one way or another, both men and women, helped to boost morale (and enlistment) with song and verse. Some of the more popular war ballads were composed by Georgians, among them "All Quiet Along the Potomac Tonight," "The Homespun Dress," and "When Upon the Field of Glory." Troops marched to the rhythm of "Goober Peas," a light-hearted tribute to Georgia's lowly peanut (Georgian soldiers were called "Goober Grabbers"), while couples danced, when there was dancing, to "The Secession Quickstep."

In Atlanta, bookseller Samuel Richards printed and distributed the *Soldier's Friend*, a journal for the comfort and entertainment of the men in gray, while in the critical closing months of 1863, with Union armies massing to the north—Atlanta papers and those of other Georgian cities circulated a bit of doggerel that was something of a battle cry:

> Sons of the Empire State, awake!
>   Your country calls you forth;
> Go forth to make the tyrant quake,
>   Go forth to show your worth. . . .

> Go forth and meet him as he comes,
>   With muskets true in hand,
> O, drive him back from Georgia's shores
>   Ye noble! patriot band!

Regardless of poetic merit, the lines were timely. For that autumn of 1863 brought the war indubitably into northern Georgia, with Braxton Bragg driven by Rosecrans out of central Tennessee to Chattanooga and then forced to evacuate that city. While Chickamauga was a tactical success for Bragg, his frightful losses made it a Pyrrhic victory for the South. He withdrew to the mountain fastness around Dalton, to try to make peace with his conscience and with a troubled Jefferson Davis.

In obstinate blindness to reality, the Confederate President first exhorted Bragg, and then Bragg's successor, Joseph Johnston, to take the initiative—plunge back into Tennessee and rout the enemy from Southern soil. Those closer to the action realized that the problem was not the recovery of Tennessee, but the prevention of losing still more territory through a fateful invasion of Georgia by the enemy in Chattanooga.

Mary Jones, wife of Charles C. Jones of Liberty County, received two letters from widely separated parts of Georgia that seemed to recognize this likelihood better than did those in Richmond. From Atlanta in mid-December, 1863, Mrs. Jones's daughter, Mary Mallard, wrote to her mother:

> The report today is the Yankees have fallen back to Chattanooga and have burned and destroyed everything in the country. Our army is at Dalton. Atlanta is being fortified. Some think the next fall back will be to this place. Very dark days may be in store for us, but I trust God will in His merciful kindness keep the enemy from this place.

The second letter to Mary from her brother, John Jones, at his seacoast plantation far to the south of Atlanta, struck the same note. John had lost his overseer and was hard pressed by the care of his slaves and the burden of taxes exceeding his income from cotton. "Sometimes," he wrote, "I think that Providence by this cruel war is intruding to make us willing to relinquish slavery by feeling its burdens and cares." And he added:

Our future often looks dark; the enemy draws nearer. If he passes the mountain barriers of Georgia, the whole state will be most probably overrun. And if Georgia is lost, the Confederacy will scarcely survive, for Georgia is the keystone state of our young republic.

In Atlanta as in Savannah, both on an almost straight line from the Union citadel of Chattanooga to the coast, the true peril was, at first, better recognized than in Richmond. The goal of the Federal armies gathering in southern Tenneseee was to strike through the heart of the Confederacy—toward the city of Atlanta, gateway to the Deep South and the sea.

The Gate City

Atlanta, the greatest spot in all the nation . . .
The very center of creation!

So ran two lines of a quatrain circulated by the town's persistent publisher of short-lived journals, Cornelius R. Hanleiter, in the early 1850s. At that period of the city's booming growth and undeniable promise, no one challenged the hyperbole. For Atlanta was indeed the center of creation—cradle and keystone of the New South born from the union of an older era of plantations and traditions with the inventive vigor of the early nineteenth century.

There had been little on this Middle Georgia ridge in 1835 except pine forests, undulating soil, meandering streams. Even the Cherokees had been driven from their hunting grounds by General Winfield Scott assisted by two cavalry officers, James M. Calhoun and his brother Ezekiel, who would some day become, respectively, mayor and distinguished physician in the city to be established here.

The first settler, however, bore the appropriate name of Hardy Ivy, one to become entwined with history and legend.

Ivy planted his roots on the site in 1833 with "a double log cabin," but did not survive enough winters to see his property soar in value. And soar it did, proving perhaps the most profitable real estate investment of its time. For this was the selected site of two projected railways—the Western & Atlantic snaking down from Tennessee and the Georgia Railroad moving westward from Augusta. More would come later. Where the tracks were to meet, a stake was planted in 1837, labeled "Terminus," and Terminus the little settlement was called throughout its period of germination.

At Zebulon, thirty-five miles to the south, young Samuel Mitchell had made a modest fortune in real estate and merchandising with his partner, John Neal. A visitor took a fancy to Mitchell's horse and proposed a trade. Mitchell considered the bargain uneven until his guest threw in a sizeable area of land at Terminus. The deal was settled and Samuel Mitchell, though not visiting his land till some years later, owned sight unseen a large part of a future town. His partner, John Neal, unaware of it then, would become one of the community's substantial citizens.

When Terminus was no more than a small log cabin community living on hope, few saw a future in the settlement. True, it was slated to be a railroad town, but as of now, the settlers observed, "The railroads don't start nowhere or don't go nowhere." Young Samuel P. Richards of Penfield, Georgia, riding by, saw nothing worthy of note on passing through the village, and had no premonition that he would someday be in business here.

Oddly enough, Stephen Harriman Long, chief engineer of the Western & Atlantic Railroad pushing toward the site, had little faith in the hamlet's future. "Terminus," he declared, "will be a good location for one tavern, a blacksmith shop, a grocery store, and nothing else." But there was one dissenting voice. Young Alexander Hamilton Stephens, riding through the village, observed to a companion that he could not help thinking "what a magnificent inland city will at no distant date be built here." Some forty years later, after a distinguished career as Vice President of the Confederacy, Stephens would occupy the governor's mansion in that magnificent city.

As the railroad tracks approached Terminus, Georgia's Governor Wilson Lumpkin got in touch with Samuel Mitchell at Zebulon regarding the purchase of some of his land for a depot and a right of way. "Speculators and sharpers" had gotten wind of the selected site, wrote Lumpkin, "but how I never knew." The sharpers had, in fact, been plaguing Mitchell with offers, but Lumpkin found Mitchell "a sensible . . . citizen of Georgia, who . . . had accumulated an ample competence of the good things of life," and hence his and Mitchell's transactions were "of a most pleasant character." Pleasant was an understatement. Mitchell donated "all the ground that might be necessary for public purposes free of charge. . . ."

Terminus was on its way. The railroads that "don't go nowhere" were now going somewhere, though it was something of a letdown when the first locomotive to arrive at Terminus in 1842 came in from Madison, Georgia, on a lumbering wagon drawn by sixteen mules. On Christmas eve, however, the engine did haul a passenger coach and a single freight car up the twenty miles of track to Marietta, thus becoming the first train to depart the future city of Atlanta.

Governor Lumpkin made the trip from Milledgeville to see the train arrive at "the rough plank depot with a shed room equipped with a fireplace where all sorts of good liquor could be bought, etc." After the ceremonies, all the visiting celebrants piled into the single coach to be towed up to Marietta to enjoy a bit of festive drinking, while the governor went off to bed. "The joyful folks danced all night," Lumpkin recollected. "There were relays of fiddlers to keep the tunes going. . . ."

Railroads . . . key to America's growth . . . key to the future city of Atlanta. The inhabitants of Terminus were sufficiently inspired by the funnel-stacked locomotive to apply for a charter the following year, renaming the village "Marthasville," in honor of Governor Lumpkin's daughter.

Commercial enterprise came to the town with a young railroad contractor, John Thrasher, who for some obscure reason would always be known as "Cousin John." Thrasher sold his gold watch and carriage to raise capital, then went to work "building and fixing up a store." He observed the arrival, one by one of new settlers, "until we had a right smart little town."

But most of these people, he noted, "were very poor. There were a great many of the women wore no shoes at all. We had dirt floors to our houses."

The same winter that "Cousin John" opened his doors to customers, a lanky red-headed lieutenant in the United States Army visited the area, and made a point of riding his horse up and down the countryside. He etched into his memory, with the would-be artist's eye, the rugged beauty of the mountains, streams and woods; while his military instincts told him how difficult such terrain would be for military operations. But such operations, at this point, were furthest from his conscious mind. William Tecumseh Sherman scarcely knew that Marthasville existed. Nor did he dream that a city named Atlanta, rising miraculously from that wilderness, would be, in precisely twenty years, the target of his ultimate ambition.

As the community's leading benefactor, Samuel Mitchell had a hand in plotting the town, laying out streets and lots, providing for a five-acre State Square in the center of the city. He was assisted by Maine-born Lemuel P. Grant, engineer and surveyor for the Georgia Railroad, who assigned himself a plot on Ivy Street on which to build his future home. Seven thoroughfares were settled on as being adequate for the town: Marietta, Decatur, Peachtree, Pryor, Loyd, and Alabama Streets—reflecting, in their irregularity, the individual independence of the citizens. "The reason why the streets are so crooked," explained Jonathan Norcross, one of the town's early mayors, "is that every man built on his land just to suit himself."

Not surprisingly, many of Marthasville's early citizens were connected in one way or another with the railways. Like Lemuel Grant, Jonathan Norcross came to the vicinity from Maine, to cut and sell ties and other lumber products to the Georgia Railroad. His sawmill, or treadmill, was powered only by a plodding, blind, decrepit horse, but it won distinction as the village's first industry.

Railroad contractors and cousins, George W. Adair and William F. Adair, built homes in the new town, as did Richard Peters, civil engineer from Pennsylvania. Thomas J. Perkerson, who served for many years as county sheriff, settled south of town, while Joseph Willis erected a flour mill some miles west, in a countryside he was certain would remain peaceful forever.

The time was not far off when he would be burrowing into his hillside to protect himself, his family, and neighbors from the ravages of war.

If the arrival of the first Western & Atlantic locomotive failed to bring instant fame to Marthasville, the completion of the Georgia Railroad in 1845 did much more in this direction. For one thing, its first train arrived not by mule power but under its own steam generated by the wood-burning locomotive; and it made the six-mile trip from Decatur in less than three quarters of an hour, uphill all the way.

Descending from the cars to salute the waiting crowd, John P. King, president of the railroad, provided some diversion by stepping into an open well near the tracks. There was some debate as to whether he had actually fallen in, or been snatched back from the brink, but a companion pitched to the bottom and was killed. The incident, however, failed to chill the town's enthusiasm. Marthasville was now a railroad town in truth, and, later, the official city seal would show a locomotive in a circle.

The occasion called for another change of name. Since the railways had sired the community, they felt they had a say in such matters. Richard Peters, superintendent of the Gerogia Road, wrote to "the distinguished civil engineer and railroad king," J. Edgar Thomson, former chief engineer of the Georgia Railroad, asking his suggestion for a name.

Thomson replied: "Eureka—Atlanta, the terminus of the Western and Atlantic Railroad—atlantic masculine, Atlanta feminine—a coined word, and if you think it will suit, adopt it."

The name forthwith appeared on railroad circulars distributed throughout the state, in capital letters above the depot and on public buildings. Newspaper editors, assuming a mythological origin, spelled the name Atalanta after the Greek goddess of the chase, "fit prototype of a worthy namesake." In time the extra "a" was dropped, "though ignorant people continued to call it by the goddess' name." Twenty miles south of Atlanta another future railroad town was inspired to change its name from Leaksville to the better-sounding "Jonesboro."

Things were moving fast now. Two railroads already, and a third was on its way, the Macon & Western entering the city from the south. Jonathan Norcross, rapidly becoming one of

Atlanta's leading merchants, witnessed the arrival of the first train and was hypnotized by that most haunting of all sounds, the locomotive whistle:

> I shall never forget it. It was a clear night and the whistle commenced blowing way out by the Whitehall . . . and the minute I heard it I started on a full run for uptown, waving my hat above my head and shouting, Lord! It was a good large whistle—none of those little penny pipes—and it could be heard everywhere. When I got to the depot I found everybody in town was on hand, and there was more enthusiasm than I ever saw in Atlanta. The engineer blew the whistle for all who wanted to hear it, and it was late before the crowd dispersed.

Jonathan's absorption with a seeming bit of trivia was not misplaced in history's annals. For the locomotive whistle would soon be orchestrated with the rebel yell in a drums-and-cannon Götterdämmerung that Georgians would long remember.

More practically, Norcross noted, "I believe that the real growth of Atlanta began right then." Possibly; but the little city had a ways to go yet, to reach full maturity. A volume entitled *Statistics of Georgia*, covering the year 1848, set the community's population at below 3,000 and described Atlanta as "a place of bustle and business. At this time there are four churches, and another will be erected in the course of the year; six schools, about twenty dry goods and grocery stores, etc. Immense quantities of produce pass through Atlanta. Amount of business done is over 200,000 dollars."

George Gilman "Pete" Smith, a youth of eleven, had just arrived in town with his parents, renting rooms in a multiple dwelling on Marietta Street. Of the first night, he wrote, "I was alarmed by the yelling of the drunken wagoners, who, after selling their cotton and loading up the goods they were to carry to the west, proceeded to fill up themselves. There was no marshal or policeman to tell them nay, and they had a free and easy time. The next day I began my tour of exploration. . . ."

The account of his tour describes what was essentially a typical Western frontier town, lusty and brawling on the one hand, pious and purposeful on the other. Whitehall Street was the principal thoroughfare, he noted, and "There were but few buildings of any pretensions along Marietta Street or Peachtree at that time." The limits of the city stretched for one mile in all directions from the Union Station, called "the car shed," and "the larger part of the infant city, or rather the city in prospect, was a forest."

If the city left something to be desired, the setting and atmosphere did not, and to these Pete Smith responded during his first April in the town:

> I never saw more beauty than there was in the springtime in the groves all over Atlanta. All the undergrowth except the azaleas and dogwoods had been cut out. The sward was covered with the fairest woodland flowers, floxes, lillies, trilliums, violets, pink roots, primroses. . . . Honeysuckles of every beautiful hue, deep red, pink, golden white, were in lavish luxuriance. The white dogwood was everywhere; the red woodbine and now and then a yellow jessamine climbed on the trees. When a stream was found it was clear as crystal. I have seen few things so fair in this world of beauty, as were the Atlanta woods in 1848.

In contrast, however, the city had its seamy quarters, three of them in fact. Murrel's Row, a block of Decatur Street near Pryor, was named for a Southern outlaw whom the district's rowdies sought to emulate. Here grog shops flourished beside gambling dens, and daily cockfights attracted hundreds of the Row's habitués. A section of Whitehall Road was called Snake Nation, haunt of thieves and cutthroats and every type of renegade, male and female. Further out, around the Jonathan Norcross mill, was "Slabtown," shabbily built of cast-off lumber from the mill, and occupied by those whom poverty had made nefarious.

Any one of these, on any Saturday night, was good for a brawl that often turned into a riot. As a result, Atlanta's first mayor and City Council in 1848 ordered the construction of a jail, with walls of hand-hewn timbers three feet thick. The jail, wrote city historian Franklin Garrett, "did not serve its purpose too well."

> Every day or two there was a delivery. Sometimes the prisoners would burrow out. Again, if enough were incarcerated at one

time, they would simply turn the structure over by main strength and return to their haunts. Once, when a general row had packed the calaboose, the comrades of the prisoners visited the jail at night and lifted it off its foundations, holding it suspended while the inmates crawled from under.

In more positive fields the city was making rapid progress. New industries were coming into town, new buildings, hospitals, and churches were going up. There was scarcely time to tidy up a street, before another street was laid, one way or another, on the grid. There was a sort of frantic, un-Southern sloppiness about it, symbols of drive and intense desire to get on with it, no matter what the project was. "Those Georgians will tackle anything," had been a saying in the North; and it was true —as the red-headed lieutenant who had visited this countryside a few years earlier would soon discover.

What had been tackled and finished by 1850 was a tunnel up north through Chetoogeta Mountain, later renamed Tunnel Hill. It made the railroad tracks continuous from Chattanooga to Atlanta, and from Atlanta via the Georgia Railroad to the coastal ports of Charleston and Savannah. The tunnel was christened with a magnum of water from the River Jordan, and Mark A. Cooper, owner of an iron works in Etowah, brought a cannon to the mountain top and fired seven salutes. Cooper also addressed the crowd as to what the tunnel meant for Georgia, saying in part:

> This, the Western and Atlantic Railroad, is the first connection of the Atlantic and the Mississippi. The chain is now complete. This quiet opening of its grand tunnel is emblematical of its peaceful finish. The roar of Georgia's native cannon over that mountain top indicates that in time of peace we are prepared for war.

It is hard to believe that Cooper foresaw the role that the Western & Atlantic would ultimately play in time of war, or that his listeners were even contemplating such a possibility. Their eyes were turned toward a glowing future of unlimited prosperity. The earlier prophecy of John C. Calhoun, champion of Southern causes, that Atlanta was destined to become the greatest transportation center in the Deep South had come true.

In February, 1853, the first map of Atlanta was prepared at a cost of a hundred dollars, a type of project considered generally unnecessary and expensive by most Georgian communities. It showed the city in the shape of a perfect circle, two miles in diameter, its center being near a spot where five main thoroughfares met: Peachtree, Whitehall, Marietta, Decatur, and Line streets, a star formation later dubbed "the Five Points." The city council took impish pleasure in sending copies of the map to other Georgian cities, such as Savannah, Macon, and Augusta, in what one civic historian called "a spirit of nose-thumbing to the older communities."

It was still, to some extent, a city in a wilderness, with primeval forests reaching to the town's back yards, and streams meandering through the streets to be crossed by wooden bridges. Citizens, conscious of their more sophisticated image, began petitioning the city council for improvements. "I live on Cain Street intercepted by brooks and rivulets," one resident complained, "void of access to my house." What could the council do about it?

Another reported personally filling a cavity in one of the city's streets with ninety yards of dirt and "if you think it will do any good please pass me a check." A group of residents asked the council to pass an ordinance "compelling all owners of cows and cattle to have them stabled at night, as there are many citizens of the city who are greatly annoyed by cows lying around their gates and Lots."

This spirit of civic improvement brought gas lights to the city's streets with 80 lampposts installed and serviced by the privately owned Atlanta Gas Light Company. Individual homes, however, remained lighted by the traditional pine knots and tallow candles. An enterprising businessman tried to popularize the sale and use of kerosene lamps, with a two-week trial offer to leading citizens. At the end of that period, the project was summarily rejected with the report that "The oil filled the room with a bad odor and smoked the chimneys. In fact it was a dangerous nuisance, anyway."

With the railroads came also the telegraph, its wires generally following the tracks and used to a large degree in railway operations. The wires were also used for the rapid transmission of news, and Atlanta, which had had a rash of short-lived journals, acquired two substantial daily papers. Foremost and first of these was the *Intelligencer*, published by Jared I. Whitaker and edited by John H. Steele. Before the end of the decade the *Intelligencer* had a competitor in the *Southern Confederacy*, published by the ubiquitous Cornelius R. Hanleiter and pioneer citizen George W. Adair. Though much of their space was given to "business cards," the two papers, especially the *Intelligencer*, came as close as anything could to being the "Voice of the People" in this central city of the South. And that voice rang with confidence up to and through the fateful year of 1861.

For this was Atlanta's golden decade, starting in midcentury, when the city lost much of its innocence but gained much in stature and importance. Wrote Elizabeth McCallie, a descendant of the publisher and civic booster, Cornelius Hanleiter:

> The Atlanta Spirit, that elusive quality, born of the union of the hearts and brains of her citizens, of their loyalty and love, of their idealism and realism, of their cooperation and unselfishness, grew to full maturity during the 50's. . . .

So much happened in Atlanta in those halcyon years, so many changes, so many new faces, that it was hard to keep track of them: new businesses, new buildings, new hotels, new homes and parks. Residents of suburban Decatur, which at first had looked askance at this boisterous infant at its knee, were so drawn to the new metropolis that it was said that in a five-year period Atlanta absorbed two thirds of Decatur's population.

Atlanta's climate, brisk, cool, bracing, was a factor in its growth. It seemed to instill an extra element of sprightliness and vigor in its citizens. It also brought from the lower savannah regions a certain number of wealthy planters anxious to escape, for a time at least, the less healthy and more sultry climate of the southern coastal zone. Some maintained second homes within the city, for temporary residence, but were hardly assimilated into the native population.

For Atlanta was a different breed of city from Savannah and South Carolina's Charleston. It may have lacked much of the latter's continuity of breeding, culture, and sophistication, perhaps because it was dedicated more to the future than the past.

It had the same pride that invested Georgians and Georgia as a whole; but its pride was based less upon yesterday's memories than upon today's achievement and tomorrow's aspirations.

There were some who recalled when Atlanta's social life got off the ground. And that, like so much in Atlanta, went back to the coming of the railroads. When the wife of a railway foreman, remembered only as a "Mrs. Mulligan," demanded a plank floor for her cabin, and lumber and labor were clandestinely appropriated from the railroad to provide it, Atlanta made its debut in society. To celebrate the laying of the floor, the community held its first ball, regarding which John Thrasher took some notes.

> It was a *crème de la crème* affair and the function established Mrs. Mulligan as the leader of the Four Hundred. She was quite a fine-looking woman of strong physique and, if anybody had questioned her leadership, could have established her claim to the championship as well as the leadership.

Perhaps Mrs. Mulligan's hardy qualities set something of a pattern for Atlanta's women. Certainly they seemed made of sturdier stuff than the popular concept of the delicate, over-protected, blanched, and perfumed Southern belle. They lived in a tougher, more realistic atmosphere—a world that combined the drive and ambition of the North with the natural good breeding and refinement of much of the South. They were not wealthy enough to be self-indulgent, even if so inclined. Yet they had enough of the inherent graciousness and sensitivity of Southern women to avoid becoming hardened by their virtue as in Northern Puritan society.

Elizabeth McCallie said it well in her recollections of *Atlanta in the 1850's:*

> There was no leisure class in Atlanta—no ladies who trailed silken garments over polished floors or gentlemen who walked the streets clad in fine broadcloth and satin waistcoats. There were no plantations in the Atlanta area, such as the term denoted in the antebellum South, where hundreds of slaves worked on thousands of acres planted to a single money-making crop. . . .

This does not mean that some of the men and women in Atlanta had no broadcloth suits or silken dresses, but these were worn only on festive occasions. The Atlanta woman in the 50's, like the one in Proverbs, rose "while it was yet night," looked "well to the ways of her household," "ate not the bread of idleness," and dressed properly for the occasion.

While it was true that Atlanta boasted no vast plantations on its borders, there were many profitable farms outside the city, some with as many as several hundred acres worked by 10 to 20 slaves. Most raised food and livestock principally for home consumption, to provide for their owners an abundant and rewarding life. Typical of these was the widespread farm of Jeremiah Huff on high ground northwest of the center of Atlanta. Jeremiah and his wife had bought the property in 1847 and on the foundations of an older house had built their two-and-a-half-story frame and gabled home that would be known in Atlanta's history as "The House of Three Flags."

The farm produced corn, yams, beans, peas, wheat and barley; raised chickens, ducks, and hogs; and maintained an extensive livestock population of cows, mules, and horses. But the Huffs' pride was their daughter Sarah, born in 1856 when Atlanta was, in Sarah's dawning mind, just a mythical "place on a wide road" —the wide road being the Marietta wagon road running past their farm.

Not far from the Huff farm was the 230-acre property of Dexter Niles with its six-room weatherboard house surrounded by a New England picket fence. Niles had come south from Massachusetts to take up farming "Southern style." As anti-Northern sentiment grew in Georgia, especially after the Kansas-Nebraska Act admitted Kansas as a free state, Niles discreetly departed as hundreds of militia volunteers poured out of Atlanta in an "On to Kansas!" drive to battle the decision. Presumably Niles returned with his family to New England, never to realize that his home would become a center of operations against the armies of his native North.

Most of the families with names embedded in Atlanta's history, however, lived within the limits of the town. "Atlanta from its earliest days," wrote Franklin M. Garrett, preeminent

among the city's historians, "attracted men of the highest ranks
... people seemed to sense its coming greatness ... the ambition
of Atlanta's leaders knew no bounds." They came from other
parts of Georgia, North and South Carolina, Alabama, even
Germany and Ireland—but more often than not from nearby
towns which had enviously watched Atlanta's growth.

Up from Macon came Samuel Pierce Richards to join his
brother Jabez in a prosperous book and paper store on Whitehall
Street. The sanctimonious, somberly attired Richards had been
born in the North, and his religiously tended diary showed a
certain ambiguity of sentiment. Lemuel Grant, the engineer,
built one of the town's more beautiful homes on his land southeast of the city. Maxwell Berry, son of a distinguished Georgian
legislator, moved into a house on Fairlie Street with his wife,
Hattie, and five children. Berry, with patriarchal beard and
manner, became one of Atlanta's busier builders and contractors, constructing a good portion of the city's mercantile establishments and churches.

The Calhoun brothers, James and Ezekiel, settled in town on
Washington Street, James as attorney and Ezekiel, having acquired the necessary skills, as combination doctor and apothe-
cary. Edward Everett Rawson of Vermont had left for Georgia
in 1837, and twenty years later settled in Atlanta. Here he became partner in a flourishing hardware business; and on acreage
overlooking Pryor Street, Rawson built perhaps the city's most
handsome residence for his wife Elizabeth and daughter Mary.
Known as "The Terraces" for the terraced hill it stood on, the
home was beautifully landscaped with shrubs, trees, gardens,
bordered paths and well-kept lawns.

John Neal of Zebulon, having built a tidy fortune in partner-
ship with Samuel Mitchell, since deceased, followed his erstwhile partner's footsteps to Atlanta with his wife and seven
children. Anxious to keep his ample family, expanding with
marriage, under one roof, Neal built two homes in the city, one
on Pryor Street, the other ("large, double brick, very handsome") at Washington and Mitchell. He could afford to. Considered "a preeminently big man and as such successful," he was
rumored as being worth half a million dollars, acquired from
mercantile and real estate transactions.

But as with Jeremiah Huff and Maxwell Berry and E. E. Rawson—as with Georgians generally, in fact—Neal's pride was in his children, especially his three young, spirited sons, James, Thomas, and Andrew Jackson Neal. Andrew for one, like Sarah Huff, would hear the marching beat of armies down "the wide road." Thomas would fight for the South on more remote fields, as would his older brother, James. James, however, would be the first of the brothers to don uniform, as an initial member of the long-to-be-venerated Old Guard in Atlanta.

As Atlanta's first military organization, the Guard was composed of the city's leading citizens and sons. Its uniform was described as "a remarkably brilliant one, being dark blue, with dark epaulettes and trimmings, edged with gold. The hat was a black French shako, with drooping white plume. . . . The company, even in antebellum times, were well drilled, and noted for their proficiency in the manual of arms. . . ." Their service, in those early years, was mostly a matter of entertaining their admirers at ceremonial and gala functions.

Entertainment during this period turned from the innocent amusements of the forties to the more sophisticated pleasures of the fifties. There were still those who excursioned to Stone Mountain to climb the Cloud Tower on its top, play in the ten-pin alleys of its four hotels, watch the traveling freak and animal shows of P. T. Barnum, and possibly purchase a white candy dove with buckshot pellets for eyes. Or in the other direction, picnic parties would travel by foot or buggy to Walton Spring, a combination health spa and amusement park. There a Frenchman had mounted a mammoth wooden wheel, rimmed with suspended packing crates for passengers, which could be slowly revolved by the muscle power of two husky blacks—a contraption said to be the prototype of Ferris Wheels to come.

Walton Spring was the source of an unscheduled bit of drama enacted by the future Vice President of the Confederate States and one of the city's noted jurists. A mass meeting and barbecue was held at the Spring to promote the Taylor-Fillmore presidential campaign, and during the festivities Judge Francis H. Cone was heard to remark that the political posture of visiting Alexander Hamilton Stephens branded him "a traitor to the South."

This was repeated to Mr. Stephens, with results recounted by George Smith, present at the time:

> The fiery little commoner said that if Judge Cone said that to him he would strike him in the mouth. As bad fortune would have it, as Judge Cone stood paring his nails on the steps of Dr. [Joseph] Thompson's Atlanta Hotel, Mr. Stephens walked briskly up from the car shed. He saw Judge Cone and at once asked him if he said "he was a traitor." Judge Cone said he did and Little Aleck struck him. The infuriated Judge stuck the knife in hand and knocked Mr. Stephens to the floor and stabbed him repeatedly. He escaped the fury of the mob by a quick flight. Then gave himself up and stood his trial in Decatur and was fined.

The South was no place, then or ever, to accuse a man of treason.

But the picnics and the barbecues and pony rides at Walton Spring, the street performers, hypnotists and magic lantern shows in downtown Atlanta, gave way in the fifties to amateur and semiprofessional musicals, dramas, and stage entertainment. And the city by 1854 had its own legitimate theater. Named the Athenaeum, it occupied the second floor of a building on Decatur Street, between Peachtree and Pryor, built by businessman James Etheldred Williams from Tennessee. Here the family troupe of Mr. and Mrs. William H. Crisp, "the South's most accomplished Shakespearean actors," performed the more serious dramas of the master, unperturbed by the odors of hay and corn, the clatter of carts and iron-shod horses from the wagon yards and stables in the street outside.

On acreage deeded by John Neal's former partner, Samuel Mitchell, a "magnificent depot" (still obstinately referred to as "the car shed") was built between Pryor and Loyd streets to serve the several railroads entering the city. To a large degree the depot was the city's heart, through which its lifeblood of provisions, not to mention people, flowed. Together with the almost adjoining State Square it formed the core of the metropolis.

At Washington and Hunter streets a new brick City Hall and Court House were built by contractor Maxwell Berry and his partner. It was designed to be "commensurate with . . . that importance among the cities of the South which seems indubitably indicated by the signs of the times." On inspection, the brick walls proved to be indifferently constructed, but the city council settled for having them thoroughly "rubbed down" at Berry and company's expense.

The combination City Hall and Court House distinguished Atlanta as seat of the newly formed Fulton County, named for Robert Fulton whose link with Georgia was somewhat tenuous. (Fulton's invention of the steamboat led to the first trans-Atlantic steamer, *Savannah*, leaving Georgia for Liverpool in 1819.) But attempts to have the state capital moved to Atlanta from Milledgeville, as promoted by such citizens as Lemuel and Frederick Grant, was defeated in the Georgia legislature by a ratio of five to three. The capital would come in time, but not until late in the next decade.

Meanwhile, however, Atlanta gained another title, unofficial but enduring. With the completion of connecting railway lines from Charleston on the coast to Memphis on the Mississippi River—with the Atlanta-Chattanooga run a key link in the chain—another railroad ceremony was in order. A hogshead of Atlantic Ocean water was carried to Memphis to be dumped into the Mississippi. Memphis reciprocated with a keg of Mississippi River water to be dumped into the Atlantic.

Mayor William Ezzard of Atlanta joined this exchange of waters on the way, traveling as far as Charleston to attend a banquet there. All the cities on the route of the completed railway chain were ceremoniously toasted—hopefully, for the mayor's sake, in alphabetical order. In any event, he remembered the toast that was drafted for Atlanta:

> The Gate City, the only tribute which she requires of those who pass through her boundaries is that they stop long enough to partake of the hospitality of her citizens.

The Gate City title caught on quickly, in the North as well as in the South. It was more than catchy, it was eminently true. No one could travel by rail from the Mississippi to the Southern coast, from Maine to Florida, without passing through Atlanta. The Old Guard changed its name to the Gate City Guard; a newspaper known as the *Gate City Guardian* appeared (to be later merged with the *Southern Confederacy*); and the cognomen became almost interchangeable with Atlanta.

Along with the passenger depot, the City Hall and Court House, and a new and stouter jail, two institutional buildings appeared in Atlanta which would play important roles in subsequent events.

The Atlanta Medical College at the corner of Butler and Jenkins streets was established largely through the efforts of Doctors John G. Westmoreland and Willis F. Westmoreland, his younger brother. Its faculty included the leading physicians of the town. The college not only started the city toward its future reputation as a leading medical center, but was destined to play a large part in the care and relocation of wounded in the war to come.

Also, toward the end of the decade, the high plot of land at the corner of Collins and Ellis streets, purchased twenty-six years before by Atlanta's first settler, Hardy Ivy, was put to unexpected use. On it rose the Atlanta Female Institute, for the education of a few select young ladies of the city. It was not hailed with universal approbation; there were those considered in greater need of education than select young ladies. But it was pushed into being by the persuasion and contributions of such citizens as Dr. John Westmoreland, his associate Dr. Valentine H. Talliaferro, and one of the "Calico House" sons of Marcus Bell.

The Calico House was virtually the last antebellum home of elegance to rise within the city, built by lawyer-realtor Marcus A. Bell on the corner of Wheat and Collins streets. Three stories high with twelve large chambers finished with oak paneling, its walls were built of native stone, its cupola-topped roof of native slate. One of the contractors, formerly a bookbinding apprentice, painted the house with splashes of blue, red, and yellow— hues used to "marbleize" the inside covers of books. Resembling a currently popular design of calico, the house was appropriately named.

With the influx of visitors from neighboring cities and from other states, new inns and hostelries arose to supplement Dr. Thompson's Atlanta Hotel, erected beside and by the Georgia Railroad—the Gate City Hotel, The Washington Hall, the

Planters Hotel, and, proudest of all, the Trout House, Jeremiah
F. Trout, Prop., at the corner of Pryor and Decatur. Four stories
tall with a hundred rooms, the Trout House made newspaper
headlines by serving the first shad of the season on January 8,
1854.

Most of the business buildings, offices, and stores were built
on Whitehall, Decatur, Alabama, and Marietta streets where
these thoroughfares approached the State Square. Er Lawshe
erected, in 1857, one of Atlanta's leading retail stores; but largest
of all was the block-sized, multiple-business structure of Jonathan Norcross, in the cellar of which Norcross kept a keg of
ginger beer for the refreshment of his personnel. When the keg
stood too long, and the ginger beer became too strong, the clerks
poured it out into the street to be lapped up by an attentive sow
accustomed to this rite, who would then sleep off the effects on
Norcross's sidewalk.

In 1859–60 the first edition of the *Atlanta Directory, City Guide,
and Business Mirror* appeared, noting in its preface: "The incorporated shape of the city is a circle two miles in diameter" and
"The geographic position of Atlanta, being nearly in the center
of the southern section of the American Union, at the point of
great railroad crossings in a right line from New York to New
Orleans . . . give to Atlanta facilities for the commerce of the
country . . . greater than can be claimed for any other inland
city in the South."

The Directory listed 13 churches covering almost every de-
nomination, most of them located near the State Square; 17
insurance agencies, six banks, and a lottery office in the financial
section centered around the intersection of Whitehall and Alabama streets; 17 major commercial buildings, some of them of
block-long size on Peachtree, Whitehall, Marietta, Alabama, and
Washington streets; and a population, "remarkable for its activity and enterprise," estimated at a modest 10,000. A breakdown of population, according to the U.S. census of 1860,
showed expectedly a preponderance of railroad personnel (126),
along with 90 merchants, 49 prostitutes, 41 doctors and physicians, a like number of attorneys, and, at the bottom of the list,
the smallest category: "Young lady, 1."

The population would more than double in the next five

years. Of greater importance, the peaceful pursuits of the city were to change to almost furious militancy in the same short period. To pinpoint a beginning, one might select "old Osawatomie" (John) Brown's raid on Harpers Ferry in October, 1859. By early 1860, rage at the North had fired a growing demand for nonintercourse with the Northern states. An article in the *Intelligencer* for January 14 closed with the paragraph:

> Strike, merchants of Georgia, at the black Republican and Abolition trade of the North! Repudiate it . . . spurn it, and spit upon it. . . . The times demand that no black Republican or Abolitionist shall profit by Southern trade, either directly or indirectly, from cupidity nor from avarice.

When merchants were called upon to sign a resolution to this effect, however, they pulled in their horns, condemning instead the discrimination against Atlanta practiced by Charleston and Savannah, and demanding preferential treatment from these ports. Aside from this sidestepping of the issue, the attitude of Atlantans was spiralling toward secession. The city favored John C. Breckinridge's Democratic candidacy for the White House, and chairman of the Breckinridge Committee, Jared I. Whitaker, issued the enunciation:

> States' Rights men of Georgia, will you sustain the abominable Federal government? Are freemen of the South slaves of the Federal government? Are you to be punished as rebels and traitors, when acting under the sanction and mandate of our own State?

The election of Lincoln, as Mary Chesnut noted, "settled the hash." A group in Atlanta known as the Minute Men of Fulton County was pledged "to stand by the States' rights of the South, their honor, their homes, and their firesides against a black Republican government." The council voted funds to the Gate City Guard for camp equipment, and additional moneys to a quasi-social military unit known as the Atlanta Grays. Georgia's Governor Brown called on the state legislature for $1,000,000 as a "military fund."

A final bombshell was dropped by Georgia's Senator Robert Toombs, addressing the General Assembly at Milledgeville. Of the administration in Washington, Toombs declared:

Hitherto it [the Federal government] has been on the side of the Constitution and right; after the fourth of March it will be in the hands of your enemy. Will you let him have it? *(Cries of "No, no, never!")* Then strike while it is yet today. Withdraw your sons from the army, the navy, and every department of the federal public service. Keep your own taxes in your own coffers. Buy arms with them and throw the bloody spear into this den of incendiaries and assassins, and let God defend the right. . . .

Georgia's Alexander Stephens followed Toombs with the caution that "The greatest curse that can befall a free people is civil war." But Stephens added that, of any decision reached by the people of Georgia, "I am not afraid. . . ."

Arsenal of the Confederacy

The tolling bells had scarcely ushered in the New Year, 1861, when an unfamiliar tremor shook Atlanta—rattling crockery and tinware in the kitchens, sending housewives rushing to their windows, startling the thrushes from their roosts around the State Square.

Earthquake!

No cause, however, for serious alarm, after that first startled recognition. Atlanta was a city where the unexpected happened. Yet people wondered about this eerie visitation, on a sunny, cloudless afternoon, in a latitude not normally afflicted by such spasms. Next morning's *Daily Intelligencer* hailed the phenomenon as a promising omen:

> May not its coming and passing away so easily with the clear and bright sky, be symbolic of the present political convulsion in the country, which, in the South, will pass away so easily, leaving the spotless sky behind. . . ?

The editor's rose-colored vision recognized at least one hard reality. Atlanta was in a turmoil over the issue of secession. All the more so because many of its citizens hoped for some peaceful settlement with Washington. The Honorable Charles Murphey, delegate to the Montgomery convention, prayed that he would never live to see Georgia out of the Union. His prayer was granted. Murphey died on January 16, three days before the Convention met to vote unanimously for secession.

The profile of the South, the gracious life of Georgia, the city of Atlanta would never be the same again.

The news reached Thomas Maguire's Promised Land plantation east of Atlanta primarily by sound waves, Maguire writing in his journal for January 20th, "Sunday—it is thought Georgia is out of the Union as James heard cannon fire last evening towards Atlanta, hope it is so." Later James, one of his servants, returned from Atlanta to confirm the news that "Georgia pulled out of the Union Saturday the 19th. . . . The cannons were heard on Saturday night in honor of the occasion."

Strangely enough, except for the ceremonial salute of cannon, there was none of the exuberant, abandoned celebration in Atlanta which had followed the secession of South Carolina—when a hundred guns were fired, a mile-long torchlight procession was held with fireworks exploding overhead, and Lincoln was hanged in effigy before the Planters Hotel. Perhaps Atlanta had let off enough steam in that earlier jubilee; or perhaps the awesome meaning of secession had struck home.

It was striking home all through the North and South. In Louisiana Episcopal Bishop Leonidas Polk wrote to President Buchanan cautioning against the use of force to prevent secession, for the resulting conflict would end "only after the most ruthless carnage had devastated the land." William Tecumseh Sherman, head of the Louisiana State Seminary, a military institute, thought that "I might have to go to California, or some foreign country where I could earn the means of living." Sherman, with deep roots in the South, resigned his position to think the matter over.

Tom Maguire, over sixty now and temperate by nature, accepted secession with sadness. He turned to the unpleasant task of tying several of his slaves to trees to grill them on who set fire to the barn ("It was Wash"); then prepared for the forthcoming meeting of his home debating society, subject: "Resolved: There is more pleasure in the pursuit than in the possession of an object." Maguire defended the affirmative.

That month, January 1861, Dr. Ezekiel N. Calhoun was nominated for mayor of Atlanta. He withdrew his name because of the "strife and foul means" resorted to in the campaign, and Jared I. Whitaker won the election. Whitaker would not serve long; nine months later Governor Brown appointed him Commissary General of Georgia Troops. But during his administration Atlanta entertained its most distinguished visitor, President Jefferson Davis, arriving via the West Point railroad in "an elegant private car, free of expense."

Little Elizabeth Hanleiter McCallie was among the school children assembled in two rows before the Union Station to greet the President. "It was our privilege to scatter flowers in Mr. Davis's pathway as he rode along between our lines," wrote Elizabeth some years later. "My only remembrance of our great chieftain was that he was tall and thin and rather tired looking as he bowed right and left to the admiring and enthusiastic citizenry."

At a reception in the parlors of the Trout House, the Confederate President spoke of a wish for peace—a sentiment Abraham Lincoln would echo at his inauguration some weeks later. But should the North attempt to coerce the seceded states back into the Union by means of arms, Davis warned, "We shall strike for our rights as our fathers did in 1776."

The President's visit aroused a fervor of patriotism in the city, not yet fully geared for war, but feeling it was ready for it. To celebrate Washington's Birthday, companies of volunteer militia—the Gate City Guards, Atlanta Grays, Fulton Dragoons, Atlanta Cadets, and Fulton Blues—paraded from Marietta Street to the Female Institute on College Hill where the young ladies performed calisthenics in their honor.

All over the split but not yet wholly separated nation, on this last national holiday, men exchanged peaceful gestures over the widening abyss. At West Point, the United States Army Band played *The Star Spangled Banner* and followed it with *Dixie*. At Fort Sumter, in Charleston Harbor, Federal commander Major Robert Anderson ordered the firing of a 13-gun salute, and a Confederate battery on shore returned the courtesy. It was, in each case, like two people toasting one another in farewell.

Two weeks later Vice President Alexander Stephens visited the city to extol preparedness as a guarantee of peace and to assure his listeners that the United States would surrender Fort Sumter to the South within ten days.

In Atlanta and the surrounding villages of Fulton County the militia companies began to mobilize in response to Jefferson Davis's call for 100,000 volunteers. There was a dashing, sporting flavor to these units, mostly youthful, mostly drawn from those who represented Southern "quality." The young officers brought along their own horses and their own slaves as body servants; and their smart gray uniforms were distinguished by a home-stitched scarf, a knitted belt, a smartly crocheted vest provided by sister, wife, or sweetheart.

Their colorful names derived from their leaders, their place of origin, or their imaginations—The Stephens Rifles, The Silver Grays, the Confederate Continentals, the Stone Mountain Volunteers. And almost every prominent name in Atlanta appeared among the roster of officers: Hanleiter, Adair, Neal, Berry, Thrasher, Willis, Mitchell, Hunnicutt, Calhoun. Young Mary Gay of suburban Decatur, who would prove to be one of the unsung heroines of the war, recorded her impressions of one of these volunteer units, writing of

> . . . this company of noble, handsome young men mustered into the military service of their country. It was a beautiful sight! Wealthy, cultured young gentlemen voluntarily turning their backs upon the luxuries and endearments of affluent homes, and accepting in lieu the privations and hardships of warfare; thereby illustrating to the world that the conflict of arms consequent upon secession was not to be "a rich man's war and a poor man's fight."

The first militia unit to be accepted that spring into Confederate Service was Captain George W. Lee's First Regiment of Georgia Volunteers. The occasion called for a parade to the State Square, and the first raising in Georgia of the new Southern flag: a circle of white stars on a field of blue, with two red bars and one of white—the initial "Stars and Bars" of the Confederacy.

First to take off for the wars was the Gate City Guard which assembled at the depot in April to leave for Pensacola. Undiscouraged by a drenching rain, 7,000 citizens crowded the sidewalks, the roofs and windows of the Concert Hall, the Atlanta

Hotel and the Trout House, to cheer the thirteen-car train on its way. Cannon fired a farewell salute; the Honorable Thomas R. R. Cobb gave a valedictory address; and Miss Josephine Hanleiter, daughter of the publisher, presented the company with the new Confederate flag fashioned by the women of Atlanta.

For women, like their husbands and brothers, were mobilizing for the cause. A Soldiers Relief Association was formed at the home of Mrs. Maria (Willis F.) Westmoreland, to provide bandages and lint for the Georgia troops at Pensacola. In anticipation of Atlanta's role as a center for the care of the wounded, the Atlanta Hospital Association and Hospital Aid Society were organized.

At the same time, a group known as the Atlanta Amateurs was created to present concerts and stage plays to raise money for the soldiers and their families. Mary Gay slipped into her diary one of their 1861 program notices:

> Twelfth musical soiree of the Atlanta Amateurs, Monday evening, June 24, for the benefit of Atlanta volunteers, Captain Wooddail, and the Confederate Continentals, Captain Seago, who are going to defend our land. Let all attend and pay parting tribute to our brave soldiers. . . . Doors open at half past 7 o'clock. Tickets, fifty cents.

Governor Brown moved to Atlanta for a stretch, to establish headquarters for the state militia in the city, and to encourage local gunsmiths, blacksmiths, and machine shop operators to produce, along with firearms, 10,000 of his famous "Georgia Pikes." The Confederate Government erected, at Peachtree and Houston streets, a building to house the offices of the Commissary Department, with supply depots on the surrounding streets.

News of the victory at Manassas Junction in July, 1861, brought joy to Atlanta and to its soldiers serving on other fronts. Andrew Neal, in one of his early letters from camp near Pensacola, wrote "I have never seen anything to equal the enthusiasm created . . . [by] the glorious news of our complete triumph at Manassas. Regiment after regiment hurrahed for Jeff Davis and the Southern Confederacy. . . . It seems to me that this ought to put an end to this wicked and unholy war."

Atlantans agreed with Andy Neal and with the words of General Joseph Johnston to his troops, that their heroic performance spelled an early victory for the South. But the community was shortly sobered by the arrival of casualty lists, showing that sixteen of Atlanta's leading citizens had died—a small number compared with the total of 387 Confederates killed, but large in proportion to the city's volunteers. With the necessarily hasty and primitive treatment provided by army surgeons in the field, a condition that would prevail throughout the war, others, too, would die of their wounds in days to come.

Hard upon this report came news of the Gate City Guard which, after brief service at Pensacola, was shifted to Virginia and placed in General Robert S. Garnett's command. After a series of skirmishes with McClellan's forces near Laurel Hill, Garnett attempted to withdraw but was himself killed, while the Gate City troops were cut off from the main body of the army and sought to escape across the mountains through uncharted wilderness. Some died of starvation and exposure; others became mentally deranged by the ordeal; the rest reached Lynchburg, Virginia, with their ranks too decimated to be reorganized. They were mustered out, never again to serve as a unit, although some survivors enlisted in other branches of the service. It was a sad and bitter ending to Atlanta's proudest military unit.

As the year drew to a close, Atlanta had reason to feel hope, if not elation. There was a sneaking suspicion that the war might last a little longer and that victory might come a little harder. Thomas Maguire noted on Christmas day that "There is not near so much bustle among the young folks as usual on this occasion," and went on to record in his journal for December 25:

Abe's government has cast its shadow of war around the country, and gloom and seriousness is the effect, even among the young and thoughtless. It is to be hoped that this misfortune will not long oppress our country, but that peace will soon be established & rejoicing once again resound throughout our country. I shall devote this day to writing to the soldiers that are enduring the hardships of camp life & standing between us as a wall of fire and the vandals of the North, so we comparatively are enjoying peace and the pleasures of home. All honor to the volunteers of the Confederacy—they deserve well of their country.

The acceleration of the war in 1862 put Atlanta on a full-scale wartime basis. Strong leadership was measured by the reelection of Governor Brown and Mayor James Calhoun, which helped to cushion a few shocks to come. Grant's victories in Tennessee, the fall of New Orleans to Farragut, even Bloody Shiloh, did not startle Atlantans as much as James Andrews's raid on the Western & Atlantic Railroad—a cops-and-robbers affair too close to home to be amusing; or the simultaneous surrender of Fort Pulaski in Savannah and the occupation by Federal forces of Huntsville, Alabama. Huntsville was only fifty miles from the Georgia border, while Union control of Fort Pulaski threatened the inflow of war goods through Savannah.

The Andrews raid was a spectactacular but passing affair. The "thieves" (they were not honored with the title of military agents) were jailed in Chattanooga for execution later in Atlanta, but the seizure of Huntsville was a personal affront. The *Southern Confederacy* which had assured its readers in February that "it is probable we will be the last to feel the tread of invasion," now received an unsigned letter proposing two steps for tightening preparedness: the appointment of a citizen vigilante to hunt out and expose "suspicious persons," and the arming of all men over the age of 35 to form a "home guard."

> If we were thus prepared, no three thousand men could hold Atlanta, as they are now holding Huntsville; and knowing that we were thus prepared they would not attempt it. . . .

Perhaps it was only natural that Atlanta was on something of a witch hunt when it came to unknown or suspicious persons. Mary Boykin Chesnut, whose husband was now an aide to Jefferson Davis in Richmond, was visiting Atlanta when she met a family friend, John Darby. Darby had just returned from lecturing in Philadelphia where they "came within an ace of hanging him as a Southern spy." In Atlanta he made the mistake of mentioning that he had been in Philadelphia, and came within an ace of hanging as a Northern spy.

"Lively among you on both sides," he remarked to Mrs. Chesnut, while Mary's comment in her diary was, "What marvelous experiences a little war begins to make."

In May the city was declared a Military Post under the command of Colonel George W. Lee, and with GENERAL ORDER NO. 1 the citizens were handed a new set of rules: military details to patrol the streets and watch the railroad depot for suspicious persons entering or leaving town; cotton, hay, and other combustibles to be removed at a safe distance from army supply depots; no liquor to be sold to uniformed personnel, and drunkenness to be punished by arrest; no blacks to be allowed out after dark.

Mayor Calhoun's young son, Patrick, helped ease the rule affecting the after-dark liberty of blacks. "Sometimes," he later wrote, "the young Negro men would want to visit their sweethearts . . . they would come to me about it, and I would write passes for them and sign my father's name." Playing a benevolent Cupid, Patrick also wrote and delivered love letters to and from the separated lovers, no doubt helping to make his father's administration eminently popular among the blacks. Among whites that popularity was solid. Calhoun was elected and reelected for the duration of the war.

"Our city is in a measure under Martial Law now," Samuel Richards wrote after Atlanta became a military post, "and we have all had to obtain passes to prevent our being taken up at night and put in limbo." His comment was something of a prophecy. In August, Atlanta was officially placed under martial law by order of Braxton Bragg, commanding the Department of the West. A few days later Bragg appointed Mayor Calhoun "Civil Governor" of the city—a title so bewildering to the mayor, since its attendant duties were not defined, that he simply ignored it and carried on as always.

Federal victories in Tennessee, marked by the fall of Nashville and Memphis and Grant's conquest of the rivers, made an angry gash in the northern rim of the Confederacy. The fighting in that state brought trainloads of wounded down the Western & Atlantic Railroad to Atlanta, and the city was fast becoming the most important medical center in the South. Sooner or later some 75,000 wounded would be cared for, or would die, in the Gate City.

The Female Institute on College Hill was converted to a hospital, and the school moved to a house on the John Neal estate. The Medical College, which had suspended operations in 1861 for want of students, was converted to hospital use, as were the Concert Hall, a number of business buildings, and several hotels —the Gate City being used as a distributing center. On the little-used Fair Grounds began the construction of forty buildings to comprise a new General Hospital. Somewhat callously, Samuel Richards recorded in his diary early in the winter:

> Our city is now full of sick soldiers, many of the large hotels and public buildings being appropriated as hospitals . . . we went to one of the hospitals, but soon got enough of seeing such miserable beings as the sick soldiers are—dirty and ignorant as well as sick. One poor fellow died today, who in coming here passed within thirty miles of his wife, and prayed to be put out there that he might go home to die, but the rules of war would not permit, so he had to die among strangers. . . .

Richards' wife, Sallie, more sympathetically involved, was helping to make "comforts" for the 4,000 wounded in the city, presently in need of blankets. In fact, few women of standing were not occupied in either the Hospital Aid Society or Mrs. Willis Westmoreland's Ladies' Sewing Circle which provided lint and bandages and clothing for the patients. Even teen-aged ladies of the town became involved. Among them was Sally Clayton whose father, William Wirt Clayton, was one-time city treasurer and a respected merchant in the community.

The Claytons, like the Neals—like so many families in Atlanta and the cities of the South—were deeply involved in the war, in one way or another. Sally's brother, William, was a sergeant (later, lieutenant) in the Confederate army; an uncle, Paul J. Semmes, was a brigadier general; a cousin, Joseph Benedict Semmes, was a commissary general in Joe Johnston's army; and a second cousin, Raphael Semmes, was captain of the Confederate raider *Alabama*, already helping to rid the seas of Federal vessels and blockaders.

Recently, Sally's father had moved to their present residence at 91 Marietta, and Sally recorded in her journal:

As we were now very near, as soon as the hospital days began, we went every morning, accompanied by a servant, with a large tray of different things prepared for the sick and wounded. None of us, however, went into the wards, except our younger sister, Gussie. We older ones simply assisted in arranging what was to be sent in by the servants and nurses.

How young sister Gussie got into the ward is not explained by Sally; all nurses and stewards were men. Possibly Gussie was considered too young to be conscious of the misery around her. Some women, however, were assigned to the distributing center and even the depot to register the wounded on arrival. Sally noted one "pathetic incident" in which a soldier, shot in the mouth, was unable to speak. Asked where he came from, he could only point north, and once identifying himself as a Federal, the righteous ladies insisted that the wounded enemy should not partake of their bounty.

The steward told Sally that "the ladies were not acting right in not being willing for him to have a part of what they brought; that our men who were near enough, would reach over and divide with him what was given to them. After that . . . the steward was told to provide for him from our tray whenever there was need for so doing, and my sister was instructed in going around with fruit never to omit him." The sister, Lucy believed that they should "try not to let hatred of a cause extend to its advocates, and especially to any one of them who was suffering."

The Soldiers Aid Society—and to some extent the efforts of the various societies were intertwined—was similarly active, reporting for one week in April, 1862, the distribution of:

68 shirts, 75 pairs of drawers, 18 pairs of pants, 6 vests, 9 collars, 72 pairs of socks, 25 towels, 7 handkerchiefs, 5 comforters, old cloths, 15 bottles of wine, 4 bottles cordial, 5 bottles brandy, 8 doz. eggs, hams, beer, butter, milk, coffee, tea, sugar, dried fruit, corn starch, gelatine, meal grits, flour, rice, jelly, pickles, preserves, all-spice pepper, sage, etc.

Besides their contributions to the hospitals, the societies sent gifts to the soldiers in the field, including such curious items as "slippery elm salve" and "six spitoons," along with bottles of ether, tomato beer, cherry pectoral and castor oil. Atlanta's belles volunteered to wrap and ship these articles, and though shy of signing their names were apt to include an inspiring message with, irresistibly, a more intimate postscript:

> This above all—to thine own self be true,
> And it must follow as the night the day
> Thou canst not then be false to any man.
>
> As sure as the vine twines round the stump,
> You are my darling sugar lump.
>
> M.A.C.

Private homes were beehives of activity, the multipleroom Calico House being something of a factory and depot for the various aid societies. Only the square stone Ponder House on the north corporate limits of the city stood apart. From it came strange, gothic rumors of its alcoholic mistress, who "devoted her whole attention to illegitimate pleasures," its independent and ambitious slaves, and the outraged husband, Ephraim G. Ponder, who threatened to shoot his wife, then settled for divorcing her, and left the city for good. His move proved wise in unexpected ways. Cannon and rifle fire would shortly try to reduce the Ponder House to rubble.

Despite the bountiful contributions of the ladies aid societies, wartime shortages were becoming a major problem. Metal for armaments was in particular demand. In an advertisement headed, NOTICE! BELLS WANTED! a surrogate of the secretary of war announced that he was requested "to get all the bell metal I can for cannon. Will the churches hold back their bells? The foundries are stopped for want of metal. . . . Don't delay, for delays are dangerous."

The churches would and did hold back their bells. For at this period, and increasingly throughout the war, Atlanta, among its many other roles, was becoming a center of religious revival in the Confederacy. The church bells were the voice of God, the Holy Ally of the South.

Shortages brought soaring prices. Though Samuel Richards

recorded in his diary that business was good, "printing paper is three times its usual price. . . . All kinds of foreign goods and supplies are getting scarce and selling high." And some time later: "Sallie bought a calico dress of Mr. [Sidney] Root, a part of the goods that ran the blockade lately in the *Memphis* at Charleston. It cost $6.50 instead of $1.00 as formerly. The shoe-maker here asks $12 to make a pair of common shoes; boots $20."

Of necessity, a practice of do-it-yourself prevailed throughout the city. Sam W. Small, a youngster at the time, remembered:

> We made substantial hats and caps from jeans cloth, with corded and quilted brims . . . We carefully shaped, sawed out and polished wooden combs for the family and for buttons we punched out leaden, tin, or wooden forms and covered them with circlets of serge or silk from mother's pre-war scrap-bag. We twisted our own wicks and molded our own candles. We dug up the dirt floors of our smoke-houses and rescued the salt that had soaked into them for years from the overhanging meat.

Sugar was scarce, due to the blockade, and coffee and tea, if available, were drunk "bearefoot"—minus sweetening or milk. Basic necessities were often scarce and, as Sam Small wrote, "increasingly the people were without medicines, thread, imple-ments and personal articles of necessity until a blockade-runner could make a successful entry into one of our ports and bring welcome, but meagre, relief."

Business as usual, where it existed, was given a patriotic flavor. James McPherson, longer established in the book and stationery trade than Samuel Richards, expanded his stock to include "Southern rights towels—of Georgia cotton and made by Georgia hands." Following the Southern trend to music, especially war-oriented ballads and Confederate marching tunes, McPherson also stocked pianos and song sheets to go with them, the latter bearing such titles as "The Southern Marseil-laise," "Dixie Polka," "The Confederate Flag," "God Save the South," and one written by an Atlantan and considered "proba-bly in poor taste" "Adieu to the Star Spangled Banner Forever."

On the whole, however, business and industry were convert-ing almost totally to war production, with machinery brought in from Charleston as required. A revised City Directory, if one were available, would have shown existing in Atlanta by the end of 1862: a pistol factory; a machine shop for the rifling of guns and cannon; a foundry for turning out "buttons, spurs, bridles, bits, buckles, etc., for the army"; a sword factory and a plant producing "Joe Brown's Pikes" for the militia; several factories making guns; Winship's Foundry producing freight cars, railroad supplies, "and other iron products in great quantities"; and, above all, the Confederate Rolling Mill, east of the center of the city on the Georgia Railroad, turning out vast amounts of cannon, rails, and armor plate—some of the latter used on such ironclads as the C.S.S. *Virginia (Merrimack)* at Charleston.

As the campaign in the West slipped slowly eastward toward Chattanooga, Beauregard made Atlanta his principal base, with the Army of Northern Virginia also relying on the city for supplies. A Confederate Arsenal was established at Walton and Peachtree Streets, and from it came many of the shells and cannon that were pounding Grant's and Sherman's armies in the North. Sherman noted the markings on the casings of the shells. He began to see, as he would later openly declare, that the enemy's heart was not the broad, expansive South, nor the tidy capital of Richmond. It could be better pinpointed at Atlanta—from which derived the instruments of war that he contended with.

Despite its military commitments, its overcrowded hospitals, its casualty lists, all was not gloomy in Atlanta. William Crisp's troupe presented Shakespeare's dramas, among them *King Richard II*, "following which, by desire, Mrs. Jessie Clark will sing ROCK ME TO SLEEP." The popular comedian Harry McCarthy thrilled audiences at the Athenaeum by singing his lyrics to "The Bonnie Blue Flag," music from an Irish ballad. Itinerant showmen presenting acts of "riding, tumbling, sleight-of-hand, legerdemain and exhibitions of wild animals" were licensed to appear on the streets or wherever they found room to perform. Atlantans were urged not to miss "Barton's Southern moving panorama & diorama of the great Yankee Stampede at Manassas Plains," while Samuel Richards noted in his diary, "Went to hear Blind Tom, the wonderful negro pianist, at City Hall. He is just twelve years old, and little better than an idiot, but he is truly one of the seven wonders."

For the young people, Lizzie McCallie remembered, "there

was Professor Agostini's dancing class with a free soiree every Saturday afternoon. . . . The old DiGive's Opera House on Marietta St. was a place of enchantment. . . . To find a seat in the mob which charged the door when it was opened was a proof of endurance and skill. It was here I saw at the expenditure of twenty-five cents every artist from Blind Tom to Ellen Terry and Henry Irving, to say nothing of Joseph Jefferson, Bernhardt, Patti and numerous others."

But these pleasant recollections were marred by some unpleasant encounters typical of the open saloon neighborhoods of Southern cities under stress. "The sight of intoxicated men," wrote Lizzie, "the odor of stale whiskey, the swinging doors revealing men in disgusting condition, all combined to make this remembrance one of horror."

In Atlanta, as in other Southern cities at this period of the war, revelry was often not far in emotion from despair.

January 1, 1863. As Lincoln's Emancipation Proclamation met with acclaim in the North, derision in the South, Samuel Richards noted in his diary:

> We enter upon the new year with renewed hope that ere many months the dark tide of war will have passed away, and the blessings of peace be again restored to us. The tidings of another great victory have come to us from Tennessee; the invading army of Gen. Rosecrans, one of the enemy's most successful officers, has been hurled back with the loss of thousands of his men. This is the day for Abe Lincoln to issue his dreadful ukase which will set the sable sons of Africa all free and independent! In the face of the defeats which his grand armies have met with recently the world will laugh to scorn such a Proclamation.

Richards was wrong on almost all counts. The battle of Murfreesboro which had started well for the Confederates, had shortly turned sour. Rosecrans had indeed suffered heavy losses, but so had the Southern general, Braxton Bragg, who was forced to yield more territory to the Federals. Lincoln's Emancipation Proclamation, far from being greeted with derisive laughter by the world, was generally commended overseas; yet few blacks were actually freed by the pronouncement, since it could not be enforced in the Confederacy where the vast majority of slaves was held.

There were occasions for elation and times of apprehension for the city. The Confederacy needed heroes to sustain its spirit, and the South provided many of them. Nathan Bedford Forrest came out of the West with a record of twenty-nine horses shot from under him and thirty of the enemy killed in hand-to-hand combat. When Union cavalry Colonel Abel Streight slashed into Georgia to cut Atlanta's railroads, Forrest pounded after him, "firing at everything blue," until Streight surrendered his entire force of 1700 men near the Alabama border on May 3. Though Streight later escaped from Richmond's Libby Prison, he was never seen again in Georgia.

In thanks for deliverance from this first real threat to its lifeline, Atlanta subscribed to the purchase of "a magnificent charger, completely caparisoned with fine bridle and halter" to be presented to General Forrest when he visited the city in July.

But hard upon this local triumph came the news of Lee's retreat from Gettysburg (where Sally Clayton's uncle, General Semmes, was mortally wounded). And, more alarming to Atlanta, the fall of Vicksburg after six weeks of terrifying siege. The collapse of this Gibralter of the West, the *Intelligencer* cautioned, "would enable Grant to cooperate with Rosecrans in the latter's design of invading Georgia, not with parties of raiders, but with a powerful army." Bragg was already holing up in Chattanooga, having been driven from central Tennessee, and the *Intelligencer* further warned that he could resist an invasion of Georgia only if reenforcements reached him from Atlanta and surrounding territories:

> The proper authorities should realize that if Atlanta should fall, the backbone of the Confederacy would be, for a time at least, broken. For ourselves we would rather be a dog and bay the moon than see our proud old commonwealth overthrown by our Abolition foes.

The proper authorities were duly concerned. In answer to Governor Brown's call for 8000 new militiamen, qualifying citi-

zens in Atlanta below the age of 45 were ordered to appear and
register at City Hall. Mayor Calhoun issued a proclamation
urging all citizens able to bear arms to enroll with one of the
existing military units. Captains of these companies conferred
with Colonel Marcus J. Wright, commander of troops defending
Atlanta, on the deployment of men, arms and ammunition in
the event of an attack on the city.

New companies were organized, while groups claiming ex-
emption by reason of their essential employment, such as the
printers' union, were threatened with conscription when they
dared to go on strike. Even the venerable Silver Grays, cap-
tained by ex-mayor William Ezzard, were slapped on the wrist
for failing to show up for drills, believing perhaps that wealth
and social standing carried certain privileges. And there were
ever the deserters, the laggards, and the able-bodied who adver-
tised for substitutes to take their places in the Confederate
ranks. "Those who talk about shedding the last drop of blood for
the Confederacy," protested the *Intelligencer*, "are strangely silent about the first drop."

The most significant move toward defense, however, came
with the actual fortification of the city. Captain (later Colonel)
Lemuel Grant, now chief engineer of the Department of
Georgia, conferred with Marcus Wright regarding plans for
turning Atlanta into an impregnable stronghold. Grant surveyed the terrain, and started by building minor fortifications
on the Chattahoochee River, north of the city, particularly in
the vicinity of likely fords and crossings.

But, Grant reported, the fortification of the city itself was as
big a problem as the fortification of Richmond. Perhaps bigger.
He envisioned a saw-toothed line of many angles, ten to twelve
miles long, encircling the city. A dozen or fifteen demi-forts, or
major points of resistance, would be placed at equal intervals
around the cordon within supporting distance of each other.

Labor was no great problem. Slaves were requisitioned from
their masters in and around Atlanta, and the owners were paid
a dollar a day for their services. Work progressed rapidly, and
the project was completed by year's end, the saw-toothed line
and its many angles conforming to the contours of the hills. It
was shaped roughly like a circle, averaging one and a quarter

miles from the center of the city, and a little more than ten miles in length, completed on December 1, 1863.

There would be more refinement, auxiliary forts, and trenches, before the line was ready to be tested, but Atlanta was becoming a walled city. Besides the Commissary Department on Pryor and Peachtree streets, the Signal Corps established headquarters in the Gate City Hotel with Atlanta's Charles W. Hubner its director. The Transport Office was located on Whitehall, the Provost Marshal's office on Wadley Street, while the garrison of the Military Post of Atlanta was stationed over a wide area north of Walton Street.

The four volunteer fire departments, normally "a gay, happy lot," occupied their stations in the spartan manner of a military garrison. There was a Remount Depot where army horses and mules were kept on the west side of Pryor Street, and a camp for recruits on the north side of the Georgia Railroad. Almost every conceivable office for the conduct of the war, outside of the capital city of Richmond, was crammed into this fortified inner city of Atlanta.

Private homes, as well as serving as auxiliary hospitals, were also put to military use. Marcus Bell's Calico House became "a beehive of war activity." Its basement rooms and ground-story halls and chambers were used for making and storing supplies for the army, for sewing and packing clothing and foodstuffs for the army and even ammunition for the military. Other rooms were reserved for groups of women knitting and sewing and making bandages, while one long wing was converted into a temporary hospital for Confederate wounded. Citizens were encouraged to meet all trains arriving from the North, and help transport the incoming casualties to the improvised hospitals throughout the city.

The flow of wounded turned into a flood in late September after the battle of Chickamauga. On the 26th, Sam Richards noted in his diary:

Hundreds of wounded soldiers have been brought to our city this week, for a severe battle has been fought since last Friday and during several succeeding days, between our forces under Gen. Bragg and those of the Federals under Rosecrans. We were completely victorious they say, though the loss of men was very great on both sides. Rosecrans was driven back to Chattanooga, where he has entrenched himself it is thought. We took some eight or ten thousand prisoners, 36 cannon and a large quantity of small arms. The battle is called after the stream near which it was fought— "Chickamauga" or "Stream of Death."

Perhaps not many in the city were aware of it, but that battle near the "Stream of Death" signaled the beginning of the struggle for Atlanta. Rosecrans was indeed in Chattanooga and would not be driven out. The city was a Union bridgehead on the Tennessee across which lay the mountains and valleys of north Georgia and the railway leading to Atlanta. Sherman and Grant were on their way from western Tennessee and soon the Confederate troops in Georgia would be heavily outnumbered. What then? The Tennessee would be just one more river to cross, before one of the mightiest armies on the continent would be on Georgia soil.

In Atlanta people complained of the autumn cold and wet, "fit ending to a year of gloom and death." Citizens were outraged at the seizure of their horses by the military, without compensation. War taxes soared, and prices became prohibitive on many items, if they could be had at all: flour $35 for a hundred pounds, eggs $1 a dozen, beef $1 and bacon $1.50 a pound, butter $1.75, and potatoes $12 a bushel.

The price of slaves rose 59 to 100 per cent due to the demand for labor. Samuel Richards thought that his 14-year-old Ellen might sell for $2,000 if he were willing to let her go; and he often felt so inclined, for she and the others were getting insubordinate and impudent. "I am disgusted with negroes and feel inclined to sell what I have. I wish they were all back in Africa or Yankee Land. To think that this cruel war should be waged for them!"

Yet there were those like Sally Clayton and the other young girls of Atlanta who still saw glamor and excitement in the wartime city—in the marching bands as the troops went off to war, the drums and bugles of the state militia drilling in the square, the innumerable uniforms and officers' regalia on the streets. Sally found that this, the last year of her wartime schooling, offered many opportunities for deliciously unorthodox encounters. She had started out from home and passed a regiment of cavalry on Marietta Street, when—

> I suppose the opportunity for a little fun was more than they could resist, for the soldiers began to call "good morning" to me, and then, not only to compliment me in the the highest terms, but to claim me as personal property in terms equally endearing, and laugh, oh! so heartily while I was trying not to be offended and to conceal my embarrassment as best I could, just as though the crimson hue of my face did not show that every remark was having telling effect.

While the Athenaeum was finally closed for the duration, stage plays being considered inappropriate to the times, scarcely an evening passed without a ball or informal dance to raise money to purchase food and other comforts for the troops now wintering at Dalton. The younger girls tended the stalls, selling cake and punch and homemade articles for the benefit of the soldiers, while the more adult young ladies served as dancing partners, carefully chaperoned by dowagers and mothers. Even those women whose men were away at war broke precedent by dancing with the officers.

As LaSalle "Sally" Corbett Pickett, wife of a Confederate officer at the front, expressed it, "They danced as only the women of the Confederacy, at that time and in that place, could dance—waltzing over the crater of a volcano, on the brink of a precipice, with the rumbling of an earthquake only a minor tone in the desperate music of their lives. For if people could not dance in the crises of life, the tragedy of existence might be even darker than it is.

"So they danced through the beautiful bright September night. . . ."

The Army of the Lord

From Dalton, 85 miles north of Atlanta, Lieutenant Andrew Neal wrote to one of his sisters on March 8 about the battle that began with minor skirmishing at 9 o'clock, followed within minutes by the "rattle of musketry, roar of artillery and the yell of charging troops. . . . At times the firing became terrific. . . ."

One time my battery came near being captured by a charge from Cleburne's division. They massed their lines and made a steady advance for our position. I fired rapidly but they came on, and were within thirty paces when they started a rabbit—and everyone took after the rabbit. I thus gained time to limber up my guns and retire to the rear.

The mock battle, one of many staged as an antidote to surplus energy and pent-up spirits, was, as Andy described it to Ella, "a grand and imposing affair . . . lots were cast for victory and Cheatham's and Walker's divisions won against Cleburne, Bate, and Stevenson. . . .

The ground for miles was covered with soldiers and spectators. Thousands of ladies had congregated from all parts of the Confederacy to witness the Military Pageant. . . . Soon the hostile lines began advancing and all the Brigade bands struck up. Ours played "Dixie" and "Bonnie Blue Flag", the other side "Yankee Doodle" and "Hail Columbia." But the sickening sight of the killed and wounded was absent, and their presence was not needed to enliven the scene.

The mimic battles with blank ammunition, the military exercises, even the strict inspections, polished weapons, and clean uniforms were measures of the improvement in spirit and morale within the Army of Tennessee since its defeat at Missionary Ridge. With a new commander and reenforcements present or expected, raising its numbers to close to 40,000, it was, with Lee's forces in North Virginia, one of the two great armies on which the Confederacy pinned its hopes.

Constituted under Braxton Bragg in November, 1862, the Army of Tennessee had fought almost incessantly for twelve months, often against superior numbers, too often under inferior command. It had been engaged in a running battle for over half of Tennessee, on a long road of retreat to Chattanooga, with the Union army under Rosecrans on its heels.

There had been a time of hope at Chickamauga, when the army had fought with brilliance and valor, but when Bragg had failed to take advantage of the Federal confusion. Then came the disaster at Missionary Ridge, from which the troops stumbled back to the valley between Tunnel Hill and Dalton, to pitch their tents on the muddy flats and brood through the long winter—all battles lost, and seemingly all hope forsaken.

Yet they never quite lost heart. "I am where I want to be above all places," Andrew Neal wrote to his mother, "I desire once more to strike for my country and Independence." And to his other sister Emma: "I hope you will not grow despondent at home or think it possible for the South to be subjugated. The men who are doing the fighting have the right to decide when they are whipped, and until they cry enough, others should be silent." And elsewhere to Emma: "Rather than affiliate with the North again I hope our rivers may run with blood. . . ." And again, the footsteps of the enemy, Neal vowed, "shall not desecrate our soil."

There was one thing still remaining in the army's favor: the troops were battle-hardened veterans. Private Sam Watkins, like Neal of Hardee's corps, had been one of the first to enlist in his company and had never been absent from its ranks. He had fought at Shiloh, Murfreesboro, Chickamauga, and "the Battle in the Clouds." His strongest recollection before reaching Dalton was of falling asleep, from total exhaustion, in Ringgold Gap —and remaining asleep through the battle in which the Confederates had held the gap against pursuing Federals. He had waked to see, with surprise, the facing side of the ravine covered with blue-coated bodies, "all lying on their faces. It had the appearance of a roof of a house shingled with dead Yankees."

Sam's exposure to the hardships, horrors, and follies of war had given him a certain armor of philosophy. He was an excellent marksman, coming from Tennessee hunting country, and accepted the need for killing in combat. But "I always shot at privates . . . I looked upon officers as harmless personages." Viewing the scattered dead at Chickamauga, Watkins concluded, "Dying upon the field of battle is about the easiest duty a soldier has to undergo."

And he also realized what every combat soldier since time began had realized, that "Glory is not for privates such as die on the field, or in the hospitals being eat up by the deadly gangrene. . . . Glory is for generals, colonels, majors, captains, and lieutenants. . . ."

Sergeant John W. Hagan, a native of Georgia, described as representing "the sturdy yeoman group . . . that gave tone and character to the Confederate Army" was recovering from "cramp colic" which had overtaken him at Chickamauga. His letters home revealed that common, curious Southern blend of tenderness and toughness; and battle conditions were never allowed to interrupt his correspondence. "You must excuse this scribbled up letter for my knees is my writing desk," he once explained, and on another occasion, "I must close for the shells is bursting too near to me."

Captain Thomas Key of Cleburne's division in Hardee's corps, having left a wife and three children to enlist in 1862, was another veteran of many battles waged by the Army of Tennessee. An artillery officer, he had fought at Chickamauga and Missionary Ridge, and had been part of the rear-guard action which had saved Bragg's army at Ringgold Gap, where Watkins had waked to see the bodies lying like the shingles of a roof.

Deeply devout, Key found that one of the great hardships of the war was the absence of a proper place to worship; he turned to the scriptures as other men might turn to whiskey. And understandably he shunned the little frontier town of Dalton, with its single muddy street of limping factories, bars, and brothels. Here he observed with concern,

> . . . the girls smoke and drink whiskey as if they are fond of the aricle. The war appears to have demoralized everybody, and rumor says that almost half the women in the vicinity of the army, married and unmarried, are lost to all virtue. Oh, what are we coming to! How shall we preserve our character when the women—gentle, kind and good women—forsake the path of virtue?

Even at his own birthday party, arranged by his battalion commander, Major Thomas Hotchkiss, Key was revolted by the behavior of guests, both officers and ladies. "The men had their arms around the girls' waists or necks, and the girls appeared to enjoy the sport as much as the men. Women should have an elevating influence upon men; for this reason alone I visit their society."

Key religiously kept a daily journal of his campaign life in Georgia, characterized by literary flourishes not untypical of soldiers' letters and diaries of the time, among both Northerners and Southerners. In Sherman's army, Major James Connolly, writing to his wife of the sun returning after an April shower, noted that "in a few minutes the rain was stealing away to the clouds, like a bashful lover, after having kissed all the little flowers and caused them to blush scarlet. . . ."

In the Confederate army, Tom Key was similarly eloquent. Night did not fall, "darkness enveloped the earth." Dawn was a time when "the luminary of day shook his locks over the eastern horizon." Others, however, saw daybreak at camp in less lyrical, but still imaginative terms, one infantryman recalling reveille at Dalton in the quatrain:

> Our bugles had roused up the camp
>   The heavens looked dismal and dirty,
> The earth was unpleasant and damp,
>   Like a maid on the wrong side of thirty.

Key, Watkins, Neal—in fact every thinking man among the troops—was depressed, if not overcome, by the feeling of malaise at Dalton. Watkins found the Army of Tennessee

> . . . depleted by battles; and worse, yea, much worse, by desertions. The men were deserting by tens and hundreds, and I might say by thousands. The morale of the army was gone. The spirit of the soldiers was crushed, their hope gone. The future was dark and gloomy. They would not answer at roll call. Discipline had gone. A feeling of mistrust pervaded the whole army.

On top of it all, corruption was rampant in the commissary department, with the troops getting second best while the commissaries helped themselves to the choicer cuts of beef, the better foods, for their own enjoyment or for sale at an outrageous profit. Things got so bad that when a supply train was due in Dalton from Atlanta, the troops boarded the train before it reached the station, broke open the cars and helped themselves to bacon, flour, sugar, meal, on the basis of first come, first served.

Crusaders for the Soldiers Aid Society in Atlanta depicted the troops at Dalton as in dire need of food and clothing; their marching feet, devoid of shoes, were staining the snow with blood. Actually, camp conditions were not unendurable. With time on their hands, a rare experience, the men could forage the countryside for provisions, build mud chimneys onto their conical Sibley tents, and gather firewood for winter warmth. Captain Key permitted his men, once they had built a stable for the horses, to construct log cabins for themselves and a cabin for the mess. Not all were clothed as warmly as they should have been for that chilly mountain country, yet Andy Neal's only request in this department was for a cap to be sent him from Atlanta "at the earliest opportunity. I am literally bareheaded and must have a cap this week else I'll have to tie my head in a handkerchief."

Despite the corrupt administration of the commissary, there was generally enough to eat, with a preponderance of starches —bread and rice, dried peas and potatoes. The ladies of Atlanta and the families of the soldiers sent boxes of foodstuffs that were often subject to plunder in transit or on arrival—containing as they did such coveted treats as sorghum syrup, cakes, pies, sometimes wines and brandies. Occasional foraging around the countryside, though officially frowned on, yielded chickens, turkeys, and at times a pig or two.

Before the organized mock battles, the men killed time with snowball fights, waged with hot-blooded earnestness. Whole brigades and regiments might be engaged, and officers found it helpful to their reputations to participate. The snowballs were often packed with pebbles or spent bullets, turning them into deadly missiles, and causing serious casualities. Combatants boasted of "enemy" personnel put out of action; two men reportedly died of wounds. But most of the "war communiqués," generally in the form of diaries, recorded fairly minor injuries and modest gains or losses. "Capt. C. H. Slocomb lost two front teeth—Lieut. Challeron a black eye—all the men more or less bruised. The captured property is the flag of the Ga. Regiment, 8 or 10 caps and hats, 1 frying pan and 4 or 5 pones of corn bread."

The sport was somewhat spoiled for Private Watkins when the battleground was momentarily cleared, and a convicted deserter was brought to the field. The doomed man was seated on a tree trunk, and the execution squad fired but failed to kill him. A captain tried to deliver the *coup de grace* but his pistol misfired. The bleeding, screaming deserter was propped back up on the stump, and the firing squad had a second chance at executing him. This time they succeeded. The body was carried off the field, and the snowball fight resumed.

Often civilian audiences from neighboring homes and towns, as well as officers with their families, came to witness the snowball fights. In one instance the presence of "Gen. Wright, his wife, and daughters & other young ladies," turned the tide of battle between several Georgia regiments. "We got whipped but the ladies were the cause. The boys all turned to look at them, and the other side took advantage of this, and charged us, and took the general and his ladies prisoners."

At night, when the snow-laden winds of northern Georgia assaulted Sibley tents and cabins, the men hovered around their fires, writing letters, playing cards, and above all singing. The more popular officers were sometimes serenaded by the instrumental groups and choristers. Captain Key recorded that "the band of General Polk's brigade surprised me with a serenade. Composed of one cornet, one bass horn, two violins, two flutes, and one guitar, its music was beautiful and sweet, and its stirring strains moved my heart and aroused sacred and dear memories." From a company surgeon, Key obtained a bottle of whiskey for the players, and "sliced a loaf of bread for their refreshment."

It was a musical war, a singing war. Pocket songbooks shipped up from Atlanta provided the lyrics of sentimental ballads, "Home Sweet Home," "Lorena," "The Girl I Left Behind Me," and "Listen to the Mocking Bird"—the latter with its haunting couplet:

> Why sings the swan its sweetest notes,
> When life is near its close?

Invariably, as the evening waned the emphasis shifted to religious favorites: "Rock of Ages," "All Hail the Power of Jesus' Name," "Just as I Am Without One Plea," and "Amazing Grace, How Sweet the Sound." For, in this late year of the war, a wave of spiritual revival had swept the armies of the South.

"The great unexampled revival is fast increasing in interest," wrote Lieutenant Thomas J. Stokes to his half-sister, Mary Gay, in Decatur. "I have just returned from the creek, where I saw thirty-three baptized in Christ, acknowledging there before two thousand persons that they were not ashamed to follow Jesus in his ordinance." And on another occasion to Mary, "This spirit pervades the whole army. God is doing a glorious work, and I believe it is but the beautiful prelude to peace."

The less reverent Sam Watkins attended a meeting held beneath a shaky, dead tree, in which a group of converts was called to kneel in a line before the improvised altar and dedicate their souls to God. At that moment, providence decreed that the dying tree should also relinquish its earthly ties. Crashing to the ground it struck ten of the converts, killing them instantly. "God had heard their prayers," Watkins concluded philosophically. "Henceforth there was no marching, battling or camp duty for them. They had joined the army of the hosts of heaven."

Captain Key also observed this religious awakening, noting in his diary, "There appears to be a wonderful reform among the soldiery, for they are leaving off card playing, profanity, and other vices, and are humbling themselves before God. May the good work deepen and widen." But Key was enough the military man to see, as well, the need for a human instrument to guide the rudderless Army of Tennessee. Since Braxton Bragg had removed himself, William Hardee had been in provisional command, not wanting the job and not expecting to retain it.

Andy Neal shared this feeling of need for a new and resolute commander, writing to Ella that "for this great purpose it is necessary to have unity of action and unbounded confidence in our leaders." For that "esprit de corps which is essential to success, we want now at the head of this army some General who will act with boldness and follow up every advantage he may gain." Granted such a leader, Andy believed, "This army will fight with all the desperation and valor displayed at Chickamauga. . . ."

Two days after Christmas, 1863, a train from Atlanta rolled into the Dalton depot, and Joseph Eggleston Johnston, aged fifty-four, stepped down into the ankle-deep mud of the squalid town. Pelted by rain which gusts turned into an aerial maelstrom, he was too absorbed in thought and a sense of responsibility to consider the inclement weather and the damage it was doing to his natty Confederate gray tunic with the two stars on its collar. For he had arrived to take command of the Army of Tennessee.

One Georgian soldier, writing home, may have expressed the feeling of most of the army. "The joyous dawn of day seemed to have risen from the night."

Among the first to welcome the new commander was Benjamin F. Cheatham's division, which marched through the rain to Johnston's tent behind its regimental band. When the new commanding general appeared in answer to a courteous summons, Cheatham stood beside him, patted Johnston's head two or three times, and told his troops, "Boys, this is Old Joe."

Three thousand voices responded with a roar that could be heard as far as Tunnel Hill.

From then on he was known affectionately as "Old Joe,"

"Little Joe," or "Uncle Joe"—the man who rode from camp to camp with a feather in his cap, and a smile and a personal word for each that seemed more friendly because of the natural gravity of his features. "He passed through the ranks of the common soldiers, shaking hands with everyone he met," wrote Private Watkins. "He was loved, respected, admired; yeah, almost worshipped by his troops."

Controversy had swirled around his head throughout his long career like the gusty storm attending his arrival.

At West Point where he had been graduated high in the class of 1827, Johnston had been a fellow cadet with Robert E. Lee, with whom he became close friends, and with Jefferson Davis whom he disliked apparently by chemical reaction. Their mutual distrust, whatever the cause, continued and developed through the years.

In his subsequent military service, Johnston's only evident failing was an attraction for lead. In battle after battle against the Seminoles in Florida and during the War with Mexico, though he was cited for "gallant and meritorious conduct," he seemed to absorb more bullets than the action warranted. "Johnston is a great soldier," declared General Winfield Scott, then commander in chief, "but he has an unfortunate knack of getting himself shot in nearly every engagement."

In a brief interlude of administrative work in Washington, he became close friends with George B. McClellan, whom he referred to in his correspondence as "Beloved McC," and more importantly met and married Lydia McLane, sister of a West Point classmate, and a woman of uncommon loyalty and understanding. It was to Lydia that General Winfield Scott appealed, when secession began to divide the generals in the army. "Get him to stay with us," Scott urged. Lydia didn't even consult her husband. "He won't," she said. "Not with your army about to invade Virginia."

She was right, though Johnston's decision was his own. He resigned from the United States Army in April, 1861, and was made a brigadier general of the burgeoning Confederate Army which he whipped into shape while arguing with President Davis over adequate supplies and reenforcements.

At First Manassas he shared with Beauregard the credit for

that early victory, his mere presence seeming to electrify the troops. After his words of welcome and encouragement before the battle, "the soldiers rent the air with cries of joy," recorded Stonewall Jackson, "and all was eagerness and animation."

Next commanding the Army of Northern Virginia, he opposed his old friend George B. McClellan, "beloved McC," in the Peninsula Campaign. Here Johnston evinced his basic strategy in the field. While he respected geography, the mere taking or holding of territory was of no importance to him. He was a thrust-and-parry artist, retreating or shifting as necessary, waiting for the enemy to make his first mistake, then striking with concentrated power when the opportunity arrived. This principle he practiced on the Virginia peninsula, defending Richmond, until shot in the chest and shoulder at Fair Oaks.

During his convalescence in Richmond, the capital's society was divided in opinion about "Little Joe" as it was about the President. One had to be on one side or another in this senseless rivalry, as Mary Chesnut noted in her witty, literate, sometimes caustic diary in which she proposed to tell the story of wartime society "in my own way" ("like a spider spinning my own entrails"). Mary acknowledged the statement that Johnston was popular among the officers and men but when it came to President Davis, "He hates not wisely, but too well."

Her husband, James Chesnut, on the other hand, though adviser to the President, seemed to admire the little gamecock general. He agreed that Johnston "has qualities which attract men to him; that is a gift of the Gods." And he considered Johnston disciplined and courteous, yet "brave and impetuous in action." There were those who thought he matched Robert E. Lee as the prototype of the perfect Virginia gentleman, well-born, well-read, well-educated, courtly of manner, quiet but authoritative.

After Johnston had recovered from his wounds Davis, having passed him over once for a rank that was due him, placed him in command of the armies of the West. "Don't accept it," Lydia warned her husband, "they will crucify you." Johnston accepted it; the army was his life, and part of army life was taking orders. But he would rail against his superior just as Lydia did. In fact, the story of Lydia's fierce loyalty to her husband was in itself a saga of the war. She stood by him throughout, she understood him, and right now, "I think my old soldier shines brightest when clouds are blackest above him," she told a friend.

The clouds were indeed black over Tennessee, where Pemberton surrendered Vicksburg and Braxton Bragg retreated to Chattanooga, and Johnston somehow felt responsible (and was held responsible by some) even though there was nothing he could really do about it. His authority was that of coordinator, more specifically a mediator between the fractious commanders in the West. While he was critical of Bragg's campaigns, he kept that criticism to himself, and shied away from any suggestion that he should replace that hapless general—even though Bragg's own officers were favorable to the move.

The inevitable could not be postponed. When Bragg resigned in December, 1863, in the face of being fired, and William Hardee refused to retain command of the Army of Tennessee, President Davis was left with little choice but Johnston. He could hardly have been left with a better choice, though it would take him a good year or more to come to that conclusion.

On a wintry Tuesday, January 26, Captain Key ordered every man in his battalion to clean and scrub their quarters for inspection. That evening he noted in his diary:

> General Joseph E. Johnston reviewed General Cleburne's command and after he passed the battery I was honored with an introduction to him by General Polk. He complimented my horses highly, and said the men were fine looking soldiers. General Johnston is about 50 years of age—is quite gray—and has a spare form, and an expressive blue eye. He was very polite, raising his cap to me after the introduction.

Key's appraisal of his new commander was more restrained than most. Perhaps the mere change from Braxton Bragg was reassuring. Johnston looked and acted the part of a confident commander. "In his dress he was a perfect dandy," Sam Watkins wrote, "carrying out in every point the dress and paraphernalia of the soldier . . . never omitting anything, even to the trappings of his horse, bridle, and saddle. His hat was decorated with a star and feather . . . and he wore a bright new sash, big gauntlets, and silver spurs. He was the very picture of a general."

Johnston, for his part, saw troops that were sadly lacking in discipline, spirit, and morale. He sensed quickly the despondency that permeated the Army of Tennessee, following its months of disappointments and defeats. He made its reconstruction his immediate goal, shuffling units and commanders to restore a sense of harmony and unity within the ranks. Men and officers had the feeling that, at long last, something was being done to salvage the army and erase the stain of past humiliations.

Discipline was tightened, but that was something the professional responded to. In contrast, amnesty was offered to men absent without leave, and furloughs were granted to one man in every ten, on a system of rotation. Thus Captain Key was permitted to make a perilous visit to his family in Arkansas, traveling with a negro servant through enemy territory to Helena. Finding his home town occupied by Yankees, he had slept in the woods instead of with his wife, and returned disconsolate and ten days overdue. He was not censured for having overstayed his leave.

Morale improved as men began to oil and polish their weapons and take pride in their appearance. Dress parades were held, to the martial beat of smartly stepping regimental bands. Mock battles were staged, and military exercises designed to draw applauding crowds of citizens from Marietta and Atlanta—including a harvest of peach-complexioned Georgia belles who stayed to compliment the troops on their performance. Absentees began returning to their units, and Captain Key, for one, was gratified to note that many of his men were reenlisting for the duration of the war.

"A new era had dawned," Sam Watkins wrote of this resurgence of the army under Johnston's new direction. "He has restored the soldier's pride." Andy Neal wrote to his father, "I never saw this army in such fine spirits, everything is hopeful and confident," while a captain of Joseph Wheeler's cavalry division wrote to his wife, "I doubt whether a volunteer army could be more perfect in its organization than the Army of Tennessee. General Johnston seems to have infused a new spirit into the whole mass, and out of chaos has brought order and beauty."

High praise for a job accomplished in three months of bitter winter.

There were, however, problems other than morale. Johnston estimated his army's strength at 36,000 "effectives," with almost as many absent due to illness, furloughs, and desertions. Opposing him, the enemy command at Chattanooga was gathering more than 100,000 Federal troops with all of the West to draw on for supplies and reenforcements. He appealed to Richmond for more men, and was ordered, instead, to send some of his own men to Mississippi to aid Leonidas Polk in checking Sherman's advance across that state from Vicksburg—thereby weakening his forces in north Georgia.

The cavalry under Joseph Wheeler was short of horses and the army needed more mules and wagons for mobility. The artillery lacked sufficient guns, with more than half the existing number out of commission. Food and supplies from Atlanta via the Western & Atlantic Railroad were subject to continual mixups and delays—it took 36 hours to make the 85-mile run to Dalton, and the railroad refused to operate at night. The troops lacked adequate winter clothing and good boots and shoes.

Johnston began bombarding Davis and Secretary of War James Alexander Seddon for men, arms, horses, and supplies; for rifles, bayonets, blankets, shoes. He argued for the use of slaves in military occupations, to release more men for combat duty. All he got in response were promises and the implication that he had better make do with what he had.

He could not complain of his three army corps commanders —Hardee, Hood, and cavalry general Wheeler—though at least one was actively undermining his position. John Bell Hood had wanted the command, and smouldered inwardly at seeing it in Johnston's hands. Yet no one could question Hood's devotion to the Southern cause, his courage in combat, his gallant disregard of self and safety which had led to maiming injuries at Gettysburg and Chickamauga. He was undeniably a Southern hero, of whom his biographer wrote:

Except for those who gave their lives, few had made greater physical sacrifices than Hood. He went into the war, at twenty-

nine, with a face and physique that were the despair of men and
the delight of women. He emerged with his left arm shattered and
useless, his right leg missing, and his features lined and aged far
beyond his thirty-three years.

Though he could not mount a horse unassisted and had to be
strapped into the saddle, Hood had lost none of the fire that
prompted President Davis to speak of him as "the gallant Hood,
a true hero, worthy of . . . the highest trust." What he had lost
was the perspective and detachment to see a situation in its true
light. His physical handicaps, a tragic love affair during his
Richmond convalescence, and disappointment at not receiving
the top command, had made him bitter, vengeful, and sometimes petty.

Commanding the second corps was Georgia-born General
William Joseph Hardee, a brilliant military theorist who had
authored a book referred to as *Hardee's Tactics*. While he had
fought at Shiloh, Murfreesboro, and Missionary Ridge, he
seemed to be not so much a field commander as an intellectual
student or remote-control director of the operation; also a self-
appointed critic of his fellow officers. Though he was instrumental in having Braxton Bragg replaced by Johnston, he reserved the right to stand in judgment over Bragg's successor.

Commanding the third corps, "Fighting Joe" Wheeler, a native of Georgia, ranked close to Nathan Bedford Forrest and J.
E. B. "Jeb" Stuart among the South's great cavalry generals. But
the cavalry itself was something of a problem, tending to operate as free-lance buccaneers and raiders, independent of the
army as a whole. Wheeler had that spirit of independence to the
point of rashness, and his cavalry at Dalton lacked discipline,
cohesion, and above all, horses. They grabbed every horse that
they could buy or steal from farmers and planters in north
Georgia.

It was hard, under those circumstances, to make the cavalry
an integral part of the Army of Tennessee. The average foot
soldier wanted no part of them and, fairly or not, made that
position clear. After a mock battle at Dalton, Andy Neal wrote
to his father: "It was comic to see the cavalry splashing around
and hear the taunts and jeers of the infantry. Cavalry never has
and never will fight and is heartily despised by the men who do

the fighting. I had rather run any gauntlet than be a cavalry man and ride by a brigade or battery." It was little wonder that the cavalry felt it had to fight its own war on its own terms.

But such was the nature of armies; and Johnston, after three months at Dalton, had unreserved confidence in the Army of Tennessee because the men, due partly to his leadership, had recovered confidence in themselves. He believed his generals to be first rate, and he counted on them. But he made one pertinent observation: "The importance to the Confederacy of defeating the enterprise against Atlanta was not to be measured by military consequences alone. Political considerations were also involved, and added much to the interest of the campaign."

The comment was typical of Johnston's understatement of a problem.

Mary Gay was as meticulous in her records as in the performance of her wartime duties. Thus she noted in her account book:

> From Atlanta to Dalton, $7.75. From the 23d to the 26th of April, 1864, to Mrs. John Reynolds, for board $20.00.
> This trip was taken for the purpose of carrying provisions and articles of clothing to my brother, and his comrades in Joseph E. Johnston's command.

The provisions in this case, which Mary thought safer to deliver in person, consisted of "Good sorghum syrup, and baskets with bread, pies, cakes and other edibles, sacks of potatoes, onions, and peppers." These she worried over like a mother hen on the thirty-six-hour train ride up to Dalton accompanied by her servant Toby, "my faithful aide-de-camp of African descent." The following day her half-brother, Tommy Stokes, obtained leave from his regiment to meet Mary in her furnished room and received this bounty with gratitude.

He had only enough time, however, to eat his fill and take a nap on Mary's bed while she kept the flies away with a handkerchief, "studied his manly young face, and . . . wept to think that God had possibly required him as our sacrifice upon the altar of our country."

Only a woman as spirited and independent as Mary Gay

would have dared to make that trip to camp alone. Others went from Atlanta to Dalton in groups, to bring gifts to the soldiers and watch the military exercises. Sally Clayton had missed a sham battle at Dalton "to which a large number of the young people of Atlanta had gone. My sister, Julia, and I were among those who failed to see it, for we were absent on a visit to friends in Alabama, and could only know from hearsay about the sights and the scenery." She further observed:

We were told of the delightful time had by all who attended, of the beautiful military maneuvers, and especially of the great ex- citement in the crowded rail coach in which they were returning home when it was found to be on fire. While they told me about their fright we could not understand how such a thing could happen at that time of year, when it was too mild for stoves, or other heat in the car, nor could they tell if the fire had been caused by sparks from the engine.

Sally, however, did not miss the excitement when Atlanta turned out to welcome the swashbuckling cavalry raider, John Hunt Morgan. Morgan was already something of a legend in his time. He had rampaged and pillaged over thousands of miles in five Northern states before his gallant band of three hundred and sixty men was forced to surrender on the Ohio-Pennsyl- vania border to a pursuing force five times their number.

Treated and imprisoned like a common criminal, Morgan escaped from the Ohio State Penitentiary in November 1863 by sliding down a rope made of bedclothes. When he visited At- lanta on this early February day, the enthusiastic citizens un- hitched the horses from their shafts so that the people might have the honor of drawing Morgan's carriage through the city. It was, in Sally's estimation, "about the greatest day ever seen in Atlanta."

Sam Richards, too, was among "the large concourse of citi- zens" who went to hear the dashing Morgan speak at a reception in the Trout House. Afterward, the Richards family held an unrelated celebration of their own: "We had our big calf killed as it cost too much to feed her, and beef is so high that we thought it best to make her feed us."

Prices were indeed high, and Confederate currency plummeting in value. A week in one of the remaining Atlanta hotels not converted to hospital use cost $150; while a farmer supplying the city turned all forty of his hogs loose in the woods rather than accept Confederate money for the pork. Large-scale planters such as Howell Cobb offered to sell their produce to the Confederacy at any price, then gave up, and presented it to the government free of charge. Samuel Richards observed that people were coming to his store to buy books that they would never read, simply to get rid of their rapidly depreciating paper currency.

In the face of a warning from the *Intelligencer* that "Georgia is the next state on the Yankee program for invasion," and that "most of the available force of Yankeedom will be hurled against this devoted state as soon as spring comes," people turned to the Church for spiritual strength—as the soldiers were turning to revivalism at the front. Dr. Charles Todd Quintard, Confederate minister and army surgeon, was first to preach at the newly erected St. Luke's Episcopal Church on Walton Street, and was surprised and gratified to see the pews filled with soldiers and officers.

Dr. Quintard's reputation had followed him from Dalton where, as chaplain of the Army of Tennessee, he was a pillar of strength among his many followers. "He was one of the purest and best men I ever knew," wrote one generally irreverent private. "He would march and carry his knapsack every day the same as any soldier." He was said to inspire the troops with the "most sincere emotions of love and respect."

The Episcopal minister had much to do with maintaining morale among the soldiers. When not attending to daily services, he would scour the countryside for clothing and provisions for the troops, administering to their physical as well as spiritual needs. He had written a prayer and song book, published in pocket edition in Atlanta, which was the *vade mecum* of the army. Many, after their tour of duty had ended, cherished the book as a lifetime keepsake.

There were others like him, coming up from Atlanta to preach and otherwise minister to the army—among them Dr. Robert Quarterman Mallard, husband of Mary Jones of Liberty County. Dr. Mallard had come to Atlanta the previous September to take over the Central Presbyterian Church on Washington Street. Mary had come with him, leaving behind the snug plantation life she had enjoyed since childhood, and the couple had settled in the home of Dr. Ezekiel N. Calhoun. Dr. Mallard made frequent visits to Dalton, some of many days' duration, taking with him food and clothing contributed by the various Atlanta aid societies.

This attention from the Church was not lost on the Army of Tennessee. Every soldier in every army in every war in Christendom has believed, or been told, that God was on his side. But it was a conviction more widely held at Dalton than at any other time and place in recent history. "I have never seen such a spirit as is now in the army," wrote Lieutenant Tom Stokes to his sister Mary Gay. "I feel confident that if the enemy should attempt to advance, God will fight our battles for us, and the boastful foe be scattered. . . ."

The enemy did attempt to advance the last few days of February, 1864, and was indeed repulsed. General George H. Thomas hurled units of his Army of the Cumberland against Johnston's defenses at Ringgold and Tunnel Hill, found them too strong, and withdrew, giving added heart to the Army of Tennessee. These thrusts, however, were an omen of trials to come. With the two armies poised on a collision course, baptisms in numbers of forty, fifty, and sixty a day continued at Dalton, and Stokes wrote to Mary that if sufficient time remained the vast majority of soldiers would be consecrated, and "the glad tidings may go forth that the Army of Tennessee is the army of the Lord."

Take the offensive, was Richmond's advice to Johnston at Dalton. Blast the enemy out of Chattanooga before he has a chance to consolidate his forces there. Invade Tennessee and recover lost Confederate territory. And while doing so, check Sherman before he joins the Federal troops already threatening Georgia from the north. Whatever you do, move! Advance! Strike while the opportunity exists!

Johnston was irked by this total misunderstanding of his situation. He had not the troops or wagons or supplies for an invasion of Tennessee. Should he undertake it, he would leave exposed the valleys of northern Georgia, the Western & Atlantic

Railroad, and Atlanta itself with no garrison to defend it but George Smith's militia. Not only that, but his army would run the risk of being cut off from its base, Atlanta. The best he could do was hope to hold his position at Dalton, with which he was not altogether happy.

To a great extent, Johnston knew, he was the victim of misleading reports from his army generals, Hardee and Hood. Hardee, on turning over the command to Johnston, had reported to Davis that the Army of Tennessee was in splendid shape, well provisioned, with morale high. Hood had more or less secretly echoed these assertions, writing to both Braxton Bragg and Davis that the time would never be more favorable for taking the offensive. "The enemy is weak, and we are strong," insisted Hood.

Unaware of the content of these messages which passed behind his back, Johnston made his position plain in a letter to Secretary of War James Alexander Seddon: "This army is now far from being in condition to 'resume the offensive.' It is deficient in numbers, arms, subsistence stores, and field transportation." In point of fact, the Army of Tennessee had lost 18,000 at Chickamauga, 17,000 at Missionary Ridge. True, many absentees had returned; he could look for reenforcements, including Leonidas Polk's Army of Mississippi; and Johnston himself had greatly improved army morale and discipline since he had taken over the command. But the Union Army of the Cumberland at Chattanooga outnumbered his own forces by a ratio of three to two.

That was not all. Sherman was moving toward Chattanooga with the Army of the Tennessee and would shortly be joined there, if reports were accurate, by General Schofield's Army of the Ohio. Johnston would do well if he could cling to Dalton and he was not certain that he could.

Northwest of Dalton ran Rocky Face Ridge stretching south as far as eye could see. It was a formidable barrier, in places 1,400 feet in height, with a few tight passes which could probably be held by well positioned troops and guns. Chief of these was Mill Creek Gap through which the railway ran, now purposefully dammed and partly flooded. Overlooking the gap was Buzzard's Roost, commanding the valley to the west. To the east lay rough and thickety terrain, sliced by innumerable streams, making unlikely a flanking movement from that quarter.

Yet with a certain homing instinct, Johnston turned his eyes toward the south. His army was based on Atlanta, and eighty-five miles was a lengthy distance over which to bring supplies. The Union army was based on Chattanooga, with provisions flowing in from Memphis on the Mississippi and Knoxville in east Tennessee. Should Johnston move closer to Atlanta he would shorten and strengthen his supply line; and force Sherman, when the latter took command at Chattanooga, to lengthen and weaken the Federal supply line. Sooner or later, Johnston might gain an advantage in position that he did not have in numbers.

His goal, as he would later declare, was to "hold Atlanta forever." But just where he started holding would depend upon the movements and intentions of his adversary—William Tecumseh Sherman.

"Atlanta Must Be Destroyed!"

Newspaper correspondents spoke of the "half-wild expression in his eye," the maniacal spirit which possessed him. Others simply called him "mad." Yet to the Federal troops in northern Georgia, camped between Ringgold and Chattanooga, William Tecumseh Sherman was a giant among men. Perhaps the restless, ever-pacing body and the brilliant but erratic mind made him difficult to pigeonhole. So much the better; it kept people guessing.

His fellow cadets at West Point in the class of 1840 remembered "Cump" Sherman as he still appeared in these, his adult years—a tall, spare man with ruddy hair and beard, charged with a nervous, restless energy. He seemed never to eat or sleep, never to pause in his compulsive pacing toward some unseen battleground. His active mind "exuded thought at every pore."

At the Academy he met many whose names would be linked with his in history. Some would be figuratively at his side in time of crisis, such as Henry Halleck and Joseph Hooker. Others would be arch opponents, such as Jubal Early, Braxton Bragg, and Pierre Gustave Toutant Beauregard, the beau ideal Creole from Louisiana. And in his senior year he met one on whom he would depend above all: a slouching, untidy plebe named Ulysses Simpson Grant.

After graduation Cump Sherman spent much of his military service in the South—some weeks of it in northern Georgia above Marietta—but after the Mexican War he resigned for a fling at civilian life. He failed at law and banking, aspired briefly to become a painter, then more practically married the daughter of his guardian, Brigadier General Thomas Ewing, a man of compassion and understanding. (Ewing would later make an eloquent defense of one of the alleged conspirators in the Lincoln assassination plot.) Sherman's subsequent appointment to the superintendency of the Louisiana Military Academy seemed to have him set for life.

Then came the war, one of many traumas in this stage of his career. He loved the South, was steeped in its traditions, and many of his close friends were Southerners. But he loved the Union more. In May of 1861 he rejected a high command with volunteer troops and enlisted as a colonel in the United States infantry, preferring to serve among professionals. Raised to brigadier general after First Manassas, he was sent to Kentucky to take over the army post of General Robert Anderson, former commander at Fort Sumter.

Kentucky was a pitfall in a life beset by the highs and lows of mercurial temperament. In a curious surge of defeatism he so greatly exaggerated the problems facing him, demanding such extravagant concessions, that he was replaced and furloughed from the army. Thoroughly despondent, Sherman contemplated suicide. It took the personal therapy of General Henry Halleck, a close friend since his West Point days, to steer Cump back toward recovery.

On his feet again, Sherman fought well at Shiloh in April of 1862 and joined with General Grant in the assault on Vicksburg, the conquest of which in July returned the lower Mississippi Valley to the Union. He and Grant made a formidable team. Their contrasting natures—Grant pragmatic and practical, Sherman mercurial and visionary—complemented one another. A strong bond developed between them. "Grant stood by me when I was crazy," Sherman later said, "and I stood by him when he was drunk."

When in March of 1864 Grant was appointed commander in chief of all the armies of the United States, he named Sherman his successor as commander of the armies in the West, headquartered earlier at Chattanooga. They were still a two-man team, now with a common goal, the total destruction of the South's capacity to fight. Their respective forces must work together, Grant decreed. He would demolish Lee's army in Virginia and take over Richmond, while Sherman would strike into the Heartland of the South, and seize its second capital, Atlanta.

"You I propose to move against Johnston's army," Grant wrote to his lieutenant, "to break it up and get into the interior of the enemy's country as far as you can, inflicting all the damage you can against their war resources. I do not propose to lay down for you a plan of campaign but . . . leave you free to execute it in your own way." In his memoirs Sherman noted: "It was the beginning of the end as we foresaw it."

In Sherman's eyes the immediate end was not the destruction of Joe Johnston's army; it was the destruction of Atlanta and all that the Gate City stood for. During months of frustration on the battlefields of Tennessee, his troops had stumbled over abandoned munition crates and casings marked "Made in Atlanta." Most of the military hardware hurled against him, most of the shells and minnie balls that had bloodied his army had come from Atlanta's factories and arsenals. Richmond might be the symbolic capital of the South, but Atlanta was its throbbing heart.

Sherman arrived at Chattanooga on April 10, having spent the previous weeks at Nashville on matters of organization and supply for the forces to be brought to his command. For the first time since 1861, in better-forgotten Kentucky, he was once again a full commander in the field, confident, elated, convinced that he was riding on the high tide of his revivified career.

While all great men and, peculiarly, military men, tempt the verbal portrait painter, there seem to be more descriptions of General Sherman than almost any other figure of the war. Perhaps a fascinating factor was the contradictions in the man himself—the Andrew Jackson syndrome—the strange mixture of elements which biographers and painters tried to reconcile:

sensitive, coarse; sentimental, ruthless; blunt and gallant, amiable and humorless. One could take almost any personality-defining adjective, couple it with its antonym, and apply it to this Yankee general.

John Chipman Gray, barely out of Harvard Law School when he joined the general's staff as aide, saw Sherman almost as a cigar-smoking caricature:

> . . . the most American looking man I ever saw, tall and lank, not very erect, with hair like a thatch, which he rubs up with his hands, a rusty beard trimmed close, a wrinkled face, sharp, prominent red nose, small bright eyes, coarse red hands; black felt hat slouched over the eyes . . . dirty dickey with the points wilted down, black, old-fashioned stock, brown field officer's coat with high collar and no shoulder straps, muddy trowsers and one spur. He carries his hands in his pockets, is very awkward in his gait and motion, talks continually and with immense rapidity, and might sit to *Punch* for the portrait of the ideal Yankee.

Henry Hitchcock, like Gray an educated fledgling lawyer, joined Sherman's staff in March and saw him as "a man of power more than any man I remember. Not general intellectual power . . . but the sort of power which a flash of lightning suggests— as clear, as intense, as rapid. Yet with all his vigor, his Atlanta campaign showed . . . abundant caution and the most careful forethought."

Again, a balance of conflicting characteristics; yet this was Sherman's season for abundant caution and most careful forethought. Too much was at stake, for him and for the Union. Though he had not known Joe Johnston personally, their fighting careers had been conflicting since First Manassas, and Sherman saw Johnston as "a most wily and dangerous adversary." But he remained, without arrogance, supremely confident. "Give me men enough and time to look over the ground," he said, "and I'm not afraid of the devil himself."

He had men enough, more than a hundred thousand of them, composing three unequal armies. As with statistics for the Confederate forces, precise numbers varied according to the source and method of computation. Sherman's own tabulation showed the Grand Army of the West as comprising: The Army of the Cumberland, General George Henry Thomas commanding, 60,778 men; the Army of the Tennessee, under Major General James Birdseye McPherson, 24,415; General John McAllister Schofield's Army of the Ohio, 13,559—or an aggregate of 98,707 men, plus 254 pieces of field artillery. Again, a reminder that Union and Confederate army names can be misleading. Thus Johnston's Army of Tennessee is subject to being confused with McPherson's Army of *the* Tennessee.

Thomas's Army of the Cumberland would be the force around which Sherman would build his campaign for Atlanta, the pivotal anchor of his armies as they, hopefully, advanced toward their goal. The lighter, more mobile armies of Schofield and McPherson would generally hold the two ends of his line and be used for flanking maneuvers and lightninglike attacks.

Sherman's total of almost 99,000 troops as of May 1, 1864, did not include several cavalry units still engaged in collecting horses (a constant problem for the cavalry) and yet to join the army. These included a division of about 4,000 mounted troops under Brevet Major General George Stoneman attached to Schofield's Army of the Ohio, and Major General Kenner Garrard's division of roughly 4,500 with the Army of the Cumberland. Also with General Thomas's command were the irregular divisions under Generals Daniel McCook and Judson Kilpatrick. All in all, Sherman's forces camped near Chattanooga probably totaled close to 110,000 men, approximately double, by April 1864, the number under Johnston bivouacked at Dalton.

Sherman had every reason, apart from superior numbers, to have confidence in this tough, hard, seasoned Army of the West. It was western in more than name. Most of the men came from the backwoods regions of Ohio, Illinois, Missouri, Indiana, and Kentucky, with very few regiments from Eastern states. His own former division which he had commanded at Shiloh and Vicksburg, was a pattern for them all, comprised of tall, well-muscled veterans who were used to living off the land; could march with a swinging walk for miles, and did; slept on the bare ground and were primed for action by the first sound of a bullet.

They were not strong, perhaps, on discipline and army ritual, and that was Sherman's fault, if fault it was. The shine on a man's boots or buckle were not as important as his conduct under fire. Precision drilling, in Sherman's mind, had little relation to battlefield maneuvers. Rugged independence made the men resourceful under fire. If the troops good-naturedly hooted and bleated at their commanders (fond of "Bla-a-a-air"-ing at General Francis Blair), and if they often failed to salute or keep in step, in combat they responded to commands like a cracked whip.

As in the Confederate army, most of the troops were young, though not as many were in their teens—there was more manpower in the North than in the South. Charles E. Benton had been barely out of school when he enlisted, in 1862, in the 150th New York Volunteers, inspired by a regimental band parading through Poughkeepsie. Being something of a trumpeter, he visualized himself as marching with that band to battle, leading his army to glorious victory. When war overtook his regiment, Benton was disillusioned to find that bands were dispensable and musicians did double duty as stretcher bearers, often serving at field hospitals instead of at the front.

Benton had seen some action at Gettysburg, however, and looked for more in Hooker's corps under Sherman—a "fighting general" about whom Benton wrote, "no man more completely commanded the confidence and esteem of his men."

Daniel Titus of New Hampshire, twenty-four, had also enlisted in 1862, and was now a lieutenant of artillery in the Army of the Cumberland. He had been in the thick of things at Missionary Ridge, and though he admired General Thomas, he wrote to his wife Emeline that he found the commander "cold and unapproachable . . . he seldom or never indulges in merriment or speaks without weighing his words before he utters them."

As in the Confederate army, and to the same degree, some of the troops were extraordinarily naive, born and raised in a nation that had not experienced a major war in fifty years. Young Elisha Stockwell of Connecticut thought that a battle continued until all on one side or another were dead; he was amazed to see troops disengaged with men on both sides still left standing. Similarly Ted Upson found it hard to believe the soldiers really fired to kill. "Them Rebs got so careless shootin' off their rifles," he complained in a letter home, "they lief to hit us!"

But they had hardened and grown wiser under combat, and

Sherman felt fully confident of them—confident too of his generals whom he had alerted before leaving Nashville and who were with him now at Chattanooga. Major General George H. Thomas, "a high-toned Virginia gentleman," was the reverse of Sherman in manner and appearance. Square of frame, with short dark hair and beard now tinged with gray, he was by nature slow and ponderous, conservative and cautious, commanding strictly by the book. And yet solid as a rock. It was Thomas who, after a railroad accident early in life, was told he would never walk again—then climbed out of bed, walked out of the hospital and back to his career. And it was Thomas who had turned the September tide at Chickamauga Creek, earning the sobriquet, "the Rock of Chickamauga."

His only failing, apart from his exasperating caution, was at worst diverting. Sherman's men, and the general as well, slept in the open or in simple "fly tents," making short shrift of camp amenities. Thomas, fond of comfort, pitched his command in a veritable carnival of wall-tents which Sherman referred to as "Thomasville—a very pretty place—appears to be growing rapidly." Thomas had been slated for command of the Western armies before Sherman got the sign from Grant. But this did not damage their mutual esteem. Asked if he thought that Thomas resented his subordinate position, Sherman replied, "I would take orders from Tom just as he takes orders from me; it doesn't matter which of us is in command." In his memoirs Sherman would write, "Never since the world began did such absolute confidence exist between commander and commanded. . . ."

Though Thomas was often referred to as "Pap" or "slow-trot Thomas" behind his back, just as Sherman was nicknamed "Uncle Billy" by his troops, neither inspired his men with warm familiarity or a sense of fellowship. There was an abrasive wall around them; their personalities appeared to bristle at the touch. But devoted loyalty—especially in Sherman's case—they did inspire. One Federal infantryman, asked to which corps he belonged, replied indignantly: "Corps? What do you mean, 'corps?' I belong to General Sherman's army!"

Sherman was more than satisfied, too, with John McAllister Schofield, commanding the Army of the Ohio—a plump, blond, scholarly ex-professor with a flowing beard who looked a little like Socrates and wore red underwear. His men looked at him askance at first, until they discovered that he chewed tobacco. That compensated for his professorial oddities. Sherman considered him an able man, though sometimes too easy-going and in need of firm direction.

Among the more popular generals in the Union army was James Birdseye McPherson, thirty-six, described as "a noble-looking man of fine, dignified appearance," with dark flowing beard and hair. His charm had captivated even the Yankee-hating belles of Vicksburg when Union forces occupied that town. Of high moral principles and fortitude, he could be, when he chose, lighthearted, gay, companionable. Sherman loved him as a son, and valued his association with McPherson as much as that which he enjoyed with Grant. "If he lives, he'll outdistance Grant and myself . . . a noble, gallant gentleman," said Sherman —knowing that McPherson's chances of survival were diminished by his reckless courage.

At the moment, in late winter of 1864, McPherson was engaged to Mary Hoffman of Baltimore, "a girl of rare beauty and worth," and requested a furlough to enable him to marry her before the campaign for Atlanta started. "Mac, it wrings my heart, but you can't go now," said Sherman; McPherson's presence at Chattanooga was essential. But according to Willard Warner, Sherman's aide, the commanding general "wrote a kind and touching letter to the girl, taking the whole responsiblity, and begging her to consider that General McPherson had no option but obedience or soldierly dishonor, and promising him leave as soon as the service would allow."

Sherman regarded all three of his principal army leaders as "generals of education and experience, admirably qualified for the work before us." There were, of course, numerous others, corps and division commanders, in the cast of the drama he was directing—among them:

Artillery genius Jacob Dolson Cox, former schoolteacher, lawyer, and author, who had an uncanny knack of being in the right place with his cannon at the right time;

Oliver Otis Howard, "a Christian, elegant gentleman," somewhat delicate and slight of frame (and minus an arm lost at First Manassas), but imbued with a deep sense of responsibility;

William B. Hazen, now commanding Sherman's old Second
Division in Howard's corps, whose moment of glory would
come late in the campaign;

John A. "Black Jack" Logan, hard as nails, Celtic in his bronze
complexion and quick temper. Logan was a fighter by inspiration rather than by training, a non-West Point "civilian" soldier,
as was political-minded ex-postmaster John White Geary.

And there were others. To note a few: Grenville M. Dodge
who, as fort commander in Kansas, would later give his name
to the "wickedest town in the West," Dodge City; Joseph
Hooker, known among his men as "Fighting Joe" and "the beau
ideal of a gentleman soldier," handsome, portly, dignified, and
almost excessively courteous—and to Sherman a potential trou-
blemaker. And joining Sherman's staff as volunteer aide, along
with John Chipman Gray and Henry Hitchcock, David P. Conyngham who was moonlighting as war correspondent for the
New York Herald.

The only branch of his army toward which Sherman had
reservations was the cavalry. He considered that arm of the
service flashy, reckless, and too independent-minded to perform
with discipline and purpose. (In strange contrast, Sherman respected Confederate cavalry as much as John Neal, for one,
despised them, and as much as Sherman mistrusted his own
mounted troops. Of Southern cavalry he wrote to "Old Brains"
Halleck: "War suits them, and the rascals are brave, fine riders,
bold to rashness, and dangerous subjects in every sense." He
singled out John Hunt Morgan, Nathan Bedford Forrest, and
William Jackson as "the types and leaders of this class. These
men must all be killed or employed by us before we can hope
for peace.")

Regarding his own cavalry, however, Sherman felt that they
might be good for reconnaissance, but were dreadful at his favorite objective of wrecking enemy supply lines and destroying
railroads. To be effective at the latter, the rails had not only to
be torn up; they had to be wrapped around the trunks of trees
or telegraph poles, then knotted, to make them irredeemable.
The cavalry had neither the time nor patience for the job.

Cavalry general George Stoneman he tolerantly branded

"crazy." Judson "Kill" Kilpatrick deserved his nickname, Sherman thought, for the number of horses worked to death or shot from under him. Typical of Kilpatrick's cavalier attitude toward the war was his note delivered to Confederate general Joe Wheeler, whom he had known at West Point, challenging Wheeler to a duel between their two divisions on the plain below Tunnel Hill, at which time "I will annihilate you and your minions." It was signed, "Your Classmate." Wheeler ignored the proposal.

Kenner Garrard became the butt of Sherman's exasperation with the buccaneering mounted troops. In moments of irritation with the cavalry he would shout, "Gar'd! Where's Gar'd!?" When that officer appeared and inquired what was wanted of him, Sherman would bellow, "What I want is for you to get out of here! Go kill some rebels!"

In general, however, Sherman had few doubts about his officers or troops; they were the finest the North could field. His great concern was readying his massive army of a hundred thousand men for an advance upon the enemy by the end of April —when he expected to get from Grant the order that would launch their joint offensives against Richmond and Atlanta. He became the quartermaster's nemesis, demanding almost impossible quantities of food, fodder, saddles, uniforms, and thousands of horses and mules to haul supplies and field artillery. He was heard storming at one quartermaster:

"I'm going to move on Joe Johnston the day Grant telegraphs me he is going to hit Bobby Lee; and if you don't have my army supplied, and keep it supplied, we'll eat your mules up, sir—eat your mules up!"

Just as Grant's campaign in Tennessee had been a "river war," Sherman's invasion of Georgia would, of necessity, be railroad-oriented. Virtually all provisions came from Nashville, 140 miles west and north, over a single-track railway to Chattanooga, and from Chattanooga south to whatever bases he established on his march toward Atlanta. To increase the capacity of the railroad Sherman ordered the seizure of trains and engines from connecting lines, almost doubling the number of cars and locomotives reaching Chattanooga daily. To make all possible room for war materiel he banned the transportation of civilian goods and passengers, raising a howl of protest among railroad managers and patrons. What of the Biblical tracts that were shipped in large quantities to the men in camp? "Bullets are better than Bibles," was Sherman's terse reply.

He stripped his army to the bone. No need for wagons to carry tents or equipment; let the troops sleep in the field as they advanced, carry their own food on their backs and forage for extras on the way. Beef cattle would be transported on the hoof. The troops, as far as possible, would be self-sustaining. The more they did without, the faster they would move. Sherman's impatience was infectious. As time progressed the men became tensed, primed, eager for action. Even the mules, it was observed, were braying from excitement.

Still there were weeks of waiting to be coped with, waiting for spring to come to Georgia and for word to come from Grant. There was less religious feeling among Union troops, fewer revival meetings to keep the men preoccupied with prayer and contemplation. The sanctimonious General Howard was an exception among major officers; when Sherman remarked that it was "a damn cold day," Howard gently rebuked his commander in chief with the reply, "Indeed, a *very* cold day." As a rule the soldiers felt, as Sherman felt about the Biblical tracts, one's soul was not of paramount concern.

So the days at Chattanooga were spent in rest, recreation and amusement. Races on horseback and foot were held, hunting parties organized—forbidden nighttime coon and possum hunting being highly favored. Gambling was universal, but on a private's pay of eleven dollars a month, as in the Confederate army, the stakes were low. Drinking was hardly a problem since liquor from the commissary was sold to officers only.

Female companionship? Well, some—if one could get an overnight leave in Chattanooga. But like Confederate Captain Tom Key, Private Benton shared the general disgust at the Southern female's addiction to tobacco—repelled to "see the other sex chew 'navy plug' while they mixed bread, or indulge in smoking, varied by rubbing snuff on the gums."

Lieutenant Titus also found Chattanooga a dreary base for an army, and a grim example of a city wrecked by siege. Braxton Bragg's guns, the previous October and November, had destroyed many of the finer homes and the rest had been converted into hospitals. The citizens, wrote Titus, "are killed, prisoners, or refugees in a strange land. A few lame and decrepit old men and women and occasionally a crippled slave alone remain of this unfortunate city." Few Southern cities that Sherman passed through, Titus had yet to learn, would be left in any better shape.

Among the officers in the Federal bivouac, "visiting parties" helped to pass the time, and David Conyngham noted that "Generals and officers, in their gayest uniforms, rode from camp to camp, making it a pleasant and exciting scene." There were also, Conyngham was grieved to note, "foraging parties," foreshadowing events to come. Since his supply line was long and vulnerable, and corn would not ripen in Georgia for several months, Sherman ordered that "the army, as far as practicable, should live on the country." Soldiers took this as license to forage at will, plunder the grain fields and arbors of the countryside, and in many cases pillage the homes of local farmers. Conyngham witnessed "a disgraceful scene of rifling houses, breaking up furniture, ripping up bedticks, and, after making a general mess of things, setting fire to the building."

By the end of April, however, a sense of sober apprehension gripped the army. Sherman, who had operated largely out of Nashville, now set up headquarters in Chattanooga where the warehouses bulged with ammunition and provisions gathered for the spring offenses. The troops were ordered, the first week in May, to fill their haversacks with "five days' bacon, twenty days' bread, and thirty days' salt, sugar, coffee, nothing else but arms and ammunition. . . ." In spite of Howard's objection to profanity Sherman declared he was "damned if he was going to have several hundred wagons slowing down the march" for the sake of carrying supplies; let the troops carry their own supplies.

Expectancy ran high, especially in Thomas' Army of the Cumberland where Private Benton of Hooker's corps swore that the mules were braying for their commander: "HOOK-ER, HOOK-ER, HOOK-ER." On May 5 Thomas led his troops down to Ringgold, eighteen miles south of Chattanooga. Short-cutting across the battlefield of Chickamauga, Benton was disturbed by the gruesome residuals of war, the dead and shriveled trees, "and still a stench of decaying flesh in the air. . . ."

> Some of the slain had been buried, though it had been hastily and imperfectly done. Protruding shoes here and there showed the bones of the foot inside, the flesh having disappeared, and not infrequently a hand would be seen extended above the ground, with the skin dried to the bones and weathered to the color of granite . . . I picked up a skull which had a smooth, round hole through it; small it was, yet large enough to let a life pass out.

Major James Austin Connolly, also of Thomas' command, had a more pleasant experience after the army had fought its way through moderate resistance toward Ringgold:

> . . . after dark, while we were yet lying on the field of the fight, a little lamb came up to me bleating most piteously; I took it in my arms, petted it until it fell asleep like an infant, and lay sleeping in my lap an hour. I couldn't think of leaving it there to starve, and I couldn't take it with me, so I carried it to a house, about a half mile distant, and gave it to a little girl who promised to take good care of it. . . .

Connolly's compassion overcame him again, shortly afterward, when he stumbled upon a Confederate private hiding behind the Union lines, and took him prisoner. The frightened soldier explained that he was only trying to visit his wife and their home was now in Federal hands, a few miles distant. Connolly's sense of responsibility would not allow him to release the man, but he took him to his home, allowed the soldier to spend some time with his wife, then took him back to the Federal camp at Ringgold.

By the first week in May, Thomas was poised at Ringgold, ready to advance, with Schofield on his left and McPherson on his right—the troops of all three straining like bulldogs on the leash. Then, on May 6, came the word. Halleck telegraphed Sherman that Grant was moving against Lee. And in northern Georgia one of the mightiest armies on the continent began to

stir and move with a rumble of wheels and tramp of feet and
hooves toward the south. Thomas pushed through Tunnel Hill,
surprised to find the railroad and tunnel left intact, and paused
before Rocky Face Ridge and the forbidding pass at Buzzard's
Roost.

Shortly Sherman stood beside his senior general and surveyed
the "sharp palisade faces" of the ridge. He could plainly see the
enemy strategically placed in Buzzard's Roost or Mill Creek
gap. Further down, two other passes had been blocked with
troops and guns. "The position was very strong," Sherman observed, "and I knew that such a general as was my antagonist,
Jos. Johnston, who had been there six months, had fortified it to
the maximum." Private Charles Benton also turned his eyes
toward the mountainous ridge, and thought with dread of trying to move against such a position and his chances of survival
if so ordered. Hovering over Buzzard's Roost was what appeared to be, or what he hoped was, just a hawk. No, a companion told him, it was just what he might expect, a buzzard.

"But why does he stay so quiet and so motionless?"

"He's counting us," his friend said cheerfully.

No army in the world, thought Sherman, could assail that
citadel without terrific loss of life. And at this, the very start of
his campaign, he could not afford the cost. Then General
Thomas, reaching into the back of his mind, came up with an
idea. Or was it Joe Hooker who proposed it first? Both would
claim credit; Sherman gave credit to neither. According to his
memoirs, he had simply come to a decision. . . .

In Atlanta, rumors that Sherman was about to make his first
move toward the city were as widespread as the flowering dogwood. Shortly after her return from Dalton, where she had
delivered the baskets of food to Tommy Stokes, Mary Gay was
advised of impending developments—and simultaneously
found herself involved in a strange, somewhat exciting bit of
intrigue. A letter from Tommy informed her that General Johnston was "on the eve of an important move, or change of base."
The regiment had been warned that no equipment or supplies
should be left behind for the comfort of the enemy.

With warm spring weather, much of the army's personal

paraphernalia was no longer needed until fall came round again —notably winter clothing, overcoats, and extra blankets, all precious and in short supply. Tommy and friends had wondered if Mary could secretly store these in her home, against the time when they would be badly needed in the autumn. Tommy cautioned her:

> Consider well the proposition before you consent. Should they be found in your possession by the enemy, then our home might be demolished, and you perhaps imprisoned, or killed on the spot. Are you willing to take the risk, trusting your ingenuity and bravery to meet the consequences? Let me know as soon as possible, as war times admit of little delay.

Mary responded without hesitation. Yes, she would guard with her life the articles sent to her, and would personally meet the shipment at the depot in Atlanta. "If I were willing to enjoy the fruits of your valor and sacrifice without also being willing to share your perils, I would be unworthy indeed."

Shortly thereafter, nine large packing boxes, unmarked except for her name, arrived at the depot, and Mary brought them by wagon to her home. With Toby's aid they were stored in the formal dining room, no longer used for entertaining. The blinds were closed, the sashes drawn, and the dining room door locked and bolted. Thus it would remain—Mary Gay's clandestine cache of supplies for the Army of Tennessee. Sooner or later, she believed, the stores would play a significant role in her life and that of her brother's regiment.

Sam Richards, too, sensed the gathering of storm clouds in the north, noting in his diary on May 6, "At Dalton the enemy seems to be making a demonstration. If we are defeated in these battles, I fear the bright and cheering hopes of peace that now animate all hearts in the South, will be dissipated quickly." Mary Mallard, whose minister husband was at the front, wrote to her mother in Arcadia:

> We all fear the next terrible struggle. . . . A battle is daily expected at the front, though some persons think this will be chiefly a diversion to prevent troops being sent to General Lee.

The Yankees are thought to have about eighty thousand troops at Chattanooga, and General Johnston about sixty thousand, all in fine spirits and expecting a victory. . . .

Mary's letter expressed a common feeling in Atlanta and in the Army of Tennessee at Dalton, namely: that Sherman's forces were considerably smaller than they actually were, and that Johnston would have little trouble holding his defense line a safe eighty-five miles from Atlanta.

The center of activity in the city was still the railroad depot, through which supplies and troops flowed northward to the front. Even Confederate troops sometimes disturbed what little peace and quiet the Gate City might at times enjoy. Sally Clayton recorded a visit to the car shed with her cousin Lucy, to witness the arrival of a unit of Louisiana Zouaves, and found this to be "the only time any of us ran into danger. . . ."

As the troop train reached Whitehall Street, the colorfully uniformed soldiers "began to jump or swing themselves off the cars like so many monkeys and just as the train came under the shed some of them began to shoot off pistols or whatever firearms they had." The depot was under siege, with Lucy and Sarah hiding behind "anything that would protect us from the bullets."

A family friend rescued the two girls, and saw that they got safely home; but home, Sarah discovered, was no longer safe, either. The Zouaves were finally brought to order and "shut up in the City Hall" just opposite the Clayton home. But "the men had no trouble in forming human ladders so they could come and go at pleasure. There was a strong guard around the square on which the hall stood but I don't know how successful they were in keeping them in the enclosure."

In a less lethal manner Atlanta was, at first, besieged more by its own troops than the enemy's. Soldiers passing through, and more specially deserters, burglarized homes and plundered gardens. One farmer just outside the city complained that a group of Confederates knocked at his door and asked to borrow a carving knife. Though they returned the knife with commendable honesty, the farmer later discovered that they had borrowed it to skin a pig that they had stolen from him.

* * *

In the valley below Rocky Face Ridge, Sherman weighed the tactic by which he might save his men from "the terrible door of death that Johnston had prepared for them in the Buzzard's Roost." A half mile away, Captain Thomas Key, with his battery placed on the side of the ridge, noted with grim satisfaction the Union maneuvers on the plain below. The entry in his diary that night exuded confidence:

Let them come! In the justice of our cause, with the memory of dear ones at home and in the name and power of God, we shall meet them with determined and brave hearts and fight until the God of Battles shall give us the Victory.

The Great Chess Game

Saturday, May 7, 1864. Warm and sunny in Atlanta, with more than a hint of summer in the air. Samuel Richards' garden was off to a good start with early plantings of corn, tomatoes, and butter beans, while the spring wheat on Jeremiah Huff's farm was a foot high. Mary Mallard wrote to her mother of the wild azaleas in her yard, "three varieties of pink and one of orange; I have never seen anything so beautiful." As for the war, "no one seems to apprehend danger for this place, for falling back is not General Johnston's policy."

Eighty-five miles to the north, the wind was still brisk across Rocky Face Ridge. From the top of the ridge Lieutenant Lawrence D. Young who had fought for two years with Hardee's corps surveyed the Union troops deployed below. With mixed emotions the young Confederate lieutenant noted:

> . . . we could see extending for miles the enemy's grand encampment of infantry and artillery, the stars and stripes floating from every regimental brigade, division and corps headquarters and presenting the greatest panorama I ever beheld. Softly and sweetly the music from their bands as they played the national airs

were wafted up and over the summit of the mountain. Somehow, some way, in some inexplicable and unseen manner, "Hail Columbia," "America" and "The Star Spangled Banner" sounded sweeter than I had ever before heard them, and filled my soul with feelings that I could not describe or forget. It haunted me for days, but never shook my loyalty to the Stars and Bars or relaxed my efforts in behalf of our cause.

Joseph E. Johnston, on the crest of Rocky Face Ridge, had no such ambiguous emotions. As he saw the orderly advance of Federal troops from their encampment—lines of blue a mile long, punctuated by their regimental bands—he realized this was zero hour, not another of Sherman's many feints. This was real, and he felt the weight of a nation on his shoulders.

Throughout his military life, it seemed, the odds had been against him. He had had to make do with what little he had, stretching his resources to the limit, using terrain in place of numbers, strategy in place of overwhelming force. He was in the same situation now: forty-five thousand men against at least a hundred thousand. Soon, hopefully, General Leonidas Polk would join him with his three-division Army of Mississippi, reducing the adverse odds to less than two to one. Meanwhile he would have to pray for luck, and for his army, without the Bishop-General's aid.

Already James Cantey's brigade, 4,000 strong, the first of Polk's troops, had reached Resaca to strengthen the small Confederate force now guarding the town and the bridge across the Oostanaula River. Johnston had ordered that breastworks be raised to protect the river crossing. Not that he had decided to withdraw from Dalton, but he took no chances. While Rocky Face Ridge provided him with strong protection, it also screened enemy movements on his western flank, making Dalton a potential trap. If he had to withdraw, he would do so to a prearranged fortified position, with his army and supplies intact.

Right now the principal question was just where the massed United States forces would assault his line. Hood and Hardee were well positioned on Rocky Face Ridge, with strong detachments protecting Buzzard's Roost or Mill Creek Gap. Wheeler's cavalry was scouting the other mountain passes, notably Dug Gap six miles farther south. To the east lay difficult terrain, heavily overgrown and webbed with treacherous creeks and marshes. A flanking attack from that direction seemed unlikely. The Confederate position seemed impregnable from east and west.

Sherman's plan of campaign, as revealed to Grant and later reported in his *Memoirs,* was so closely followed that it seems to have been based on hindsight. He would hurl the mighty Army of the Cumberland, in full force, against Johnston's front, to keep the Confederates locked in position. Schofield's Army of the Ohio would add muscle to the Cumberlanders whenever and wherever needed. Meanwhile, McPherson's Army of the Tennessee would slip to the right of Johnston, threaten his rear, and force him to withdraw across the Oostanaula, first of three main rivers between Dalton and Atlanta.

Sherman forewarned Grant, "Should Johnston fall behind the Chattahoochee [the third of these principal rivers], I will feint to the right, but pass to the left and act against Atlanta or its eastern communications, according to developed facts. This is about as far ahead as I feel disposed to look. . . ."

Now, on this seventh day in May, with his troops deployed for the attack, an initial problem had been solved: how to flank Johnston's strong position behind Rocky Face.

Whoever came up with the suggestion hardly matters, though it was General Thomas who knew the terrain best and most probably indicated on the map the secretive course of Snake Creek Gap that twisted through the western mountains from Ringgold to the Oostanaula River. Even Confederate cavalry, preoccupied with reconnoitering close to Rocky Face, would hardly detect an army marching through that mountain passage. Emerging at the southern end of Snake Creek Gap, McPherson would take Resaca by surprise.

No need to think twice. Sherman gave the word to McPherson: Go! At the same time, Thomas and Schofield advanced, flags streaming, bugles sounding bravely, upon Rocky Face.

The campaign for Atlanta had begun.

The storming of Rocky Face Ridge was, to Sherman, princi-

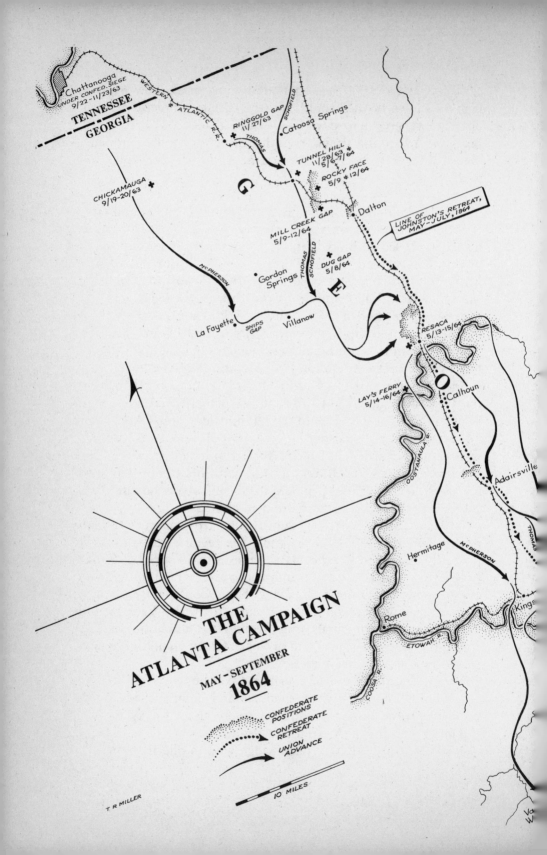

Chattanooga
UNDER CONFED. SIEGE
9/22 – 11/23/63

TENNESSEE
GEORGIA

WESTERN & ATLANTIC R.R.

SCHOFIELD

RINGGOLD GAP
11/27/63

Catoosa Springs

THOMAS

TUNNEL HILL
11/28/63
5/6–7/64

ROCKY FACE
5/9 & 12/64

Dalton

LINE OF JOHNSTON'S RETREAT,
MAY – JULY, 1864

CHICKAMAUGA
9/19–20/63

MILL CREEK GAP
5/9–12/64

THOMAS

SCHOFIELD

DUG GAP
5/8/64

McPHERSON

Gordon
Springs

La Fayette

SHIPS
GAP

Villanow

RESACA
5/13–15/64

LAY'S FERRY
5/14–16/64

Calhoun

OOSTANAULA R.

Adairsville

THOMAS

Hermitage

McPHERSON

THE
ATLANTA CAMPAIGN

MAY – SEPTEMBER
1864

Kings

Rome

ETOWAH R.

COOSA R.

············ CONFEDERATE
POSITIONS

⟶ CONFEDERATE
RETREAT

⟶ UNION
ADVANCE

T R MILLER

10 MILES

Va
W

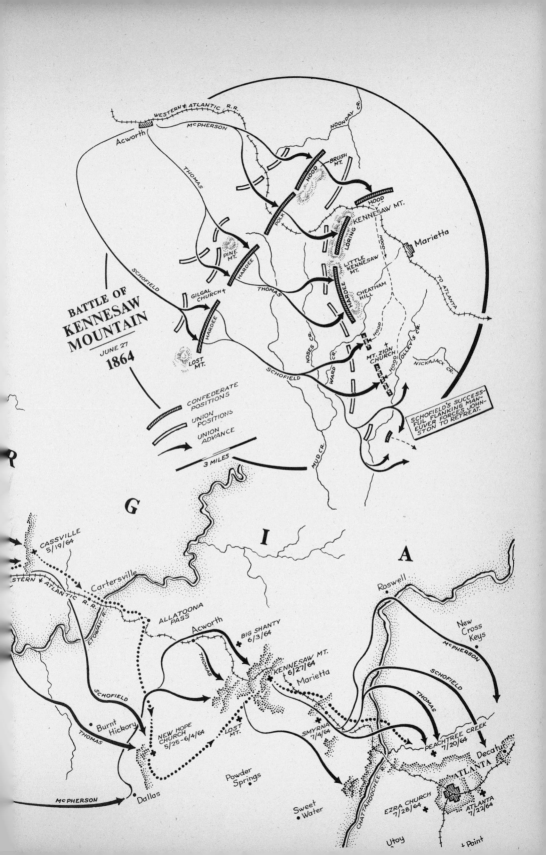

BATTLE OF
KENNESAW
MOUNTAIN
—————
JUNE 27
1864

CONFEDERATE
POSITIONS

UNION
POSITIONS

UNION
ADVANCE

3 MILES

SCHOFIELD'S SUCCESS-
FUL FLANKING MAN-
EUVER FORCES JOHN-
STON TO RETREAT.

WESTERN & ATLANTIC R.R.

Acworth

McPHERSON

THOMAS

SCHOFIELD

GILGAL
CHURCH

PINE
MT.

HARDEE

HARDEE

LOST
MT.

SCHOFIELD

POLK

HOOD

BRUSH
MT.

NOONDAY CR.

HOOD

KENNESAW MT.

LORING

LITTLE
KENNESAW
MT.

CHEATHAM
HILL

Marietta

TO ATLANTA

HARDEE

THOMAS

HOOD

NOSES CR.

WARD CR.

MT. ZION
CHURCH

HOOD

OLLEY'S CR.

NICKAJACK CR.

SCHOFIELD

MUD CR.

R

G

I

A

CASSVILLE
5/19/64

Cartersville

STERN & ATLANTIC R.R.

ETOWAH R.

ALLATOONA
PASS

Acworth

BIG SHANTY
6/3/64

THOMAS

KENNESAW MT.
6/27/64

Marietta

Roswell

New
Cross
Keys

McPHERSON

SCHOFIELD

THOMAS

SCHOFIELD

THOMAS

Burnt
Hickory

NEW HOPE
CHURCH
5/25-6/4/64

LOST
MT.

SMYRNA
7/4/64

PEACHTREE CREEK
7/20/64

Decatur

McPHERSON

Dallas

Powder
Springs

Sweet
Water

CHATTAHOOCHEE R.

EZRA CHURCH
7/28/64

Utoy

ATLANTA

ATLANTA
7/22/64

Point

pally a diversion, but a costly one. Standing beside his general in the valley, David Conyngham watched the blue-coated Federals hurl themselves against the mountain. Their repeated assaults, he recorded, "were met by a fierce fire behind every cliff or rock. Huge rocks were even rolled from the top of the ridge, which came plunging down from crag to crag, crashing and tearing among the trees, and sweeping through the advancing line."

The Union advance was, as expected, stopped in its tracks at the base of Rocky Face Ridge. Only General Hooker's corps achieved some brief success at Mill Creek Gap, piercing the Confederate defenses and obliging Johnston to send Hardee to the rescue. Confederate cavalry general Wheeler, meanwhile, had gone off on his own—an incurable addiction. Without orders from Johnston and with less than 3,000 men he took his cavalry north and east of Dalton with the vain idea of flanking Sherman's left—when he should have been watching the unprotected mountain passes.

The following day Confederate scouts reported a Union force in the vicinity of Snake Creek. Johnston was slow to respond; he could not believe Resaca was in serious danger; he still believed the main threat was to Dalton. However, he sent Hood to Resaca with portions of three divisions to reenforce Cantey's meagre forces in the town.

That afternoon, debouching from the gap, McPherson reported to General Sherman that all had gone as planned—he was within a mile and a half of the railroad at Resaca.

Raising his fist in a gesture of triumph, Sherman shouted: "I've got Joe Johnston dead!"

He ordered Thomas and Schofield to be ready to hit Johnston's army the moment the latter abandoned his line at Dalton.

Sherman's jubilation was premature. Approaching Resaca, McPherson noted sturdy Confederate earthworks bristling with cannon, curving protectively around the west side of the town. How many men were behind those breastworks he could only guess; but he would take no chances. He sent a second message to Sherman reporting that Resaca was too strongly fortified to risk an assault by his army alone. He was pulling back into Snake Creek Gap to wait for the rest of the army to arrive.

It was becoming a comedy of errors. As Sherman later wrote, McPherson with 23,000 veteran troops could have walked into Resaca thumbing his nose at the tiny garrison defending it. Instead, he had cringed before an imaginary foe and slunk back into his burrow at the mouth of Snake Creek. Confederate General Hood, meanwhile, arrived at Resaca, heard that McPherson had come and gone, reported the same to Johnston, and was ordered back to Dalton.

Only Sherman seemed to know what he was doing. McPherson had failed to take Resaca by surprise (later Sherman would tell that general gently, "Mac, you missed the opportunity of your life"), but there was still time for the rest of the army to follow McPherson's route through Snake Creek Gap and intercept Johnston before he reached the Oostanaula.

Johnston, alerted now to this danger to his flank, barely beat his opponent in the race south. As Schofield and Thomas plodded down through Snake Creek Gap, slowed by the single narrow road, the Confederate army sped by foot and train down the railroad to Resaca, where they were joined by Leonidas Polk and his Army of Mississippi. Polk added 18,000 veterans to Johnston's forces, but the ex-bishop's first assignment was to baptize General John Bell Hood in the latter's candlelit field tent, using holy water from a rusted tin can.

By the following day, May 13, Johnston had his troops deployed on high ground north and west of Resaca, his right protecting the railroad on the north, his left anchored on the Oostanaula River below the railroad bridge. It was a strong defensive position, a three-mile arc over knolls and hills, concealed by overgrowth and forest. When his troops arrived, Sherman took up a corresponding position to the west; and the next two days, May 14 and 15, saw what David Conyngham considered the first real battle in the campaign for Atlanta.

Except for one initial thrust against the Union line by General Hood, which might be called successful without consequence, Johnston's posture at Resaca was defensive. Yet he himself stayed in the center of things, riding up and down the line in a "light or mole-colored hat with a feather in it," oblivious to the bullets from Federal sharpshooters on his front. As the troops observed him, Sam Watkins wrote, "there is one little cheer to start with, then the very ground seems to shake with cheers. Old Joe smiles as blandly as a modest maid, raises his hat in acknowledgment, makes a polite bow, and rides toward the firing."

General Sherman made no such display, got no such reception from his men. Arriving at Resaca weary and unshaven after many hours on the march, he stretched out for a catnap in the underbrush. A Federal private spied him.

"Is that man a general?" he asked incredulously. "He looks drunk!"

Aroused by the remark, Sherman raised himself on an elbow and told the soldier without rancor. "Young man, I'm not drunk. I am napping. While you were sleeping last night, I was planning for you, sir. And now I'm tired." The word went through the army that "Uncle Billy sleeps with one eye and one ear open." It was figuratively true.

Sherman had indeed been planning. He sent portions of the cavalry south, to reconnoiter the Oostanaula river for a possible crossing farther south and a way to trap Johnston from the rear. Meanwhile, on midnight of May 14–15 Hooker's corps launched the first of several assaults on the Confederate position. His troops were dead tired from forced marches and insufficient rest, and Daniel Titus was lost in "sweet sleep" when:

> . . . suddenly, unexpectedly the air trembles violently with the din of battle, and the darkness is chased away by the fitful flashes of the musket. Volcanic fires leap forth from the cannon's mouth, and their Apocalyptic thunders startle the weary sleeper from his slumbers. In a moment the enemy's fire is returned & the storm of battle rages with terrible fury.

With the Confederate artillery, Andy Neal wrote a more succinct, less colorful account of the engagement. "Yesterday evening the enemy attempted under cover of night to assault our works. We fired a large building and lit up the field and opened on them with a dozen pieces of artillery, repulsing the attack."

The following day the Union forces renewed the assault. David Conyngham watched as "the column advanced up the hill, steadily, bravely, as if on parade, driving back the rebel sharpshooters and skirmishers to their works . . ."

Over the hill they swept; down the valley in double quick time; across it, raked by a withering fire from the rebel artillery; up the opposite hill toward its crest, where they met a regular shower of shell and bullets. Yet on they swept; plunged through the woods, striving desperately to gain its ascent.

Shells from concealed Confederate batteries seemed to come from all directions, until the attacking troops became so confused that they started firing at each other, unable to distinguish friend from foe. A few intrepid officers, trying to straighten out the mess, inspired and directed their men, charged up to the rebel parapet, and fell dead on its brim. The entire corps, disheartened, started to fall back.

Believing the enemy routed, the Confederate troops climbed to the top of their fortifications to cheer lustily. Their taunting gesture reversed the course of battle. A lone color bearer of the Illinois Infantry turned in his tracks, charged back to the rebel breastwork and planted the Stars and Stripes on its crest. He was shot dead—but his example caused his comrades in the rear to renew the assault, "to be met in the same manner with similar results." According to Lieutenant Young on the Confederate line:

> Three times during the morning and early afternoon were those attacks made upon our lines. It was a veritable picnic for the Confederates, protected as we were by earthworks and with clear and open ground in front. Had Sherman continued this business during the entire day (as we hoped he would) the campaign for Atlanta would have ended right there.

Both sides, however, remained dormant throughout the rest of the day and evening, taunting one another across the narrow no-man's land dividing them. "We had some rich conversation," Andy Neal reported to his father:

> Our boys hollered the news [of Confederate victories] to the Yankees—they asked "What is Confederate money worth?" Our boys answered "What niggers command your brigade?" "Have the niggers improved the Yankee bread?" and all sorts of things

—it was a rich scene. There is a creek about 100 yards from our front. Yankees swear we shall have no water from it tomorrow. We'll see.

Nobody stopped for water from the creek that following day. Union General McPherson had finally brought his guns within range of the railroad bridge across the Oostanaula, while Federal cavalry had managed to cross the river at Lay's Ferry six miles to the south and west. Once again a strongly held Confederate position was imperilled. Once again, over the still surviving bridge and pontoons thrown across the river, Johnston started to withdraw his troops, heading south down the railway line toward Calhoun.

The following morning, before Sherman took off in pursuit, David Conyngham tramped over the battleground to assay the cost to the Union of two captured cannon—all they had to show for two days' fighting during which two generals, Hooker and Kilpatrick, had been wounded. He found the field before Resaca

... thickly strewn with the dead and wounded. Inside and around the earthworks, rebel and Union officers and men lay piled together; some transfixed with bayonet wounds, their faces wearing that fierce contorted look that marks those who have suffered agony. Others, who were shot dead, lay with their calm faces and glassy eyes turned to heaven. One might think that they were sleeping. . . .

Others had their skulls crushed in by the end of a musket while the owners of the muskets lay still beside them, with the death grip tightened on the pieces. Clinging to one of the guns, with his hand on the spoke and his body bent as if drawing it, lay a youth with the top of his head shot off. Another near him, his body cut in two, still clung to the ropes.

Burning the railroad bridge below Resaca, after his withdrawal from that city, Johnston had hoped to make a stand at Calhoun, catching and fragmenting Sherman's army as it crossed the river piecemeal. But on second thought he rejected the position. Above Calhoun lay only an open plain divided by a swollen stream which would in turn have divided any line he formed there. He decided to move farther south toward Adairsville, but meanwhile established an overnight camp, set out pickets, and gave his troops an 18-hour rest.

For the first time since rejoining the Army of Tennessee, Private George W. Hagan of the Twenty-ninth Georgia Volunteers found time to write to his wife. Private Hagan lacked the eloquence of Captain Key or the blunt repertorial talent of Sam Watkins, but his letters—which disregarded syntax, spelling, and punctuation—reflected the general confusion of the common soldier in this running battle that appeared to have no definition, no start, no middle, and no end:

> I can not give you any news that is good. the yanks have flanked us from Dalton to Calhoon 25 miles our forces have fought them very hard & in some places whiped them our line of Battle now is about 30 miles long & we are compeled to fall back I do not Know how far we will fall back, our forces have done some of the hardest fighting I ever heard we have not been in the fight but we have been held in reserve & Some of our boys have been wounded, . . . I come near geting struck with grape Shot it mist my head 2 inches & the[r]ew Splinters in my face I do not Know how the fight is going on some times they whip us & some times we whip them & they Keepe flanking us & compeling us to fall back some times our line is fighting for 15 miles at a time.

The following afternoon the army reached Adairsville. At first glance the site looked promising. A high ridge encircled the town. Through it flowed the Oothcaloga Creek, forming a gap which Johnston's engineers assured him would be easy to defend. The steep sides of the pass offered a good position for artillery as well as solid anchors for the two ends of his line.

The Army of Tennessee was reaching its maximum strength. Leonidas Polk's cavalry arrived with 3,700 mounted troops under General William H. Jackson. Another division under General Samuel French was on its way. Nathan Bedford Forrest's cavalry was reputedly about to strike at Sherman's communications in the north. Everything boded well for making a stand at Adairsville.

As Andy Neal reported, not altogether accurately, to his mother, "We have about as many men as the enemy and if they would give us a fair fight we could sweep them from the face of the earth. Gen. Johnston has not yet drawn them far enough. Some think he will fall back to Atlanta. I think he will turn upon the enemy half way between here and Marietta and we will race for the Tennessee."

Johnston himself was gnawed by doubts. The pass at Adairsville appeared, in his eyes, too wide for his troops to hold against still superior Union forces. He had in mind, however, an alternative maneuver, a scheme to divide and ambush Sherman's forces.

At Adairsville the railway and adjacent turnpike forked slightly south and east. The railroad continued south to Kingston; the turnpike branched southeast to Cassville. A third road connecting Kingston and Cassville formed the base of an equilateral triangle, the keystone of his plan. Sherman, arriving in pursuit at Adairsville, would be forced to choose between two routes to follow. Most probably he would divide his army, sending one column to Kingston, the other to Cassville, to cover both lines of escape. By settling for only one route he would risk the chance of losing Johnston altogether.

Johnston would bait the trap at Cassville. He, Hood, and Polk would march directly to that town. Hardee and Wheeler would act as decoys, luring half of Sherman's army down the railroad tracks to Kingston, tearing up the tracks in Sherman's path to hamper his progress. Then Hardee would hasten via the base of the triangle to join Johnston's troops awaiting the other half of Sherman's forces at Cassville. At this point the united Confederate army would confront and destroy, by superior numbers, the divided enemy.

Calling his generals into conference Johnston received their agreement to the plan—then led the small group to his field tent to fulfill a promise to his wife. Lydia had written to Polk requesting the former Bishop to "lead my soldier nearer to God." Following Hood's example, Johnston was baptized by Polk before an improvised altar, to the background music of distant firing in the north. The next morning the two columns of the army went their separate ways, Johnston following Hood and Polk to Cassville.

Previously, at both Dalton and Resaca, Johnston had hoped to stop the enemy while still far distant from Atlanta. He had retreated thirty miles from Dalton. His troops, he knew, were tired of withdrawing and were eager for a showdown. John Hagan confirmed this attitude in a letter to his wife from Cassville: "The truth is we have run until I am getting out of heart & we must make a Stand soon or the army will be demoralized, but all is in good spirits now & beleave Gen. Johnston will make a stand & whip the yankees badley &c."

Johnston's confidence and spirits soared as he surveyed the country around Cassville. High ridges rising behind the town protected his rear and offered a strong defense position for artillery and troops. The plain in front, down which the enemy would come, was open and exposed. Perfect! He sent Hood's corps to the right of the road from Adairsville; placed Polk in the center, in front of the town; positioned Hardee, when he arrived from Kingston, on the left—all three forming the triple steel jaws of the trap.

This was the time; this was the place; this would be the turning point in the campaign for Atlanta. He issued a long-awaited battle order to his troops, assuring them that their rear was at last secure from the enemy. "You will now turn and march to meet his advancing columns. Fully confiding in the conduct of the officers, the courage of the soldiers, I lead you to battle." Recently consecrated, he felt qualified to add that God Almighty would reward their strife with victory.

His words electrified the army, as Sam Watkins noted in his diary:

> I never saw our troops happier or more certain of success. A sort of grand halo illuminated every soldier's face. You could see self-confidence in the features of every private. . . . We were going to whip and rout the Yankees . . . the soldiers were jubilant. Gladness was depicted on every countenance. I believe a sort of fanaticism had entered our souls. It seemed that whoever was killed would be carried to the seventh heaven.

Even in Atlanta there were echoes of this optimism, despite the retreats from Dalton and Resaca. The *Atlanta Intelligencer*, a bellwether of Southern confidence if not of realistic Southern prospects, found the situation promising on all fronts. "The silver lining is visible . . . and by the touch of the Almighty, the golden cloud will be rolled up like a scroll and the beautiful world of welcome peace lies within view."

Not all readers shared this blue-sky outlook, some accusing the paper of presenting a false picture of the situation. Johnston was falling back; Atlanta was threatened. Wrote one subscriber: "You are misleading the people by holding out to them hopes which will be dashed to the ground." Editor John Steele was prompted to reprove these "doubting quidnuncs. . . ."

> On the street, every minute, the ravens are croaking. Do you hear them? There is a knot of them on the corner, shaking their heads, with long faces and restless eyes. They say that General Johnston is falling back, that the greater portion of our army is at Resaca and Calhoun. Doubtless a considerable portion of our army is at these points, in the rear of Dalton, which requires attention. But we have no fear of the results, for we keep it constantly and confidently before us that General Johnston and his great and invincible satellites are working out the problem of battle and victory at the great chess game at the front.

Atlanta, regardless of optimism, was mobilizing for a crisis. The second week in May all persons between the ages of 16 and 60 not in the Confederate service were ordered to appear at City Hall "for the purpose of being armed and equipped for local defense. Herein fail not under penalty." As one authority noted, "The process of robbing the cradle and the grave had begun."

Ten days later on Marietta Street, as Johnston was setting his trap for Sherman at Cassville, General Marcus J. Wright reviewed the civilian militia in what was pronounced "the finest military display in every respect, ever witnessed in Atlanta."

Meanwhile "an immense number" of wagons and provisions were being sent daily to the front, accompanied by members of the various Soldiers' Relief Associations carrying food, tobacco, and other comforts to the troops, including especially arrowroot, believed to be of special benefit to the wounded and the indisposed. The relief workers were replaced every day or two, to avoid excessive fatigue, by other volunteers. Their efforts and sacrifice were genuine, if their own appraisal of results accomplished seem exaggerated.

"Day before yesterday," wrote one, "the lives of forty men were saved by the timely assistance of the committees. Humanly speaking, they would all have died."

Back to Atlanta flowed carloads of wounded from the battles around Dalton and Resaca, some 2,500 arriving in mid-May. To provide for them the hospitals were cleared of their civilian patients, these generally being sent home, while volunteers went from house to house throughout the city collecting rags for bandages, blankets and sheets for bedding.

"There is," wrote Mary Mallard, "a great demand for old sheets to spread over the wounded who are brought down on the cars. You can imagine the necessity for these; when limbs are amputated and the clothing cut off a foot or two above the place, something cooler and lighter than their blankets is necessary to throw over them."

Freshly turned earth in the burial ground on the edge of the city, and the funeral corteges wending through the streets, were grim reminders that the cost of Atlanta's security was being paid in human lives. On May 15 Samuel Richards recorded in his diary, "After dinner Sallie and I and the children rode out to the cemetery. The saddest sight that I have seen is the acre of fresh dug graves that are filled by dead soldiers, the result of this terrible war. Not a blade of grass left growing there."

Mary Mallard's husband, the Reverend Robert Quarterman Mallard, served as ex-officio chaplain to the Army of Tennessee, as did several other Atlanta ministers, dividing his time between Atlanta and the front. During the week of May 14 Atlanta surgeons were also ordered to the front to prepare for the impending engagement implicit in Johnston's order to his troops that he would shortly lead them into battle. Mary learned from her husband, and wrote to her mother in Arcadia, that:

> The men are in the highest spirits, and express the utmost confidence in General Johnston. . . . Whether they will fall still further back no one knows, though it is conjectured that the great battle will be fought at the Etowah River . . . I trust our Heavenly Father will fight the battle for us and crown our arms with suc-

cess, for a reverse would be terrible: in all probability this place would go next.

Mary was quick to correct the implied doubt in her final sentence. The following day, as Union and Confederate forces were prepared to come to grips at Cassville, she wrote to her cousin Susan Cumming in south Georgia, "If General Johnston is victorious, the Yankees must suffer terribly. All think he is able and will follow up any advantage he may gain."

At Cassville on May 18 all was going as planned. General Sherman, scouts reported, had divided his pursuing forces at Adairsville as anticipated—one column proceeding toward Kingston, the other toward Cassville. Hood was positioned east of the Adairsville-Cassville Road; Hardee was approaching from the west, both poised like the steel jaws of a trap. Polk was entrenched before the town, primed to deliver the coup de grace when Sherman's isolated unit became overwhelmed.

With his army ready to pounce on the approaching enemy and with, for once, odds appearing in his favor, Johnston prepared for the decisive battle. His spirits, like those of his army, were high. Telegrams from Virginia reported that Grant had been repulsed with heavy losses in the Wilderness; Johnston would soon have similar news to report concerning Sherman. Women and children were ordered to leave the town of Cassville, and promising buildings, including the dormitories of a woman's college, were converted into hospitals.

The next morning, after a night of tension and emotion, Johnston waited impatiently for word of Hood's attack. Nine A.M., no message. Ten A.M., no sound of fire from any direction. Then came an extraordinary report. Hood had been surprised and flanked by the enemy "in heavy force" approaching from the east, and had abandoned his position!

Johnston, stunned by the news, consulted the map. Such an enemy maneuver seemed impossible. Yet Hood's retreat was an accomplished fact; the element of surprise had been erased; Johnston cancelled his battle plans and pondered how to salvage his position.

The "Cassville Affair" would be extensively debated in the

post-war years, in what would be referred to as the "Battle of the Books." From the morass of contradictions, charges and denials, it was impossible to extricate the truth. Hood blamed a confusion of orders, a breakdown of communications. There had been no enemy on his flank; no enemy anywhere in view. For that reason, Hood asserted—having received no specific instructions otherwise—he had withdrawn in good order just to tighten up the line. That was one simple, if inadequate, explanation; later elaborations would not solve the mystery.

At the moment, Johnston was more resigned than vindictive. He wrote to President Davis, naming no names: "Yesterday having ordered a general attack, while the officer charged with the lead was advancing, he was deceived by a false report that a heavy column of the enemy had turned our right and was close upon him, and took a defensive position. When the mistake was discovered it was too late to resume the movement."

Making the most of a subverted situation, Johnston regrouped his forces on a ridge behind the town, a hundred and forty feet or more above the valley floor. Hardee was stationed on the left, Polk in the center, Hood's corps on the right end of the line. Thus deployed, Johnston's muskets and artillery commanded the entire valley, and the general considered his new position "the best that I saw occupied during the war." There was reason for renewed hope, a good chance for decisive victory in spite of all.

Sherman had repaired the railroad from Kingston in record time and had reunited his army before Cassville. His new line, in the valley, paralleled that of Johnston on the ridge, and his guns began shelling the entrenched Confederates. That evening came another curious twist in Johnston's plans. As he reported:

> On reaching my tent soon after dark, I found an invitation to meet the Lieutenant Generals at General Polk's quarters. General Hood was with him, but not General Hardee. The two officers, General Hood taking the lead, expressed the opinion very positively that neither of their corps would be able to hold its position next day; because, they said, a part of each was enfiladed by Federal artillery. . . . On that account they urged me to abandon ground immediately, and cross the Etowah.

Hardee, when he arrived, protested against this defeatism, but to no avail. Johnston was dumbfounded. Here he was strongly entrenched in an ideal position, the troops eager and ready to make a stand. Yet his lieutenants voted for retreat! Though he argued vehemently against this folly, he finally yielded, "in the belief that if the commanders were convinced of their inability to resist the enemy, that conviction would inevitably be communicated to their troops, and produce that inability."

Again, Johnston's hopes were dashed. A strong and likely bid for victory had been surrendered. His aide-de-camp, General W. W. Mackall was moved to tears, partly for Johnston's sake because, "This retreat will damage the General in public estimation." The following morning the bewildered Army of Tennessee was ordered to pick up its arms and march south toward the Etowah, crossing the river by the railroad bridge, taking up a strong position at Allatoona Pass while Johnston established his headquarters farther down the line at Marietta.

The pass was a steep and rugged gap through the thousand-foot-high Allatoona Range, almost impossible to penetrate if strongly fortified. Here perhaps the troops might have a brief but needed rest. For nearly three weeks the Confederates had been engaged in a running battle with Sherman's army, over some fifty miles of rugged terrain from Dalton to Allatoona, more than halfway to Atlanta.

With their retreat a refugee problem was developing. Hundreds of families fled their homes in the wake of the Confederate army, clogging the roads with their mules and wagon trains. More important, however, than this disruption of civilian life, was the loss of certain valuable territories—"the best part of Georgia," as Andy Neal wrote to his mother, adding that "nearly the entire Population is moving off, taking their negroes south. There will scarcely be any provisions raised about here this year, which will seriously affect us another year whether the war continues or not."

Johnston, however, was operating according to plan despite the rupture of that plan at Cassville. He was luring Sherman deeper and deeper into Georgia—forcing the Union general to extend his supply line perilously and to leave behind more men to guard it—while he himself was drawing ever closer to Atlanta, base of supplies and the point beyond which Sherman's armies could not pass. Not that he hoped that point would be reached, but Captain Grant's Atlanta fortifications were, Johnston knew, impregnable.

What Johnston did hope was that Sherman would attack him here in Allatoona where the narrow gorge through the Allatoona Mountains, studded with Confederate cannon, might become a slaughterhouse for Union troops. Cheated of making a stand at Adairsville, this might be the Confederate army's turning point in the campaign.

In Richmond, in both civilian and military circles, there were growing doubts about affairs in Georgia. Was Joe Johnston the right man to check the Federal invasion and defend Atlanta? He had fallen back before Sherman's army from Dalton almost to Allatoona. There was talk among Mary Boykin Chesnut's intimates of the indubitable courage of Sam Hood, perhaps a better choice to lead the Army of Tennessee.

General Josiah Gorgas, Chief of Ordnance, made waspish by Johnston's demands for more guns, more ammunition, more horses, more everything, was becoming increasingly disillusioned about the Confederate general. In his diary he wrote, "Johnston will reach Macon in a few days at the rate he is retreating—I trust the country will sooner or later find out what sort of general he is. I don't think he will suit the emergency."

Gorgas found nothing in future events to change his mind, writing some time later, "Johnston verified all our predictions of him. He is falling back as fast as his legs can carry him . . . and will, I fear, give up Atlanta. . . . Where he will stop Heaven only knows!"

But that was Richmond. And as Andrew Jackson once said of Washington, a nation's capital is the last place to reflect the public thinking or judge events intelligently.

News that the Army of Tennessee had withdrawn across the Etowah and had established defenses within only twenty-five miles of Atlanta had disturbing repercussions in the city. On May 23 Mayor Calhoun issued a proclamation:

In view of the dangers which threaten us . . . I require all male citizens of Atlanta, capable of bearing arms, without regard to occupation . . . to be organized into companies and armed, and to report to General Wright when organized. And all male citizens who are not willing to defend their homes and families are requested to leave the city at their earliest convenience, as their presence only embarrasses the authorities and tends to the demoralization of others.

The response was more than satisfactory, for Atlanta was losing its illusion of security. It was no longer merely threatened from a distance; it was the immediate target of impending battles. Noted Samuel Richards in his diary: "The past week has been one of great excitement in our city, the army having fallen back continually and refugees from upper Georgia constantly arriving. Our forces are said to be in good condition yet and are still facing the foe about 25 miles west of Atlanta. For several days past some of our citizens have heard the report of the Artillery at the front."

Closer than Atlanta to the scene of military action and experiencing what most Atlantans dreaded, possible abandonment of their city to the Federals, Mary Eliza Robarts of Marietta was busy making bandages and tending the wounded from the front. Described as "one of nature's noble women—a queenly character of cultivated intellect and sparkling wit," the fifty-nine-year-old spinster found the immediate future dark, as she reported to her cousin in Atlanta:

The Confederate army is now on this side of the Etowah River. The families from above are fleeing before the enemy—the streets filled with all sorts of vehicles, people moving their property of all kinds: cattle, sheep, Negroes. And the stampede has commenced in Marietta: streets filled with movables, neighbors packing and going off. . . .

You will ask what we are going to do? My dear cousin, we were constantly assured the Yankees would never get here! So, thinking we were in no danger from the enemy, we thought best to stay home and protect our property. . . . But oh, those horrid Yankees! How can I see them enter this place and live? I am so afraid of them!

In Atlanta, Miss Robarts' cousin, Mary Mallard, shared the general apprehension, writing, "We are passing through times of intense anxiety. We hope for a favorable issue, but none know how this campaign will end. The enemy are certainly very near us. . . . It has been a great disappointment to all that they should have proceeded thus far without a battle. . . . It is said that they are laying waste as they come through."

Once again John Steele took pen in hand to reassure the citizenry. The Army of Tennessee, reported the *Intelligencer*,

> remains in cheerful spirits. There is no sign of disorder or straggling. . . . Our troops are enjoying the shades and reveling in the magnificent scenery along the Etowah. . .resting from the fatigues of late maneuvers. If there is really a formidable advance threatened upon Atlanta, it would be more advisable for every man who can resist the onset, to arm for the purpose, rather than exhaust themselves with foolish exertions to save property by removal.

Editor Steele closed his admonition with what had become the watchword of the city:

"Atlanta must not fall!"

Sherman was in possession of a new horse. It had been shipped to him from Nashville, a roan mare, spirited and lively. He vowed that he would ride it across the Etowah River which he called "the Rubicon of Georgia." But the river, like others in his path, was swollen by the spring rains. He settled for crossing it on pontoon bridges hastily assembled by his engineers.

Contrary to Johnston's hopes and expectations, Sherman had no intention of assaulting Allatoona. As an artillery lieutenant back in 1844, stationed briefly at Marietta, he had reconnoitered the countryside on horseback and, he recorded, "had noted well the topography of the country, especially that about Kennesaw, Allatoona, and the Etowah River. . . . I therefore knew that the Allatoona Pass was very strong, would be hard to force, and resolved not even to attempt it, but to turn the position by moving from Kingston to Marietta via Dallas."

It was a somewhat reckless maneuver in that he would be cutting loose from his railroad supply line and leading his army through difficult terrain. But once at Dallas he would have two options. He could either move against Johnston's flank and force him to abandon Allatoona, then occupy that railroad town himself. Or he could move by several roads directly to Atlanta. If he beat Johnston to Atlanta he would have little more than green militia to contend with.

Johnston's "lynx-eyed watchfulness"—the words were Sherman's—anticipated his opponent's move. On May 23 his cavalry scouts reported a Union crossing of the Etowah some seven miles west of Allatoona. He shifted his army in that direction to intercept the enemy, and two days later had established a defense position across the projected route of the Federal advance, slightly north of Dallas, between Pickett's Mill and New Hope Church.

Checkmate.

Dance of Death

Cannon exploded.

The blast shook the clouds.

Down came the rain.

It was as simple as that, the troops believed. What else could account for the constant downpour but the bursting of Union and Confederate artillery, shaking the heavens loose of their accumulated moisture? All of north Georgia, that last week in May, was a vast morass. Especially at New Hope Church, northeast of Dallas, the rough land was a quagmire. Troops, horses, caissons became mired in a sea of mud.

But "Fighting Joe" Hooker had his orders. Though the joke in camp was "Fighting postponed because of rain," he prepared to hurl his three divisions against the Confederates which his skirmishers, the day before, had found entrenched below the little chapel. In fact, Joe Johnston's line extended on May 25 from New Hope Church to Pickett's Mill on Pumpkinvine Creek, with the mud like a glutinous moat before his breastworks.

The union troops had learned to divine the future from the personal idiosyncracies of their generals. Alpheus S. "Pop" Wil-

liams, commanding Hooker's first division, habitually bit on a
cigar. If the cigar was lit and smoking, no action was expected.
If it was unlit but being chewed, some plan or movement was
in the works. "But when it was shifted from side to side and kept
rolling over and over between the lips, there would surely be a
fight. . . ."

This morning the cigar was whirling "like a log in the
peeler."

Hooker's attack fell on General Alexander Stewart's division
of Hood's corps, whose entrenchments were flanked by powerful Confederate artillery. Three times in succession, starting in
late afternoon, Hooker's forces tried to storm the line, only to
be repulsed with frightful losses. "No more persistent attack or
determined resistance was anywhere made," recorded Johnston;
while the Federals, finally withdrawn at midnight, irreverently
christened New Hope Church "the Hell Hole."

The next day both sides clung to their trenches in the mud
and rain, the lines so close that taunting catcalls traveled back
and forth.

"Hey, Reb! How far is it to Atlanta?"

"Too far for you to ever get there!"

Sherman, seated on a log below Pumpkinvine Creek and
grinding the ubiquitous cigar between his teeth, marveled at
how quickly Little Joe had moved his entire army to New Hope
Church to intercept him. The Confederate general was wise to
his ways and becoming difficult to flank. But one thing had been
accomplished. He had forced Johnston to abandon Allatoona
Pass. Now, keeping his infantry in position, he sent Stoneman's
and Garrard's cavalry sneaking east to occupy the railroad town
of Acworth. It would bring him no nearer to Atlanta, but would
make his supply line once again secure.

There was not much more than skirmishing and artillery fire
throughout the day. Sam Watkins' company trudged back to
New Hope Church for rations that had been stored in the little
meetinghouse. He found that "the stench and the sickening odor
of dead men and horses were terrible." Not terrible enough,
however, to quell his appetite. "I ate dinner with the boys and
filled my haversack with hardtack and bacon."

The following afternoon, May 27, Sherman's forces tried

again. This time Oliver Otis Howard's divisions were pitted
against General Hardee's corps on the left of Johnston's line.
Confederate troops had been primed with news reports circulat-
ing in the North, stating that the Southern armies were demoralized. It had made them fighting mad; and "demoralized" became a Southern battle cry at New Hope Church.

Mary Gay's half brother, Tommy Stokes, was in the thick of
that twilight battle and considered it "the hottest engagement
so far of this campaign. . . . You could see a pleasant smile
playing upon the countenances of many of the men, as they
would cry out to the Yankees, 'Come on, we are *demoralized!*' "

Commanding Tommy's regiment was Major James M. Ken-
nard, a devout man who generally rallied his troops in battle
with the exhortation, "Put your trust in God, men, for He is
with us!" He changed it on this occasion to conform to the new
slogan, shouting, "Come on, boys, we are demoralized!" A bullet
caught him in the chest and he was carried, seriously wounded,
to the rear. To the men attending him he said apologetically,
"My fault, boys. I told a lie. No wonder I got shot."

The fighting lasted until after dark, Lieutenant Stokes recorded. "About 11 o'clock at night, three regiments of our brigade under [Brigadier General Hiram Bronson] Granbury
charged the enemy, our regiment among them. We went over
ravines, rocks, almost precipices, running the enemy entirely off
the field. We captured many prisoners, and all of their dead, and
many of their wounded fell into our hands. This charge was a
desperate and reckless thing, and if the enemy had made any
resistance they could have cut us all to pieces."

As in the "Battle of the Hell Hole," more politely, New Hope
Church, the Federal losses were staggering. Captain Key was
one of the heroes of the day. With the Confederate line severely
dented by the force of the attack, Key's men wrestled their field
guns through the mud to reach a position where they could
enfilade the Union column. Some 1500 bluecoats fell to that
artillery fire. In Oliver Howard's ears "the very woods seemed
to moan and groan with the voices of the suffering." The
Confederates swarmed out of their trenches to capture any of
the enemy left standing.

Stokes was slightly wounded in the nighttime fighting and,

trying to find his way back to the lines in the dark, became lost
"and completely bewildered between the two armies. Here I
was, alone at midnight, with the wounded, the dying, the dead.
What an hour of horror! . . . My feelings in battle were nothing
to compare with it." A cruel dawn, as he recalled it, revealed a
field strewn with corpses:

> . . . hundreds upon hundreds, in every conceivable position; some
> with contorted features, showing the agony of death, others as if
> quietly sleeping. I noticed some soft, beardless faces, which ill
> comported with the savage warfare in which they had been en-
> gaged. Hundreds of letters from mothers, sisters, and friends were
> found upon them, and ambrotypes taken singly and in groups.
> Though they had been my enemies, my heart bled at the sickening
> scene. . . . It is said to be the greatest slaughter of the enemy of
> any recent battle.

The engagements at New Hope Church and Pickett's Mill,
which cost Sherman 3,000 men against Confederate losses of
300, changed the character of the campaign. From now on,
trench warfare as opposed to fighting in the open, would be
practiced by both armies. While Confederate General Hood,
supported by West Point tradition, deplored the change as detri-
mental to the fighting spirit of the army—it emphasized
security, destroyed initiative—the lesson of New Hope Church
was plain. Outnumbered Confederates, strongly entrenched,
had delivered a stunning blow to the exposed, attacking Union
forces.

Johnston had blocked Sherman's path to Atlanta but he had
lost his former strong position at Allatoona Pass. Now Sherman
sent his cavalry to take possession of the Western & Atlantic
Railroad from Allatoona to the little hamlet of Big Shanty. As
both Union and Confederate armies began shifting back toward
the railroad, skirmishers were left behind to hold each other in
check at New Hope Church. No one took this duty too responsi-
bly. Private Ted Upson, patrolling the wooded front of the
Union line, stumbled on a Confederate private patroling the
front of the Southern line. They glowered at one another, fon-
dling their rifles uneasily. The Confederate was first to break the
silence.

"Say, Yank, got anything to trade?"

Upson explained that he had left his haversack in camp.

"Go get it," the other suggested.

Upson did. When he returned he found the Confederate soldier had been joined by others from his regiment. They swapped "Lincoln Coffee" for Southern "flat tobacco," and then parted amicably, mission completed.

"Good luck, Yank!" one of the soldiers called after Upson. "I hope you don't get hurt in any of our fights."

The move back to the railroad south of Allatoona concluded what Sherman considered the first stage of his campaign for Atlanta, summed up in his *Memoirs:*

> Thus, substantially in the month of May, we had steadily driven our antagonist from the strong positions of Dalton, Resaca, Cassville, Allatoona, and Dallas; had advanced our lines in strong, compact order from Chattanooga to Big Shanty, nearly a hundred miles of as difficult country as was ever fought over by civilized armies; and thus stood prepared to go on, anxious to fight, and confident of success as soon as the railroad communications were complete to bring forward the necessary supplies.

Actually, the Union forces were no closer to Atlanta—now twenty-five miles south—than they had been at New Hope Church; and between them and the city were a number of forbidding mountain ranges. Johnston, matching Sherman's movements step by step, was quick to establish a new defensive position along the Kennesaw Mountain range, last great geographical barrier between the Union Army and Atlanta.

The left of the Confederate line, a ten-mile arc, was anchored on Lost Mountain; Pine Mountain formed a salient in the center, while the right flank rested on Kennesaw, an 1800-foot-high peak of rugged granite. Johnston still maintained headquarters in the town of Marietta, a mile or so south of the mountain range. By June 4 with the rain still coming down in torrents, the positions of both armies were consolidated and the stage was set for the next and final act in Sherman's campaign for Atlanta.

There were those in Marietta who, once they had adjusted to the shock of finding Sherman's army on their doorstep, put on their Sunday-go-to-meeting clothes and excursioned to the top of Kennesaw to view "the burrowing Yankees" in the trenches on the plains below. It was the last time, they felt certain, that they would see the Stars and Stripes and the blue-coated uniforms on Georgia soil. Foxy Joe Johnston had lured Sherman almost a hundred miles from his base of supplies at Chattanooga, and was poised like a vulture on the ridges, waiting to pounce when the Union army made a move, or pursue the bluecoats if they saw the wisdom of retreating.

But some, like Mary Eliza Robarts on the outskirts of Marietta, were not so confident. "Day after day," she wrote to her cousin Susan Cumming, "we kept hoping that the battle would be over and the enemy not permitted to invade our homes," but with the Yankees just beyond the mountain, they would wait no longer. They had started sending their furniture down to Macon where they hoped to find refuge, stopping on the way to visit with the Robert Mallards in Atlanta.

In a last look at the adjacent town Eliza found Marietta "one vast wagon yard," with "hundreds and hundreds" of vehicles passing to and from this railhead to the front. It was rumored that the Yankee cavalry was pushing east toward the important manufacturing town of Roswell and "if they are not checked, perhaps in a few days that enterprising village may be in ashes." In a closing paragraph Eliza wrote to Susan from Atlanta:

> I fear our army will be worn out marching and countermarching. Would that the great battle could have been fought before they were brought so near to us! I do not believe in this falling back; it brings too much misery on those left within the lines. All the crops of corn and wheat have been destroyed. I expect every night to hear that Marietta is in ashes. Mr. Mallard and Mary do not expect to leave unless the army falls back to the Chattahoochee and the battle comes very near Atlanta.

In the Gate City, Mary Mallard wavered between doubt and apprehension. The increasing hordes of refugees and wounded kept her busy with the Relief Associations, but she had time to write to her mother in Arcadia:

> Our Army is about three miles from Marietta, and was in line

of battle yesterday; but whether it will result in an engagement it is idle to conjecture, for no one has the slightest idea of General Johnston's plans. . . . It would be a great relief to us could we be assured General Johnston would not fall back to the Chattahoochee. . . . The armies may keep their present positions for half the summer. Everyone feels unbounded confidence in General Johnston, and the condition and spirit of the army is as good as could be desired.

Sally Clayton felt a certain thrill at the proximity of the armies. Parties of civilians had visited Kennesaw to view the opposing camps, and there had been a few fatalities from carelessness. Still, Sarah hoped for a chance to see the soldiers. "There was said to be a finer view of them there than at Missionary Ridge," she wrote, "and a party of us began to make preparations to go on another viewing expedition. But just as we were about ready another civilian was added to the list of those who had been killed, and an order was issued forbidding the visits of any more citizens."

Atlanta had a hero by reflected glory: Sally Clayton's second cousin, Joseph Benedict Semmes, Johnston's chief depot commissary in the city. Benedict's cousin, Raphael Semmes, was, as noted, captain of the Confederate raider *Alabama*. While the Confederacy won few naval battles, having nothing one could call a fleet, its raiders and blockade-runners had posted an enviable record. For two years, ranging from Newfoundland to Singapore, the *Alabama* had been the terror of the high seas, sinking or capturing 380 Union vessels and destroying more than $10,-000,000 worth of Federal shipping. Now, in mid-June, cornered off France by the U.S.S. *Kearsarge*, the ship was sunk in a two-hour battle. Benedict's cousin Raphael, however, was rescued by an English yacht and returned to sea as a Confederate rear admiral.

Although people complained about "the most terrible rains and interminable depths of mud" around Atlanta, Mary Gay's spirits soared with the burgeoning of summer. "Gay, laughing Flora had tripped over woodland and lawn and scattered with prodigal hands flowers of every hue and fragrance, and the balmy atmosphere was redolent with their sweet perfume. . . ."

In the midst of this bucolic reverie, Mary and her sister, Missouri, were confronted with a reminder of Lincoln's Emancipation Proclamation—specifically, how it might affect their slaves, now that Sherman had invaded Georgia. One they knew only as "King" now stood before them, hat in hand, and asked if they would like to sell him.

No, he was told. "Why do you ask?"

"Because Mr. Johnson wants to buy me."

"Would you rather belong to Mr. Johnson?"

"When this war is over," King argued sensibly, "none of us will belong to you. We'll all be free, and I would a great deal rather Mr. Johnson would lose me than you. . . . He says he'll give you his little old store on Peachtree Street for me . . . and when Marse Tommy comes out of the war, it will be mighty nice for him to have a store of his own to start business in, and if I was in your place I would take it for me. . . ."

King's consideration for Tommy Stokes's welfare deeply moved his mistress. Touched her so deeply, she confessed, that she could not let King go. No she would not sell him.

In a surprise move Governor Brown announced that he was placing General G. W. Smith's division of 3,000 Georgia State Militia under Joseph Johnston's command at Marietta; Johnston requested that the troops be sent to guard the fords and bridges of the Chattahoochee leading to Atlanta. Mayor Calhoun, "in view of the perils of the times," declared June 10 a day of fasting and prayer, although daily prayer meetings were already being held in many churches in Atlanta, while fasting, to a degree, was being imposed by shortages and soaring prices.

In fact, the normally sanguine *Intelligencer* declared, "Our city is in a state of siege"—adding, however,

> But what a humbug the siege is. At every corner we find sentinels. . . . They watch you like a spider does a fly. They explode into your face a small vapory cloud of tobacco juice as they shout at you the horribly discordant word—'PASS'—at every turn. The nuisance has become intolerable. . . . The guards are only an annoyance.

In summary, the press reported Atlanta was a maelstrom of activity:

Relief committees are seeking to aid those destitute of food, clothing and shelter; aid is sought from the countryside as well as adjacent states. Their condition is touching, their position sorrowful, their hearts desolate.

Trains seem constantly in motion, carrying freight to and fro; wagons clog the streets, the noise of their wheels deafening; the voices of citizens, children, newshawks, mules, and the clatter of soldiery create a Babel and a Bedlam. Rumors fly thick as minie balls.

As to the situation at the front: "With Sherman dominating the area of Big Shanty, it is likely he will give the order soon for a massive assault which may be regarded as the major thrust for Atlanta itself."

"All things are now as near our calculations as possible," Sherman wrote from Allatoona at the beginning of the second week in June. But he was concerned that he had not seriously damaged Johnston's army, and that the Confederate general had drawn him so deeply into Georgia while keeping his own army intact. "My long single line of railroad to my rear, of limited capacity, is the delicate point of my game. . . . It is a big Indian war; still thus far I have won four strong positions, advanced a hundred miles, and am in possession of a large wheat-growing region and all the iron mines and works of Georgia."

The relative strength of the two armies remained about as it had been at the start of the campaign. Though Sherman had lost a tenth of his forces engaged during May, or more than 9,000 men, he had received another corps of two divisions under Major General Francis P. Blair, to add to McPherson's Army of the Tennessee. Johnston had lost roughly eight per cent of his troops during May, or approximately 6,000 men, but had been reenforced by an equivalent amount. Moreover, Confederate cavalry was threatening Sherman's supply lines in the north. Nathan Bedford Forrest's mounted troops were rampaging in mid-Tennessee, while John Hunt Morgan's raiders had been destroying Federal supplies and railroads in Kentucky.

However, rain, not military force, continued to be the dominant factor in the sluggish situation above Kennesaw, permitting nothing more than minor skirmishing between the armies as Sherman probed for soft spots in the Southern line. "It had rained so hard and the ground is so boggy that we have not developed any weak point or flank," he reported to Halleck at the end of the first week in June. Still he pushed his army forward against tough Confederate resistance, taking possession of Big Shanty, and placing his forces in a position roughly corresponding to Johnston's line on Lost and Pine Mountains and Kennesaw.

He had expected that Johnston would choose this point to make a stand, and observed that "on each of these hills the enemy had signal-stations and fresh lines of parapets. Heavy masses of infantry could be distinctly seen with the naked eye, and it was manifest that Johnston had chosen his ground well, and with deliberation had prepared for battle. But his line was at least ten miles in extent—too long, in my judgment, to be held by his force, then estimated at sixty thousand. As his position, however, gave him a perfect view over our field, we had to proceed with due caution."

He could appraise the situation from both sides, a rare advantage for a general contemplating battle. On his visit to Marietta twenty years before, Sherman had often ridden to the top of Kennesaw and knew the strength of the Confederate position. "I expect the enemy to fight us at Kennesaw Mountain," he wrote to Halleck, "but I will not run head on against his fortifications."

The sight of Kennesaw staring him in the face, defying his Grand Army of the West, was a source of constant irritation to the Union general. Conyngham found him more than usually quick-tempered and impatient, running his fingers nervously through his thatched hair, smoking cigars incessantly, pacing behind his lines impervious to both the rain and bullets from Confederate skirmishers on his front.

Yet on one occasion, at least, he showed a recrudescence of wry humor. Seeing one of his infantry cowering behind a tree, fearful of the constant fire from enemy pickets, the general watched him for a moment in deep thought. Then he circled furtively around the tree, crept a little closer through the bushes, and began to pelt the trunk with rocks.

After several moments of this barrage, the timid soldier seeking to make himself invisible, the general shouted reassuringly: "All clear, friend! You can come out now."

The soldier peered cautiously from behind the tree and saw, confronting him, the unmistakable slouched hat, the perennial cigar, and the two stars on the general's shoulder—and fled to the rear as if the whole Confederate army were behind him. Sherman resumed his pacing in much better humor.

But the troops as a whole were getting edgy from the constant downpour which increased the incidence of scurvy and the prevalence of gangrene in the hospitals. Private Elisha Stockwell, twenty-two-year-old volunteer from Connecticut, had rejoined the army at Big Shanty, after having been wounded and separated from his regiment at Chickamauga. The bullet wound in his shoulder had not bothered him; in fact he concealed it from his comrades; but now he was plagued with adolescent pimples and these bothered him immensely. He consulted the post surgeon "about a bad boil under my right arm. He told me to come and have it lanced when I thought it ready to open."

Stockwell, who had refused to expose his battle wounds to medical treatment, thought the surgeon's attitude toward his boil an outrage. He complained in his diary: "The army doesn't think any more of a man than of a mule." Then he added, "Perhaps not as much."

On June 14 the weather cleared slightly, visibility improved, and Sherman reconnoitered his and the Confederate lines. He surveyed the enemy-held Brush Mountain and Pine Mountain, conical in shape, their steep sides ringed with double trenches revetted with timber and topped with *chevaux-de-frise.* Johnston's engineers had done a thorough job. Behind these lesser hills, like a brooding sentinel, stood Kennesaw Mountain, 1800 feet high, monarch of the range. On its crest was a Confederate signal station. Union officers had long since broken the Confederate code, and the semaphored messages had been as useful to Sherman's army as to Johnston's.

Standing near General Howard's breastworks, Sherman caught sight of a group of Confederate officers atop Pine Mountain. They appeared to be studying his troop deployment with field glasses. He called to Howard to give them a couple of shots from his battery, to force them to take cover.

Howard demurred; Thomas had ordered him not to waste ammunition.

Fire at them anyway, Sherman suggested, just to let them know we're here.

Howard's battery discharged three volleys. The rebel officers scattered, except for one who remained in position, glass in hand; then in slow motion crumpled to the ground. Sherman wondered who the officer was. Back at his headquarters in an abandoned house at Big Shanty, he received the answer. A signal officer informed him of a message intercepted from the Confederate semaphore station on Kennesaw Mountain: "Send an ambulance for General Polk's body."

An unfortunate consequence of this intercepted message was that, while informing Sherman of the general's death, it was picked up by a newspaper correspondent with Thomas's Army of the Cumberland who dispatched it for publication in New York—betraying the fact that the Federals had broken the Confederate code. As a result the code was quickly changed by the signal corps in Atlanta, denying the North any further use of this leakage of Southern military secrets. Sherman demanded that the reporter be hanged; Thomas settled for shipping him back to the North.

Like his opponent, General Sherman, Johnston had been aware of the unwieldy length of his position. He could shorten and strengthen it by withdrawing from Pine Mountain, and anchoring his line on Kennesaw. On the morning of June 14 he rode with Hardee and Polk to the crest of Pine Mountain to look the situation over. Three quarters of a mile below, a Union battery, looking like toy cannon tended by toy soldiers, lobbed two shells in their direction.

Johnston and Hardee took cover, as did other officers who had joined the group from curiosity. Polk remained unruffled, viewing through his glass the scene below. A third shell whistled from the Union guns. It struck the bishop-general squarely in the chest, tearing his lungs out. For a second or two he remained erect—even in death he would not be hurried—then slipped to the ground without a sound. Ignoring the Federal cannon, Johnston ran to his side, raising the head of the fallen general on his arm. Weeping unrestrainedly he whispered, "I would rather anything than this."

An ambulance was summoned by the signal station. While waiting, his fellow officers discovered in Polk's bloodied tunic a copy of Dr. Quintard's poems, *Balm for the Weary and Wounded*, with the corner of a page turned down to mark the stanza:

> There is an unseen battlefield
> In every human breast
> Where two opposing forces meet
> And where they seldom rest. . . .

Later a sad and silent cavalcade wound down the mountain, with Johnston riding bareheaded beside the body of his general. Polk's remains were carried to the Marietta depot to be taken to Atlanta; and Johnston returned to the front to break the news to his assembled army. "In this distinguished leader," he told the troops, "we have lost the most courteous of gentlemen, the most gallant of soldiers. The Christian patriot has neither lived nor died in vain. His example is before you; his mantle rests with you."

Polk's loss was not a major military tragedy to the defending army. His fellow officers agreed that he was "more theoretical than practical," and even the troops considered him a little ineffectual. Yet they loved him withal, as even hardened troops can love a man for his humanity rather than his skill in combat. Perhaps the most eloquent tribute was found by Federal troops who occupied Pine Mountain two days later. Greeting them was a crudely lettered sign: YOU YANKEE SONS OF BITCHES HAVE KILLED OUR OLD GEN. POLK

Johnston placed Major General William W. Loring in provisional command of Polk's corps till a permanent replacement could be found. Then, having abandoned Pine Mountain, he reshaped his line closer to Marietta, in trenches which his engineers had been preparing for a week. The new defenses occupied a shorter arc to the west and north of Marietta —Hood on the right, protecting the railroad; Loring with Polk's corps in the center resting on the flank of Kennesaw; Hardee on the left or south end of the line entrenched in rolling, hilly country.

The only weakness in his new position, as he saw it, was the Chattahoochee River at his back, but he had the bridges guarded by General Smith's militia released for this assignment by Governor Brown.

Johnston also ordered his chief of artillery, General Francis A. Shoup, to construct, as a precautionary measure, fortifications and gun emplacements south of Kennesaw—one line running through the railroad town of Smyrna, another and stronger line along the north bank of the Chattahoochee River. Not that he planned or foresaw a withdrawal at this time; his defenses on Kennesaw Mountain were more than satisfactory. But knowing from past experience Sherman's tendency to flank impregnable positions, he would take no chances.

By June 18 his position at Kennesaw was consolidated, and Johnston moved his headquarters to the Thomas M. Kirkpatrick home near Marietta, beyond range of Federal artillery. To the house that evening came two dark and undistinguished looking horsemen in the rough dress of Kentuckians or backwoods Tennesseeans. Their "road names," to use a Western frontier term, were J. Milton Glass and John C. Moore. Both were traveling through Confederate territory on passes issued by Johnston's provost marshal, Colonel Ben Hill (not to be confused with Senator Benjamin Hill).

Both men had been employed as spies by Colonel Hill, and were here to report on the strength of Sherman's armies above Kennesaw and whether or not the Union general was receiving rumored reenforcements. But Moore was troubled on seeing a man being held under guard at Johnston's quarters. The stranger, he learned, was from Kansas but carried no identification papers and was suspected of being a Union spy. Trying to ignore the prisoner, Moore gave his report on Sherman's strength. The figures he quoted were staggering—between 140,-000 and 150,000 veteran troops.

Colonel Hill, plainly cynical regarding the probity of spies, declared Moore's figures absurdly high. His own information placed Sherman's number closer to 105,000. Johnston was even more skeptical. He declared that Moore was "either an honest man or an infamous rascal," and asked Moore, sarcastically and irrelevantly, if the Union General Thomas had told him to dress in that outlandish fashion. He suggested that the spy obtain a decent set of clothes, and gave him a pass to Atlanta to do so.

Following this strange consultation, Glass and Moore left the house, still troubled by the presence of the Kansan at the interview. They had reason to be. Both were double agents, allegedly working for the South but, in truth, serving as spies for Thomas's Army of the Cumberland under General Sherman. Right now they were engaged in feeding Johnston whatever false information General Thomas wanted the Confederates to have. Had the Kansan recognized them and exposed them, both would now be hanging from the nearest tree.

Moore gave his pass to Atlanta to his partner—he was not concerned with Johnston's criticism of his mode of dress—and returned to the Federal lines to report what he had seen and heard at Confederate headquarters. Glass, with Moore's papers, headed for Atlanta, crossed the Chattahoochee River, and circled the Gate City to approach it from the south. He noticed that Jonesboro was well garrisoned; that the two contiguous railway lines, the Atlanta & West Point and Macon & Western which fed Atlanta from the south, were strongly guarded; and that, in short, the southern approaches and flanks of the city were well fortified. He also saw northbound trains, loaded with troops, headed for Atlanta and quite probably the front.

By June 22 he was inside the city, spending three hectic hours viewing everything he could. He took no notes; an unfamiliar wanderer writing observations in a notebook would be suspect. What he saw, he filed in his head. He surveyed enough of Lemuel Grant's fortifications around the city to get a good idea of their strength—earth embankments revetted with stone and timber, ten feet high and up to fifteen feet in depth, with artillery emplacements linking rifle pits. No artillery was yet in place, but the fortifications were still being strengthened by slave labor. Proceeding north he observed that the railroad to Marietta and the bridge across the Chattahoochee were being strongly fortified with extensive earthworks and that these were being further enlarged by armies of black laborers.

The spy then proceeded north up the Marietta road, and Atlanta historian Wilbur G. Kurtz, who studied his activities as closely as records permit, observed:

At that time, this road was very much astir. It was the direct
route from the supply depots to the front lines. An endless procession of mule-drawn provision wagons traversed the road—
choking the way with their snail-like progress amid the debris and
rack of rear-line activities. Adding to the confusion of up-traffic,
there was a downward drift of Confederate wounded, also con-
veyed in wagons. Just why none of this traffic was handled by the
railroad, puzzled the spy.

Glass's bewilderment as to why more traffic was not handled
by the railway was unfortunately pertinent. The Western &
Atlantic was operating to full capacity and that capacity was
limited. Cars and equipment had been lost in the long retreat
from Dalton; replacements were impossible, repairs difficult;
there was a dearth of experienced engineers and trainmen.
Though the road was under the jurisdiction of Joe Brown, state
ownership versus War Department supervision applied to other
lines, making things no better. The tired Western & Atlantic,
with its rails worn and rickety, its cars in disrepair, beset by
confusion in priorities, was suffering from all the wartime ail-
ments of the Southern railroad system. Perhaps Glass was judg-
ing from his acquaintance with the better run railway operations of the North.

Back at Marietta the spy brashly called on Colonel Hill to
report his observations on Atlanta. Everything was as Hill
would like to hear it. The fortifications were strong and getting
stronger. The arsenal and other war industries were operating
to capacity. Few citizens were leaving the city, and slave labor
for war activities was plentiful. Hill was encouraged by the
report. General Sherman might not be encouraged; but at least
he would find the information useful, and Glass left immediately for the Union lines to relay a duplicate report, in further
detail, to the Federal commander.

Johnston had no great use for spies. One of the best, daughter
of a Confederate captain, ordinarily lived near his headquarters
here in Marietta: Fanny Fraser, described as "a young woman
of discretion, poise, and courage." Fanny posed as a nurse to
"gather information on the movement of Union troops" and to
"carry dispatches and other documents." Now, however, her

motives and identity were too well known in Federal camps, and Johnston's generals relied on their privates to infiltrate Union lines and learn what they could by observation.

Sam Watkins was an old hand at this. The trick was to learn the Federal countersign for the day. Once that was obtained, he could roam around at will. Wearing the battered uniform of a dead or captured Union soldier, he slipped behind the forward enemy pickets, and waited for one of them to be relieved. As the relief guard came, and the picket started back to camp, Sam would stop him with his rifle. "Advance and give the countersign!" The picket, accustomed to this routine precaution, gave the countersign, providing Sam with his passport for the day.

He learned that Sherman had been reenforced by two divisions under Blair, and was extending his flanks to embrace Johnston's defenses at Kennesaw. Johnston was all too conscious of this pressure on his front. As fast as Sherman advanced and entrenched, he threw up corresponding trenches, shortening and strengthening his curving line. It was as if Sherman's forward movement were compressing Johnston's defenses into harder and more durable composition.

Johnston was aware of pressure from other sources, too. While troop morale was high, and the men showed a canny understanding of their general's methods and motives, Richmond and Atlanta were uneasy over his retreats. Braxton Bragg, ever jealous of Little Joe, warned Jefferson Davis that "The condition of affairs in Georgia is daily becoming more serious," and that if Sherman should hurl his full weight against the Army of Tennessee "we may well apprehend disaster." Davis needed no such warning. For weeks he had wondered if Johnston would ever stand and fight. He realized how the fall of Atlanta would boost Lincoln's chances for reelection. The Gate City—even more than Richmond, not immediately threatened —was the key to Confederate survival.

Yet, approaching the last week in June, it was Sherman's move in this giant game of chess, and Johnston's knights and kings and pawns were strongly positioned on the mountain checkerboard. Hood's corps was on the left in fairly open country, with Jackson's cavalry extending the defenses further south. Polk's corps, commanded since that general's death by General

William Loring, occupied the right, embracing the twin mountains, Big and Little Kennesaw, with Wheeler's cavalry guarding Loring's flank. Hardee held the critical center, where several angles bent the line from north to south.

On June 23 Sherman telegraphed to General Halleck, Army Chief of Staff in Washington, as to his situation after three weeks of sparring before Kennesaw:

> We continue to press forward on the principle of an advance against fortified positions. The whole country is one vast fort, and Johnston must have at least fifty miles of connected trenches, with abatis and finished batteries. We gain ground daily, fighting all the time. . . . Our lines are now in close contact, and the fighting is incessant, with a good deal of artillery-fire. As fast as we gain one position the enemy has another all ready, but I think he will soon have to let go of Kennesaw, which is the key to the whole country.

What made him think that Johnston would have to let go of Kennesaw, he did not state. Sherman had often expressed himself regarding the folly of attacking, head on, strongly fortified positions. Now, however, he was thinking of making an exception. The flanking maneuver that had worked so well at Dalton and Resaca, and at Allatoona, seemed dangerous to undertake in this rain-soaked terrain. He would be forced again to leave his supply line, giving Johnston a chance to recapture Allatoona, sever the silver railway cord, and cut the Union army off from all supplies. Even if Sherman went on to reach Atlanta, he might be hanging on a dead vine. Nevertheless—

"I am inclined to feign on both flanks and assault the center," Sherman concluded in a telegram to Halleck. "It may cost us dear but in results would surpass any attempt to pass around." He rationalized the change of policy by reasoning that Johnston, fearful of being flanked, had strengthened both ends of his line and left the center relatively weak. Sherman would drive through the center, split the Confederate forces, and then devour the two halves piecemeal. He expounded this plan to his army generals. Thomas and Schofield agreed or acquiesced. McPherson questioned the necessity of such a gamble and believed that "the assault would be too dear."

But Sherman would not brook a stalemate. He had been stalled before Buzzard's Roost at Dalton. Stalled again at Allatoona, and forced to alter his intended course. For fifty miles he had followed Johnston's lead in a sort of nineteenth-century *pas de deux* or dance of death, one step forward to the other's one step back, side-slipping to the east, side-slipping to the west, losing with every movement men, supplies, and above all precious time.

No more delays were tolerable. With Lincoln nominated for a second term, a decisive Union victory was essential to the President's reelection. Sherman wrote to his brother in Ohio that what he did before Atlanta "would probably decide the fate of the Union." And what he had to do was as clear as it had been when he started his campaign at Dalton.

Atlanta must be taken and destroyed.

9

"Hell Broke Loose in Georgia, Sure Enough!"

They came in their gigs and phaetons to watch the Battle of First Manassas or Bull Run. Later they climbed, as Sally Clayton did, the heights of Missionary Ridge to view the pageantry below. Now "the linen coated gentlemen and gaily dressed ladies"from Marietta and Atlanta crowded the top of Kennesaw Mountain to see (for what would surely be the last time in this part of Georgia) "the burrowing Yankees" in the plain beyond.

Major James Connolly of the Army of the Cumberland resented their civilian presence and their obvious "disdain for the legions of the North"—as did every other soldier in the Union army. Sherman ignored them. He directed his field glasses at the position of Confederate troops along the range, and concluded that Johnston had "chosen his ground well." Miles upon terraced miles of trenches, rifle pits, and breastworks studded the slopes and intervening gaps, spiny with cheveaux-de-frise and protected as well by natural woods and thickets.

For a week Atlanta had heard the boom of cannon echoing from Kennesaw as Union field guns pounded the Confederate position, and Johnston's artillery replied. General Thomas, with forty long-range cannon, direced his shells at the center of

Johnston's mountain line, held by General Hardee and considered as one likely point of penetration. Atlanta's Andy Neal believed that his battery drew most of the fire because they kept their flag aloft while other flags were lowered by command. Neal's gunners refused to lower their standard so long as the Federals kept "their striped rag" floating in the Georgia breeze before their very eyes. A Confederate rifleman noted:

> We would work hard every night to strengthen our breastworks, and the very next day they would be torn down smooth with the ground by solid shots and shells from the guns of the enemy. Even the little trees and bushes which had been left for shade, were cut down as so much stubble. For more than a week this constant firing had been kept up against this salient point. In the meantime, the skirmishing in the valley below resembled the sounds made by ten thousand wood-choppers.

To Sherman's infantry, bored with inactivity, the artillery duel was something of a spectacle. The troops climbed to the top of their breastworks to sit "like crows on fence rails"and to observe the fireworks. Occasionally a Confederate gunner, irked by their sanguine indifference to danger, would lob a shell in their direction. Head over heels went the spectators, somersaulting to safety, only to climb back to their perches when the shell had passed.

By the last week in June, Sherman's plans for conquering the mountain fortress blocking his path to Atlanta were complete. It would be a two-pronged assault. McPherson's Army of the Tennessee would strike at the right of Johnston's line where a shallow gap separated Little Kennesaw from Pigeon Hill. General Thomas' Army of the Cumberland would move against the center where the junction of two Confederate divisions formed a salient that could be enfiladed by Federal artillery. Thomas was strong for using heavy guns to supplement ground action. June 27 was the date set for the operation.

A day or so earlier, Schofield's Army of the Ohio would make a "demonstration" against General Hood's corps on the far left of Johnston's line—primarily to draw attention from the real intended targets and to prevent Hood's troops from coming to the aid of Hardee and Loring holding the center and right, respectively, of the Confederate defenses.

In Atlanta, people would long remember the services for General Leonidas Polk, "the biggest funeral of the war," conducted by Dr. Charles Quintard. The body of the bishop-general, killed on Pine Mountain, was brought from the depot and placed in an open casket in St. Luke's Church. Before the altar the general lay in his worn gray uniform, sword by his side, a cross of white roses on his breast. Over the casket was draped the Confederate flag, while hundreds of magnolia blossoms made a bower of the transept.

To Sally Clayton it seemed almost like a funeral for the Confederacy. She joined the long line of mourners filing past the casket, and the scent and beauty of the flowers, the radiance of the summer day outside, "seemed to mock the gloom and sorrow of Atlanta." She noticed that many of the passing mourners bent over the casket to take a leaf, a flower, or a twig, as a memento of the fallen general. The funeral seemed to underscore in Sally's mind the changes that the war had brought. "Life, Joy, and Mirth," so native to Atlanta, had given way to "Gloom and Sorrow, Suffering and Death."

The tragedy was very personal to Sally. As a student at the Ladies Seminary, she realized now that she "would never be graduated at the mouth of the cannon." A few days later, her class knelt on the hardwood floor to pray together before the school was closed for good. "We had little hope of ever meeting again," wrote Sally. With good reason. Many of the Claytons' friends were packing up to leave Atlanta for a safer haven farther south.

Building contractor Maxwell Berry's daughter, ten-year-old Carrie, also worried about the closing of her school. Her active mind and busy nature missed the daily classes, the companionship, the affection of her teacher, Fannie Holmes. Would all resume again in the fall? She could only hope so. Meanwhile, with her father doing repair work in the city (there was little building going on), and her mother working for the Soldiers Aid Society, Carrie spent her time caring for her younger sister, Zuie—knitting and sewing things for her to wear and playing with her in the yard behind the house.

Already a supply and military depot, the city was rapidly filling up with military personnel and offices servicing the Army of Tennessee. One of the first of the newcomers to arrive was Major Charles W. Hubner, of the Telegraph Corps, who arrived ahead of his telegraphers and couriers to set up headquarters in the American Hotel near the railroad depot. Jared I. Whitaker had temporarily forsaken publishing to become Commissary General for the Confederacy offices on Whitehall Street; while Howell Cobb, now a major general commanding the districts of Georgia and Florida, maintained headquarters in the new Confederate Building.

The continued presence of Governor Brown, in offices on Whitehall Street, renewed conjectures that before too long Atlanta might become the capital of Georgia. Brown had more immediate concerns in mind. One was to add 10,000 men to the Georgia State Militia by drafting virtually every able-bodied male, sixteen to sixty, and barring all exemptions. New recruits were drilling now in the City Park, in response to the Governor's clarion call:

> Your state is invaded and a portion of its most valuable territory overrun by a vindictive enemy of great strength who is laying waste and devastating the country behind him. Unless this force is checked speedily, the property and homes of thousands must be destroyed and they driven out as wanderers in destitution and beggary. Our noble army needs further reenforcements.

Perhaps to keep his readers' minds from too much gloom of war, John Steele of the *Intelligencer* complained about the weather: seventeen days of rain in June, followed by intense heat covering the city and its occupants with a patina of red dust, followed in turn by further frequent cloudbursts.

And "the mud! O the mud!" the editor complained, calling attention, tongue in cheek, to "the hundreds of beautiful ladies that float like mists of glorious clouds, in gorgeous colors along our streets . . . sneering at the contemptible parsimony of a city that obliges them to wade through mud up to their ankles."

Mary Mallard wrote to her mother that officers were combing the city for blacks to work on fortifications being erected along the Chattahoochee River. One of her two male servants had

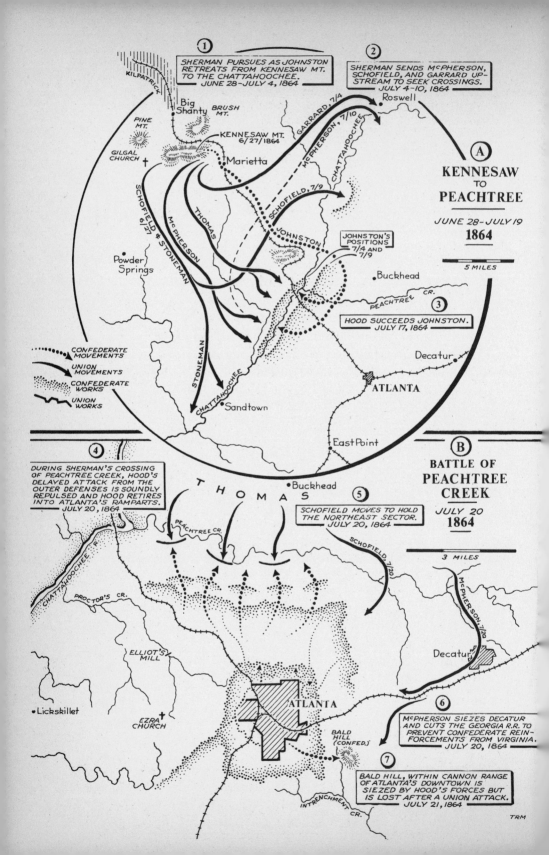

1 SHERMAN PURSUES AS JOHNSTON RETREATS FROM KENNESAW MT. TO THE CHATTAHOOCHEE. JUNE 28-JULY 4, 1864

2 SHERMAN SENDS McPHERSON, SCHOFIELD, AND GARRARD UP-STREAM TO SEEK CROSSINGS. JULY 4-10, 1864

A KENNESAW TO PEACHTREE

JUNE 28–JULY 19 **1864**

5 MILES

3 HOOD SUCCEEDS JOHNSTON. JULY 17, 1864

CONFEDERATE MOVEMENTS
UNION MOVEMENTS
CONFEDERATE WORKS
UNION WORKS

KILPATRICK
Big Shanty
BRUSH MT.
PINE MT.
KENNESAW MT. 6/27/1864
GILGAL CHURCH
Marietta
GARRARD, 7/4
McPHERSON, 7/10
Roswell
SCHOFIELD, 7/9
SCHOFIELD 6/27
McPHERSON & STONEMAN
THOMAS
McPHERSON
JOHNSTON
JOHNSTON'S POSITIONS 7/4 AND 7/9
Powder Springs
Buckhead
PEACHTREE CR.
Decatur
ATLANTA
STONEMAN
CHATTAHOOCHEE
Sandtown
EastPoint

4 DURING SHERMAN'S CROSSING OF PEACHTREE CREEK, HOOD'S DELAYED ATTACK FROM THE OUTER DEFENSES IS SOUNDLY REPULSED AND HOOD RETIRES INTO ATLANTA'S RAMPARTS. JULY 20, 1864

5 SCHOFIELD MOVES TO HOLD THE NORTHEAST SECTOR. JULY 20, 1864

B BATTLE OF PEACHTREE CREEK

JULY 20 **1864**

3 MILES

T H O M A S
Buckhead
PEACHTREE CR.
SCHOFIELD 7/20
CHATTAHOOCHEE R.
PROCTOR'S
ELLIOT'S MILL
Lickskillet
EZRA CHURCH
McPHERSON 7/20
Decatur
ATLANTA
BALD HILL (CONFED.)

6 McPHERSON SIEZES DECATUR AND CUTS THE GEORGIA R.R. TO PREVENT CONFEDERATE REIN-FORCEMENTS FROM VIRGINIA. JULY 20, 1864

7 BALD HILL, WITHIN CANNON RANGE OF ATLANTA'S DOWNTOWN IS SIEZED BY HOOD'S FORCES BUT IS LOST AFTER A UNION ATTACK. JULY 21, 1864

INTRENCHMENT CR.

TRM

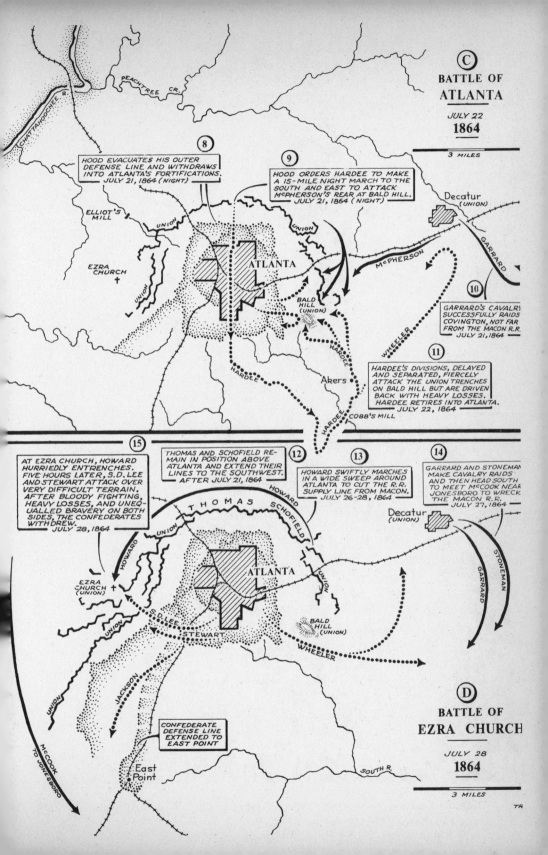

C

BATTLE OF
ATLANTA

JULY 22
1864

———
3 MILES

8 HOOD EVACUATES HIS OUTER DEFENSE LINE AND WITHDRAWS INTO ATLANTA'S FORTIFICATIONS. JULY 21, 1864 (NIGHT)

9 HOOD ORDERS HARDEE TO MAKE A 15-MILE NIGHT MARCH TO THE SOUTH AND EAST TO ATTACK McPHERSON'S REAR AT BALD HILL. JULY 21, 1864 (NIGHT)

10 GARRARD'S CAVALRY SUCCESSFULLY RAIDS COVINGTON, NOT FAR FROM THE MACON R.R. JULY 21, 1864

11 HARDEE'S DIVISIONS, DELAYED AND SEPARATED, FIERCELY ATTACK THE UNION TRENCHES ON BALD HILL BUT ARE DRIVEN BACK WITH HEAVY LOSSES. HARDEE RETIRES INTO ATLANTA. JULY 22, 1864

PEACHTREE CR.

CHATTAHOOCHEE R.

ELLIOT'S MILL

EZRA CHURCH +

ATLANTA

UNION

BALD HILL (UNION)

McPHERSON

Decatur (UNION)

GARRARD

WHEELER

Akers

HARDEE

COBB'S MILL

15 AT EZRA CHURCH, HOWARD HURRIEDLY ENTRENCHES. FIVE HOURS LATER, S.D. LEE AND STEWART ATTACK OVER VERY DIFFICULT TERRAIN. AFTER BLOODY FIGHTING, HEAVY LOSSES, AND UNEQUALLED BRAVERY ON BOTH SIDES, THE CONFEDERATES WITHDREW. JULY 28, 1864

12 THOMAS AND SCHOFIELD REMAIN IN POSITION ABOVE ATLANTA AND EXTEND THEIR LINES TO THE SOUTHWEST. AFTER JULY 21, 1864

13 HOWARD SWIFTLY MARCHES IN A WIDE SWEEP AROUND ATLANTA TO CUT THE R.R. SUPPLY LINE FROM MACON. JULY 26-28, 1864

14 GARRARD AND STONEMAN MAKE CAVALRY RAIDS AND THEN HEAD SOUTH TO MEET McCOOK NEAR JONESBORO TO WRECK THE MACON R.R. JULY 27, 1864

THOMAS

HOWARD

SCHOFIELD

UNION

ATLANTA

EZRA CHURCH (UNION) +

S.D. LEE

STEWART

UNION

BALD HILL (UNION)

WHEELER

Decatur (UNION)

GARRARD

STONEMAN

JACKSON

TO McCOOK JONESBORO

CONFEDERATE DEFENSE LINE EXTENDED TO EAST POINT

East Point

SOUTH R.

D

BATTLE OF
EZRA CHURCH

JULY 28
1864

———
3 MILES

TR

Jefferson Columbus Davis (1828–1879), President of the Confederated States of America. *(National Archives)*

Alexander Hamilton Stephens (1812–1883), Vice-President of the Confederated States of America. *(National Archives)*

Joseph E. Brown as he appeared in 1860 during his first of four terms as Governor of Georgia. *(Courtesy Mrs. Albert S. Anderson, Jr.)*

Howell Cobb, key advocate of Georgia's secession, became in 1863 a major general commanding the District of Georgia. *(National Archives)*

Robert Augustus Toombs of Georgia, Confederate Secretary of State who resigned in July, 1861, to serve as brigadier-general in the army. *(National Archives)*

James M. Calhoun, Mayor of Atlanta during the siege and at the time of its surrender. (*Atlanta Historical Society*)

Bird's-eye view of Atlanta, 1864; oil painting by Wilbur G. Kurtz, Sr. (*From the private collection of Beverly M. DuBois, Jr.*)

Atlanta Railroad Passenger Station in 1860, from a watercolor by Wilbur G. Kurtz, Sr. *(From the private collection of Franklin M. Garrett)*

"The Old Calico House," home of Marcus A. Bell and center of volunteer war relief activities, from an engraving in *Century Magazine,* July, 1887.

Portrait photograph of Mary Rawson, daughter of E. E. Rawson of "The Terraces." *(Courtesy Mrs. Robert L. Foreman, Jr.)*

Portrait photo, "in her early 'teens," of Carrie Berry, author of the often-quoted diary of Atlanta's siege. *(Courtesy Mrs. Dan Franklin)*

"The Terraces," landmark home of Edward E. Rawson and his daughter Mary on South Pryor Street. *(Atlanta Historical Society)*

Elizabeth ("Lizzie") Perkerson, daughter of Thomas Jefferson Perkerson of one of Atlanta's pioneer families. *(From the estate of Mrs. Angus Perkerson)*

Oil portrait, artist unknown, of John Neal, father of Lieutenant Andrew Neal, whose house served as Sherman's headquarters in Atlanta. *(Atlanta Historical Society)*

General Braxton Bragg, C. S. A., commander of the Army of Tennessee at Chickamauga and Missionary Ridge, replaced by Joseph Johnston in December, 1863. *(Library of Congress)*

General Joseph Eggleston Johnston, C. S. A., commander (until July 17, 1864) of the Army of Tennessee. *(National Archives)*

General John Bell Hood, C. S. A., commander (after July 17, 1864) of the Army of Tennessee. *(Library of Congress)*

General William J. Hardee, C. S. A., corps commander in the Army of Tennessee. *(Library of Congress)*

General Leonidas Polk, C. S. A., former Bishop of Louisiana and commander of the Army of Mississippi, killed at Pine Mountain in June, 1864. *(Library of Congress)*

General Patrick R. Cleburne, C. S. A., division commander in the Army of Tennessee, killed at the Battle of Franklin, November 30, 1864. *(Library of Congress)*

General Joseph Wheeler, C. S. A., commander of cavalry with the Army of Tennessee. *(Library of Congress)*

Ulysses S. Grant, after March, 1864, Lieutenant General of the Union Armies. *(Mathew Brady photo, National Archives)*

William Tecumseh Sherman, U. S. A., general commanding the armies in the campaign for Atlanta. *(Library of Congress)*

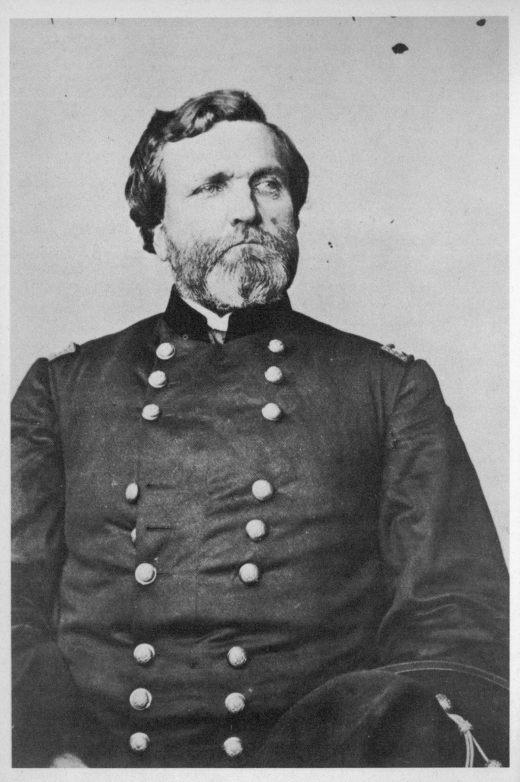

General George H. Thomas, U. S. A., commander of the Army of the Cumberland.
(Library of Congress)

General James B. McPherson, U. S. A., commander of the Army of the Tennessee, killed near Atlanta, July 22, 1864. *(Library of Congress)*

General Sherman (armchair center) and his staff: L. to R., O. O. Howard, J. A. Logan, W. B. Hazen, (Sherman), J. C. Davis, H. W. Slocum, J. A. Mower. *(National Archives)*

General John McAllister Schofield, U. S. A., commander of the Army of the Ohio. *(National Archives)*

General Oliver Otis Howard, U. S. A., corps commander with the Army of the Cumberland. *(National Archives)*

General John A. Logan, U. S. A., corps commander with the Army of the Tennessee. *(National Archives)*

Battle of Kennesaw Mountain, June 27, 1864, from a late nineteenth century lithograph. *(Library of Congress)*

Distant view of Atlanta from Federal signal station at Vinings during Sherman's advance upon the city. Generals Hooker and Logan, standing, at right. *(Atlanta Historical Society)*

"Cheveaux-de-frise" or spiked stakes protect the Confederate earthworks before Atlanta, some of the timber obviously coming from the dismantled houses in the rear. *(Library of Congress)*

Segment of Atlanta Cyclorama painted by T. R. Davis in 1886, depicting fighting east of Atlanta near the Georgia Railroad on July 22, 1864. *(Library of Congress)*

Battle of Atlanta, July 22, 1864. Lithograph inaccurately shows death of McPherson, right of center; McPherson was actually shot some distance from the scene of battle. *(Library of Congress)*

Union soldiers occupy captured Confederate fort outside of Atlanta, August, 1864.
(Library of Congress)

"Sherman's chimneys," symbols of destruction wrought by the shelling of Atlanta. (*Atlanta Historical Society*)

Entrance to typical "bombproof" or dugout "back of the house and kitchen," used by civilians during the siege, from a pen and ink drawing by Wilbur G. Kurtz, Sr. (*Atlanta Historical Society*)

Contemporary woodcut captioned, "Interior of a bombproof in a garden at Atlanta during the bombardment. *(Atlanta Historical Society)*

The square, massive Ponder House on the northwest line of Atlanta's fortifications bore the brunt of heavy shelling. *(Atlanta Historical Society)*

View of abandoned Confederate fort and camp on the outskirts of Atlanta looking southward toward the city. *(Library of Congress)*

All that was left after the destruction of General Hood's ordnance trains, Sept. 1, 1864, prior to the evacuation of Atlanta. *(Library of Congress)*

Lithograph of sketch of Atlanta, looking west from breastworks on the Georgia Railroad, just before the city's occupation by Sherman's army. *(Atlanta Historical Society)*

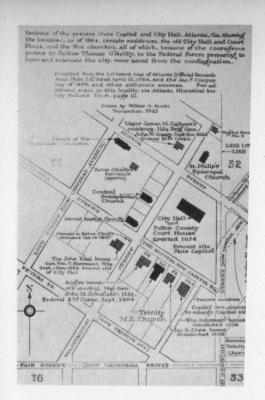

Map of central section of Atlanta in 1864, drawn by Wilbur G. Kurtz, Sr. *(Atlanta Historical Society)*

Mayor James M. Calhoun (on white horse) surrenders Atlanta to Colonel John Coburn, U. S. A. (left foreground), Sept. 2, 1864. From a drawing by Wilbur G. Kurtz, Sr. *(Atlanta Historical Society)*

Contemporary woodcut showing Union troops in Atlanta "tearing down buildins [*sic*] shattered during the bombardment." *(Atlanta Historical Society)*

Tents of Second Massachusetts Infantry encamped in front of the Atlanta Court House after Sherman's occupation of the city on September 2. *(Atlanta Historical Society)*

Woodcut showing evacuation of civilians from Atlanta in mid-September. *(Atlanta Historical Society)*

View of the "Car Shed" (depot) looking west toward Peachtree Street during September evacuation of civilians from Atlanta. *(Atlanta Historical Society)*

The last train to leave Atlanta in September carried boxcars loaded with refugees and their belongings, shown here waiting at the depot. *(Library of Congress)*

Looking north on Peachtree Street from railroad tracks as Union supply train leaves the city prior to its destruction. *(Atlanta Historical Society)*

Contemporary woodcut captioned, "View of the city of Atlanta, looking south, on the eve of its evacuation by General Sherman, November 12, 1864." *(Atlanta Historical Society)*

View of Peachtree Street looking north from railroad tracks, showing destruction by Federal troops and looters. *(Atlanta Historical Society)*

View from southwest of "Old Car Shed" or Union Depot prior to its destruction by Federal troops. *(Atlanta Historical Society)*

Ruins of the central Atlanta railroad depot, blown up by Sherman's army before abandoning the city in November. *(Library of Congress)*

Woodcut depicting destruction of the depot, public buildings, and factories at Atlanta, Nov. 14, 1864. *(Atlanta Historical Society)*

Sherman's troops destroy railroad tracks and equipment in Atlanta by melting them over fires. Western & Atlantic Railroad depot at left rear. *(Library of Congress)*

"Cutting loose from the base." Sherman's troops destroy Atlanta's railroads before marching to the sea. *(Atlanta Historical Society)*

Woodcut view of the burning of Atlanta on November 14. Federal soldiers in foreground destroy railroad tracks. *(Atlanta Historical Society)*

Troops of General Thomas' Army of the Cumberland evacuate the burning city on November 12. *(Atlanta Historical Society)*

already been impressed. But there was no immediate danger to the city, Mary assured her mother. "I think even supposing the army falls back to the Chattahoochee, it will not do so for some weeks yet." She urged Mrs. Jones to come up and visit them, and enjoy the bounty of their vegetable garden. Her husband, Robert Mallard, was back in Atlanta after visiting the front, and was holding daily prayer meetings in the Central Presbyterian Church.

Eight o'clock. *The* day. Monday, June 27, 1864.

For once the morning broke clear and gentle in the valley below Kennesaw, with a promise of summer heat to come. Private Sam Watkins, stationed on the central spur of the Confederate line, noted that "the heavens seemed made of brass, the earth of iron," and the only audible sound was the rat-a-tat-tat of a woodpecker working on a felled tree. On the plain below they could see the bluecoats assuming their positions, the caparisoned officers riding to and fro, the Stars and Stripes and regimental colors marking the even rows of columns.

"It seemed that the arch-angel of Death stood and looked on with outstretched wings, while all the earth was silent," Private Watkins wrote. Then, like a clash of Brobdingnagian cymbals, the Union batteries broke loose—a hundred and forty big guns hurling round after round of grape and solid shot and shrapnel into the Confederate defenses.

For a full hour the barrage kept up, aimed at softening the Southern lines. A newspaper correspondent wrote, "the ground seemed to heave, the torrent of lead seeming to empty the heavens, as this greatest of battles on Georgia soil unfolded." One Confederate soldier expressed it more simply: "All hell broke loose in Georgia, sure enough."

As the fire echoed from the mountainside, iron clashing against rock, Sherman issued last instructions to his troops. This was the assault that must not fail. Pierce the line, conquer the mountain, and Atlanta falls. Thomas was poised in two compact columns, four lines deep, representing two corps of the Army of the Cumberland. They would thrust against an angle formed by the junction of Cheatham's and Cleburne's division in dead center of the Confederate defenses.

On Thomas' left, McPherson was forming for a thrust against the Confederate right on Little Kennesaw. "About half way up the mountain," Sherman told McPherson, "there is a peach orchard where the men can stop and catch their breath for the assault." He explained to McPherson the fine points of growing peaches. Planted on the north side of a mountain, they would not bloom too soon and run the risk of being killed by early frost.

Stout heart was given to McPherson's men by their appointed leader, Colonel Dan McCook—of fourteen brothers and first cousins known throughout the Union army as "the Fighting McCooks." Now above the din of the barrage, Colonel McCook was reciting to his men the words of Horatius defending the Tiber bridge against outnumbering Etruscans: "How can man die better than facing fearful odds. . . ." The odds against the Federals here were partly steep slopes, rocks and crevices and trunks of trees, which gave a murderous advantage to the guns and rifles of Confederate commanders Samuel French and William Walker.

As the Union guns fell silent and the smoke began to clear, the temperature rising to ninety degrees, the bluecoats were seen moving forward in two mighty waves. Confederate sharpshooters at the foot of Kennesaw brought them down in scores; Confederate artillery on the mountain tore gaping holes in their ranks; but on they came. From the top of Little Kennesaw, rebel infantry began hurling stones and rolling boulders down on the advancing troops; still on they came, swearing and fighting their way over rocks and underbrush to reach the main Confederate entrenchments. To Samuel French the battle raging below "became a pageantry on a grand scale . . . one of the most magnificent sights ever allotted to man."

As "Fighting Dan" McCook's men reached the top of Little Kennesaw, the defenders had scarcely time to reload their rifles after firing, and relied on their bayonets or swung their muskets at the enemy like clubs. Here the fighting was close and vicious, men clawing, screaming, using bayonets and Bowie knives in primitive hand-to-hand encounters. In one Confederate rifle pit, nine out of eleven Georgians were bayonetted to death. Eighty of Walker's men were similarly slaughtered or subdued, like penned sheep in their rifle pits.

Most of the Union troops, however, were stopped within twenty to thirty feet of the Confederate entrenchments, with 600 Union dead sprawled out along the slope of Little Kennesaw. Among them was Colonel Dan McCook who had died like Horatius at the Bridge and lessened the ranks of "the Fighting McCooks" by one. Some of the survivors made it back to Union lines, but most were pinned down in the crevices and hollows of the hillside, threatened with death if they raised their heads.

Just to the west, Thomas' Army of the Cumberland fared little better, suffered still more bitter fighting as the several divisions thrust toward the angled junction of Cleburne's and Cheatham's two divisions. Advancing in close formation in the manner of European armies, the compact Federal columns made a vulnerable target for Confederate artillery, while the rifles of Cheatham's and Cleburne's defenders became so hot from rapid firing that they discharged while being loaded. In two hours, Sam Watkins noted, "every man in our regiment killed from one score to fourscore, yeah, fivescore men . . . all that was necessary was to load and shoot."

With Cleburne's division at what later became known as the "Dead Angle," Watkins was in the center of the action which, in his estimation, dwarfed all previous battles for ferocity:

> The sun beating down on our uncovered heads, the thermometer being one hundred and ten degrees in the shade, and a solid line of blazing fire right in the muzzles of the Yankee guns poured right into our very faces, singeing our hands and clothes, the hot blood of our dead and wounded spurting on us, the blinding smoke and stifling atmosphere filling our eyes and mouths, the awful concussion causing the blood to gush out of our noses and ears, and above all, the roar of battle, made it a perfect pandemonium.

To add to the pandemonium, bursting shells from both sides set the undergrowth afire, and flames raced toward the wounded trapped upon the slopes. A Confederate colonel, waving a white flag on his sword, stepped out to drag one man to safety. Soon, by common consent, both armies swarmed across the burning fields to save the wounded, friend and foe alike, from the enveloping flames. When this mission of mercy was completed, a Union officer handed the Southern colonel, who had inspired the truce, a brace of pistols in appreciation. Then each withdrew to order that the battle be renewed.

Few of the attackers reached the Confederate breastworks. This, the Southerners believed, was partly due to the difficulty they encountered in climbing over the bodies of their dead, "piled up like cord wood, twelve feet deep." Union Colonel Robert Fulton, however, believed that Confederate resistance was the most deadly and decisive of the war to date:

> The Rebels fought with a desperation worthy of a better cause. The conduct of our soldiers and officers on this occasion needs no comment; never did men show more gallantry, mounting the works, shooting the enemy, and beating them over the heads with the butts of their guns.

Though they held their breastworks, the Confederates did indeed take bitter punishment. Wrote Sam Watkins:

> When the Yankees fell back, and the firing ceased, I never saw so many broken down and exhausted men in my life. I was as sick as a horse, and as wet with blood and sweat as I could be, and many of our men were vomiting with excessive fatigue, over-exhaustion, and sunstroke; our tongues were parched and cracked for water, and our faces blackened with powder and smoke, and our dead and wounded were piled indiscriminately in the trenches. There was not a single man in the company who was not wounded. . . .

There were, however, reports of one Federal success from an unexpected quarter. Schofield's attack on Johnston's left had been designed primarily as a feint—to prevent Hood's corps from coming to the rescue of the hard-pressed Southern forces in the center. Actually, advance units had succeeded in encircling the Confederate defenses and establishing a bridgehead across Olley's Creek, southwest of Marietta and the nearest approach yet to Atlanta. Sherman would keep a close eye on this salient.

The battle was over shortly after noon, with 2,000 Federal

dead and wounded beneath Kennesaw, against 500 lost to the defenders. Watching the action from the crest of the mountain, Johnston compared the Union disaster with one he knew only from history, ". . . more of their best soldiers lay dead and wounded than the number of British veterans that fell in General Jackson's celebrated Battle of New Orleans." Complained a Federal officer, "for all our loss we did not gain a *single* thing nor probably killed one man among the enemy." Though he was wrong on the last count, his gloom was warranted.

Even after the fighting had ceased, Ted Upson and his fellow Union soldiers found themselves in "a bad fix. We could not go ahead and we could not get back." Even after dark the glow of burning brush and the flame of guns kept the slopes too well lighted for a safe withdrawal. Upson and his companions huddled behind the shelter of a massive boulder where "The Johnnys might have killed every one of us as we hugged its base, but they only yelled and threw stones at us."

Meanwhile the cries of the wounded from all sides, and the stench of burning flesh as the flaming underbrush ignited clothing, tormented the Union infantry more than the threat of bullets. As many as possible of the wounded were taken to field hospitals behind the Union lines, where General Oliver Otis Howard recorded the grim scene:

> There were temporary operating tables with men stretched upon them; there were diligent medical officers, with their attendants and medical helpers, with coats off and sleeves rolled up, and hands and arms, clothes and faces, sprinkled with blood. The lights outside and in were fitful and uncertain; smoky lights for the most part, from torches and pine knots. It was a weird, horrible picture, and the very heavens seemed to be in sympathy with the apparent confusion.

For two days, hundreds of Union troops remained pinned to the mountain slopes, clinging to crevices, logs, boulders, anything that offered cover from the Confederate riflemen above them. Unable to move, they were not completely helpless. Many resorted to a weapon so far little used in the campaign. Though hand grenades had been around since the seventeenth century, employed by elite regiments of "grenadiers," they were unfamiliar to Confederate troops. Now the Yankees began hurling "these little shells" at enemy rifle pits, but so ineffectually, as one Confederate observed, that "they would either stop short of us, or go over our heads, and were harmless."

The Yankees had developed, too, a form of periscope, with mirrors mounted on the barrels of their rifles, which the British had found "devilishly unsportsmanlike" in 1815 at the Battle of New Orleans. Thus they could fire without exposing heads or arms. The Confederates offered them obliging targets. Placing their caps on the tips of their bayonets, they raised them above the rims of the trenches, causing a useless expenditure of Yankee ammunition—then made a game of counting and comparing the relative numbers of bullet holes in their headgear.

On the third morning a truce was declared to bury the dead. "I get sick now when I think of it," one private noted. "Long and deep trenches were dug, and hooks made of bayonets crooked for the purpose, and all the dead were dragged and thrown pell mell into these trenches . . . finely dressed officers . . . were thrown into the ditches with the rest." The personal possessions of the dead, however, were carefully saved and turned over to an officer for shipment to their families. Finally, a prayer was said by a chaplain of one of the armies, it did not matter which, and the pits were filled with earth.

A cannon blast announced the ending of the truce, and the combatants parted amicably.

"Hope I miss you, Yankee, if I have to shoot in your direction."

"Same here, Johnny, if we fight again."

Kennesaw had been a Federal disaster, the worst defeat of the campaign.

Sherman blamed no one but himself for having deviated from his normal policy of not assaulting strongly-held entrenchments. As to the dreadful slaughter of his troops he wrote to his wife, Ellen, "I begin to regard the death and mangling of a couple of thousand men as a small affair—and it may be well that we become hardened. . . . The worst of the war is not yet begun." However, he sought to defend his action in a letter to General Halleck:

The attack I made was no mistake; I had to do it. The enemy and our own army and officers had settled down into the conviction that the assault of lines formed no part of my game, and the moment the enemy was found behind anything like a parapet, why, everybody would deploy, throwing up counter-works, and take it easy, leaving it to "the old man" to turn the position. . . .

Yet to turn the position—to flank or to force Johnston back —was precisely what he now began to plan, inspired by the fortuitous success of Schofield against General Hood's position on Johnston's left. The bulk of Thomas' army lay entrenched below Kennesaw, exchanging fire with Confederate pickets. Some of the Cumberlanders started digging a tunnel through the base of Kennesaw to blow the mountain up, antedating by precisely one month a similar venture at Petersburg. Sherman ordered McPherson to slip behind Thomas and join Schofield's forces south of Olley's Creek. Meanwhile he ordered fodder and provisions hurried down from Chattanooga to enable his whole army to cut loose from the rails and flank the Confederate position by a wide sweep west and south toward Atlanta.

On July 3 the Union general trained his glass on Kennesaw, delighted to see some of his pickets cavorting on the crest. Johnston, as expected, had learned of the Federal maneuvers threatening his flank. He had abandoned his mountain citadel, had probably quit Marietta and was retreating across the Chattahoochee River, for "no general, such as he, would invite battle with the Chattahoochee behind him."

Sherman ordered Thomas and Garrard's cavalry to press on to Marietta, and arrived there himself that afternoon, surprised and angered to find that he and his staff had beaten the army to the city. "Old Slow-trot Thomas" was running (if "running" was the word) true to form.

He was also surprised to learn that Johnston had not withdrawn across the Chattahoochee but was occupying newly built fortifications around Smyrna, eight miles above the river, and had brought up General Smith's Militia to help hold the line. It was the pattern repeated: Johnston, forced to abandon one strong position, had slipped into another stronghold and was still in Sherman's path. After four punishing weeks, during which, at Kennesaw, the Union army had suffered its worst defeat of the campaign, Sherman was only five miles closer to Atlanta.

On the Confederate line at Smyrna, Sergeant Hagan found himself behind "tolerable good breastworks . . . the Yankees . . . are shelling us furiously but haven't as yet done us any harm . . . we thought this morning being the 4th of July we would have a hopping time with them but they Seem to Keep their proper distance . . . I am now siting in full view of their line of Battle & there wagon trains bringing Supplies they Seem So cheerful & full of fun Some of our troops grow despondent but is only those who are all ways despondent all good Soldiers will fight harder the harder he is prest. . . ."

News that Johnston had abandoned Kennesaw and retreated closer to the Chattahoochee River caused alarm but not despair in the Gate City.

"Atlanta cannot be lost and we have an abiding faith that no victorious enemy will ever occupy it," the *Intelligencer* assured its readers. Regarding the forthcoming Anniversary of Independence: "The enemy seems to be somewhat confounded in his plans and perfectly foiled in his proposition to celebrate the national anniversary in our city . . . Our success has infused new life into our gallant army. They know and feel the pervading influence of the great necessity . . . in preventing the enemy from occupying this great center of the Confederacy."

On the Sunday before July Fourth, Samuel Richards wrote in his diary of "the church bells pealing out their call to sanctuary, while mingling with their peaceful sound comes the deep booming of the distant cannon telling of war and its dreadful scenes of blood. It is said that the enemy is very desirous of taking Atlanta by the Fourth of July, and a battle has been expected to come off today."

In view of that expectancy, Richards, who had been attending prayer meetings daily for nearly two months, deplored the scant attendance at Dr. W. T. Brantley's Second Baptist Church. "It would seem as if all Christians in this extremity would be both ready and anxious to seek a throne of grace to implore God's protection from our cruel foes, but alas! how few there are who evince any such desire."

Perhaps Atlantans were too concerned with immediate problems to spend much time in church. Down from Marietta, since Johnston's evacuation of that town, came scores of refugees with tales of woe that presaged what might happen if Atlanta should succumb to Sherman's army. Irby and Julia Morgan had been fleeing the Federals since early May in the wake of Johnston's army, and had hoped that Marietta was secure behind its mountain. But on the second of July, Julia noted:

> Our town was almost in a frenzy of excitement. Our house was crowded with soldiers as the army was almost in town. . . . We could hear the boom, boom every moment, resounding from hilltop to hilltop. We could see the smoke from the firing. O, it was a grand but awful sight! . . . we were nearly crazy.

Julia was worried about her sister and aged father living north of town, when an ambulance stopped at the gate, and there they were, muddy, bedraggled, and soaked to the skin. "They told us that Federal batteries were planted so that they swept their house, and shell after shell was sent crashing and shrieking through the roof. At intervals they tried to get their precious clothes and succeeded and tied them in bundles and then started to run."

Julia's sister and father had escaped but were desperate at the thought of what might happen to their home. Julia's two sons visited what was left of the house and concluded that its destruction was "premeditated cruelty on the part of the Federals. . . . The enemy in passing had raided the house, and as they could not carry off things, had deliberately ripped open feather beds and had the contents flying in every direction; they had knocked in the heads of several barrels of molasses and did all the damage they could."

Of more concern to Atlanta than the refugees, however, were the wounded—who came from the front in box cars, freight cars, or on wagon trains, to be dumped at the depot like so much damaged produce, then rushed by volunteer citizens to the various hospitals. Every one of the hospital buildings was crowded to overflowing, and tent-sheltered medical communities sprang up like mushrooms in the city's parks and on the Fair Grounds. The air reeked of disinfectant and less sanitary odors.

The Soldiers Aid Societies did their best at supplying bandages and blankets to the wounded, but some of the younger
volunteers lacked the necessary stamina and ended up needing
help themselves. Among those assigned to call on soldier-
patients, Mary Rushton wrote:

> Sister Eva and I were going across town to make some visits.
> The train had just come in with the wounded and dying and these
> were being carried on litters or stretchers to the hospitals near the
> square. Just as Sister and I were opposite the depot—it was indeed
> a heart-rending sight—she fell in a dead faint on the street. But
> several surgeons from the hospitals came to our relief, soon had
> her all right, ordered a carriage and took her home.

More stalwart, professional help was needed, and this was
imported from surrounding towns. Thirty-year-old Kate Cumming, whose brother had been in the Confederate army since
the start of the war, had volunteered for medical service in the
Army of Tennessee in 1862, and had been a peripatetic nurse,
moving from battle area to battle area, ever since. Now she came
up from Newnan to serve in whatever hospital she was assigned
to, moving from one to another as required.

Kate was not likely to faint on duty. She had seen and tended
"gray-haired men, men in the prime of manhood, bearded
youths, Federals and all, mutilated in every imaginable way, just
as they were taken from the battlefield." While "the foul air
from this mass of human beings at first made me giddy and sick,
I soon got over it . . . the same sad scenes, men dying all around
me . . . we think nothing of it at all." At Atlanta she observed
that most of the injured, having fought behind breastworks,
were wounded in the head and upper limbs.

In the Gate City Hospital the bloodied and battered soldiers
stood in the halls, sat or lay on the floors, waiting to have their
wounds dressed. As soon as tended to, they were dismissed—if
they could walk—to make room for others. Kate admired the
assembly-line operation, but the daily scene at the depot as the
trains arrived was given more attention in her diary:

> Old gentlemen and ladies were there to meet the poor fellows
> with baskets full of edibles and buckets full of milk, coffee and

lemonade, and some had wine. I noticed one aristocratic looking old gentleman who wore a large white apron, serving out the rations with as much zest as the youngest there. I was told that this work had been going on since the war commenced. Many a time, tables were set at the depot for the benefit of the well soldiers going from and returning to their command.

Behind the facade of hospitals and wounded was a grim pursuit, epitomized in the increasing signs of traveling morticians. These grizzly opportunists followed the armies like vultures, setting up business in stores vacated by Atlanta merchants who had sought refuge in safer cities. There was little to cheer the passers-by on Whitehall or Peachtree streets in signs conspicuously lettered: *Embalming—Free from Odor of Infection.* The fabrication and sale of coffins became a thriving industry.

If Atlanta did not have enough to worry about, with its population doubled by the refugees and wounded (more than 75,000 wounded would have passed through the Gate City before summer ended) there was, in spite of martial rule, a general breakdown of law and order in the town. Thievery and vandalism became rampant among young delinquents. Even worse were deserters and stragglers from Johnston's army, "prowling horsemen and mulemen," the *Intelligencer* labeled them. "There are thousands who are imposing on our people in every outrageous manner. . . . About our city they have become an unmitigated annoyance."

With no military police existing, there was little way of spotting and controlling the offenders. "They respected the property rights of no one," wrote Sarah Huff, alone in the house with her mother while her father was fighting in Virginia. Consequently, the two women were "at the mercy of robbers who claimed to have a right to whatever would aid maintenance or supply individual craving. . . ."

These marauders, calling themselves soldiers, and wearing ragged gray garments, killed and skinned mother's two hogs intended by her for the next year's bacon, which was a vital item of family supply. . . . With tears in her eyes she remonstrated with the killers; only to be told if they didn't take them the Yankees would.

She replied that they were "laying the Yankees a poor pattern."

To save her chickens mother had them brought into her bedroom. There, chicken-housed in a big covered basket, they proceeded to lay eggs, crow, cackle and cluck to their yellow legged brood. And . . . made the best they could of a very unfamiliar environment.

Mrs. Huff also had her beehives carried upstairs, leaving the windows open so the bees could come and go in search of honey. The buggy horse and the two mules named "Beck" and "Kit" were stabled in the smoke house and escaped detection.

Strange fires in the city were attributed to saboteurs and spies. Atlanta newsboy L. C. Butler, who lived alone with his mother in the Connally Building, was certain that Yankee spies had burned their home, forcing them to move to Pryor Street. A number of enemy suspects were confined to a stockade on Alabama Street, and young Butler went to inspect the malefactors. "As a ten-year-old boy I had a curiosity to see what a Yankee looked like, but upon investigation found that they had neither hoofs nor horns, and were just like the Johnnie Rebs. . . ." Military prisoners were easier to distinguish because "they wore blue and our boys gray."

Andy Neal's other sister, Emma, received a letter from the lieutenant at the front that threw confused light on the future of the city, and expressed some doubt, which was rare among the rank and file, as to the leadership of the defenders:

> Johnston can save Atlanta by fighting for it but the preservation of the Army is infinitely of more importance than Atlanta. As long as our Army continues in the field Sherman can do little damage in Georgia and I cannot believe it is possible for him to remain in Georgia much longer. If we had a good General at the head of our army we would have the bulk of Sherman's army in twenty days. I don't believe Johnston ever did or ever will fight unless he gains some decided advantage and I look for nothing in that direction while . . . Sherman commands the Yankee Army.

Sherman's arch spy, Milton Glass, however, was on the move again. His boss had called him to Marietta where the Union General was studying Johnston's new defense line below Marietta. Sherman would not repeat his mistake at Kennesaw; he would not assault fortified entrenchments. But with Schofield and McPherson pressing hard on Johnston's flank, the Confederate general might be tempted to withdraw across the Chattahoochee River—a good time to catch his army unprepared and separated, if only Sherman knew where such a crossing might take place. He instructed Glass to reconnoiter the north bank of the Chattahoochee and see if the Confederates had constructed any pontoon bridges, especially downriver from the railroad.

Crossing Confederate lines with Colonel Ben Hill's pass, Glass followed usual procedure. He paid a courtesy call on Hill —it was good to stand in well with both sides—feeding the colonel misinformation on the state and intentions of the Union Army. Then he proceeded down to the river and along its northern bank to Baker's Ferry, noting no pontoon bridges but some likely fords. On his way back to the Federal lines, he stumbled on a revelation. Chugging down the railroad tracks, southbound from Smyrna, came trainloads of Confederate soldiers, the vanguard of Johnston's army withdrawing to the Chattahoochee.

This was big news! Glass hastened toward the Union line when he was abruptly stopped by Shofield's pickets. He explained the urgency and nature of his mission, but was not believed; he begged to be taken to Sherman, under guard if necessary. An arrogant sergeant ordered him detained until his story could be checked. The biggest coup of the spy's career was thwarted. Glass made himself a solemn promise: to get even with that sergeant if it took a lifetime. But typical of a double agent's promise it was short-lived. Two days later he had forgotten the man's name.

By the time Glass was released to report to Sherman, Johnston's withdrawal from the Smyrna line was no news to the Federal commander. Had Glass put two and two together some time earlier, he might have known it would not be. Colonel Hill had told him that he might not be at Smyrna when the spy came back again. Making no obvious deduction, Glass thought nothing of it.

Johnston's prepared defense on the north bank of the Chattahoochee was as strong as, even better than, the Smyrna line. Sherman regarded it as "one of the strongest pieces of field-fortification I ever saw." Throwing a unit of infantry against it was like poking at a hornet's nest; it released a stinging swarm of shells and bullets ("I came very near being shot myself"), convincing the Federal general, once again, that frontal assault would not be worth the effort.

Sherman had written earlier that if he reached the Chattahoochee he would feint to the right and cross the river on his left where least expected. Now he sent Garrard's cavalry northeast to the manufacturing town of Roswell, twenty miles upstream, to take possession of the factories and, more importantly, secure the bridge that crossed the river at that point. Garrard reported on his arrival that the bridge had been destroyed but that the three major factories, turning out cotton and woolens for the Confederacy, were going full blast and had raised on their roofs the French tricolor as a devious means of securing protection for property of a neutral government.

The flags had just the opposite effect on Sherman. He ordered that the factories be totally destroyed, the owners charged with treason, and sent with their employees under guard to Marietta. As to any party which had hoisted the French flag, "Should you, under the impulse of anger, natural at contemplating such perfidy, hang the wretch, I approve the act beforehand." He further instructed Garrard to hold his position for now while Schofield tested possible river crossings further down, adding with ominous satisfaction: "Atlanta is in plain view."

Major James Connolly described that view from bluffs overlooking the Chattahoochee River, writing to his wife that, "Mine eyes have beheld the promised land. The 'domes and minarets and spires' of Atlanta are glittering in the sun before us, only 8 miles distant." And he added:

> Generals Sherman and Thomas ... were with us on the hilltop, and the two veterans for a moment gazed at the glittering prize in silence. I watched the two noble soldiers—Sherman stepping nervously about, his eyes sparkling and his face aglow—casting a single glance at Atlanta, another at the River, and a dozen at the surrounding valley to see where he could best cross the River, how he best could flank them.

Eight miles upriver from where Sherman stood, the problem was on its way to being solved. Schofield's third division under

General Jacob Cox had been probing for river crossings south of Roswell. On July 8 Cox discovered a fish dam lying astride the river at a tributary called Soap Creek. Pontoons were brought up and hidden in the creek, and the next morning an infantry unit groped and slithered across the dam, driving off Confederate pickets who fled with the first exchange of shots. The pontoons were laid across the river, and before dark most of Cox's division had been planted on the left bank of the river.

It was a small bridgehead, but a giant step in Sherman's campaign for Atlanta. Federal troops had at long last crossed the Chattahoochee river which, more than the Etowah, qualified for Sherman's definition of "the Rubicon of Georgia"— the last significant barrier between the Union army and Atlanta.

In the Executive Mansion in Richmond, Jefferson Davis, older and whiter since the previous summer, awaited a visitor from Georgia. And Georgia was foremost of the worries in his mind. While Grant appeared stopped before Richmond, Atlanta seemed on the verge of falling to the enemy. Joseph Johnston's Army of Tennessee had fallen back from every strong position it had established, failing to check Sherman's drive toward the city. Would Johnston ever stand and fight?

On the President's desk were scores of letters and telegrams from apprehensive citizens demanding or suggesting steps to be taken to save the threatened city. Atlanta had now become the critical center of the war. It was, in the President's eyes, "the spine of the Confederacy" and "the back door to Richmond." Its railroads, arsenals, factories, and military stores were of "incalculable value." More than these tangible considerations was the fact that the Republicans demanded Atlanta's conquest as the price of Lincoln's reelection which in turn meant four more years with an uncompromising Abolitionist in the White House. Atlanta must not fall; and the key to its survival was Joe Johnston.

For that reason, particularly, Davis welcomed today's call from Senator Benjamin Hill who had visited Johnston just before the latter withdrew from Kennesaw to his lines above the Chattahoochee. Hill had asked Johnston, as he now reported to the President:

"How long can you hold Sherman north of the Chattahoochee River?"

After some deliberation, Johnston settled for an estimate of "at least fifty-four days, and perhaps sixty days." This, Hill had agreed, would give time to bring John Hunt Morgan's cavalry from Virginia and to take all other possible steps to keep Sherman from driving Johnston back into Atlanta. General Hood, who had been present at the interview, disagreed with his commander—stating that once the Confederates had abandoned Kennesaw, Sherman would gain a never-to-be-lost initiative in his drive toward the city. Johnston, in turn, disagreed with Hood; he had two strong lines above the Chattahoochee "from which I can hold Sherman a long time."

After listening to this recounting of the conversation, Davis asked the Senator from Georgia:

"How long did you understand General Johnston to say he could hold Sherman north of the Chattahoochee?"

"From fifty-four to sixty days."

Wearily the President leaned across his cluttered desk and handed Hill a telegram. It was dated the day before, July 9, and reported that Johnston had retreated across the Chattahoochee. The sixty days had shrunk to five, and the hopes of a nation had dwindled in proportion.

10

Dropping the Pilot

Most Georgians, in their schooldays, became acquainted with the Chattahoochee through Sidney Lanier's poem about that river:

> Down the hills from Habersham,
> Through the Valleys of Hall,
> I hurry amain, to reach the plain,
> Run the rapid and leap the fall. . . .

Now, in Atlanta especially, children and adults alike were aware of the river for a grimmer, more immediate reason. Johnston's army was on one side of it; Sherman's army was on the other, threatening Atlanta from the general direction of Habersham and Hall. In addition, units of Sherman's army had crossed the swollen river south of Roswell—which had forced Johnston to evacuate his strong position on the north bank, withdrawing his forces on July 9, and burning the Chattahoochee railroad bridge behind him.

On the very day that Johnston had pulled back to the left bank of the river, Andy Neal wrote to his mother, "Gen. Johnston has published an order to his troops saying we must now fight the enemy and can pull back no more." The *Southern Confederacy* assured its readers in Atlanta that "The army is in an immensely strong position north of the bridge. . . . There is some little uneasiness manifested on the part of civilians, but the military are more than confident. . . ."

Joseph Semmes, Johnston's chief of commissary, was also confident—to a degree. Writing to his wife Jorantha, whom he addressed as "Eo," Semmes told her of enemy movements across the river aimed at flanking Atlanta and cutting the city's communications on the south:

> I tell you this to prepare you and prevent you from feeling any alarm. . . . It is possible that Atlanta may be evacuated but do not be discouraged. Remember Moscow and Napoleon's splendid advance and miserable retreat. We are all in fine spirits tho we hated to fall back from Marietta.

A few hours later, Johnston had withdrawn to his last position of defense before Atlanta, one from which to strike at Sherman's forces if and as they crossed the river in pursuit. Peachtree Creek, a wide and muddy tributary running roughly east to west, provided a natural barrier five and a half miles above the city. High ground overlooked the valley of Peachtree Creek, just south of the stream. Here Johnston ordered the construction of breastworks, at the same time keeping artillery and troops along the south bank of the Chattahoochee to watch for, and inhibit, any Union crossing of the river. He also sent William Jackson's cavalry downriver to watch the fords below the railroad bridge, and sent Wheeler's cavalry to guard the fords and ferries upstream from the railroad, and the vulnerable area between the Chattahoochee and Decatur.

Johnston himself rode into Atlanta and set up headquarters in the former home of Dexter Niles near Jeremiah Huff's farm. Three miles from the center of the city, the location was convenient to the front since it adjoined the Western & Atlantic Railroad and the Marietta wagon road. The general's wife Lydia, who had been in Atlanta almost since the campaign started, moved in with him to bring hospitality and order to the six-room house.

From the inflated optimism of preceding weeks Atlantans awoke to the knowledge that their city was no longer merely threatened from a distance; it had become a battle zone. The enemy was six miles away; the defending army less than that. Government stores and offices were being moved to Milledgeville and Macon. Howell Cobb, commanding the military department of Georgia and Florida, moved his headquarters to Macon. Frightened families in Atlanta were packing their belongings with a view to fleeing farther south, while the last of the refugees poured down the Marietta wagon road from their abandoned homes above the Chattahoochee river.

"This has been a sad day in our city," Samuel Richards wrote on Sunday, July 10, "for it has been quite evident for some days past that there is a great probability of Atlanta falling into the hands of the enemy, and the city has been in a complete swarm all day and for several days. All the Govt. Stores and Hospitals are ordered away and of course the citizens are alarmed, and many have left and others are leaving. . . ."

George Adair's *Southern Confederacy*, which the day before had seen little cause for apprehension, changed its tune:

> We shall not attempt to lull to a fancied security the readers of the *Confederacy* by declaring that Atlanta is not in immense peril. Its capture, however, cannot be considered a foregone conclusion. The withdrawal of stores from the city may appear ominous, but the activity and vigilance of Gen. Johnston, as at present displayed along the Chattahoochee, indicates at least a determination to hold it at all hazards. Save the rumble and dust of wagons upon her pavements, Atlanta appears today as quiet as if there was not a Yankee in North Georgia. There is no panic or any existing excuse for it.

The paper belied its own report by promptly suspending publication and moving to Columbus, on the Alabama border.

The Daily *Intelligencer* also declared that while there was cause for apprehension in Atlanta, there was still "no panic." The paper predicted, however, a future of trial and hardship for the city and blamed President Davis for not supplying Johnston with sufficient troops to cut off Sherman's vulnerable supply line in the north. "Should Atlanta fall, fearful indeed will be the responsibility. . . . The Richmond in Virginia is the political Richmond, but the Richmond in Georgia is Atlanta, which to the Confederacy is a more important point. . . ."

Having said which, the *Intelligencer* took the cue from its rival paper and left the city, moving its presses down to Macon and publishing in its last edition a bit of chin-up poetry as a farewell to its readers:

> Hoot away despair,
> Never Yield to sorrow,
> The blackest day may wear
> A sunny face tomorrow.

Atlanta was now without a daily source of news apart from dubious stories from soldiers at the front and still more dubious rumors circulated in the streets. Little wonder that the city was electrified to hear of General Sherman's capture. He had been reconnoitering along the Chattahoochee River on his own, and accidentally stumbled upon a company of Walker's cavalry. The prisoner was being brought into Atlanta under heavy guard.

False alarm. The wrong Sherman had been captured. William Tecumseh Sherman had indeed been reconnoitering the river on that day, and reported that he almost had been captured: "I came near riding into a detachment of the enemy's cavalry; and later in the same day Colonel Frank Sherman, of Chicago, then on General Howard's staff, did actually ride straight into the enemy's camp. . . . He was carried to Atlanta, and for some time the enemy supposed they were in possession of the commander-in-chief of the opposing army."

Nevertheless, Sherman's troops were reported everywhere around the city, and the ubiquitous sound of guns and rifle fire up and down the Chattahoochee gave credence to these alarms. In anticipation of the city being shelled, which now seemed likely, citizens began building bomb shelters in their yards, not unlike the hurricane cellars in the Plains states.

Called variously "bombproofs" and more derisively, "gopher holes," these were generally excavations of from six to eight feet deep, and eight to twelve feet square—but might be larger according to the size and collective muscle of the family. Stout planks were laid over the subterranean chamber, covered with three or four feet of earth. The entrance was always on the south side, the only direction from which enemy missiles were not likely to arrive.

Between the Chattahoochee River and Atlanta many such shelters had already been prepared. Southwest of the city an area pioneer, Joseph Willis, owned extensive land and a grist mill on Utoy Creek. With Confederate troops now south of the Chattahoochee, he saw the handwriting on the wall and constructed, with the help of two neighbors, Laban Helms and William White, a bombproof behind his home large enough to accommodate the twenty-six members of their families.

It was an ambitious enterprise, for citizen Willis had no intention of quitting his property whatever came. The room was sixteen feet square, excavated from a hillside, with a roof of timbers covered with several feet of turf and overlaid with evergreen boughs to keep the earth in place. Nonperishable foods and containers of drinking water were stowed in the compartment to provide, if need be, for a lengthy siege.

Some families, however, were leaving the city altogether—not in a lemminglike rush to the sea, for not enough towns in southern Georgia could provide for refugees. In many cases only wives and children left to stay with relatives, leaving husbands and fathers behind to care for their homes and business in Atlanta. Mary Rushton would work no more as a hospital volunteer. Her father, William Rushton, a master mechanic for the Georgia Railroad, had been pulling strings to get passage for Mary on the overcrowded trains:

> Finally father managed to get hold of an engine not being used for other purposes, and he put Eva and me in the cab with the engineer and fireman, piled our trunks on the tender, and sent us off down the road to Madison, while he went back to Atlanta. Before we left Stone Mountain, as we were laughing and talking with some of the young officers, who perhaps laughed and talked no more after that day, we could hear the cannonading in the distance and the gunshots of the pickets and outposts who were falling back.

Mary Mallard, prompted by her husband Robert, made plans for taking her children to Augusta, but misfortune overtook them at the start. They had borrowed a four-wheeled dray from a neighbor, and on an incline leading to the depot, "I think something gave way about the cart." The wagon lunged into the hindquarters of the horse, the animal took off, and the occupants were thrown out, the more fortunate incurring only bruises and abrasions. "Mr. Mallard's foot caught, and he was dragged for some distance, but sprang back into the cart and disengaged his foot. I was seriously injured, being bruised in every part of my body . . . and my collarbone was dislocated."

Dr. Logan was summoned to the scene of the accident, bandaged everybody up, and advised Robert to ship his wife off in the freight car with their furniture, enabling Dr. Mallard to unpack their blankets and make a bed for Mary on the floor. "Thus you see," she wrote to her cousin in Augusta, "how narrowly our lives were preserved . . . Mr. Mallard returned to Atlanta and will abide the issue. If the town is evacuated, he will of course come away. I hope we may be able to return to Atlanta, but of course we will have to be governed by the movements of the army."

Every day in the City Hall park the new recruits for the militia went through their drill. Governor Brown in conjunction with the city council agreed that, in view of the impending crisis, "every male, excluding the senile and infirm," should be called to arms. The sixteen-to-seventy age limit, previously designated, was rescinded. There were some curious reactions. One man, exempt because of infirmity, brought in his fifteen-year-old son, received a bounty for the youngster, and left him with the recruiting agent, happy to have done his part. An able-bodied youth chopped off the tips of his fingers with an ax to avoid conscription, but was taken anyway and assigned to kitchen duty.

Atlanta was becoming an unpleasant place to be. Prices were shooting sky high, and the bare necessities of life were hard to come by. Drunkenness in the streets was common, especially among soldiers visiting the city on an overnight pass. Decent women were warned to keep to their homes; those walking the streets plied an old profession that followed the armies everywhere. Humbug Square gained new vitality from the influx of tawdry opportunists. Wrote Dr. John S. Wilson, Atlanta physician and druggist:

Here is a kind of camping ground for lotterymen, patent medi-
cine vendors, and all kinds of small shows. Here flourish the
prize-package business, the educated hogs and uneducated men;
monsters of all kinds, human and inhuman, corn doctors, root
doctors, and all kinds of doctors except regular doctors. Here are
the microscopemen, the balloon-men, the telescope-men, the sham
jewelrymen.

In suburban Decatur there were refugees, recuperating
troops, and agitating rumors. To the more apprehensive citizens, the capture of Roswell indicated that the enemy might
advance upon Atlanta by way of Stone Mountain, with Decatur
next en route. Only Wheeler's cavalry stood between the Union
army and Decatur, and even now the Federals were creeping
closer to the Georgia Railroad running from Decatur to Atlanta,
forcing families to flee their homes for safety everywhere. As
Elizabeth Wiggins wrote to her mother:

There is a great many refugees from above gone down the
railroad and there is a heap in Atlanta just in tents. It is frightful times on every side. Everything is so high that people can't
buy much: corn is 13 dollars a bushel, meat four dollars and a
half a pound, flour 80 cents per pound and everything in propor-
tionate. . . .

Not far from the Wiggins home, Mary Gay was engaged in
the second act of the drama that had started back in May when
half-brother Tommy Stokes had shipped army overcoats, blankets, and other Confederate supplies for safekeeping in her
home. He had warned her of the danger if this cache should be
discovered by the enemy. Now, with news that Sherman had
crossed the Chattahoochee below Roswell, Mary and her maid
Telitha began opening the crates and sorting out the contents.
This done, Mary climbed upon a pyramid of chairs with ham-
mer and chisel, pried loose several loose boards in the ceiling,
and stowed in the aperture the contraband articles that Telitha
handed up to her.

When the last article had been laid on this improvised shelf, I
gazed upon them in silent anguish and wept. Telitha caught the
melancholy inspiration and also wept.

The boards were replaced, and Mary turned to the pressing problem of saving her own possessions. She summoned the young slave, Toby, from her mother's house, and together they packed every trunk available with linen, silver, china, cut glass, "treasured relics, etc.," between quilts and blankets. Then she and Toby took them by wagon to the depot and rode with the trunks by freight car to Atlanta where a friend had agreed to keep them in the basement of his home.

They hurried back to catch the next train home. But there was no next train. Union cavalry raiders were tearing up the tracks between Atlanta and Decatur. "I'll race you home," said Mary to Toby, and the two began the long trek east on foot. Half way there, with darkness closing in, Toby called from behind: "Look, Miss Mary! Soldiers! And they're ours, too."

> To my dying day I shall never forget the scene to which he called my attention. In the weird stillness it appeared as if the Lord had raised up from the stones a mighty host to fight our battles. Not a sound was heard, not a word was spoken, as those in the vanguard passed opposite me, on and on, and on, in the direction of Decatur, in what seemed to me an interminable line of soldiery . . . once the moon revealed me so plainly that a cheer, somewhat repressed . . . sounded through the woods, and I asked:
> "Whose command?"
> "Wheeler's Cavalry," was the simultaneous response.

Two hours later, when the road-weary couple reached Decatur, Wheeler's regiment was there ahead of them. "They were lying on the ground, asleep, all over the place; and in most instances their horses were lying by them, sleeping too. And I noticed that the soldiers, even though asleep, never released their holds upon the bridles."

The next morning, Mary was up early planning to prepare a feast for the Confederate soldiers but found them gone and the town deserted. Wheeler's cavalry, obviously, had been sent to check Sherman's attack on the Georgia railroad; and now, hope whispered to Mary, "Some strategic movement that will culminate in the capture of the entire Yankee army, no doubt is engaging its attention."

Along the Chattahoochee the war arrived at a bucolic pause. Union troops stripped and plunged into the river for the first good bath they had enjoyed in eight weeks, and were joined by naked Confederates from the south bank. Those remaining in the rifle pits on both sides simply sunned themselves and placidly watched the water carnival. This sort of behavior was not in Private Elisha Stockwell's books. Gesturing toward the Confederate fortifications across the river he asked a fellow Union private:

"Don't they ever shoot?"

"No. We let them alone, and they leave us alone."

While a few of the more sporting-minded soldiery on both sides might exchange shots in a gentlemanly show of marksmanship—riddling an enemy's hat with carefully directed bullets—most of them on both sides of the river refrained from firing or even aggravating their opponents. In a divisional camp of McPherson's army, General Mortimer Leggett was puzzled by the silence on the river front. He sent one of his escorts to investigate. The man returned to report that the Union troops were "having a chat with the Johnnies." Recorded Private Stockwell:

> It made the General mad. He said he didn't put us up there to talk but to shoot, and ordered every man be given one hundred rounds, and if they didn't use them up, they were to be put on extra duty. It was impossible to shoot them away, so they threw them away. But it almost broke up the fun. . . .

Lieutenant Andrew Neal, getting ever closer to his birthplace in Atlanta, was with one of the last Confederate units to cross the Chattahoochee, burning the pontoon bridge behind them. Andy was not convinced of the wisdom of this camaraderie between the opposing lines. "We are not fifty yards apart," he wrote to sister Emma. "Yet we walk along the river banks talking as friendly and courteously as if to old acquaintances. The men laid aside their guns and are scattered up and down the river swapping canteens and hats and bartering one commodity for another. All day we lie in the shade of the banks and act very becomingly. . . ."

As the day wore on, however, Andy noted that the conversations became "rich" and the profanity offensive.

At night as campfires glowed on both sides of the river, singing groups and regimental bands performed as much for the enemy's benefit as their own, aunting each other with such improvisations as "We'll Hang Jeff Davis from a Sour Apple Tree," and hearing in return the challenging strains of "The Bonnie Blue Flag" and "Dixie." But as night wore on the tunes became more sentimental, more reflective of the weariness of war, the wish for peace, as the haunting measures of "Tenting Tonight" crossed with the cadences of the favorite ballad of the South, "Lorena."

In general, the officers of both contending armies averted their eyes from this communal swimming and fraternization at the front. For the Federals, this tolerance had a purpose. Union agents mixed with the bathers to sound out the river bottom, look for possible fords, and relay this information to their high command for future use. Ts Joseph Semmes wrote to his wife, "I have been obliged to order the guards to fire on the cavalry when they go into the river to bathe with the Federal cavalry. Federals never venture in unless our men are bathing. Our men are not seeking fords; they are. That is what they are looking for."

After five days of inaction near the Chattahoochee bridge, during which Sherman had strengthened his forces on the left, established strong bridgeheads near Roswell and attacked and virtually cut the Georgia Railroad supplying Atlanta from the east, the Union general was ready to advance. Infantry up and down the river line began to force crossings to the southern bank. It was a game of snap-the-whip, with Thomas's Army of the Cumberland as a pivotal point in the center, and McPherson sweeping in a wide arc from west to east and down toward Decatur to approach Atlanta along the Georgia Railroad from the east. Up and down the river line, Thomas's army began crossing the river opposite Atlanta.

Troops of one division had been issued special Spencer repeating rifles, using waterproof cartridges, that worked as well under water as in the air. Firing as they stepped into the river, they ducked beneath the surface as the Confederates fired back, loaded their rifles under water, raised the barrels to fire again, then pulled them back beneath the surface—making themselves alternately lethal and invisible. According to Captain Joseph Vale of Thomas's command, the astonishment of the defenders "knew no bounds. We could hear them calling to each other.

" 'Look at them Yankee sons of bitches, loading their guns under water!'

" 'It's no use to fit agin fellus that'll dive down to the bottom of the rivah an git that powdah and ball!'

"Something over two hundred in number remained on the bank, quit firing and surrendered as soon as we got on the south side, anxious only to see the guns that could be loaded and fired under water."

By mid-July most of the Union troops had crossed the river, disposed according to Sherman's preplanned strategy. Thomas's Army of the Cumberland was on the right, facing Atlanta from almost due north. Schofield was in the center but slightly to the rear of Thomas, since he had crossed the river farther upstream. McPherson was swinging down between Stone Mountain and Decatur to advance upon Atlanta from the east. This slightly concave line enveloped, and overlapped, Johnston's fortified defenses overlooking Peachtree Creek.

Johnston had remained curiously quiet during the four-day hiatus. In fact, Sherman believed that the Southern commander had missed a chance in not strongly opposing the Union crossing of the Chattahoochee or attacking the Federals as fast as they reached the other side. Now the Confederate general arranged his troops to correspond roughly with Sherman's line above Atlanta. Former division commander General Alexander Stewart had assumed command of Polk's old corps, relieving the temporary Loring. He was placed on the left of the Peachtree line; Hardee held the center, Hood the right, with Wheeler's cavalry keeping an eye on Decatur and the Georgia Railroad.

In Atlanta the Federal secret agent, John C. Moore, was assigned to report to Sherman on conditions in the city. Not all of his information seemed, at first glance, relevant. Stationing himself in front of Johnston's headquarters on the Marietta road, he reported to Sherman its precise location and added that, "They seem to be having a jollification."

What "jollification" he referred to, it is hard to say. But at that

THE HEART OF ATLANTA
—— 1864 ——

time Johnston had an unexpected visitor from Richmond. Braxton Bragg, military adviser to Jefferson Davis, had come to Atlanta to report on General Johnston's situation and prospects for holding the Gate City.

On arrival, Bragg wired Davis: "Our army all south of the Chattahoochee, and indications seem to favor an entire evacuation of the place. Shall see General Johnston immediately."

He did not see Johnston immediately. The general was at the front. He had not expected a visit from Bragg, and never knew why Bragg had come. But he had received a hint from Senator Benjamin Hill who had warned Johnston, after Hill's talk with President Davis, that requests for more aid from the government were futile. Now Hill telegraphed from Richmond, "You must do the work with the present force. For God's sake, do it."

The wires hummed between Atlanta and the capital, letters and messages crossed in transit. John Bell Hood, holding a reciprocated grudge against Joe Johnston, crept into the cloudy picture. In a plain bid for the generalship, Hood wrote to Bragg on the latter's arrival in Atlanta that Johnston had grossly understated his losses; the figure should be raised from ten to twenty thousand. He qustioned both Johnston's policy and competence. Indicating that he himself had consistently advocated taking the offensive—a statement far from true—he added: "I regard it as a great misfortune to our country that we failed to give battle to the enemy many miles north of our present position."

Bragg was no help in the matter. His own past record and relations with Johnston and the Army of Tennessee made him vulnerable, and he tried to straddle the fence. After talking with Johnston, twice but briefly, he telegraphed Davis that the army was "greatly reduced, now very little over 50,000," but added that morale was good. He must have confused the president still more regarding Johnston's plans. "He has not sought my advice and it was not volunteered. I cannot learn that he has any more plan for the future than he has had in the past."

Davis found little comfort in Bragg's report. He sent another telegram to Johnston, expressing alarm at Sherman's nearness to Atlanta, adding: "I wish to hear from you as to present situation, and your plan of operations so specifically as will enable me to anticipate events."

Johnston had a plan. He had Sherman just exactly where he wanted him. His new line overlooking the valley of Peachtree Creek enabled Johnston to watch for enemy crossings of the stream; then promptly descend on, and destroy, each isolated unit as it reached the southern bank, before reenforcements could be brought across the creek. But he failed to explain this to Davis "specifically" as the President had requested. Instead he telegraphed to Richmond:

> As the enemy has double our number, we must be on the defensive. My plan of operations must, therefore, depend upon that of the enemy. It is mainly to watch for an opportunity to fight to advantage. We are trying to put Atlanta in condition to be held for a day or two by the Georgia militia, that army maneuvers may be freer and wider.

The last sentence was unfortunate. Davis interpreted it to mean Johnston was planning to turn Atlanta over to the militia while he himself retreated farther south. Actually, Johnston intended using the militia to hold the city's fortifications while the bulk of his army advanced against the enemy.

There were other misunderstandings between the President and Johnston. So many that Davis sought the advice of General Robert E. Lee at Petersburg regarding the "sad alternative" he was considering: "Genl. Johnston has failed, and there are strong indications that he will abandon Atlanta. . . . It seems necessary to *relieve him* at once. Who should succeed him? What think you of Hood for the position?"

Lee's reply reflected his personal sadness at the situation. "It is a grievous thing to change the commander of an army situated as is that of Tennessee. Still, if necessary, it ought to be done. . . . Hood is a good fighter, very industrious on the battlefield, careless off. . . . may God give you wisdom to decide on this momentous matter."

Davis decided.

Across the railroad from Johnston's headquarters, on July 17, Jeremiah C. Huff sat on the porch of his house with his daughter Sarah and listened to a regimental band serenading the Confederate commander. The band ran through the familiar favorites,

"Dixie," "The Bonnie Blue Flag," "The Homespun Dress." But General Johnston was not listening. He was discussing with Colonel Presstman, his chief engineer, the matter of extending his breastworks overlooking Peachtree Creek, the better to withstand enemy attempts to cross that stream. Their conversation was interrupted by Major Charles Hubner of the telegraph corps with a message for the commander, signed by the President's adjutant:

> I am directed by the Secretary of War to inform you that as you have failed to arrest the advance of the enemy in the vicinity of Atlanta, far in the interior of Georgia, and express no confidence that you can defeat or repel him, you are hereby relieved from the command of the Army and Department of Tennessee, which you will immediately turn over to General Hood.

The troops at the front heard the news in the most dismal fashion possible—from the enemy, who had learned it from decoded Southern semaphores. "It came like a flash of lightning, staggering and blinding everyone," recorded one soldier in the ranks. "It was like applying a lighted match to an immense magazine." Relayed from the Federal pickets above Peachtree Creek, the disclosure was prefaced by the customary, taunting Yankee call:

"Johnny, O, Johnny, O, Johnny Reb!"

"What do you want?"

"Joe Johnston is relieved of the command."

"*What!?*"

"General Joseph E. Johnston is relieved, and Hood appointed in his place."

"You're a damned liar! Come out and show yourself and I'll shoot you in your tracks."

After several bitter exchanges, the Federal picket accepted the challenge. Both men stepped out into the open, rifles at the ready, and simultaneously started firing—and kept on firing until the Confederate spun to the ground with a bullet in his heart.

The tragic demonstration was in keeping with the stricken feelings of the Army of Tennessee, which had been raised from winter despair by "Uncle Joe" and had campaigned with him with undiminished confidence for four embattled months. Not once had they been defeated. Heavily outnumbered, they had lost ground. But no lives had been wasted uselessly. They were a tougher, better, more inspired army than they had been six months earlier.

The relief unit which brought the news to another Confederate outpost on Peachtree Creek introduced it with the words, "Boys, we've fought all the war for nothing." When told that Johnston was leaving the Army of Tennessee, all five pickets at the outpost threw down their guns, their haversacks, their cartridge boxes—remarking that they would have no further use for them—and crossed the creek, presumably casting their lot with Sherman's Federals.

John Bell Hood had got what he wanted, but at an inopportune time. The fate of Atlanta was suddenly thrust upon his shoulders; the blame for any false move would be his. He would have preferred to have Johnston retain the command at this critical point, and told the general so. Hardee and Stewart also urged Johnston to delay observing the order for a few days (and later Hood would accuse the general of "deserting" him in time of crisis). But Johnston's only choice, however painful, was at once to relinquish the command to Hood. In a farewell address to his troops the following day, he told them:

> I cannot leave this noble army without expressing my admiration of the high military qualities it has displayed. A long and arduous campaign has made conspicuous every soldierly virtue, endurance of toil, obedience to orders, brilliant courage. The enemy has never attacked but to be repulsed and severely punished. You, soldiers, have never argued but from your courage, and never counted your foe. No longer your leader, I will still watch your career, and will rejoice in your victories. To one and all I offer assurances of my friendship, and bid an affectionate farewell.

There was no real sound whatever from the troops, only a murmur of grief and denial like ripples in a pool of silence. A pall of gloom enveloped the army, Halsey Wigfall wrote to his parents, arising not so much from distrust of Hood as love of

Johnston. As the different regiments began returning to their posts, they marched past their former general. "We lifted our hats," wrote Colonel J. C. Nisbet of the Georgia Volunteers. "There was no cheering. We simply passed silently, with heads uncovered. Some of the officers broke ranks and grasped his hand, as the tears poured down their cheeks."

For years to come, the wisdom of Johnston's removal would be debated. There were those who thought Davis was justified in his decision, if only because of Johnston's failure to communicate properly with Richmond and to keep his superiors informed. But the feeling in the army was unequivocal. Captain Key, stationed with his battery at Peachtree Creek, wrote in his diary on July 18:

> Every man looked sad and disheartened at this information, and felt that evil would result from the removal of Johnston, whom they esteem and love above any previous commander. His address touched every heart, and every man thought that his favorite General had been grievously wronged. The cause for this procedure on the part of the President, at this eventful moment when the enemy is pressing us, we have been unable to conjecture. General Hood is a gallant man, but Johnston has been tried and won the confidence of the soldiery.

Key's sentiments were echoed throughout the ranks. Sam Watkins considered Johnston's removal "the most terrible and disastrous blow the South ever received," and added, "I saw thousands of men cry like babies—regular old-fashioned boo-hoos." Sergeant Hagan wrote to his wife Amanda: ". . . all moan the loss of our grate Leader he would have been retained in prefferance to any one else. Gen Hood now commands us & I hope he will be successful but the releaving of Gen Joe is dampening to his troops."

Among the commissioned officers, Lieutenant Robert M. Gill wrote to his wife, "Hood is the most unpopular Genl in the army & some of the troops have been called together to forestall anything like an outbreak. Maj Genls and Brig & all regret that Johnston is gone, Johnston has made himself very dear to the soldiers."

Higher in the command, Generals Cleburne and Stewart, in

their own ways, believed the move was "a death blow to the army." Hardee later wrote that the spirit of the troops had been "buoyant" under Little Joe, and regarding his own corps that "I led them into battle with more confidence" when Johnston was in charge of things. Stewart was even more positive, considering Johnston "the only commander . . . whom *men* and *officers* were disposed to trust and confide in."

Hood himself, as of the moment, was equally concerned. He had not expected the burden of command to be deposed so quickly on his shoulders. Better it had happened later, when and if the situation was more favorable. With Stewart and Hardee he composed and signed a telegram to Jefferson Davis, "stating that, in our judgment, it was dangerous to change commanders at that juncture, and requesting him to recall the order removing Johnston, at least until the fate of Atlanta should be decided."

Davis replied that it was too late; Johnston's Fabian policy had "proved disastrous. The order has been executed, and I cannot suspend it without making the case worse than it was before the order was issued." Richmond as a whole, far removed from conditions in Atlanta, generally approved the change. General Josiah Gorgas wrote of the people's reaction to the news of Johnston's displacement: "They have praised him and waited for him to fight until he has lost all Georgia, and they have got tired of him."

Mary Boykin Chesnut believed that Johnston's refusal to listen to advice constituted the "madness of self-conceit" and if he had been a Yankee, Washington "would have lodged Joe Johnston behind triple walls in the twinkling of an eye." Sally Buchanan of Richmond who, for reasons to come, had played an important part in Hood's life, exclaimed to Mrs. Chesnut: "Now they will blame Sam for Johnston's mistakes. I have prayed as I never prayed for him before. . . . And I went to the convent and asked the nuns to pray for him too."

In and around Atlanta there was corresponding gloom. Kate Cumming had been transferred to the hospital in Newnan, a town 40 miles south of Atlanta, where all wounded soldiers and convalescent patients able to move about at all were set to work digging entrenchments and throwing up breastworks in anticipation of the crisis. Kate's companion among the nurses, Fanny Beers, recorded the reaction in the hospital to the news of General Johnston's removal from command:

> The whole post seemed as if stricken by some terrible calamity. Convalescents walked about with lagging steps and gloomy faces. In every ward lay men who wept bitterly or groaned aloud or, covering their faces, refused to speak or eat. For that hour, the buoyant, hopeful spirit seemed to die out. I do not think anything was ever the same again.

Samuel Richards the bookseller, however, was less pessimistic, writing in his diary, "All of a sudden Gen. Johnston has been relieved of the command of the Army and Gen. Hood or 'Old Pegleg' as the soldiers style him placed in command, so that there is thought to be a prospect for a fight before Atlanta is given up, as Hood is said to be a fighting man, if he *has* only one leg."

In Sherman's ranks entrenched along Peachtree Creek, the knowledge that Hood was "a fighting man," replacing Johnston's cautious but effective tactics, came as heartening news. Wrote Sherman himself, "At this critical moment the Confederate Government rendered us a most valuable service. . . . The character of a leader is a large factor in the game of war, and I confess I was pleased with the change."

Sherman's satisfaction was shared by his generals who had been forced to match wits with Joseph Johnston. Hooker recorded that the news of Johnston's removal "was received by our officers with universal rejoicing." The wily Jacob Cox, begrudgingly praising Johnston's "patient skill and watchful intelligence and courage," regarded his removal "as equivalent to a victory for us." All agreed that Hood had courage, that ultimate victory would not come easily. But that it would come in time, seemed far more certain. Sooner or later the Stars and Stripes would fly above Atlanta—if the city physically survived the fight for its existence.

The change in command would lead to a closer confrontation

among former friends. Both McPherson and Schofield had been classmates of Hood at West Point where their performance had been notably superior—McPherson and Schofield graduating first and seventh in their class, respectively. Hood had graduated forty-fourth. Such ratings might not mean much when it came to military aptitude, but as to temperament Hood confessed that he himself "was more wedded to boyish sports than books," and "after a night of merrymaking" he often relied on McPherson to help him through "the more difficult portions of my studies for the day."

But Hood was no opponent to be taken lightly. "He'll hit you like hell, now, before you know it," Schofield assured Sherman. That suited the Union general to a T. He had been baffled by Johnston's skillful retreats to prepared positions that still kept the Union army blocked and tied down to its lengthening supply line. He could never get at the man. When he had finally tried the direct approach, at Kennesaw, he had suffered a catastrophe. Now he confronted an altogether different type of enemy, one who promised to come out and meet him in the open, willing to gamble on the outcome. That was the secret—Hood was a gambler. A Kentucky trooper had once told Sherman of a poker game in which "I seed Hood bet twenty-five hundred dollars with nary a pair in his hand."

Sherman would wait for Hood to make his play, confident that he would not have to wait long.

11

Battle of Peachtree Creek

Atlanta could never quite accept the bearded, handsome, one-armed general who had to be helped from the saddle before stumping on his wooden leg to Johnston's house on Marietta road. In Richmond just a year before, John Bell Hood, "Sam" Hood, had been idolized and feted as the first real hero of the war. "With his sad face—the face of an old crusader who believed in his cause, his cross, his crown," wrote Mary Boykin Chesnut, he gave an appearance "of awkward strength" with "the light of battle shining in his eyes."

Convalescing from his wounds in Richmond he had failed to win the tantalizing hand of Sally Buchanan Preston, known among her friends as "Buck." Sally was an unscrupulous femme fatale whom Mrs. Chesnut described as "easy to fall in love with, impossible to fall out of love with." Buck added Sam Hood to her list of conquests and then, vanity satisfied, eased him out of her life—dealing that gritty soldier one more wound, perhaps the bitterest of all. He had returned to the army grimly determined to regain his self-esteem, his public image as one who conquered regardless of the cost.

Visiting Johnston at the Niles house now, the morning of July

18, Hood had in mind a telegram just received from James A. Seddon, Secretary of War: "You are charged with a great trust. . . . Be wary no less than bold . . . God be with you." Wariness was not in his nature, but bold he did intend to be. In any event, he needed to know what his predecessor, General Johnston, had in mind (if anything) for resisting or routing Sherman's army gathering like a thundercloud along the banks of Peachtree Creek just five miles from Atlanta.

Of that fateful meeting between Hood and Johnston each bequeathed to history his own account.

"In transferring the command to General Hood," wrote Johnston, "I explained my plans to him. First, I expected an opportunity to engage the enemy on terms of advantage while they were divided and crossing Peachtree Creek." If Johnston failed to defeat the Union forces in this initial action, he would fall back to the fortifications in Atlanta, "and, when the Federal Army approached, march out with the three corps against one of its flanks." If unsuccessful again, "the Confederate army had a near and secure place of refuge in Atlanta, which it could hold forever, and so win the campaign of which that place was the object."

Hood's account of the interview was very different. According to the commander, he pleaded with Johnston "for the good of the country to remain in command." Citing "the great embarrassment of the position in which I had been placed . . . I did not even know the position of the two remaining corps of the Army . . . I besought him, if he would not retain command and fight the battle of Atlanta, to at least remain with me and give me the benefit of his counsel whilst I determined the issue."

Johnston was deeply moved, wrote Hood, by the earnestness of this plea, and "he finally made me the promise that, after riding into Atlanta, he would return the same evening" and give his successor the counsel requested. "He not only failed to comply with his promise, but, without a word of explanation or apology, left that evening for Macon, Georgia."

No one will ever know precisely what was said in Johnston's house that day. Certainly Hood was not completely ignorant of where the other army corps were stationed. And he appears, in the light of subsequent events, to have had some knowledge of

Johnston's military plans, or else to have deduced them from whatever Johnston said. No doubt, Johnston was a taciturn and uncommunicative man. No doubt, too, Hood was looking for someone to blame if the greatest gamble of his life, the battle for Atlanta, failed to pay off.

That evening Johnston and Lydia left the Gate City to stay for a while at the home of Major General Howell Cobb in Macon. Cobb sensed that the retired general was deeply hurt at being relieved of his command. "Still he indulges in no spirit of complaint," he wrote, "speaks kindly of his successor and very hopefully of the prospect of holding Atlanta." After several days spent in becoming better acquainted with his guest, Cobb concluded, "I greatly fear that we shall have to regret too deeply the removal of Genl. Johnston. . . ."

Headquartered from this point on in the Atlanta home of Windsor Smith on Whitehall Street, "the finest wooden building in the city," Hood assessed his situation, difficult to say the least. With the deposition of General Johnston he was, he knew, unpopular with the rank and file. And also distrusted by his officers, many of whom he in turn mistrusted. But to a degree he had brought the command upon himself, and with it the responsibility of holding Atlanta against a vastly superior Union army flushed and spirited with almost three months of victorious campaigning.

Also, he had inherited a military posture not of his own choice or making. The zone of battle and the disposition of Confederate troops had been decided by Joe Johnston. There was no time for extensive redeployment; he would have to make do with what he had. And make do, he would. He would not only "hold Atlanta forever," as his predecessor had vowed to do; he would carry the battle to the enemy and rout or destroy the Union army in the bargain.

While Johnston was "comfortably quartered at Macon," Hood began consolidating his position. In provisional command of Hood's own corps, at Richmond's suggestion, was General Benjamin F. Cheatham, no particular favorite of Hood himself but a marked improvement in tSquarees of the troops. While so far relatively undistinguished in the war, Cheatham had endeared himself to the rank and file by one day stumbling upon a group of foragers from his division raiding a Southern apple orchard. Instead of reproving the men, the general had called to a soldier in a likely-looking tree, "Son, throw me down one of those nice looking apples, will you?"

Now, on July 19, Hood arranged his three corps in a line approximately paralleling Peachtree Creek. Alexander P. Stewart had taken over Loring's corps, formerly commanded by Leonidas Polk. Stewart's Corps was positioned on the left and Hardee in the center, both facing Thomas's Army of the Cumberland and covering Atlanta. Cheatham held the right flank, his entrenched line bending south toward the Georgia Railroad to face Union generals Schofield and McPherson operating near Decatur. For reenforcement, the Georgia Militia and Wheeler's cavalry were placed at his disposal.

Though Hood himself did not appear on the prospective battlefield, now or ever, he was kept informed of Sherman's movements by his scouts. He learned that General Thomas's divisions were already crossing Peachtree Creek, brigade by brigade, over flimsy pontoon bridges. Soon the bulk of his army would be over the stream and within the wedge-shaped pocket formed by the junction of Peachtree and the Chattahoochee River. McPherson had seized Decatur, and he and Schofield were moving toward Atlanta from the east, along the tracks of the Georgia Railroad.

Hood perceived at once that Sherman had violated a basic rule of military strategy, one that Sherman himself verbally espoused: never permit the segments of an army to become detached from one another. Now there was a hole nearly four miles wide straight through the Federal line, giving Hood a chance to strike full force at Thomas' army while preventing the left wing of Sherman's line from coming to Thomas' aid. It was the sort of Federal blunder that Joe Johnston had always prayed for, one he had tried to induce at Kingston by luring Sherman into splitting off in two directions. Now that opportunity was handed to Little Joe's successor on a silver platter.

"My object," Hood wrote, "was to crush Thomas's Army before he could fortify himself, and then turn upon Schofield and McPherson." On the morning of July 20 he issued final orders to his generals. Stewart's and Hardee's corps, each with two divisions and one division in reserve, would advance through the gap on Thomas' flank, then bear left to crush the Union forces in the pocket between creek and river, "everything on our side of the creek to be taken at all hazards." Cheatham would protect the right of the advancing troops, and keep Schofield and McPherson from coming to the aid of Thomas. The attack was set for 1 P.M. that afternoon.

It seemed a superbly simple, well considered, and effective plan—on paper—and it was. But timing was all important. Thomas should be taken by surprise before his troops had a chance to entrench and bring supplies across the creek. Everything had to adhere to schedule; and almost at once that schedule began to fall apart.

Cheatham found the right of his line endangered and was forced to extend it farther south. Stewart and Hardee were ordered to move to their right to close the ensuing gap. Hardee shifted too far, then had to move back to the left again. All this through a junglelike terrain of woods and thickets, interspersed with rivulets and ravines. The troops lost contact with one another, visibility was almost nil. One whole division of Hardee's corps, under General W. B. Bate, failed to locate the enemy and "simply dropped out of sight." Most important of all was the fact that the attack, supposedly synchronized for 1 P.M., got off at varying hours after that, and was not actually under way until late afternoon.

By four-thirty, Stewart's troops had made a gallant thrust against Thomas' line, had taken possession of portions of his hastily constructed breastworks, and were engaged in fierce hand-to-hand combat with the enemy. With the outcome in the balance, Stewart looked for support from Hardee. He saw nothing, heard only feeble firing on his right, suggesting that Hardee was meeting with little resistance and would be joining him at any moment. . . .

Even before General Thomas' army started crossing Peachtree Creek, on the direct route to Atlanta, Sherman had been astonished at the lack of Confederate resistance. He wondered briefly if Hood were withdrawing into the fortifications of At-

lanta, or even intended to evacuate the city. It made no sense.
Schofield, a classmate of the Confederate commander at West
Point, had warned that Hood would take the offensive the moment he saw an opportunity, and Sherman had agreed. In fact,
wrote Sherman, "every division commander was cautioned to
be always prepared for battle in any shape." This was the sort
of situation that Sherman welcomed; was, in fact,

> . . . just what we wanted, viz.: to fight in open ground, on anything
> like equal terms, instead of being forced to run up against pre-
> pared entrenchments; but at the same time, the enemy having
> Atlanta behind him, could choose the time and place of attack, and
> could at pleasure mass a superior force on our weakest points.
> Therefore, we had to be constantly ready for sallies.

He issued a series of field orders to his generals resulting, on
the morning of July 20, in the movement of General Thomas
across Peachtree Creek and the junction of Schofield and
McPherson's armies at Decatur, marching against Atlanta from
the east. Almost too late, he realized that the two wings of his
army were dangerously separated, with a vulnerable gap between. He sought to close the gap by moving two divisions of
Thomas' army to the left. But it always took "Old Slow-trot" a
long time to move.

In his own estimation, the siege of Atlanta had begun—implicit in a final order to his generals:

> Each army commander will accept battle on anything like fair
> terms, but if the army reach within cannon-range of the city
> without receiving artillery or musketry fire he will halt, form a
> strong line, with batteries in position, and await orders. If fired
> on from the forts or buildings of Atlanta no consideration must
> be paid to the fact that they are occupied by families, but the place
> must be cannonaded without the formality of a demand. . . .

Atlanta was to feel the consequences of that order even before
the two contending armies clashed in battle. About noon, Er
Lawshe was passing the corner of Ivy and Ellis streets and
noticed a young girl standing with her parents before Rice's
lumber yard across the way. There had been little more than the

distant sound of musket fire from the direction of Peachtree Creek; but now came a savage scream crescending from the north, a deafening explosion, and a cloud of dust and smoke enveloped Lawshe as the pavement lurched beneath him.

When the sulphurous smoke had cleared, Lawshe saw the young girl lying in a pool of blood, the dazed parents struggling to regain their feet. Crowds gathered around helplessly, but no one knew, or would ever know, the name of the dead child and her parents. Lawshe guessed that they were refugees from elsewhere; but one thing was certain—the first enemy shell had fallen on Atlanta. The Gate City was under siege.

On the Confederate front, that Wednesday morning, tension had been building to the snapping point. A rumor had circulated through the ranks, that Johnston was still in command of the Army of Tennessee. Tom Key did not believe it, concluding that "it was done to prevent desertions and to cause the troops to fight with their former bravery in the now approaching conflict." Key rode with other artillery officers of Hotchkiss's battalion along Cheatham's eastern section of the line, to select a commanding position for his battery.

The chosen site adjoined "a new and beautiful residence on the Atlanta and Decatur Road. . . . It looked as fresh as a young bride." Key was disturbed by the fact that "if the Yankees attack us here they will destroy it with their shells." He was confident that the Yankees would attack; they had already taken Decatur and were moving on Atlanta down the Georgia Railroad, while General Thomas was crossing Peachtree Creek to the north of Key's position. This was the point of no return. "We have retreated as far as policy or safety will permit," he noted.

On the Peachtree line, Sergeant John Hagan of the Georgia Volunteers wrote to his wife, Amanda, that "the grate storm is gathering. heavy Skirmishing going on in our front & the enimy crossing in heavy force &c." But Hagan's chief concern was for "the Box of Something to eat" which he had asked his wife to send two weeks before. It had not yet arrived. "I do not know what to think . . . I fear the Box is lost." He asked Amanda to make sure it had been properly sent and to try to trace it.

Private Sam Watkins, in the early morning hours, was standing watch in a sedge field in front of Hardee's section of the line. A pale moon and stars and passing clouds infected him with noble sentiments common to even hardened troops before a battle. "I thought of God, of heaven, of home, and I thought of Jennie—her whom I had ever loved, and [who] had given me her troth in all her maiden purity." In the midst of these reveries Sam suddenly noticed a moving form ten yards in front of him. He instantly raised his rifle and fired, and "the most unearthly scream I ever heard greeted my ears."

Something else greeted his ears: two shots from Confederate pickets behind him and the smack of bullets against a tree-trunk inches from his head. He shouted to the pickets to hold their fire, then raced back to their post in righteous wrath.

"Who fired those two shots?"

Two of the pickets answered, "I did." They explained that they had heard a rifle shot up forward and, believing the enemy was out there somewhere, had fired at random in that direction.

"I was on them like a duck on a June bug," Sam recorded. The three men fought and wrestled, kicked and gouged and bit, until the pickets took off and ran—leaving Sam stunned and bloodied by a blow on the head from a water-filled canteen. He carried the scars on his face and head for life, the only wounds that Private Watkins suffered in the War Between the States.

Lieutenant Andrew Neal, with his back to the city of his birth, wrote to his father that morning:

> We have been digging dirt for twenty-four hours and have good substantial works. The Yankees have crossed the river, frightened away the cavalry, and are making a noise some eight hundred yards in front with our skirmishers. The Generals, staff officers and couriers are dashing about furiously as if they expected the Yankees this evening but I have no idea they will make an attack. I hear they are already on a big flank by way of Decatur.

The big flank by way of Decatur was indeed under way, with McPherson's cavalry under Kenner Garrard circling Stone Mountain to approach Atlanta from the east. At his Promised Land Plantation, Thomas Maguire began noting in his diary the sequence of events: "July 18—Yankees at Stone Mountain—

water station burned—part of track torn up—great excitement. July 19—Fighting at Atlanta—Yankees at the Mountain—folks badly scared in this settlement. July 20—We are now cut off and are in the enemy's lines, but I do not feel so." Maguire would feel the sting six hours later.

In Decatur, Mary Gay, for the first time, felt the pure horror of the war. She was caring for her young slave, Toby, who had come down with pneumonia, when forward units of Schofield's army poured into the town.

> Advance guards, composed of every species of criminal . . . swooped down upon us, and every species of deviltry followed in their footsteps. My poor mother, frightened and trembling, and myself, having locked the doors of the house, took our stand with the servants in the yard, and witnessed the grand *entree* of the menagerie. One of the beasts got down upon his all-fours and pawed up the dust and bellowed like an infuriated bull. And another asked me if I did not expect to see them with hoofs and horns. I told him, "No, I had expected to see some gentlemen among them, and was sorry I should be disappointed."

The invaders killed their chickens and hogs, calves and cow; stole everything of value in the house; scattered the crockery over the floor, and committed "other outrages and indignities too revolting to mention." In their wake the rest of the army descended on Decatur like an avalanche, and Garrard's cavalry took possession of and set up tents in Mary's yard. Soon came a knock on the door, and an officer introduced himself as Major J.W. Campbell of General Schofield's staff. He demanded that Mary and her ménage abandon her home, to be used as head-quarters for the general.

Mary beckoned the major through the ravaged house. She showed him the seriously ailing Toby on his cot, the shattered furniture and crockery, the ransacked closets and bureaus, the emptied larder and behind the house, the carcasses of slaugh-tered fowl and livestock. The major underwent a change of heart. He assured Mary that not only could she keep the house, but he would seek out and hang the vandals to the nearest tree.

The next morning, as Mary wondered what they could eat to

survive—having been robbed of everything edible in the house and being too proud to beg from the Union troops who were breakfasting in the yard—another knock sounded on the door. She admitted a burly Union private with a large tray, "covered with a snow-white cloth and evidently filled with food." The bearer handed her a card with the inscription: "Please accept this small testimonial of regard and respectful sympathy, with the compliments of (Major) Campbell."

From his tent headquarters on slightly rising ground northeast of Atlanta, Sherman scanned the projected battle-ground. In his later report he somehow misconstrued the hour, recording that Thomas' troops had crossed Peachtree Creek and "were resting for noon, when, without notice, the enemy came pouring out of their trenches down upon them; they became commingled and fought in many places hand to hand."

Actually, it was well after noon when Stewart's troops, "with the hideous rebel yell," charged down upon the unsuspecting Federals. Beaten back at first, they charged again, and then again, with the fiercest fighting taking place at the site of Collier's Mill, held by Newton's and Geary's Federal divisions. "Pap" Thomas, watching the battle from the opposite bank of Peachtree Creek, saw his men in danger of being surrounded; the Confederates swarmed from everywhere, in seemingly inexhaustible numbers. Bayonets and bullets were not enough to check that furious attack.

Thomas had been an artillery commander in the War with Mexico eighteen years before. He had witnessed the fate of infantry exposed to heavy guns. Beside him now were six pieces of horse-drawn field artillery, awaiting action. "Old Slow-trot" forgot his sobriquet. Drawing his sword he prodded the horses across the river at a gallop, forced them to a commanding rise of ground near Collier's Mill, unlimbered the guns, and started pumping death into the ranks of the attackers. Once again Thomas was "the Rock of Chickamauga," the pivot of Federal resistance. While the Confederates had killed or wounded 1,800 of his men, mostly from Hooker's corps, Union guns left 4,800 of the enemy on the field before the hopelessly decimated Southerners withdrew.

Where had Hardee been all the time, while Stewart's men had pressed the attack and finally taken such a frightful beating? Hood would forever ask that question, and answer it himself. Hardee simply "lay down." Out of conflicting reports the facts appeared to be that Hardee, reconnoitering the Federal line, had encountered heavy firing, concluded that the Union troops were well entrenched, and hesitated openly to charge a strongly fortified position. According to Hood, "in lieu of attacking as ordered, and supporting Stewart's gallant assault, the troops of Hardee—as their losses on that day indicate—did nothing more than skirmish with the enemy."

Stewart had looked in vain for support from his confederate. But unlike Hood, he did not blame Hardee by name for the calamity. Praising instead "the special gallantry of [my] officers and men whose blood was so freely, and it would seem so uselessly, shed on this occasion," he concluded simply: "I cannot but think had the plan of the battle, as I understood it, been carried out fully, we would have achieved a great success."

Sarah Huff's home had been directly in the zone of battle. She had seen General French's division march by the house and throw up breastworks just a mile above the farm. She was fully forewarned. "For weeks," she wrote, "we had listened to the nearer-coming rumblings of exploding bomb-shells, so remindful of slowly approaching thunderstorms. . . . All at once in the early forenoon the expected storm broke over us. Within one mile of where mother and members of her family stood, trees as big as a man's body were mowed down. . . ."

We were on the edge of the battlefield, which extended for several miles around the northeastern line of the city. The reports of the cannon sounded like thunderclaps and the musketry was like hail on the roof in the time of a summer squall. I recall hearing my brother say, "If they turn their guns this way we will be torn to pieces."

Men were being, or had been, torn to pieces just a mile or so away, where Private E.B. Fenton lay wounded on the field. Fenton remembered:

The plains and the hillsides were strewn with the corpses of men where they fell. The dead and dying were lying close together. . . . There is the groaning and the crying of the wounded. In quiet tones we speak to each other. The question passes back and forth, "Where are you wounded?"

"Through the body."

"And you?"

"An arm broken."

"My knee smashed with a piece of shell," or

"A minie bullet through the foot . . ."

. . . so the low replies pass around.

The action on Peachtree Creek that afternoon was, however, only a part, although by far the greater part, of the over-all struggle for the city. Throughout the day McPherson's Army of the Tennessee had pressed toward Atlanta from Decatur, destroying the tracks and wires of the Georgia Railroad. Sherman had issued specific orders to McPherson regarding the mutilation of the rails:

Officers should be instructed that bars simply bent may be used again. Pile the ties into shape for a bonfire, put the rails across and when red hot in the middle, let a man at each end twist the bar so that its surface becomes spiral.

Though it slowed their progress toward Atlanta, this method of destroying railroad tracks had an infectious fascination for the Union troops. With every twist of the rails they felt they were wringing an opponent's neck. Some elaborated on the method, wrapping the red hot rails around the telegaph poles or trunks of saplings, and tying the ends into a sort of half-hitch, thus creating what were known as "Sherman's neckties."

Only Wheeler's Confederate cavalry, the troops dismounted, were available to check McPherson; Cheatham's corps was held to its defense position by Schofield's Army of the Ohio. Yard by contested yard, Wheeler was driven back to make a last stand on a low ridge known as Bald Hill, a mile and a half from the outskirts of Atlanta. Here he entrenched, but saw below him "masses of the enemy, fully 20,000 strong, all aligned and ready to attack. I felt that any respectable effort on their part could easily dislodge my force and leave nothing between McPherson and the interior works which had been erected for the final defense of Atlanta." He appealed to General Hood for help.

Hood had been about to send Cleburne's division, held in reserve during the battle of Peachtree Creek, into action against Thomas. Receiving Wheeler's call for aid he shot back word to "hold on . . . Cleburne's division is coming to your support." Wheeler did hold on, surviving two spirited assaults, until Cleburne arrived at his side around midnight. By that time, the fighting had subsided all along the six-mile line from Peachtree Creek to Bald Hill.

News of Confederate disaster on both fronts, north and east of the city, reached Atlanta with the retreating troops and wagonloads of wounded. Confederate Captain J.P. Austin rode into town along Peachtree Road and found time to write to his parents:

> We found the city in a wild state of excitement. Citizens were running in every direction. Terror-stricken women and children went screaming about the streets seeking some avenue of escape from hissing, bursting shells, as they sped on their mission of death and destruction. Perfect pandemonium reigned near the Union Depot. Trunks, bedclothing and apparel were scattered in every direction. People were stirring in every conceivable way to get out of town with their effects.

Several hospitals had been moved to other towns for safety, piling impossible numbers of wounded into those remaining. At the Medical College, Dr. Peter Paul d'Alvigny began operating round the clock. Dr. Charles Todd Quintard and the Reverend Thomas O'Reilly were among those who moved among the crowded cots and figures lying in the halls, ministering to the suffering and dying patients. For the first time Atlantans realized that their city was under full seige, and that they as well as the army were a military target. They had read about the ordeal of Vicksburg; they shuddered at what might lie ahead.

The following morning a truce was declared between the contending armies, to bury the dead from the battle of the day before. Sergeant Hagan was not among the casualties, though his regiment had suffered badly, and he himself had had a narrow escape. As he wrote on that hot and steaming morning to Amanda: "I come very near falling into the enimy's hands & had to lay down my gun & accutiaments & haversacks & Bedcover. I had to leave all & Swim the creek about 3 hundred yards & made my asscape." His principal concern remained the box of food, of which he noted:

> I receved the Box last night about 10 P.M. the box had been robed there was no Syrup nor honey nor cakes there was Some apples and some buiskits the Buiskits were Spoilt & the loaf of Bread was also spoilt & the Butter was also divded I got a little I was sory the Box was Robed if you should ever send more you must not cook anything & you must have the Box hooped & then it will not be opened but there was nothing to do but prize the lead [lid] off.

Sam Watkins, also luckily unscathed in the battle, was drawn by curiosity to the place where he had stood watch in the sedge field, had fired at an unseen enemy and had, in turn, been fired on by pickets in his rear. He saw that his bullet had found its mark. A dead Yankee lay on the spot, but it was hard to tell where the prowler had been hit. As so often happened with the dead, the Union soldier had been stripped of everything he carried, boots, rifle, canteen, haversack.

"He was stark naked," Watkins wrote, "and black as a Negro, and was as big as a skinned horse. . . . My hair stood up like the quills of a porcupine. He scared me worse when dead than when living."

For Sarah Huff and her mother the battle of Peachtree Creek had been a fateful one. Though the house still seemed to tremble from the cannonade, Mrs. Huff told Sarah she had no intention of leaving the only home that she had known throughout her adult, married life. But that morning a squad of military engineers arrived and began laying out entrenchments between the "big house" and the kitchen. An officer politely ordered Mrs. Huff to leave immediately; within twenty-four hours this could be the scene of an even bigger battle.

It was not, however, until "long lines of breastworks lined and wound about the estate," that Mrs. Huff accepted her impossible predicament. She and Sarah selected those belongings which they could not do without, and started packing them in the horsedrawn buggy. Sarah's two brothers were too small to help, and the slaves had run away, so some of their heavier, bulkier possessions had to be left behind. The family went to a house in Atlanta, on Railroad Street, which had been loaned to them by Mr. Charles Shearer, "one of the city's finest old-time English gentlemen." Shearer lived in another house adjoining.

At his Promised Land plantation, Thomas Maguire experienced the miseries of being caught behind enemy lines. In his journal for the 21st he wrote: "At 12 or 1 o'clock at night the Yankees came here in force. Knocked us up. The house was soon filled with the thieving Yankees—robbed us of nearly everything they could carry off. Broke open all our trunks, drawers, etc. & carried off the keys. They must have practiced roguery from their childhood up, so well they appeared to know the art."

Twenty-odd miles to the southwest, on the slope of Bald Hill, Captain Key was up at dawn, a fiery-hot sunrise, to prepare for the expected enemy attack. He did not have long to wait. At eight o'clock McPherson's rifled cannon opened fire on Wheeler's and Cleburne's troops entrenched around and atop the ridge, and Key's battery replied with shell and canister.

To Key the contest was largely an artillery duel, with the Confederates heavily outnumbered as to guns. But to Cleburne, battling with rifle and bayonet to hold Bald Hill, it was "the bitterest fighting" of his life. The Union artillery fire came from all directions, one battery of 20-pound parrot guns proving particularly deadly. Wrote James A. Smith, brigade commander under Cleburne, "I have never before witnessed such accurate and destructive cannonading. In a few minutes 40 men were killed and over 100 wounded by this battery alone. In the Eighteenth Texas Cavalry, dismounted, 17 out of the 18 men composing one company were placed *hors de combat by one shot alone.*"

Major Hotchkiss, commanding Tom Key's battalion, was shot in the hip, and Key took command of the artillery for the remainder of the fight. In spite of the "destructive cannonading" of the Union guns the battle was not entirely one-sided. Key's battery took its toll. Among the Federal wounded was Irish-born Colonel Tom Reynolds of Giles Smith's division, struck in the leg. As field surgeons prepared to amputate the limb, he relied on the Celtic gift of gab to talk them out of it. It was an *Irish* leg, he told them, imported not domestic, and thus of more than ordinary value. The doctors concluded that if, at such a time, he could make a joke of the matter, "they would trust to his vitality to save the limb." After the war, he walked with it up the driveway to his home in Madison, Wisconsin.

While this artillery duel raged, General Mortimer D. Leggett of McPherson's 17th Army Corps approached brigade commander Manning F. Force. "I think I shall have to ask you to take that hill," he said politely. Force ordered fixed bayonets and sent his brigade in two lines up the suicidal surface of the hill. More than 40 percent of his men fell under fire, but the General wrote, "they closed on their colors, and swept over the works precise as on parade." In their wake came the rest of Leggett's division, routing Cleburne's troops and artillery from what would later become known as "Leggett's Hill."

That night the Union troops entrenched atop the ridge. The Confederate breastworks which had faced east were now paralleled by newly constructed breastworks facing west, behind which Leggett's artillery had Atlanta well in range, especially the important rolling mill on the city's outskirts which McPherson informed Sherman he would set about destroying.

Sherman had moved his headquarters to the Augustus Hurt (or Howard) House east of Atlanta, behind the center of his six-mile line which curved around the city. He was well satisfied with events so far. "On the whole the result is most favorable to us," he telegraphed to General Halleck. But the bold, though unsuccessful, Confederate attack had put him "on guard as to the future tactics of the enemy." It indicated that Hood, as Johnston before him, "intended to fight us outside of Atlanta." By now, Kenner Garrard's cavalry would be tearing into Roswell, north of the city, destroying the mills and hopefully shooting those traitors who had tried to protect them by flying foreign flags. He could forget Garrard for now, and concentrate on the primary target, Atlanta. He ordered Thomas to move closer to Hood's Peachtree Line above the city; then turned his attention to McPherson's army astride the Georgia Railroad north of Bald Hill.

McPherson's supply and ammunition trains were in Decatur four miles to his rear, and the left of McPherson's line was "in air," to use a military term, or extending into unprotected limbo. Sherman didn't like the looks of it. He ordered McPherson to move farther to his right, toward Thomas and Schofield. So far the 16th Corps of General Grenville M. Dodge had been crowded out of the action around Atlanta, more by circumstance than planning. Sherman ordered Dodge to stand by in support of McPherson's Army of the Tennessee.

He pondered what Hood would do next, happily convinced that the Southern general would not stay inactive long.

In the city, Hood had not been idle. Though he refused to leave the Windsor Smith house—a forgivable attitude, perhaps, in view of his infirmity—he issued rapid-fire orders to his officers. For the last three days Colonel S.W. Presstman, chief of engineers, had been working to strengthen the fortifications originally built by Lemuel P. Grant. Now last-minute changes were incorporated in the rock-and-timber wall (a stout abutment, front and center, was named Fort Hood), and that evening the Confederate general withdrew his army from the Peachtree Line to the parapets around the city.

He was aware of Cleburne's hazardous position vis-à-vis McPherson, which, in Hood's words, "made it necessary to abandon Atlanta or check his [McPherson's] movement." He also smarted from the catastrophe on Peachtree Creek and felt it essential to recapture the initiative and strike again, and quickly, at the enemy before the Army of Tennessee became disheartened. There was still a gap in Sherman's line, between General Thomas north of Atlanta, and Schofield and McPherson on the east. The same opportunity prevailed that had prevailed the day before—to strike one portion of the Federal army before the other could come to its assistance.

Of one thing Hood was certain. He would not allow his troops to rot, morally and physically, within the snug security of fortifications. That was what had been wrong, he thought, with General Johnston's conduct of the campaign. He had fought from entrenchments till the troops became so used to this protection that they lost the will and skill for open combat. It was what happened to Hardee's troops in the Battle of Peachtree Creek; they had shrunk from advancing in the open against sketchy Union parapets. In short, he wrote, "The continued use of breastworks during a campaign, renders troops timid in pitched battle. . . ."

So he would not fight from the walls around Atlanta. He had been whipped outside them once, but that only challenged his pride to undertake another bold excursion. He formed a plan that would take the enemy completely by surprise. Risky per-haps, and one that "required no small effort upon the part of the men and officers," but then, he was a gambler. That night he issued instructions to his three commanders. Nothing could wait until tomorrow; the grand coup would begin tonight.

12

A Warfare of Giants

Hood had abandoned Atlanta to its fate. The Gate City, a key to Confederate survival, appeared open to the enemy. Rising clouds of dust along the highways leading south marked the footsteps of retreating troops; and even at this early hour, civilians gathered on the roofs to watch their departure and await, no doubt with grave foreboding, the occupying forces of the Union army.

So it seemed, at least, to Generals Blair and McPherson who rode toward the Confederate entrenchments, around daybreak of that fateful Friday, July 22. They risked exposure to look over the situation. No rebel soldiers fired at them. No Confederate forces appeared anywhere in sight. Deciding that Hood's army had withdrawn, resigned to the surrender of the city, McPherson and Blair rode back to the Howard House to report to General Sherman.

Sherman had come to the same conclusion. Through his glass from the frame house east of the city, he saw that Hood's Peachtree line appeared abandoned, and, he recorded, "I thought the enemy intended to evacuate Atlanta." He ordered General Thomas to occupy the Confederate works, then "close up on the city." Meanwhile something was going on before McPherson's front below the Georgia Railroad, where Sherman could see the Confederates raising parapets and dragging up trees and saplings for abatis. He instructed Schofield to move closer to McPherson; there was still that troubling gap between the two parts of his army.

Far from abandoning Atlanta, Hood had launched the biggest gamble of his career, one destined to send McPherson and Schofield reeling back to Peachtree Creek and free Atlanta from the threat of invasion from the east.

The evening before, Hood had outlined the plan to his three corps commanders, Stewart, Cheatham, and Hardee, along with cavalry general Wheeler and Gustavus Smith of the militia. Stewart would hold Thomas' Army of the Cumberland in check before Atlanta, keeping it from coming to the aid of Schofield and McPherson, two to four miles to the east. Cheatham and the militia would hold and extend their breastworks facing Schofield's army, north of the Georgia Railroad. Both would advance on Schofield's front on signal.

Hardee's corps would undertake the key maneuver, following a pattern that had brought success to Stonewall Jackson at Chancellorsville and Second Manassas. Hardee, that same night, would move in a wide sweep to the east as far as Decatur, to come upon McPherson's rear, attacking "at daylight, or as soon thereafter as possible." Wheeler's cavalry would act as guides and escorts on the fifteen-mile march, and join in the attack at dawn.

As fast as Hardee surprised and overwhelmed McPherson's flank and rear, Cheatham and the Georgia troops would attack from the direction of Atlanta. By this pincer movement the combined Confederate forces would drive McPherson and Schofield back against the muddy barrier of Peachtree Creek where they would be fighting, in supposed confusion, at a disadvantage. Once Schofield and McPherson were put out of action, Hood would hurl his entire army against Thomas and achieve "a signal victory for our arms."

The swiftness and secrecy of Hardee's thrust were keys to the success of the maneuver, and some cover would be provided by the woods around Bald Hill. As Hood recorded:

It was absolutely necessary that these operations should be executed that same night, since a delay of even twenty-four hours would allow the enemy time to further entrench, and afford Sherman a chance to rectify, in a measure, his strange blunder in separating Thomas so far from Schofield and McPherson . . . I was convinced that McPherson and Schofield intended to destroy not only the Georgia Railroad, but likewise our main line of communication, the Macon Railroad—our main line of supplies— [which] rendered it imperative that I should check immediately his operations in that direction; otherwise Atlanta was doomed to fall at a very early day.

Beneath Hood's gritty exterior was a human streak of vulnerability that needed understanding. Only one of his officers went out of the way to express to the general some sympathy for the stress that he was under. General William Henry Talbot Walker of Hardee's corps stopped at Hood's headquarters that evening to say "that he was with me in heart and purpose, and intended to abide with me through all emergencies." It was a gesture that Hood would recall to his dying day and that Walker would have only fifteen hours to remember.

Again timing was essential, and again the timing went awry. Though Hardee was ready to march at dusk, he was obliged to wait for Cleburne who was having trouble disengaging from the enemy below Bald Hill. Cleburne stumbled into Atlanta around midnight, his troops exhausted after two days' lack of sleep and almost constant fighting. It was an hour more before the ponderous column finally got moving, down the McDonough road and south into wooded, unmapped, unfamiliar country. Not until three in the morning did the rearguard units leave the city, with the stragglers following at dawn.

It was tedious going from the start, with frequent stops on the narrow highway to make room for artillery and cavalry. In the oppressive heat, men dropped by the wayside from exhaustion, and had to be prodded back into the column. Ammunition wagons were delayed; regiments lost track of one another in the dark, and stopped to wait for those behind to catch up. As the column veered back toward the north, six miles below Atlanta, the countryside became a wilderness of thickets, woods, ravines, and marshes, growing more impenetrable as the distance lengthened.

It was not until daybreak that they reached Cobb's Mill, still some miles from their destination. Hardee paused to ask directions of William Cobb, the owner. The Confederate general planned to divide his army into separate columns, sending two divisions with General William Walker to Decatur, these to swing back upon McPherson's rear. Hardee would take the other two divisions, including Cleburne's, due north to assault McPherson's flank—not precisely what Hood had ordered, but Hardee felt he had some option in the matter. Cobb agreed to act as guide for Hardee's wing, and assigned an employee, Case Turner, to escort the other column to Decatur.

Case Turner warned Walker of a wide pond blocking their projected path and suggested a detour to the east, since Decatur lay in that direction. Walker developed a sudden stubborn streak. He insisted on bearing to the left, and threatened to shoot his guide in the dispute. The frightened Turner acquiesced, and Walker marched not toward Decatur, as intended, but directly toward McPherson's flank and into a nest of Confederate pickets. A sharpshooter tumbled him from his horse, with a bullet through the heart. Walker would never fulfill his promise made to Hood, to serve with "heart and purpose" in the battle for Atlanta.

The scattered divisions of Hardee's corps pressed on toward the estimated Federal position, out of touch with one another, confused as to precisely where the enemy might be. Wheeler lost track of the army altogether, and plunged toward Decatur with his cavalry.

In Decatur, Mary Gay, somewhat shattered by her experience with Schofield's marauding invaders and the presence of Garrard's troops camping in her yard, was more than a little apprehensive. "The coming and going of cavalry," she wrote, "the clatter of sabre and spur; the constant booming of cannon and report of musketry, all convinced us that the surrender of Atlanta by the Confederates was but a question of time. A few thousand men, however brave and gallant, could not cope successfully with 'three hundred thousand' who ignored every usage of civilized warfare."

Mary asserts that intuition alone told her that the Confederates were near, and that the hated Yankees were about to be attacked by Wheeler's cavalry riding to the rescue. Much as she welcomed the event, she dreaded the thought of any fighting on her property which might endanger her mother, her servant Telitha, and the ailing Toby. In preference to that, she chose to warn the Yankees of their danger. Garrard and his officers were in the parlor, the troops were in the yard, "lounging about promiscuously, cursing and swearing and playing cards," when Mary shouted her warning:

"Our men must be nearly here."

An officer verified the report. A rebel force was indeed descending on Decatur, and, wrote Mary, "in a few minutes, horses and mules were hitched to wagons, and the mules, wagons and men were fairly flying from the Confederates." In a few more minutes the yard was filled with troops in butternut and gray. An officer—"Ah, how grand he looked in Confederate uniform"—ordered everyone to take cover; this house was in a battle zone. Mary, and neighbors who arrived in panic, huddled in a safe part of the building while Mary observed the battle from a window, and recorded:

> Shot and shell flew in every direction, and the shingles on the roof were following suit, and the leaves, and the limbs, and the bark of the trees were descending in showers so heavy as almost to obscure the view of the contending forces. The roaring of cannon and the sound of musketry blended in harmony so full and so grand, and the scene was so absorbing that I thought not of personal danger . . . for was not I a soldier, enlisted for the war?

Mary believed that hers was "the only feminine eye that witnessed the complete rout of the Federals on that occasion. . . . All the discouragements of the past weeks fled from me, and hope revived, and I was happy, oh, so happy! Schofield's division, I think, ignominiously fled from a little band of lean, lank, hungry, poorly clad Confederate soldiers, and I doubted not that an over-ruling Providence would lead us to final victory."

Mary had let her emotions jump to grandiose conclusion. She had witnessed only a fragment of the battle which was gathering in fury a short distance to the west. Due to its scattered and delayed approach, Hardee's corps did not get into approximate position until after noon—and then the troops were astonished to find that McPherson's line, far from being "in air" or exposed at this point, had been angled back to form an L, with an extended east-west line protecting McPherson's flank and rear. In addition to that, a whole new corps, that of Union General Grenville M. Dodge, appeared to be holding a section of these new entrenchments.

As large a number of soldiers would recall, and write of their experiences in the battle of Black Friday as remembered Gettysburg or Chickamauga or other great, decisive battles of the war. Some would embellish their recollections with forgivable hyperbole; certainly no engagement offered so much adrenalin to the imagination. "Hood's men marched out to battle seemingly on dress parade," wrote one observer. General Andrew West of the Georgia troops saw one Confederate division lead the charge "in magnificent style—officers with drawn swords, the Stars and Bars in brave hands, floating defiantly in the breeze, with a band of music on a distant hill playing 'Home, Sweet Home.'" West thought the tune ironically appropriate, since so many fought within sight of their homes and never lived to return to them.

General Grenville M. Dodge of the Federal Sixteenth Corps was early engaged by the advancing troops of Confederate generals Bate and Walker and was also moved to a degree of lyricism:

> The scene at this time was grand and impressive. It seemed to us that every mounted officer of the attacking column was riding at the front of, or on the right or left of, the first line of battle. The regimental colors waved and fluttered in advance of the lines, and not a shot was fired by the rebel infantry, although the movement was covered by a heavy and well-directed fire from artillery, which was posted in the woods and on higher ground, and which enabled the guns to bear upon our troops with solid shot and shell, firing over the attacking column.

Actually, the attack was far from disciplined and even; it was uncoordinated and sporadic, the four divisions advancing at different times against bristling breastworks they had not anticipated. But all were armed with two invaluable weapons: extraordinary fighting spirit and determination. This was one battle that they would not lose, if their lives depended on it— and thousands wagered their lives upon that vow, and lost. But when they smashed head on against the Union line, they went through, and on, and over it before the astonished Federals had time to get their balance.

Initially, the fiercest fighting took place at the apex of the angled line, where it bent around the base of Bald Hill. Here Cleburne slammed through a gap between the Union corps of Blair and Dodge and swept over Blair's men from the flank and rear, forcing them to scramble back to secondary trenches. Tom Key, with Cleburne's artillery, watched his fellow Confederates in the face of "fire so galling that many faltered in the charge. The enemy's abatis was formed of saplings and bushes cut off and bent over, leaving the butt or stump two feet high. Notwithstanding these formidable works and tangling obstructions, the brave Confederates charged over all intervening obstacles and took the enemy's dirt works with many prisoners." Key recorded further:

> This caused the Yankees to evacuate all the fortifications protecting their rear and to abandon four pieces of Napoleon guns. . . . I at once called to the men of the battery for volunteers to go with me across the fortifications and turn the enemy's guns upon them. Enough promptly came forward, and with a cheer I led them at a double quick through the abatis to the Yankee guns. However, while my men had one gun and were running it up to commence firing, the Yanks from behind the second works poured such a volley of musketry upon those brave cannoneers that they were promptly compelled to abandon the gun. The Yanks reenforced and came back with a charge, and I thought it advisable to retire, which we did in hasty steps and not in good order, knowing that artillerists are defenseless unless they can get their guns in an effective position.

Sam Watkins, with Maney's division on Cleburne's left, also witnessed Cleburne's charge and awaited orders to join in the attack. Earlier, on leaving for the battleground, Watkins noted that "Cannon balls, at long range, were falling on Atlanta. We could see the smoke rise and hear the shells pass away over our heads as they went on toward the doomed city."

Now the order reached Sam's company: Advance! Struggling forward beside Watkins was a private named James Galbraith who, to Sam's discomfort, cried unceasingly, "God have mercy on my soul!"—stopping at intervals to kneel and pray and include his family in this petition: "God have mercy on my wife and children!" Sam remonstrated with the man; such invocations were neither "inspiring or seemly." He told Galbraith, "Quit that nonsense!" But, step by faltering step, the soldier continued his supplications: "God have mercy! God have mercy!"

The Yankee batteries and rifles on Bald Hill began to take their toll, and "made the earth tremble beneath our feet," Sam Watkins noted. "A discharge of cannon, and a ball tore through our ranks. I heard Galbraith yell out, 'O, God have mercy on my soul!' The ball had cut his body nearly in two. Poor fellow, he had gone to his reward."

As the Federal forces began recovering from the initial shock, the battle seesawed back and forth, with the Confederates pounding their opponents from four sides, front, flanks and rear. Wrote General Giles Smith, holding the center of the Union line, "Rebel commanders with [their] men . . . were not infrequently occupying one side of the works and our men the other. . . . The flags of the two opposing regiments would meet on the opposite sides of the same works and would be flaunted by their respective bearers in each other's faces. . . ."

Strange, swift emotional events occurred in the confusion. At one place where Brigadier General Govan's troops crawled up the slope of the hill, on hands and knees, to spring with slashing bayonets on the enemy in their trenches, the Union forces surrendered to what they thought were superior numbers. Then, making a recount, they demanded and obtained the surrender of the Confederates. In the time it took for these transactions, both sides decided that their numbers were approximately equal, cancelled the double surrender, and fell upon each other with renewed ferocity, fighting breast to breast with bayonets, knives, and rifle butts until the Federals were killed or whipped into submission.

Other isolated, less dramatic incidents took place. Elisha Stockwell, Jr., for inexplicable reasons of his own, had lost his rifle in the middle of the raging battle. A Union officer found him hovering on the outskirts of the field, and demanded an explanation. Elisha confessed that he had mislaid his gun. The good-natured officer told him not to worry; they would shortly be capturing plenty of rifles from the enemy, so just sit tight. Gratefully Elisha went behind the lines, to the army mess, to see what the chefs were cooking up, and there he waited out the battle.

Bald Hill as a whole remained in Union hands, in spite of repeated Confederate thrusts to take the ridge. Of one charge by Hardee's troops, Federal captain George Pepper wrote, "The rebels fought with a fierceness seldom if ever equalled. . . . All our artillery opened upon them; 17,000 rifles, several batteries of artillery fired simultaneously. The whole Rebel line was crushed down like a field of wheat through which a tornado had passed."

One Union battery, in particular, wrought havoc on the Confederate attackers. Cleburne watched one regiment after another fall back until, exasperated, he shouted to Sam Watkins' brigade:

"If those men can't take that battery, then by God, you take it!"

The brigade responded with the shrill and piercing rebel yell, and as Sam Watkins noted in his journal:

> We rushed forward up the steep hill side, the seething fire from ten thousand muskets and small arms, and forty pieces of cannon, scorching and burning our clothes and hands and faces from their rapid discharge, and piling up the ground with our dead and wounded almost in heaps. Officers with drawn swords met officers with drawn swords, and man met man with bayonet and loaded guns. Blood covered the ground, and the dense smoke filled our eyes and ears and faces. The groans of the wounded and dying rose above the thunder of battle. . . .

As the Confederates reached the crest of the ridge and poured into the Union trenches, Captain Henry Dwight of Blair's Seventeenth Corps was in the center of the action. He saw

Mortimer Leggett's division almost overwhelmed by Cleburne's nearly mortal thrust, and witnessed both the utter confusion and refusal to be beaten that possessed the Federal infantry:

> When this attack was made they jumped the works to the front, or outside, and fought that way. This attack repulsed, they jumped back and repulsed an attack from the outside, or real front. Thus they fought, looking for all the world like a long line of those toy-monkeys you see which jump over the end of a stick ... firing front and rear, and to either flank, they held their works, only changing front by jumping over the parapet as five assaults were made upon them, successively from front, rear, or flank. ...

And this was only the beginning of what Union General Giles A. Smith would call "a warfare of giants" and what history would call the "Battle of Atlanta."

As the sun rose high and hot above Atlanta, civilians on the rooftops kept an apprehensive watch on Union breastworks to the north, and on the east where intermittent firing warned of possible impending action. In the streets down which the last of Hardee's haggard, weary troops had trudged from after midnight until dawn, there was an air of feverish excitement. Something was happening. That was all the people knew. Was Hood evacuating the Gate City? What was the meaning of the sporadic firing toward Decatur? Wrote Wallace Reed, keeping a knowledgeable finger on the city's pulse:

> The citizens were unable fully to understand the situation. The movements of troops had but little significance to them, because they knew nothing of what was transpiring beyond the breastworks. It was impossible for a civilian to obtain trustworthy information. That fierce fighter, Hood, was in command, and the noncombatant who dared to question him ran considerable risk of being hustled off to the trenches. The subordinate officers and soldiers had but one reply to make to all questions. They said that the policy of falling back had been abandoned. Sherman had been drawn far enough into the interior, and his men were to be slaughtered like sheep as they threw themselves upon the impregnable defences of the Gate City.

Sam Richards complained of a sleepless night during which "our city was a complete hubbub with army wagons and marauders as though the whole army was passing through. A lot of cavalry robbers broke into the stores and stole everything that they took a fancy to. They stripped our store of paper and other stationery that we had there, and about thirty dollars of money. Today our last newspaper departed, also the Postoffice, and every other establishment and individual that intended to go, as the enemy was confidently expected to take possession tonight."

Standing behind Cheatham's line, east of the city, General Hood had waited throughout the morning for the sound of musketry and cannon from Decatur. There was only dust and heat and intermittent fire signifying nothing. High noon came; and not until an hour later did the exploding din of battle reach his ears. It came not from Decatur, but from the left of the Union line which faced the city. Hardee was not only late; he was not where he was supposed to be, approaching McPherson's rear from the direction of Decatur.

"I at once perceived," Hood later reported, "that Hardee had not only failed to turn McPherson's left, according to positive orders, but had thrown his men against the enemy's breastworks."

Again that sinking feeling, that dread awareness that despite this well-conceived, infallible plan, something had gone wrong, "rendering doubtful the great result desired."

Sherman, too, was in for a surprise. Seated with McPherson on the front steps of the Howard House, he discussed with his much-loved associate the posssible meaning of Hood's evacuation of his Peachtree line. What was that incalculable general likely to do next? Both agreed, however, that everything seemed to be going well. Thomas was pressing down upon Atlanta from the north. Any minute now they might hear accelerated firing from that direction.

Instead, they heard sudden, heavy fire from the Union front below the Georgia Railroad, where McPherson had earlier dispatched two fresh divisions under Grenville Dodge to occupy the line below the railway.

General McPherson—as always smartly dressed for battle in his major-general's uniform, shiny boots outside his pantaloons, gauntlets on his hands, sword belt around his waist—promptly mounted his horse and rode toward the sound of battle to look things over. He found Dodge's two divisions holding firm against a strong attack from Walker's troops; detected trouble around Blair's corps on the right; and swung west in that direction, accompanied only by an orderly.

As they passed through a stretch of woods a squad of Confederate pickets, appearing from nowhere, ordered them to halt. Raising his hat as if in salute, McPherson suddenly wheeled his horse to gallop away and was almost instantly killed by a volley from the pickets. The wounded orderly was captured and released.

When McPherson's horse was discovered "bleeding, wounded, and riderless" by Union troops, the general's body was found and carried to Sherman's headquarters, where it was placed on a door torn from its hinges. Confederate shells had found the range of the building and now began to play a sinister dirge on the wooden roof, threatening to set the place afire. Wrote Willard Warner, Sherman's aide: "I can never forget the touching scene at the Howard House as his [McPherson's] body lay there, still and beautiful in death. . . . Sherman slowly paced the floor, frequently stopping to gaze into the lifeless form of his beloved captain, the tears meanwhile coursing down his war-worn face."

It was hard to believe that the death of one man would diminish an army or a cause, but Sherman in his grief believed it. "The army and the country have sustained a great loss," he told Warner, speaking of McPherson. "I had expected him to finish the war. Grant and I are likely to be killed, or set aside after some failure to meet popular expectation, and McPherson would have come into chief command at the right time to end the war."

Immediately, Sherman summoned "Blackjack" Logan from the front and placed him in temporary field command of the Army of the Tennessee. Logan wasted no time in avenging his predecessor's death. The army was at its most critical point in the campaign for Atlanta, severely mauled and beaten back in many places by the tireless Confederates. By late afternoon, Hood had ordered Cheatham's corps and Gustavus Smith's Georgia militia to join the battle from the west, closing the two jaws of the rebel drive on the hard-pressed Federal forces.

Logan's corps on the right of the Union line, now partially flanked by Cheatham's troops, was battling for its life, after repelling seven fierce assaults. The men of both sides were fighting "hand to hand, clubbing, stabbing, shooting, throttling. Flags were snatched away, the snatchers were shot, the flags retrieved." When Logan himself reappeared on the scene, he inspired the troops to raise again their battlecry of "Blackjack! Blackjack! Blackjack!" When he called to them of McPherson's death, they changed the cry to "McPherson and revenge!"—and turned their resistance into a savage, musket-swinging charge.

The battle ended as it had begun, at different times, in different places, in different ways. One description of the twilight of that struggle on Pat Cleburne's front was given by Brigadier General Mark P. Lowrey who made a last-minute charge against the Union corps of General Blair:

> Taking the brigade altogether, I never saw a greater display of gallantry, but they failed to take the works, simply because the thing attempted was impossible for a thin line of exhausted men to accomplish. It was a direct attack by exhausted men against double their numbers, behind strong breastworks. I lost in killed, wounded and captured about one half the men that were in the charge. . . . To add to the difficulties, my men had neither sleep nor rest for two days and nights . . . and under the oppressive heat many good men fell completely exhausted and could go no further.

That was about it. The troops in that quarter, drained of all reserves of strength and will, could fight no more, and fell back to their corners.

Yet where the fighting was fiercest, in front of Cleburne's Confederate division, it continued well into the night. Wrote Union General Smith opposing Cleburne: "In the impetuosity, splendid abandon, and reckless disregard of danger with which the rebel masses rushed against our line of fire, of iron and cold steel, there has been no parallel during the war. . . . Our lines were broken and pierced . . . and batteries and regimental colors were lost and won again and again." General Dodge, from the left of the action, saw the blue and gray troops "fighting hand to hand until it grew so dark that nothing could be seen but the flash of guns from opposite sides of the work. The ground covered by these attacks was literally strewn with the dead of both sides."

Sam Watkins was among the wounded, but a curious circumstance may have saved his life. In the midst of the charge he stooped to pick up an abandoned Union flag, knowing that those who returned with a captured flag were generally promoted. Just at that moment a shell whined over his bent form which would have killed him, while two bullets pierced his foot. He crawled into a ditch already full of Confederate wounded and there crouched for safety from the raking fire overhead.

"While I was sitting here," he wrote, "a cannon ball came tearing down cutting a soldier's head off, spattering his brains all over my face and bosom, and mangling and tearing four or five others to shreds." Watkins clung to his ditch for the rest of the battle and to his precious Union flag. If his wounds should keep him from further action, he concluded, he could have the retrieved flag made into a shirt.

Again, the point was reached where the men of both sides, each unwilling to concede defeat, broke off the fight from total weariness. By midnight the cannon and rifle fire faded like a curtain being slowly lowered on the battlefield.

Sherman had lost 3,500 men, including the irreplaceable McPherson, with instances of whole battalions being wiped out in a single charge. Hood had lost a colossal 8,000 to 10,000, including General William H.T. Walker, with all the commanders of one division, that of General John A. Smith, missing, killed, or wounded. The Confederate commander could point to the capture of 13 pieces of Federal artillery and 19 stands of colors, as token trophies soothing to his pride. He also gave a rosy tinge to his report of the affair:

Notwithstanding the non-fulfillment of the brilliant result anticipated, the partial success of that day was productive of much benefit to the Army. It greatly improved the *morale* of the troops, infused new life and fresh hopes, arrested desertions, which had hitherto been numerous, defeated the movement of McPherson and Schofield upon our communications in that direction, and demonstrated to the foe our determination to abandon no more territory without, at least, a manful effort to retain it.

Sherman reported to Halleck in Washington that though his army had suffered serious setbacks, it had "made sad havoc with the enemy." Colonel Willard Warner, Sherman's aide, recorded that "the day closed with the enemy completely foiled of his object, and everywhere repulsed and beaten with great loss." General Frank Blair whose Seventeenth Corps had been in the center of the fighting, called the Confederate attack "disastrous."

Though Hood would never admit to such an adjective, he knew he had now been twice defeated in attempts to rout the enemy before Atlanta. He blamed Hardee for failing properly to get behind McPherson's rear instead of attacking his fortified flank; but he obliquely credited Hardee's attack for stalling Sherman's attempts to get at the Macon railroad southeast of the city. If Sherman were to try again to cut the Confederate supply line, he would have to approach it from a different angle.

In Atlanta, as dusk began to fall, mule-drawn ambulances poured into the city, accompanied by columns of Federal prisoners which Samuel Richards believed "had been taken in a successful flank movement by General Hardee, making it seem likely that Gen. Hood intended to hold the city, if he could." But that thought brought no rejoicing to Atlanta. Too many friends and relatives had died that day, and too many worthy citizens, including the brother of Governor Brown, a Georgia militiaman, who had fallen early in the battle.

Sarah Huff, who had fled to downtown Atlanta the day before with her mother and brothers, recorded that "before that fiery July sun set, thousands of as brave men as ever joined battle were numbered among the dead. And I saw thousands more brought into the city in ominous black-covered ambulances to make their slow, pain-laden way up Decatur Street to improvised hospitals where Dr. Noel D'Alvigny and Dr. Logan, as well as many of Atlanta's most prominent ladies, waited to ease their suffering. . . . The dismal-looking vehicles had their side curtains lifted to let in the air, for the heat was intense. We could see . . . the blood trickling down from the wounds of the poor helpless victims."

Her twelve-year-old brother was beside her, had been beside her all day, as "his keen ears caught the sound of distant firing."

Sarah remembered his reactions:

Men were clinging to the sides of the hospital vans, trying to fan away the terrible swarms of flies which hovered over the wounded. My young brother John went into action, as he usually did when he saw a chance to be helpful. Noting that a fly brush had just fallen from the hands of a man on one of the ambulances, and had been crushed by the heavy wheels, he grabbed the slit-paper fly brush that Mother handed him, and leaping to the side of the slow-moving ambulance, became one of the most efficient fly-fanners in the procession.

Wallace Reed had been close to General Hood's "field head-quarters"—a table and tent on Decatur Street—all day and had watched the couriers come and go, sometimes with "a bright, exultant look," and falsely optimistic news: "We've got 'em . . . whipping them like hell . . . we'll capture Sherman's whole army!" Now Reed witnessed a grisly scene as tables were stretched out in the city park and surgeons arrived and started opening their instrument cases:

It was not long before ambulances and wagons rolled into the park by the dozens, and the wounded were hastily taken out and placed upon the tables. After that it was cut and slash, for the work had to be done in a hurry.

The green grass took on a blood-red hue, and as the surgeon's saw crunched through the bones of the unfortunates, hundreds of gory arms and legs were thrown into the baskets prepared to receive them. This ghastly sight was too much for the citizen lookers on . . . One by one they disappeared, and soon the park was given up to the surgeons and their patients, the grim general meanwhile awaiting the returns a few yards away.

Reed watched the face of that grim general, trying to read his thoughts, and failed. Hood was revealing nothing. Nobody knew much more that evening than they had when Hardee's troops had left the town that morning. They learned of McPherson's death and considered it a lucky omen, although General Hood himself felt the loss of McPherson as keenly as if he had been a friend, as once he had been, rather than a leader of the foe. "No soldier fell in the enemy's ranks," Hood wrote, "whose loss caused me such equal regret."

To Hood, there was one notably bright spot in the day's engagement. Wheeler still held Decatur on the city's flank, having driven Stoneman's mounted troops from town; but Union cavalry general Kenner Garrard was raiding the village of Covington forty miles southeast of Atlanta, too close for comfort to the Macon railroad.

In Covington, George Hewitt Daniel, quartermaster in Gustavus Smith's militia, was home on furlough to see his daughter and attend to things at his plantation. That morning he had been hunting east of town, and had seen smoke rising some miles north along the railroad track. It never occurred to him that farms and settlements were being burned by advancing Union cavalry.

Shotgun under his arm, Daniel returned to town and checked with the stationmaster at the depot to see if he had any news. Suddenly he found himself surrounded and arrested by a band of blue-clad cavalry. Why was he carrying a shotgun? Just for hunting ducks? A likely story! He was a damned rebel, out to ambush Union troops from woods and roadside. He was given a "drum-head" court-martial, sentenced to be shot, and taken to a grove near Colonel W.W. Clark's plantation for execution.

As he faced the firing squad, two soldiers tried to bandage his eyes. Daniel pushed them away. "A Confederate soldier can face death without a blindfold," he told them. And proved it.

At the Covington hospital Mrs. S.D. ["grandma"] Smith had heard news of the approaching Yankees and had climbed to the cupola on the roof where she too saw the smoke from burning buildings in the north. Soon she heard that the blue-coated cavalry had entered town, and, along with the rest of the hospital staff, urged all the wounded soldiers who could save themselves, to do so. As a result, she wrote, "if ever I saw what is called pell-mell I saw it there and then. Every one who could walk broke for the pine thicket." Some of the wounded were eating in the mess hall. "I told them to run with all their speed and escape if possible. And, sure, they took me at my word. . . ."

Some, however, were caught at the doors of the hospital by Federal cavalry. Banded together, the prisoners were marched off past the Covington court house, where a Union-hating citizen, Iverson Jones, stood on the steps with his squirrel rifle. As a Federal soldier warned him not to use the gun, Jones raised his rifle and shot the man dead. Then, as Colonel Clark reported:

> Reloading his rifle and changing his position to another street a second squad of prisoners came by and again his rifle brought down its game. Reloading the third time he intercepted a platoon of cavalry and fired into it, wounding two of them. They captured him, shot him to death and then beat out his brains with the butts of their rifles. He doubtless anticipated such a fate and went coolly to certain death with no hope of fame and with only the satisfaction of getting two for one.

A few miles away, at the Burge plantation, Mrs. Dolly Burge was writing in her diary with her nine-year-old daughter Sadai by her side:

> We have heard the loud booming of the cannon all day long. . . . Suddenly I saw the servants running to the palings. I walked to the door and I saw such a stampede as I never witnessed before. The road was full of wagons, men on horseback, all riding at full speed. Judge [John J.] Floyd stopped, saying, "Mrs. Burge, the Yankees are coming. They have got my family and here is all I have on earth. Hide your mules and carriages and whatever valuables you have."

The curtain was rising on a scene to be reenacted throughout all of central Georgia, as families hid, buried, or removed their silver, crystal, jewels, precious fabrics, and all the irreplaceable accouterments of gracious Southern living. Sometimes the slaves took note of the hiding places and stole the treasures themselves or revealed them to the Yankees. Just as often they helped in the secreting of possessions and kept that knowledge to themselves.

Assuring Sadai there was nothing to fear, though trembling with fear herself, Dolly went to the smokehouse, "divided out the meat to the servants and bade them hide it. . . . China and silver were buried underground and Sadai bade Mary hide a bit of soap under bricks that mama might have a little left." Though Mrs. Burge tried not to alarm Sadai, she was fearful that she and her daughter and the hundred blacks might soon be homeless, "for on every side we could see smoke rising from burning buildings and bridges."

Among the burning buildings was the Covington hospital where Mrs. Smith had saved so many of the wounded and which Kenner Garrard, who put it to the torch, described as "composed of 30 buildings . . . for the accommodation of 10,000 patients." Garrard's conscience was apparently not bothered by the nature of his target. He also burnt all carpenters' tools that might be used to repair the structure, and all auxiliary tents used to house the wounded—along with whatever commissary supplies were in the town, including 2,000 bales of cotton.

Sherman was still stalled before the gates of Atlanta. The remaining spires of its churches were in full view, as were its many angled fortifications. But in some respects Atlanta seemed light years away. For, as Sherman recorded in his memoirs, there was still "a bold, determined foe" between him and his goal, "and every soldier realized that we had plenty of hard fighting ahead. . . ."

13

The Crisis of Our Destiny

"The news of the victory at Atlanta," said the *Richmond Inquirer*, self-declared Voice of the People in the Southern capital, "delighted the public as much as any that has been received during the war. It caused a general joy throughout the city and will carry the same to all quarters of the country. Gen. Hood has signalled his acceptance of the command of the Army of Tennessee with a brilliant victory, and justified his selection by success. . . ."

Sam Hood was not so sanguine as to credit such reports. But it was good publicity, not just for him but for his troops. Let them cling to the belief that, notwithstanding dreadful losses, they had scored a measurable triumph. He helped to promote that belief as good for their morale. For Hood himself, despite the damage to his army, had no intention of remaining passive. While he withdrew his forces back into the parapets around Atlanta, it was only to regroup and rest for the next offensive.

The sight of the city packed with men in gray, the clatter of cavalry in the streets, the rumble of the ammunition wagons and the roar of their own artillery from the forts around the town, gave many Atlantans a feeling of new confidence. Noncombatants especially congratulated one another on the military situation. According to Wallace Reed, the "blow-offs" boasted that "We've got Sherman just where we want him; so far from his place of supplies that his starving troops will desert to us, surrender, scatter—anything but fight."

In the Union camp, by contrast, there was little vainglorious boasting—despite the successful repulse of the fierce Southern onslaught in defense of Atlanta. For one thing, the loss of General McPherson hung like a pall of gloom over the army. Among the men, McPherson had stood for something beyond the two stars on his collar. Gentleman soldier, gallant, cheerful, debonair, and fearless, he was known as the "Whiplash of the Army" —one who came through in a pinch.

For another thing, they had come too close to losing; the rebels seemed to fight more fiercely and with more resolve as their backs fell closer to the wall. Perhaps Atlanta stood for home to many of them, the shining city of the South in which the brave old world refused to yield. In any event, had the numbers been equal, the Confederate army might have triumphed. General Frank P. Blair, whose Seventeenth Corps had borne the brunt of the Confederate attack, concluded: "The movement of General Hood was a very bold and brilliant one, and was very near being successful."

At ten o'clock on the morning of the twenty-third, a truce was declared to bury the dead and tend to the wounded of both sides. "The sight of the great number of Confederate dead in front of our lines was appalling," recorded Willard Warner, "and never to be forgotten by those who saw it." It was never forgotten by Andrew West, who wrote: "That day in Atlanta had none of the romantic surroundings that give an artificial renown to Battlefields. . . . Many times have I prayed that visions of those upturned faces, blackened and distorted, of the staring, glazed eyeballs, of the stiffened, outstretched hands, seemingly grasping for support, those rigid forms, wrapped in gray, who had met death in one of the deadliest battles in the history of the world, might be blotted forever from my recollection."

That it had been "breast to breast fighting, such as seldom comes in any war," seemed apparent to West in the scene around him:

It was necessary in some places to climb over the heaps of the dead. The wonder seemed to be not that there were so many dead, but that any lived at all. Officers and privates made a common cause here, and rank was forever obliterated, for among the dead could be seen the shining stars and golden wreath on the collar of the coat of that great patriot and soldier, General William Henry Walker, mingled with the ordinary uniforms of the common soldier.

West stooped to pick up a letter lying beside a dead Confederate soldier. It was torn and partly illegible from bloodstains, but it was plainly in a woman's writing and sent from North Carolina. One sentence only was altogether clear: "We hope that you can come home soon and help us with the tobacco crop." West looked at the bloated, blackened face of the dead soldier, and wondered how many tens of thousands of other women had expressed their love and prayers in similar words, "We hope you'll be home to help bring in the cotton . . ." ". . . to help Josie cut the corn" . . . "to help with the tobacco crop." And waited for an answer. And waited . . .

Sarah Huff's uncle, Wilson Huff, had reportedly been in the fighting and they had had no further news about him. She and her mother went out to conduct a fruitless search of the battlefield. Sarah noted that "the ground looked as if it had been blowed up, and was literally red with the blood that had been spilled there the day before." They met another couple looking for their son who had served with Cheatham's corps and, coming upon a burial party, found the boy's body being lowered in a shallow grave. As for Wilson Huff, he was finally listed as missing, turned up in a Union prison camp where, his fellow inmates wrote to Mrs. Huff, he died of smallpox, singing to his comrades, "I am but a stranger here, Heaven is my home."

In Atlanta there was contrasting calm and confusion. Once the wounded had been taken to the hospitals or sent to the less crowded suburbs, the citizens tried to resume some semblance of their normal life. "People crowded the stores," wrote Wallace Reed, "and the roar of battle gave place to the hum of traffic." Housewives sought to stock up on provisions in anticipation of a siege, and complained of soaring prices. There were no vegetables or dairy products in the city. Coffee cost $20 a pound, sugar $15, flour $300 a barrel—where these items chanced to be available. A breakfast of ham and eggs and coffee in a restaurant was $25. One well-to-do Atlantan, intent on keeping up appearances, "bought a felt hat for $150, a pair of shoes for $100, and a sack coat of good durable cloth for $200." W.B. Young, a retail merchant anxious to close out his business, found himself stuck with 200 sewing machines he could not sell at any price.

There was some panic at the depot as frightened families sought to leave the city, with or without their possessions; and some looting under cover of this panic. Certain Confederate soldiers were said to be ransacking local stores, and citizens were detailed to stand guard in the streets. Occasional fires broke out in scattered sections of the town—some inexplicable, some caused by the shells that Sherman's batteries started lobbing across the fortifications. Wrote Samuel Richards in his diary:

> We have had a considerable taste of the beauties of bombardment today. The enemy have thrown a great many shells into the city and scared the women and children and *some* of the *men* pretty badly. One shell fell in the street just below our house and threw gravel in our windows. This seems to me a very barbarous mode of carrying on war, throwing shells among women and children.

That Atlanta was in a state of siege, nobody had any doubt. True, only a scattering of bombshells fell upon the city during the day. But enough to keep the populace alert to danger, prepared to slip at a moment's notice into their cellars or backyard "gopher holes" or dugouts. Mollie Smith had just sat down to breakfast with her family when a shell soared through the ceiling, crashed through the wall into the adjoining room, and then exploded, turning the grand piano upside down. According to Mollie:

> One end of the sofa was torn to pieces, every pane of glass broken in the windows and the blinds smashed. Pieces of shell penetrated to a closet in an adjoining room and tore some clothing. Other pieces went through the floor, and the bedclothes caught on fire. The house was so filled with smoke that we thought

it was blazing. Some soldiers who were camped near us rushed in and took part of our things into the street where they stayed all day.

It was the start of a frantic twelve hours for Mollie and her family. Mr. Smith arranged to move to a friend's house on Alabama Street, which seemed less in the range of enemy artillery. On the way, another hazard overtook them. A pack of dogs made wild by the bombardment charged the group, bowling over Mollie and scattering their possessions on the sidewalk.

The house on Alabama Street appeared to be no safer than their former home. The Smiths and their hosts had just sat down to supper, Mollie's first meal of the day, when a shell plunged into the yard outside. That was too much; no place in the city appeared safe. They packed their food into the buggy, and rode to a ridge on the outskirts of the city, to eat their supper in picnic fashion. A mounted officer rode up, exhorting them to leave at once. The hill had been used as an outpost during the Battle of Peachtree Creek, and the enemy, seeing it occupied, might place it under fire. But they were tired of running, as Mollie wrote:

> We decided to risk the shelling and finished our meal unmolested. We could see the shells flying over the city and when one exploded in the air, there was a white smoke. We could also hear the crash when the houses were struck. We remained on that hill for hours watching the shells and wondering when we could go back to our home.

Maxwell Berry, the contractor, came home with a notebook purchased at Sam Richards' stationery store. He had paid a small fortune for it—paper was scarce since the Yankees had burned the mills at Roswell—but Berry felt that, with this crisis in the family's life, someone should keep a daily record of events.

He chose for the task his ten-year-old daughter Carrie, a girl of lustrous brown eyes, auburn hair, and even disposition. Carrie was bright and conscientious, and undertook willingly any chore assigned to her, whether looking after her younger sisters or helping her mother around the house. Maxwell gave her the notebook and urged her to keep a diary of whatever happened in the weeks and months to come.

Carrie liked the idea. She would begin her diary officially on August 1. But the white, lined pages tempted her to start at once, with an undated, introductory notation:

Up to this time we have had but few quiet days. We can hear the canon and the muskets very plane, but the shells we dread. One has busted under the dining room which frightened us very much. One passed through the smokehouse and a piece hit the top of the house and fell through but we were at Auntie Markham's, so none of us were hurt. We stay very close in the cellar when they are shelling.

Joe Semmes, Hood's (formerly Johnston's) chief of commissary, watched the fuse shells soaring overhead, and timed them: One every three minutes. They had been shelling his commissary depot for thirty hours without intermission, killing one teamster and wounding another. Finally Semmes reported to General Hood that he was concerned about the safety of the depot; it seemed to be a principal target. Hood ordered him to move the provision trains out of range. Semmes did so; but, sheltered in one of the cars, he remained fascinated by the "great shooting stars above the city—a city," as he wrote to his wife Eo, "destined to become celebrated for either our glorious success or defeat. It [Atlanta] is to be held at all hazards and Sherman will try to take it at all and any cost. . . ."

Mary Mallard had finally escaped Atlanta, but the 140-mile trip reflected the hardships of those who sought to flee the embattled city. As she wrote to her sister Susan Cumming from Augusta on July 22:

My passage through the state—up one railroad and down the other—was accomplished in such haste that I have been greatly exhausted by three days and nights spent in the cars. The last thirty-six hours, between Atlanta and this place, we were detained by four crushed cars, heavily laden with government supplies and furniture of refugees, which could not be removed from the track a night and part of a day. My stock of provisions had been completely exhausted before I left Atlanta. We stopped where not a drop of water could be had. . . . The most disagreeable part of the whole was walking quite a distance in the middle of the night— up embankments and down in ditches—to reach a relief car. I do

not think my strength could have held out for the exertion had not
a kind Providence brought to my assistance the strong arm of a
young soldier, a lieutenant on furlough, who rendered me every
necessary help. In all that journey . . . I felt desolate and lonely
beyond expression.

"The siege of Atlanta began on this day," Sherman noted for
the record on July 22, although others considered that the siege
had started with the Battle of Peachtree Creek on the 20th, or
even with Johnston's retreat across the Chattahoochee on July
9; while the campaign for the city had begun in May. But of one
thing Sherman was certain. With a supply line 250 miles in
length, he could not sustain a prolonged siege. The single track
railroad from the Atlanta front to Nashville, on which he depended for food, was too vulnerable to enemy attack. Already
too many men had had to be detached from the campaign to
guard it.

His immediate problem was to find a permanent replacement
for McPherson. "Blackjack" Logan had performed well, filling
in for McPherson in the recent battle, but neither Sherman nor
Thomas—whom he consulted on the matter—considered Logan
ready to command an army. "I wanted to succeed in taking
Atlanta," Sherman wrote, "and needed commanders who were
purely and technically soldiers . . . I regarded both generals
Logan and Blair as 'volunteers' . . . not professional soldiers."
The only other eligible, senior corps commander was Joseph
Hooker. Both Sherman and Thomas considered Hooker something of a prima donna, temperamental and jealous of his au-
thority.

Sherman settled for Oliver Otis Howard as the new commander of the Army of the Tennessee. Howard was no military
genius but, through trial and error, had become a sound and
careful planner. In protest at being overlooked, Hooker
promptly resigned from the army—to be replaced, in time, by
Henry W. Slocum. Hooker immediately spread the word that
Sherman "had run up against a rock at Atlanta, and that the
country ought to be prepared to hear of disaster from that quarter."

Consulting Howard on how best to take Atlanta, Sherman

told his new commander that he thought that Hood was "finished." After two serious defeats, the Confederate general had not the troops or spirit to hold the city—not for long, at least. Howard disagreed.

"I knew him well at West Point," Howard said. "He won't give up."

In that case, there was only one course: starve him out. Cut off Hood's supply lines in the south, and make the Confederate general and his army prisoners within their walls.

In the next few days Sherman plotted his strategy. Keeping Thomas' and Schofield's armies roughly where they were, pressed tightly against Atlanta on the north, he would move Howard's Army of the Tennessee in a wide sweep east to west, to sever the railway lines below Atlanta, especially the Macon & Western, on which Hood depended for supplies.

But infantry moved slowly. Though Sherman generally placed little faith in cavalry, he would use his mounted troops in an auxiliary maneuver to help speed things up. Garrard had returned from his successful raid on Covington and was now at Decatur resting his horses and having them reshod. Also at Decatur was General George Stoneman, Sherman's principal cavalry commander, making a total force in that vicinity of 6,700 mounted troops. Sherman would send Stoneman and Garrard down through Covington again, to strike at the Macon railroad from the east. At the same time, another cavalry division under Colonel Edward M. McCook would close in on the railway from the west. These two forces would lock together somewhere around Jonesboro to slam the door on Atlanta's lifeline in the south.

Stoneman had a project of his own which he suggested to the general. There were more than 34,000 prisoners in the already infamous stockade at Andersonville. Stoneman proposed that, after wrecking the Macon railroad, he take his cavalry the extra fifty miles to Andersonville and liberate the prisoners. Provided with arms, this vengeful host would offer a terrifying threat to the already apprehensive heartland of the South. Where the arms were coming from, and the probable physical condition of these long-imprisoned men, were not considered.

Sherman relished the idea, confessing to a "natural and in-

tense desire to accomplish an end so inviting to one's feelings."
    Permission granted.

Andy Neal was back in the Atlanta that he loved, but not
under the happy circumstances of his youth. Though the young
lieutenant had survived the battle of the 22nd without injury,
his horse had been killed, and he felt the loss as deeply as he
might mourn a fellow soldier who had fallen. He also grieved
for the suffering and war-scarred city, and for those refugees
from the north, fleeing in advance of Sherman's army, who had
no gopher holes or cellars of their own to hide in. They sought
shelter in the railroad culverts or the vacant, partially wrecked
buildings.
    On a new horse obtained from the army, Neal rode over the
city and was saddened by "the ruin and desertion of the place"
and the fact that it had become a "nest of speculators, thieves,
etc. If Sodom deserved the fate that befell it, Atlanta will not be
unjustly punished for since this war commenced it has grown
to be the great capital of corruption in official and private circles." Neal did not specify the form of that corruption except
to note that one of the relief committees was "giving away
everything to a parcel of straggling soldiers who had deserted
their posts at the front and were plundering and pilfering all
over Atlanta."
    Tom Key had not lost a horse, but he had lost a gun, and it
caused him equal sorrow. It was a howitzer that had been presented to him and his battery by General Cleburne early in the
war, had been captured by the Yankees in the battle at Bald Hill,
then recaptured by a Confederate regiment which refused to
return it to Key's battalion. Key was brokenhearted. He had
stood by that gun, as by a faithful comrade, through countless
battles including those of Murfreesboro, Chickamauga, Missionary Ridge, Resaca, New Hope Church, Lost Mountain, Kennesaw, and finally "the terrible assault from the Yanks two miles
east of Atlanta on the 21st of July. So it cannot be thought
strange that I regret having separated from my command a gun
that has been my companion under such trying and bloody
circumstances."
    Of the stragglers and deserters of which Andy Neal wrote,

many were being rounded up and placed on the fortifications, while Governor Brown had issued a proclamation ordering all "aliens" unwilling to bear arms to leave the state. If they tried to leave Atlanta, however, to avoid conscription, they were often impressed into the service. One known Union sympathizer who was given a gun and assigned to picket duty, confessed:

> At first I fired blank cartridges, thinking that the Federal pickets would understand me. But they didn't, durn 'em, and I got so blind mad to think of their firing at a good Union man that I fired balls after that, and I shot to kill. When a fellow hears musket balls whizzing about his ears it is no time to stand there like a sentimental fool wasting blank cartridges.

Samuel Richards, part Northerner, part Southerner, in sympathies, simply did what he was told. "The city authorities," he wrote, "required me to do police duty, and I had to stand guard on McDonough St. from 8 to 10 and 2 till 4 this night, and carried a musket for the first time in my life. My wife and children had to put their beds on the floor behind the chimney to be secure from shells which were thrown into the city all night long. No more fell near our house, however, and but little damage was done anywhere."

Sam Watkins had rejoined his company after a record sixty hours of recuperation from his foot wound. After a night in a Montgomery hospital—with soup and bread for supper, lights out at nine, and "Ye gods, the smell!"—he had had enough of convalescence. Without permission, he hobbled out of the hospital and to the depot and caught the first train for Atlanta. Thrown off the car for having no pass, he boarded the next train, and was bounced again. He kept this up with such persistence that he finally reached Atlanta with the aid of a conniving friend.

The circle of "almost impregnable forts and breastworks" around the city had been further strengthened and improved by Captain Lemuel Grant, and thousands of blacks had been impressed to level all trees and bushes, and even houses, within a mile of the line, "in order to give the guns full play, as well as

to prevent the enemy from stealing a march upon the city."
Confederate pickets posted outside the ramparts were protected
only by their rifle pits and one-man barricades of mud and logs.
A good number of the troops were bivouacked in private houses,
the rest in tents or hastily constructed barracks.

Watkins found his company stationed on the northeast corner
of the ramparts near the stone and plaster Ponder House. Directly opposite, one of two Union batteries would periodically
send up puffs of smoke, followed by a moment's silence. Then
the report. Then the scream of the shell as it sped overhead into
the city:

> We used to count from the time we could see the smoke boil up
> until we could hear the noise, and some fellow would call, "Look
> out, boys, the United States is sending us some iron; let's send 'em
> back a little lead!" And we would blaze away at the battery with
> our Enfield and Whitworth guns until we silenced them. This sort
> of fun kept up for days.

The citizens of Atlanta, too were growing accustomed to the
sound of artillery, the shattering explosions, the rising clouds of
dust and sulphur fumes. They learned to gauge the path of the
fuse bombs by their flaming wicks and duck for shelter before
they landed. And they learned to stay away from targets visible
to Sherman's batteries—the columns of smoke from the locomotives in the railway yards, tall chimneys and church steeples.
Most of the churches had been closed for safety, and Sam Richards missed a cherished weekly pleasure, Sunday evening choir
practice. The last time church bells sounded in Atlanta was
when shells struck the cupola of the Wesley Chapel and jarred
the clapper into ringing out an angry message of defiance.

Though the bombs which exploded in the streets would blast
a hole "big enough to swallow an army wagon with its mules,"
deaths and injuries became less frequent as the people grew
more prudent and alert. "It was no uncommon thing," wrote
Wallace Reed, "for a lady to walk some distance to see a neighbor. Sometimes she would be caught on the way in a pattering
shower of shells, and then she would run merrily into the nearest yard and huddle down in a bomb-proof, perhaps with perfect

strangers. But that made no difference. A common danger made everybody well acquainted, kind and hospitable."

One family had the porch on which they were sitting blasted out from under them, as a shell ploughed through the floorboards and exploded. Mother and children scampered to the dugout; but the master of the house, a retired colonel, was absorbed in *The Life of Napoleon* and went on reading—until a massive explosion shook the neighborhood. Seconds later, somewhat shaken, he had joined the others in the bombproof.

"What happened?" he was asked.

The colonel wasn't sure. The visibility, he said, had been impaired by sulphur fumes and "debris." Fearfully his wife peered through the entrance to the dugout.

"What happened to the rest of the house?" she demanded.

"I couldn't bring it with me," said her husband testily. "It was all I could do to get here by myself."

There was little diversion in the city now, with the Athenaeum closed, food and drink too scarce for even modest entertainment, and dancing and musicals considered too frivolous for the occasion. For the soldiers posted on the fortifications—mostly troops of Hardee's corps and General Smith's militia—there was only endless watchfulness and boredom, enlivened on occasion by the chance to take a pot shot at a careless Yankee.

For off-duty hours there were cockfights at the south end of the city, out of reach of Sherman's Parrot guns. Pits had been shaped with benches for the audience. Some of the soldiers had their own rambunctious roosters, stolen from some ill-fated farmer, which they trained and trimmed themselves; while country people from points south brought their fowl to pit against the reigning champion.

It was a memorable day when Private Thomas Tuck's rooster named "Southern Confederacy"—"Fed" for short—met a challenger brought from the hinterland by "a green looking country hunk." Bets were placed in the proper hands. The gaffs were fitted to the gamecocks. The birds were placed in the pit and let loose. In an instant the challenger "popped both gaffs through the head of his opponent," and the champion was dead.

To do full honor to Southern Confederacy, and satisfy his backers that he had not lived in vain, the soldiers plucked, cooked, and ate him, dipping their home-fried biscuits in his gravy.

When General Hood chose as his headquarters in Atlanta the two-story manor of L. Windsor Smith on Whitehall Street, some snide remarks were circulated. It was to be expected, said Hood's detractors, that this vain, arrogant warrior would choose a mansion befitting his image of himself. But they were wrong. Hood turned the house over to his staff, and pitched a tent in the backyard. In this canvas shelter, furnished with only a cot and table, he conducted the business of the war. Such a setting seemed more military.

Some changes in command were necessary. Cheatham's assumption of Hood's old corps, when the latter took over the army from Joe Johnston, had been only temporary. Cheatham was replaced by Stephen D. Lee, summoned now from Mississippi, at thirty-one the youngest lieutenant general in the Confederate army—considered a little too young and rash by his subordinates. At the same time Francis A. Shoup, formerly chief of artillery, was appointed Chief of Staff, bringing him a little closer to the top command. On Lee's arrival, Tom Key found the new commander "of medium height with dark hair, blue eyes, and affable manner." But he noted that many veterans resented Lee's replacement of that "rough and ready fighter, General Cheatham; hence he assumes command with the prejudices of the army against him."

Hood would have liked a substitute for Hardee, and Hardee would have liked nothing better than to be replaced; but their mutual dislike, for now, remained a standoff.

" It is said," wrote artillery captain Tom Key on July 24, "that Sherman notified General Hood that tomorrow he will shell the city of Atlanta, and for the non-combatants to be removed. The notice was sent after he had been shelling the women and children for five days, and to cover his cruel and ungentlemanly conduct, for I saw the effects of his cannon balls several days prior to this. At dark the Yankees, with some evident intent at deception, sent up skyrockets which illuminated the heavens as they burst high in the air. This drew forth cheers from the troops of the opposing lines. Sky rockets can be used to indicate the lines so that the whole army can understand the position of their own troops, or to indicate a retreat or advance."

Hood needed no rockets to give a clue as to enemy movements on his front. The Union line extended in a semicircle from the captured and disabled Georgia Railroad, two miles east of Atlanta, to an opposite point about two miles to the west. And the weight of that line was plainly being shifted to the southwest— suggesting another of Sherman's flanking movements, this one aimed at severing the railroads which supplied the city, and Hood's army, from the south. Were this accomplished, Atlanta would become untenable.

The most critical section of this supply line was the right of way which the railroads shared from East Point, six miles south of Atlanta, to the city. To protect this double link, Hood ordered a fortified line constructed from the eastern bastions of the city, due south as far as East Point where it curved like a half-clenched fist around the railway junction.

While this was under way, the Confederate general learned of cavalry threats to the two railroads farther south, below East Point where they forked to continue, one to Macon, the other to the Alabama border. Stoneman's dragoons were said by scouts to be heading via Covington toward the Macon railroad on the east. Union General Edward McCook, with another cavalry division, had reportedly crossed the Chattahoochee via Campbelltown and was threatening the West Point railroad from that quarter.

Hood dispatched Wheeler's cavalry to break up Stoneman's sortie in the east. "Fighting Joe" Wheeler leapt at the assignment. His dismounted troops had been posted at the barricades around Atlanta, a demeaning duty for spirited horsemen. To intercept McCook, Hood relied on a newly arrived division under General William H. Jackson, an independent, buccaneer-type cavalry raider rated on a par with John Hunt Morgan and Nathan Bedford Forrest.

So far so good, but enemy threats were rising on all sides. George Thomas' Army of the Cumberland was poised just north of Atlanta like a thundercloud, ready to burst upon that front at any moment. Schofield was another menace slightly to the east or left of Thomas; while on July 26 Hood learned from his scouts that McPherson's Army of the Tennessee, now under General Howard, was moving south between Atlanta and the Chattahoochee River, with the apparent aim of attacking the city in the rear or cutting the double railway line to East Point.

Hood summoned Lee and Stewart to his tent on Windsor Smith's estate for consultation. Hardee and Gustavus Smith were not included in the conference. For the moment, Hardee along with Smith's militia would have the job of holding the parapets against a possible attack from General Thomas. Hood had concluded that Hardee, like Joe Johnston, operated best on the defensive—behind breastworks: not to be trusted to show initiative, or blindly follow orders, in the field.

Spreading a map on the gate-legged table Hood showed his two corps commanders the hypothetical line he had selected, west of the city, beyond which the Union forces must not pass: Lickskillet Road, bisected near Ezra Church by a roadway running north and south. He instructed Lee to proceed to that point with two divisions, and establish a fortified line facing north along or near Lickskillet Road. Stewart, also with two divisions, would follow and take up a position in the rear. Stewart would be on reserve, ready to come to Lee's aid if the enemy pressed too hard against his front. Or Stewart could swing to either side if Howard attempted to flank the line.

It seemed a sound and foolproof disposition of his troops. If all went as expected, Howard's army, almost obliged to take the north-south road past Ezra Church, would fall into an ambush.

At almost the same hour Sherman was giving last minute instructions to his new army commander, General Howard. They, too, noted on the map the north-south ro ad that led from Elliot's mill on Proctor Creek past Ezra Church toward the southern reaches of Atlanta. Howard pointed to the crossroads near the chapel.

"The enemy may meet me there," he said with canny prescience.

A happy thought! "If he does, entrench, and wait for him to attack," said Sherman.

There was nothing the Union commander hoped for more than another of Hood's blunderous attempts to whip him in pitched battle outside the walls of Atlanta. Sherman did not underrate Hood's fighting prowess or the courage of his troops. He expected, as he later wrote, "to have a desperate fight to get possession of the Macon road, which was then the vital objective of the campaign." But if he succeeded, the ultimate goal of the campaign, the capture of Atlanta, seemed assured. This might be the decisive battle which the other two, on the 20th and 22nd, had not proved to be. For that reason:

"Goad the enemy," Sherman advised Howard, "act offensively to show him that you dare him to the encounter."

Near Utoy Creek, east of the city, the war was coming too close for comfort for Joseph Willis and the families of Laban Helms and William White. All twenty-six members of their group crawled into the excavated bombproof behind Willis' mill, not to see fresh air and freedom for some weeks to come. Some seemed hardly fit for the ordeal of this entombment. One woman who had been bedridden for several years had to be carried into the shelter. One of the men was crippled, half of the occupants were old and feeble. Their beds were mattresses of straw; the only illumination came from precious candles; there was little ventilation.

In Decatur, Mary Gay was happy to see Stoneman and his cavalry depart, apparently on some secret mission in the south. For the first time in a week her yard was clear of the raucous, swearing, card-playing troops of Kenner Garrard who had pitched their camp there, stolen her chickens and hogs, and used the palings of her fence for firewood. But a greater misery had visited her home. Her "dusky" servitor, Toby, had finally succumbed to pneumonia. She had Toby prepared for burial "in a nice white suit of clothes," and went out to find a carpenter who could build a coffin for him, while the local blacksmith agreed to dig the grave.

In Covington, Mrs. Smith was still packing off the wounded to points farther south, after the general destruction of the hospital, when she heard a member of her staff call out, "The Yanks are back!"

What was there left in Covington to bring them back? She hurried as many patients as she could into the cellars, then came above ground to see the Federal cavalry not pausing to occupy the town, but racing through it pell-mell, a "detestable horde which disgraced the banner of their country. . . . From the manner in which they hastened off, it was very evident that something was in the rear that did not appear very attractive to them." When later her wounded patients asked what had happened to Stoneman and his "band of thieves," she told them: "I guess General Wheeler and his men are too close on his heels for his good health." Mrs. Smith was right.

General Howell Cobb, commanding the Georgia troops in Macon, and still playing host to retired General Joseph Johnston, was disturbed by rumors of Federal cavalry raids around Atlanta, and even more concerned about the future of that city. "The news from Atlanta," he wrote to his wife, "is very confused and unsatisfactory. . . . It is perhaps enough to say that the most favorable rumors indicate that there is great danger of the fall of Atlanta. . . . I must confess that I do not feel the same confidence I did when Genl. Johnston was in command."

In Atlanta, Hood addressed the Army of Tennessee before sending Lee and Stewart marching to the west to intercept the enemy, hopefully along Lickskillet Road:

> Soldiers: Experience has proved to you that safety in time of battle consists in getting into close quarters with the enemy— guns and colors are the only unerring indication of victory. The valor of troops is easily estimated, too, by the number of those received. If your enemy be allowed to continue the operation of flanking you out of position, our course is in peril. Your recent brilliant successes prove your ability to prevent it. You have but to will it and God will grant us the victory which your commander and your country so confidently expect.

Then he sent the army on its way—no streaming flags, no trumpets blowing, simply a gray column flowing west in darkness to its Armageddon. Tom Key, manning the ramparts with Cleburne's division, saw them depart and noted in his diary, "This is emphatically the crisis of our destiny. . . ." Hood would have agreed and welcomed the commitment. Like Sherman he looked for a pitched battle somewhere in the neighborhood of Ezra Church. But unlike Sherman he saw the prospects somewhat differently. For this was the point at which he meant to stop the Union army in its campaign for Atlanta and redeem all past defeats. This was to become his finest hour.

14

Tightening the Noose

It was a race, for the infantry and cavalry of both sides, as to who would get there first—"there" being one of many points on the soft underbelly of Atlanta.

As Howard's Union army shifted to the west, McCook's and Stoneman's Federal cavalry rode pell-mell around Atlanta toward the Macon railroad in the south.

From Atlanta Stephen Lee's Confederate corps moved swiftly toward Lickskillet Road to intercept General Howard, while Wheeler's and Jackson's Southern cavalry raced toward the Macon railway to check Stoneman and McCook.

All were on a collision course. All were aware of impending clashes, but none was certain of the point of contact.

Only Confederate General Hardee stayed put in Atlanta, to checkmate General Thomas' Army of the Cumberland, forever threatening the city from the north.

"This morning unusual quiet prevails along the entire line," wrote Tom Key on Tuesday, July 26, "and I am anticipating a terrible bombardment from the untiring Yanks." Key's battalion discovered that McPherson's old army had abandoned its breastworks east and northeast of Atlanta ("their fortifications were like rat holes in a curve and were thrown up on all sides"), and Cleburne moved forward to establish an outer defense line a mile from the heart of Atlanta. The enemy apparently was slipping westward and Cleburne's exhausted troops looked forward, hopefully, to quiet on the eastern front.

The following day, near dusk, the expected bombardment began as Thomas' artillery started hurling shells into the city and its fortifications and Hood's guns replied. Behind this iron screen Howard's Army of the Tennessee, its wagon wheels muffled with straw, began rolling west toward Proctor Creek. Though spirits were high, there was hardly the appearance of a conquering army on a victory parade. Twenty-one-year-old Henry Dwight with Blair's corps found the average trooper "dusty, ragged, and unshaven, his appearance far more in accord with his surroundings, far more becoming the earnest fighting man" than picture-book versions of the Union soldier published in the North.

Though Sherman had repaired the railroad from Chattanooga to the front, supplies had yet to arrive in adequate quantities. Confederate cavalry raids continued to disrupt the flow of traffic in north Georgia and east Tennessee. The army diet was hardtack, hardtack, and more hardtack, with sometimes a strip of raw pork sprinkled with brown sugar for variety. Though concentrated milk and dessicated vegetables were shipped to Sherman by the War Department, these, derided as "desecrated vegetables" and "consecrated milk," were held in abomination by the troops.

On this march, particularly, Elisha Stockwell, who regarded food as equal in importance to sufficient sleep, was outraged by the situation. "We had eaten the last hardtack that morning," he recorded, "so we went without for the next two days." When they made camp that night, the cook had only coffee to offer. He refused to grind the coffee; he simply dumped the whole beans into boiling water and let the mixture stand. At evening mess Elisha contrived to be last in line in order to get the turbid dregs. He drank the water off the top, then ate the beans.

By the following morning, July 28, Howard's troops had reached the little log chapel known as Ezra Church where they skirmished briefly with Confederate pickets. The rebels had apparently got wind of their maneuver. With no time to spare, the Union soldiers all but tore the church apart, dragging out benches, stalls and planks to build hasty breastworks facing south on rising ground above Lickskillet Road. "Blackjack" Logan held this section of the line; Blair's and Dodge's corps felled trees to construct a row of defenses running north and south, facing Atlanta and guarding Logan's flank.

Around noon Confederate General Lee swung confidently toward Lickskillet Road—suddenly to discover that he had been beaten to the punch. His orders from Hood had been to take possession of the crossroads, establish a strong defense line on both sides of Ezra Church, and "not to attack unless the enemy exposes himself in attacking us." But here was the enemy already entrenched on favorable ground that he was supposed to occupy!

Lee had not seen active combat for two years; but he knew that nothing would be gained by hesitation. With no time to organize an orderly advance he gave the order to attack, flinging his forces in uncoordinated charges, wave after wave, against Logan's front. The first units to advance, waving their muskets with defiant rebel yells, found themselves tangled in thickets and underbrush. Like trapped animals they struggled to get free, while Union rifles picked them off with cold precision. As those left standing started to withdraw, a fourth wave came up behind them, struggling over the dead and wounded.

"Hold 'em! Hold 'em!" Logan bellowed.

The Federals did more than hold them. Crouched behind their chapel pews and holy timbers they racked them up "in windrows, two and three deep"—then poured out of their breastworks to finish the slaughter with knives and bayonets. Howard ordered up his field artillery, placing it so that it could enfilade the field, and poured a rain of shells on the disjointed lines of the attackers. "I never saw fighting like this before!" remarked the veteran general who had fought with the Army of the Tennessee in every battle since First Manassas in 1861.

A mile away, Sherman got word of the Confederate attack. "Good! Fine! Just what I wanted," he exclaimed. "Tell Howard to keep them attacking, it will save us trouble. Let 'em beat their brains out, beat their brains out!"

He ordered Schofield and Thomas to move against Atlanta's front and simultaneously storm the fortifications, also suggesting that Thomas send Jefferson C. Davis' division on a wide sweep to the west to attack the Confederate flank and "win Atlanta out of hand." Sherman was hitting them on all sides now, north, south, east, and west, with infantry and cavalry.

In Atlanta, Hood had kept A.P. Stewart's corps standing in reserve, ready to swing into action against Logan's flank when Lee had thrown the Federals off balance. Now it was a matter of sending Stewart to rescue Lee's troops from disaster. Stewart arrived to hurl three more divisions into the attack. Logan, heavily outnumbered, called on Blair and Dodge for reenforcements, and Elisha Stockwell forgot his empty stomach, shouldered his musket, and double-timed toward the din of battle.

For three hours the Confederates fought with a desperation born of the trap that they had stumbled into. The battle was one that "for severity is unsurpassed by any of the campaign," recorded a Federal colonel; while another Union officer noted that "the carnage was fearful and the dead and wounded on the field must clothe many hearthstones in mourning and sorrow." With the Confederates, Private W.P. Archer watched his comrades being carried by the stretcher bearers off the field:

> Their litters, being noted, were as bloody as if hogs had been stuck on them; their flagstaffs were shot to pieces; their colors were shot into ribbons, and not more than one-half of that fine brigade that left that morning returned.

In a pause between clashes, one Union soldier called across to the Southern lines:

"Well, Johnny, how many of you are left?"

"Oh, about enough for another killing," was the dispirited answer.

It was little wonder that, in time, the heart went out of Lee's and Stewart's men. Even veteran troops could take just so much punishment, and these had taken more. Union soldiers, quoted by General Jacob Cox, agreed on the general disintegration of the Confederate offensive: "In the last attacks portions of the command refused to advance, and line officers with their drawn swords were seen from our works to march to the front of the troops that would not follow them."

General Stewart had galloped on the field, waving his men forward, when a ricocheting bullet struck him in the forehead and he toppled senseless to the ground. Division commander Loring was also wounded and disabled, as were two other southern generals. Hearing reports of the Confederate reverses, which he found hard to credit, Hood reluctantly sent for Hardee and dispatched him to the battlefield to "look things over." By the time Hardee reached Lickskillet Road, Stewart and Loring were out of action, and only scattered artillery fire kept the troops engaged.

Happily, Elisha Stockwell reached the field just as the crisis was considered over, and many of Blair's reenforcing troops were sent back. Returning to his lines, a more important matter came to his attention. "We saw our cook coming up across the open field with a box of hardtack on his shoulder, and he looked good to us. This was the third day that we had [not] eaten anything, and we gave him a lusty cheer and made a hole in the box in short order."

But they had to swallow the hardtack amid "a shower of cannon balls coming over the hill" from Confederate artillery. "Some of our boys started to catch them but were ordered back, and were told if they put out their foot, the ball would take the foot off. But it was a sight to see them. They came bounding along so thick one couldn't count a quarter of them."

By dusk the Battle of Ezra Church was over. Hood had lost 5,000 men, including the four wounded generals; Sherman had lost fewer than 700. Apart from the accident of timing, which permitted Howard to reach and occupy, ahead of Lee, the better position, what had happened? Initially, Lee's troops had performed heroically in an uphill fight over hideous terrain. "I am convinced," wrote Lee in his report to Hood, "that if all the troops had displayed equal spirit, we would have been successful, as the enemy's works were slight, and, besides, they had scarcely gotten into position when we made the attack."

In short, according to Hood's own summation of the battle, Lee had "not been able to bring about united action. Whilst one brigade fought gallantly, another failed to do its duty . . . not withstanding he himself led one or more to the attack, and had even offered to lead others. Although this affair occurred subsequent to the improvement of the *morale* of the Army and the check to desertions, which had resulted from the battles of the 20th and 22nd, the lack of spirit manifested in this instance will convey a just idea of the state of the Army at this period."

The judgment was a harsh one. Lack of spirit had not developed until all spirit had been irrevocably crushed by weight of arms.

Sherman, too, was not elated with the outcome of the action. He had not been uneasy about the probable results, he wrote, "but wanted to reap fuller results, hoping that Davis' division would come up at the instant of defeat, and catch the enemy in flank; but the woods were dense and as usual this division got on the wrong road. . . ." He had also believed that, since Hood had weakened his forces in Atlanta, Schofield and Thomas would be able to "break in." But "both reported that they found the parapets very strong and fully manned."

If there had been one single hero of the Battle of Ezra Church, it was "Blackjack"Logan who, with a single division, had stood off more than half the Confederate army. Logan was rapidly becoming a legend in his time. With "long raven hair and eyes so black that the pupils were scarcely visible"—physical attributes which had given him the nickname "Black Jack"—Logan would spur his horse among the embattled troops, waving his sword and bellowing words of exhortation like some warrior out of Götterdämmerung. That evening a newspaper correspondent added a story to the legend.

Shortly after the battle, Logan was told that a "rebel" baby had been born in a nearby shack and the mother wanted an army chaplain to baptize the child. Logan accompanied the chaplain to the wrecked and looted cabin; then, acting as godfather, held the infant in his arms while the chaplain performed the appropriate rites. Then came the question, what to name the girl? With the sound of shells still echoing in the woods, the general had a ready answer. "Shell Anna," he said, and Shellana she became. Before he left, Logan ordered his staff to tidy up the place and fix the roof, and left a goldpiece with the mother, telling her to "keep it in a safe place, or some damned bummer will steal it."

South of Atlanta, and on both sides of the Macon railway, the great race of rival cavalry was under way.

As with the foot troops, Sherman's horsemen got the jump on the Confederates. George Stoneman with 2,500 men and Kenner Garrard with 4,000 both started on the 27th, both committed to an explicit plan. They would meet at the little crossroads town of Flat Rock, southeast of Decatur, and proceed together to Lovejoy Station south of Jonesboro—there to link up with Edward McCook's division coming from the west. All three would devote themselves to wrecking the Macon road beyond repair, rendering Hood's supply line useless, and forcing the surrender of Atlanta.

Then, and only then, would Stoneman carry out his espoused plan of riding the extra fifty miles to Andersonville to liberate the 34,000 Union prisoners in the Confederate stockade.

As Garrard departed for Flat Rock, Stoneman's cavalry rode out of Covington just one jump ahead of General Wheeler who had raced out from Atlanta in pursuit. Covington got no glimpse of Wheeler; saw only the clouds of dust kicked up by his hard-riding troops on Stoneman's heels. But the town, partially wrecked and robbed of its provisions by previous Union cavalry raids, breathed a little easier. Once again Mrs. Smith had saved the Confederate wounded in her charge:

> Now the hidden boys came out in the fresh air, and all right. The sick left their beds, delighted at their speedy recovery. All were ready to join in the changing events of the day, and many were the merry laughs at the Yankees being so completely humbugged out of a number of Rebel prisoners. That night many came to the conclusion that escape was the better part of valor. Having run the risk of being captured more than once within the last few weeks, they adopted the old adage that "a burnt child dreads the fire." Therefore, several left.

On her plantation near the village, Dolly Burge wrote in her diary of

. . . sleepless nights. The report is that the Yankees have left Covington for Macon, headed by Stoneman, to release prisoners held there. They have robbed every house on the road of its provisions, sometimes taking every piece of meat, blankets and wearing apparel, silver and arms of every description. They would take silk dresses and put them under their saddles and many other things for which they had no use.

Mrs. Burge was misled on one point. The Union cavalry had boasted of freeing the captives at Andersonville, not at Macon, and had threatened the townsfolk with dire reprisals if they found that their men had been mistreated in that prison. And while Stoneman was in command of this wing of the raid around Atlanta, Stoneman had mysteriously disappeared. Kenner Garrard waited in puzzlement at Flat Rock for his ally to arrive, only to find himself surrounded on all sides by Wheeler's men.

Garrard threw up some hasty breastworks and skirmished with Wheeler for the next two days, then started pulling back toward Decatur with Wheeler in pursuit. A stalemate developed near the town of Latimer, with Garrard still wondering, Where was Stoneman?

Wheeler asked himself the same question. Garrard was small potatoes compared with his superior. The Confederate general decided to split his forces three ways. He left one brigade under General Dibbrell at Latimer to keep Garrard in check; and sent three brigades under Alfred C. Iverson to hunt down Stoneman, presumably headed for the Macon railroad. Wheeler himself swung west to link with Confederate General Jackson's cavalry to form a tight chain of defense across the all-important railroad.

West of Atlanta, Union General Edward McCook of "the Fighting McCooks," had crossed and recrossed the Chattahoochee River and had struck the West Point railroad near Palmetto. Jackson's Confederate cavalry had been tight on his heels until he crossed the Chattahoochee south of Campbellton, then had lost the trail. McCook was religiously following the same instructions Sherman had given to General Stoneman: Smash the Macon railroad near Lovejoy Station, then proceed south to

Macon, tearing up tracks, destroying supplies, and taking Confederate prisoners on the way.

So far his men had torn up two miles of tracks and telegraph lines along the West Point railroad; then, proceeding east, had met and destroyed a score of Confederate wagon trains, burning 1,160 wagons and slaughtering 2,000 mules—all badly needed by Hood's forces in Atlanta. At one point a wagon train blocked their progress, the mules sleeping in the road. An officer jabbed the nearest animal with his sword. The mules "came to life with loud snorts and other uncouth noises," according to one account. "With tails in the air, the whole train stampeded and went rushing down the road, scattering units ahead and strewing packs through the woods on either side. It was hard to straighten this out."

At Lovejoy Station, McCook was puzzled to find no sign or word of Stoneman. After waiting awhile he gave up on the appointed rendezvous, tore up several miles of track along the Macon railroad, then headed back west toward Newnan—wondering, as Garrard had wondered, where was Stoneman. McCook slaughtered a few hundred more mules, burnt several score wagons, and also took 300 Confederate prisoners en route to Newnan. The latter were mostly stragglers and deserters hiding out in the hinterland, and proved more trouble than they were worth.

In Newnan, General Philip D. Roddey with 600 Confederate troops found himself annoyingly inconvenienced. He was on his way to Atlanta to join General Hood, and had learned that the railroad line had been torn to pieces near Palmetto. Disgruntled, he would have to stick around until repairs were made. Newnan itself was in a state of panic over reports of approaching Federal cavalry. The streets were clogged with refugees from the surrounding countryside where McCook, "by his unparalleled cruelty, had made his name a horror." Many had lost their homes, and some their families, and all were seeking shelter or a means of fleeing farther south.

In the Newnan hospital, nurses Kate Cumming and Fanny Beers shared the general apprehension. The hospital was overcrowded, more and more patients were arriving every day as a result of the fight at Peachtree Creek and Atlanta. The nurses wondered what would happen to their charges when McCook arrived. Would they be shot, or taken prisoner, or, hopefully, ignored? Kate tried to focus her mind upon the wounded in her care:

> Mr. Thomas is wounded through the head; his brain is oozing out and at times he is delirious . . . one very large man named Brown, who is as helpless as an infant . . . a fine looking man from Kentucky who has lost a leg and arm, and there is little hope for his recovery . . . many shot through the spine which paralyzes them so they can use neither hands nor feet.

There were, however, some self-made victims for whom she had scant sympathy. "Among these martyrs is a young man who, the surgeons are certain, shot himself intentionally. Some time ago, a man, rather than be returned to duty, cut three of his fingers off with an ax, and a bad job he made of it."

Meanwhile, more arriving refugees confirmed the earlier rumors: McCook and his Yankee raiders were only fifteen miles away. "They go into houses and what they do not carry away they destroy. They have a dreadful antipathy to crockery, and break all the poor people's dishes." One fleeing landowner reported that "these vandals had called on him, and after robbing him of everything worth taking, took some dressed leather that he prized very highly; and before his eyes cut it into pieces."

By midafternoon McCook was at the gates and skirmishing broke out outside of town. McCook had expected little opposition, but he had cut his throat when he cut the West Point railroad. He had trapped General Roddey and his small but gallant army in the city. Now Roddey leapt on his horse, "without taking time to saddle the animal or don his uniform," according to nurse Cumming. Like a modern Pied Piper in a Hamelin besieged, he mustered behind him the young, the maimed, the halt, the hospital convalescents and attendants— anyone capable of bearing arms—and led them out to battle.

The sound of firing east of town brought nurses Beers and Cumming to the hospital roof to witness the excitement. As Fanny Beers reported:

> When the smoke cleared away, our own troops could be seen drawn up on the railroad and on the depot platform. The hill on

the opposite side seemed to swarm with Yankees. Evidently they had expected to surprise the town, but, finding themselves opposed by a force whose numbers they were unable to estimate, they hastily retreated up the hill. By that time a crowd of impetuous boys had armed themselves and were running down the hill on our side to join the Confederates.

Startled by the brisk resistance, McCook withdrew east into an unexpected trap. Joe Wheeler, having broken loose from the rest of his division which was hounding Stoneman and Garrard, was coming at him from the east. Jackson, having recovered the scent, was closing on him from the west. McCook's cavalry was spent. His men had not eaten or slept properly for two days. They were falling asleep in the saddle; their officers had grown too fuzzy from fatigue to make decisions.

McCook put every man on his own, releasing his troops to fight their way out of the trap as best they could. Some of them, including McCook himself, made it back to Sherman's camp. Others were killed or captured, with scores of their injured taken to the hospital in Newnan. Here one Confederate patient volunteered to help take care of the Union wounded. He started, with the first man to arrive, by taking him outside and shooting him. Though he claimed it was in revenge for atrocities committed by the Union cavalry, the act was considered "execrable" by the citizens of Newnan, who were unable to prosecute for lack of witnesses.

Back in the Federal camp McCook, despite all, felt he had fulfilled his mission. He had wrecked the West Point and Macon railroads. But Sherman gave him little credit. The roads were back in operation within forty-eight hours. And where, McCook still asked himself, as Sherman did, was Stoneman?

There was nothing puzzling in Stoneman's mind about his actions. Thinking things over in Decatur before he left to meet Garrard at Flat Rock, and join forces later with McCook at Lovejoy Station, he decided that these intermediate steps could be dispensed with. His ultimate goal was Andersonville and the liberation of the Union prisoners. This single act would embellish his career, so far branded a "distinguished failure," with a crown of glory. He would be a hero in the North. Why bother with the preliminaries? Garrard and McCook could take care of demolishing the Macon railroad.

He swept wide to the east to avoid detection, through Covington and on toward Macon, confident that Garrard, whom he was ignoring, was unwittingly protecting the right flank of his cavalry. He planned to by-pass Macon, maybe hurling a shell or two into the city for good luck. But otherwise—Howell Cobb was there with his Georgia militia and the home guard, and the town was fortified. To try to capture it would simply hold things up.

At Macon, Howell Cobb had a different idea. Perhaps some of the spirit of "Little Joe" Johnston, his house guest, inspired him to take offensive action—the sort of action Johnston had planned, once he had drawn the Union army far enough into central Georgia. In any event, hearing from scouts of the approach of Stoneman's cavalry, Cobb led his militia out from the fortifications and into Stoneman's projected path. Here, north of the city and straddling the Ocmulgee River, he threw up breastworks, hunkered down, and waited.

Stoneman was his own worst enemy. On the ride to Macon he began to vacillate. He saw himself being flanked by Jackson's cavalry on the west; he saw Confederate battalions, rising like mirages, in his path. And there was General Wheeler, reported as having left Atlanta. Where was Wheeler? There were rumors, too, that Hood was sending extra troops to garrison Macon. Suddenly obstacles, obstacles everywhere. Stoneman dispatched a brigade to tear up the railroad north of Jonesboro, to protect his rear.

In Atlanta, word reached Hood of Stoneman's threat to Macon and its all-important arsenal. Unsure where Jackson and Wheeler were at this point, he dispatched a brigade of infantry under General Joseph C. Lewis to Jonesboro to try to intercept the raiders. Aboard the boxcars was former private Sam R. Watkins, now a corporal by virtue of the Union flag that he had "captured" after the Battle of Atlanta.

Watkins found this chase by locomotive a diverting lark. "We were charging a brigade of cavalry with a train of boxcars, as it were." As fast as Stoneman's men tore up the tracks in front of the pursuing engine, the men piled out of the train, relaid the tracks, and chugged along after the bluecoats—the snorting locomotive bearing down upon the enemy like a fire-belching dragon. Finally Stoneman told his troops to forget the train; they couldn't wreck the railroad any faster than the rebels could repair it. He cut loose from the railway line and headed cross country for Macon.

Approaching Macon on Thursday, July 30, Stoneman's plans began to crumble. He found he could not get past the city. On high ground east of the only bridge across the Ocmulgee River stretched a line of breastworks bristling with abatis and the muskets of defending troops. He ordered his light artillery to shell the town.

Asa G. Holt, one of Macon's more distinguished senior citizens, was enjoying an afternoon siesta on the porch of his home on Mulberry Street. A bansheelike scream, crescending, seemed to pierce his eardrums. He looked up to see a 72-millimeter shell strike the sidewalk and bounce through the wall of his parlor—coming to rest, unexploded, on the floor. It was one of the few of Stoneman's shells to strike the city and did little damage. But it alerted the town like the first shock of an earthquake. Factory whistles sounded the alarm, and citizens poured from their homes in response to the emergency. Among them was Thomas Dabney, Jr., a local planter's son, who remembered:

> Father and I ran to the arsenal and got rifles and ammunition, and then ran to the bridge. . . . We were among the first to arrive, but soon old men and boys began to pour in. . . . A considerable number of convalescents from the numerous hospitals in Macon joined us. We were none too soon, for already could be seen the long lines of the enemy not over a half-mile from the bridge, and every few moments shot and shell whistled over the defenders of that bridge.

Joe Johnston, house guest of the Howell Cobbs in Macon, witnessed "the gallant defense of the place by Major-General Cobb" and the militia. "With them and as many of mechanics of the workshops and volunteers of the town as he could find arms for, in all fifteen or eighteen hundred, General Cobb met the Federal forces on high ground east of the Ocmulgee; and repelled them after a contest of several hours, by his own courage and judicious disposition, and the excellent conduct of his troops, who heard hostile shots then for the first time."

As Cobb's militia brought up their own artillery to return the Federal fire, Stoneman's dreams of glory faded. He knew that the troop train which had chased him down the railroad would soon arrive to reenforce the garrison at Macon. And rumors reached him that Alfred Iverson's division of Wheeler's cavalry was descending on him from the neighborhood of Flat Rock. He thought briefly of seeking refuge in Pensacola on the Gulf, then chose a disastrous alternative. He retreated north toward Decatur and ran squarely into the arms of Iverson who, hearing of Stoneman's predicament, had entrenched his dismounted cavalry across the enemy's escape route.

Goaded by fury and frustration, Stoneman made no attempt to slip past Iverson by one side or the other. Casting caution to the winds, he charged the Confederate barricades head-on, and was driven back, and tried again. The seesaw fight continued for four hours, until Stoneman was falsely told that troops were coming up from Macon to attack his rear. His situation, he deduced, was hopeless.

The general told his troops that he, with 500 volunteers, would keep the Confederates in check while the rest of the cavalry made good their escape. Two of the three brigades took off through the woods, eventually to reach the Union lines above Atlanta, while Stoneman surrendered himself and his band of volunteers to Iverson. Though he believed he had had no alternative, there was actually no enemy in his rear; his troops outnumbered Iverson's; had he continued the fight it might have gone the other way.

But as it was, he was hailed in the North as a self-sacrificing hero. He cherished and fostered the image, writing to Sherman from a Southern prison that he preferred to be in captivity "rather than amongst those who owe their escape to considerations of self-preservation." That the 500 volunteers agreed with him is open to some doubt. In Sherman's mind there was no doubt whatever. As remnants of all three of his cavalry divisions filtered back from Newnan, Macon, and Flat Rock, he "became satisfied that cavalry could not, or would not, make a sufficient lodgment on the railroad below Atlanta." From now on he would rely on infantry to undercut the city. Of Stoneman, who had totally disobeyed orders, Sherman's judgment was extraordinarily mild. That bungling general had simply been "bewildered."

General Lewis' troops had long since arrived by train at Macon, disgusted to learn that they had missed the action. Stoneman's capture had already been reported. Nonetheless they were treated as heroes and liberators by the grateful populace. Food and drink, Sam Watkins found, were offered on every hand, and "the libation of the boys [became] a little heavy. ... They started whooping, and yelling, and firing off their guns, just for the fun of the thing. And they would go into stores and places and do many things they should not have done. In fact, the whole caboodle of them ought to have been carried to the guard house."

Such incidents of "hurrahing" a friendly community to let off steam—precurser of the genial shooting-up of Western cow-towns in the dawning cattle era—were not uncommon. But in this case, as in others, a militia detail was organized to round up the celebrants and take them into "protective custody" until they could be shipped back to their base camp. Sam Watkins shortly found himself, with the rest of his company, on a train of boxcars headed for Atlanta. But on the whole it had been a rather pleasant expedition.

At the Windsor Smith estate, Hood pondered a letter received from President Davis after the affair at Ezra Church. It contained the admonition: "The loss consequent upon attacking the enemy in his entrenchments requires you to avoid that if practicable." The President, who had been urging him to take the initiative, now proposed to clip the eagle's wings. Hood could only accept what was patently a mild rebuke; but it was the beginning of a rift between himself and Davis similar to the gap that had divided Johnston and the President—the essentially different points of view of the Executive in Richmond and the general at the front.

The balance sheet admittedly did not look good. Since he had taken command from Johnston, Hood had lost from 12,000 to

15,000 men; his army, even with new recruits and reinstated troops, now numbered only 35,400. But in Hood's line of thinking, battle losses indicated a degree of triumph. His army had not flinched (except in the twilight hours at Ezra Church). It had stood up to Sherman's superior numbers; had given not as much as it had taken in the way of punishment, but a good deal, notwithstanding. He was aware that in his army there were cries of "Give us back Joe Johnston!" But at this point he was not concerned with popularity; time would bring him victory and vindication.

For, over all, there were these positive considerations: Sherman had been stopped cold at the point where Hood had ruled he should not pass: Lickskillet Road. His cavalry divisions had been thoroughly whipped in their attempts to cut the Macon railroad. Hood's supply line was intact, and protected by the fishhook line of breastworks that extended from Atlanta to the East Point junction. His position was serious, but far from desperate; his determination undiminished. He would hold Atlanta and let Sherman beat his brains out on the city's walls.

For Sherman, the Stoneman-McCook debacle had been catastrophic, confirming his poor opinion of the Union cavalry. His initial reaction was, for him, unusually mild. "On the whole," he wrote laconically, "the cavalry raid is not deemed a success." There was even a hint that the Confederates had rendered him a service by, as he said, "taking Stoneman out of circulation." In any event, one thing was clear. He could not quickly reduce Atlanta by attacking its supply line. While closing an iron ring around the city, everywhere but in the south, he would batter it into submission with artillery.

Sherman had been shelling Atlanta since the 20th of July, but only intermittently. Now he wrote to Halleck, "I am too impatient for a siege . . . whether we get inside Atlanta or not it will be a used-up community by the time we are done with it." In more specific words he proposed to General Oliver Howard, "Let us destroy Atlanta and make it a desolation."

Down from Chattanooga, at Sherman's orders, came the heavy cannon, to destroy the city and all human life and war machinery within it. On August 9, between key points along the Union line before Atlanta, the word was passed:

"Bring up the guns!"

15

Summer and Smoke

"The city is very quiet now," wrote Samuel Richards on that first sultry day of August. "Except," he added, "when the shelling is in progress."

Atlantans were beginning to accept the fact that their city was under siege, with no apparent end in sight. The first shock and terror caused by the falling shells, which had plunged the community into overnight despair, had worn off; the citizens "strengthened their bombproofs, and calmly prepared for the worst."

Like his neighbors, Richards had built what he called a "pit" or bombproof in his cellar to which he and his family could retreat for safety. So far no missiles had struck the house, and the bookseller had had ample time to work on the vegetable bed designed to offset the scarcity of fresh foods. His garden had not suffered much from the thieves and stragglers prevalent in the city. His corn, tomatoes, and butterbeans were growing plentifully, and he was able to give to his neighbors what his family did not need.

Since the churches had been closed as being military targets, the Baptist choir met at Richards' house to sing and practice during these early days of siege. That was some comfort to him in a war of which he disapproved. Otherwise: "I have to stand on guard every other night," he recorded in his diary, "but the duties have not been arduous and I will not complain so long as we have no other duty to perform. If they go on making us do *active service* at 'the ditches' or 'the front' I shall try to get off from it."

For the most part the people went about their business with composure. They learned that the flight path of the bombshells could be followed by the flaming wicks, giving those endangered time to duck. Shells with percussion caps emitted only a brief, shrill, warning whistle; but many—some said as many as two-thirds—failed to explode as they landed wrong-end-to or skittered sidewise into walls and buildings. There was, too, a certain pattern to the Federal bombardment, by which civilians could regulate their movements and stay off the streets or take to their shelters when danger threatened.

Sherman himself had set that pattern in an order to General Schofield: "You may fire from ten to fifteen shots from every gun you have in position into Atlanta that will reach any of its houses. Fire slowly between 4:00 P.M. and dark. I have inquired into our reserve supply and the occasion will warrant the expenditure. Thomas and Howard will do the same."

Four hours of bombardment took their toll. Nelson Warner, plant superintendent, was sleeping in his house at Elliott and Rhodes Streets, with his six-year-old daughter on the bed beside him, when a shell crashed through the ceiling. The girl's body was cut in half, and Warner bled to death with both legs severed at the thighs. An elderly refugee approaching the car shed stooped to pick up something from the street and never raised his head again. Thirty women shopping in a downtown market were covered with dust and rubble, but miraculously escaped serious injury, when a cannonball plunged through the roof. A bombshell exploding behind a wagon carrying Confederate dead to the cemetery, stampeded the mules and scattered the bodies for some distance up and down the road. Thereafter, both Sally Clayton and Mollie Smith observed that even civilian casualties were buried, not properly in the cemetery, but often in their own backyards.

A shell struck the slave quarters in Sally Clayton's yard, with less grisly results. It landed on a bed where two small girls were sleeping, burst and set the bed afire. Sally's mother rushed to the rescue, as did all the servants and several passing soldiers. At first, recorded Sally, "the smoke was so dense that it seemed impossible to reach or to even find the bed. Finally someone succeeded, and instead of bringing out mangled dead bodies they brought out two perfectly sound little girls, with only a few tiny powder marks on hands and arms." The young girls were taken into the "big house," and placed behind a thick chimney for protection.

The incident alarmed a neighbor, Oliver Jones, who fetched an ambulance and urged the Clayton family to evacuate their home. It was obviously in the direct line of enemy fire. Mr. Clayton agreed, and the girls and their parents were taken to a two-story business building, that of the Georgia Railroad Banking Company on Whitehall Street, where Mr. Clayton had worked before the war. It seemed solid and safe, but lacked cooking facilities, so that food was prepared at home and delivered to their place of refuge.

To make this service possible, Caroline Clayton, Sally's mother, timed the discharge of shells from Sherman's batteries north of the city. There was an interval of five minutes between salvos, a long enough period to carry food from Marietta to Whitehall Street. This discovery yielded limited benefits, however, since the servant assigned to carry the food, "fell flat on the ground, face down," each time he heard a shell burst from whatever quarter, and the result, as Sally wrote, was often, "goodbye dinner."

In their borrowed house on Railroad Street, where the Huff family had fled after the Battle of Peachtree Creek, Sarah Huff would lie on her bed and watch through her window the pyrotechnical display above Atlanta. She had never seen anything like it since the July Fourth fireworks exhibitions held before the war.

Sarah had a commanding view of the spectacle, since the house was in the direct line of fire from the Federal batteries on the northern outskirts of the city. It was also close to an obvious target, the railroad terminal and switch yard. Early that month, General Hood had ordered the locomotive engineers to toot their whistles frequently, suggesting to the enemy a constant flow of men and munitions into Atlanta from the south. The citizens had petitioned that the practice be abandoned; it only called the Federal battery's attention to the presence of the trains. The whistles stopped, but nothing could stop the columns of smoke which spiralled from the locomotives, making the area a target zone.

Sarah watched the shells strike and illuminate with their explosions, a house, a factory building, and the Washington Street churches. Then a second salvo, falling minutes later in the same locale, would silhouette the stark black skeleton of what had been a church, a factory, a home. Often, where once a house had stood, the clearing smoke would reveal only a single stone flue, rising from the rubble, like a finger pointing heavenward in protest, known among both Federals and Confederates as "Sherman's chimneys."

Not owning the house, the Huff family did not feel entitled to build a bombproof in the yard. When the bombardment grew intense, they sought shelter in the rock-walled cellar of Richard Peter's flour mill across the railroad from their temporary home. Sarah would never forget the curious stimulating camaraderie of those subterranean evenings in the mill. Years later she recalled:

> The more furious the firing the bigger the crowd in the basement. There was no such thing as a stranger, there never was in war-time, and I remember how the men and boys tried to rattle each other about the way they had reacted to a shrieking bombshell. Like an electric storm going over, the shelling seldom lasted more than an hour or so, and the people went home and put the children to bed.

Carrie Berry had started the diary which she had promised her father she would keep, noting for Tuesday, August 2: "Not much shelling, but the muskets have been going all day." On Wednesday she reported: "This was my birthday. I was ten years old, but I did not have a cake, times were so hard, so I celebrated with ironing. I hope by my next birthday we will have peace in our land so that I can have a nice dinner."

Most afternoons and evenings, and sometimes the whole day,

the Berry family stayed in their cellar where Carrie knitted stockings and "nurst sister." She did not feel altogether safe in the cellar, the shells "fell so thick and fast." The week's only diversion was a visit from Carrie's militiaman cousin, Henry Beatty, with some coffee he had captured from a Yankee in a skirmish. The family ground the beans for Henry and all enjoyed the only real coffee they had had for many months.

In charge of the Confederate telegraph office in the American Hotel on Alabama Street, Major Charles W. Hubner had the weighty responsibility of supervising all messages which traveled to and from the city. Across the railroad from the city square, he was in dead center of the action. "The Federal gunners got the range of the old car shed which stood near headquarters," he recorded, "consequently both buildings were severely shelled."

A shell whistled through the basement where the major and his telegraphers were sleeping on a row of cots, fortunately failing to explode. It neatly severed the legs from the cots, and dumped the sleepers on the floor. But Hubner remembered best the day "when a fragment of shell which had burst in front of the building, came through the window where I was recording a message and ripped off the page opposite to the one upon which I was writing."

Fanny Beers was another who experienced the hazards surrounding the railroad tracks and depot. She had come up from Newnan, with her servant Tempe, to visit her soldier husband stationed in Atlanta. Approaching the city, she heard the frightening roar of the bombardment, then the whistle of the locomotive which unwittingly informed the enemy of an approaching train. The Union batteries began at once to shell the depot. Fanny heard a "shrieking sound: and saw the passengers fall to the floor or duck behind the seats."

Before I could think twice, an awful explosion followed; the windows were all slivered, and the earth seemed to me to be thrown in cart-loads into the car. Tempe screamed loudly, and then began to pray. I was paralyzed with extreme terror, and *could* not scream. Before I could speak, another shell exploded overhead, tearing off the corner of a brick store, causing again a deafening racket. . . .

As the train glided into the station, Fanny felt momentarily safer; but as she started out from the depot, in search of a place to stay, her terror returned.

The shells still shrieked and exploded; the more treacherous and dangerous solid shot continually demolished objects within our sight. For a few hours I was so utterly demoralized that my only thought was how to escape. It seemed to me *impossible* that any body of soldiers could voluntarily expose themselves to such horrible danger. I thought if *I* had been a soldier I must have deserted from my first battlefield. But at last I grew calmer; my courage returned, and, urged by the necessity of finding shelter, I ventured out. Not a place could I find. The houses were closed and deserted, in many cases partly demolished by shot and shell, or, having taken fire, charred, smoking, and burnt to the ground.

Fanny finally took possession of a vacant house which had had its roof and upper story blown off and was open to the sky. She then crept cautiously along the streets, with Tempe clinging to her hand, until she found an officer going to the trenches and gave him a note to her husband telling of her arrival and her strange abode. Soon after sunset her husband joined her, followed by several of his army friends. "They were all ragged, mud-stained and altogether unlovely," Fanny noted, "but seemed to me the most desirable and welcome visitors I could imagine."

Fanny and Tempe had brought with them several boxes of food on which the soldiers feasted, stuffing the remainder in their haversacks. The next evening brought an even larger group of friendly soldiers from the fortifications, this time contributing their own provisions. The following night, the same congenial ritual; until this half-wrecked house became a home-like sanctuary in the middle of the siege, a place of warmth, and song, and laughter as important to the citadel's survival as the stone walls which surrounded it.

Atlanta's defending troops in the forts and breastworks suffered the same combination of alert anxiety and boredom which the citizens endured. Captain Tom Key, stationed near the monolithic Ponder House on the northeast section of the wall, complained of the dawn-to-dusk cannonading in his sector, and the constant "pecking away" at the pickets of both sides.

No building in Atlanta would overlook so much fighting, suffer so much shelling, as the home which Ephraim Ponder had relinquished to his wayward wife. Its hollow-eyed windows, lidded with splintered glass, faced General Slocum's corps of the Army of the Cumberland which possessed the heaviest field artillery in Sherman's command. From here, Key noted in his diary for August 1:

> Cannonading opened with the dawn, and the heavy, dull thunderings continued all day. Heavy shells are now bursting around and over the large stone house in which I am writing and which houses the headquarters of General Cleburne and his staff. Because the Atlanta and Montgomery Railroad has been cut, depriving us, at least temporarily, of our source of supplies, the artillery horses are becoming materially reduced from lack of their usual number of pounds of corn.

Key thought he could keep his horse in shape by foraging for green corn in the countryside below Atlanta. He noticed the infantry was eating it, and what was good enough for infantry was good enough for horses. He saved much of his sympathy for the beleaguered citizens of the beleagured city, writing three days later, August 4:

> Every five minutes throughout the whole night on, two 20 pounder guns threw shells in the city, striking through houses and exploding midst families, killing women and children. All day that same cruel piece of cowardice has gone on under the direction of the inhuman ungentlemanly Sherman. The citizens have excavated holes in their yards and covered them with timbers upon which they throw dirt, and when the shelling begins resort to these for safety.

Corporal Sam Watkins, having returned from the great locomotive chase of Stoneman's cavalry down the Macon railroad, found himself and his company back in the fortifications near the Ponder House complaining of a more persistent, pesky enemy than Sherman's Federals. Noted Watkins:

> We found everything exactly as we had left it, with the exception of the graybacks [lice], which seemed to have propagated a

thousand-fold since we left, and they were crawling about like ants, making little paths and tracks in the dirt as they wiggled and waddled about, hunting for ye old Rebel soldier. Sherman's two thirty-pound parrot guns were in the same position and every now and then a lazy-looking shell would pass over, speeding its way on to Atlanta.

Except for the pickets positioned outside the fortifications, most of Hood's 37,000-man army was behind the walls now, including the fish-hook-shaped parapets extending from the west side of Atlanta clear to East Point, through which the two remaining railway lines poured vital supplies into the city.

Hardee's corps faced the Union Army of the Cumberland on the north side of the city, and during the first week in August the troops along this section of the ramparts had a visitor. Battery Captain Tom Key saw "an aged man of corpulent dimensions" telling the Georgia troops to "stand by the artillerists and you will whip the Yankees like the devil." The visitor's remarks took such effect, observed Key, that "an involuntary cheer was raised, and I walked near the individual to get a close view of him. It proved to be the Hon. Robert Toombs of Georgia, who . . . now goes by the title of General of Militia. It was to the Georgia militia that he was addressing himself."

To the tough and skeptical veterans of the Army of Tennessee, the Georgia militia, 5,000 strong, had been something of an unknown quantity, and as such open to derision. Generally, in the battles around Atlanta, they had been held in reserve, and were still regarded by the seasoned troops as "Joe Brown's pets." Captain Key found them "ready to do their duty" but "it is laughable to see their awkward motions and blunders at simple military evolutions." Sam Watkins found the militia "the richest picture of an army I ever saw. It beat Forepaugh's double-ringed circus." In amplification, Watkins wrote:

Every one was dressed in citizen's clothes. . . . A few had double-barreled shot-guns, but the majority had umbrellas and walking-sticks, and nearly every one had on a duster, a flat-bosomed "biled" shirt, and a plug hat; and, to make the thing more ridiculous, the dwarf and the giant were marching side by side; the knock-kneed with the bow-legged; the driven-in by the side of the drawn-out; the pale and sallow dyspeptic, who looked like Alex

Stephens, and who seemed to have just been taken out of a chimney that smoked very badly, and whose diet was goobers and sweet potatoes, was placed beside the three hundred-pounder, who was dressed up to kill. . . .

This derisive view was changed, however, when the Georgia militia went into action in early August. A company sent on a scouting expedition beyond the walls ran into a squad of Union infantry which opened fire. Despite the hail of minie balls the militiamen charged the enemy, killing or capturing the entire squad, with eight of their own men killed or wounded. That afternoon their dead were buried with full military honors, and "Joe Brown's pets" were thereafter hailed as "gallant and noble fellows."

A less noticed visitor than Robert Toombs was Sherman's double agent, Milton Glass, still free to roam the streets of Atlanta with a Confederate pass from provost marshal Colonel Hill. He was able to report to General Sherman, still at Howard's House above the city, that Southern reenforcements were arriving in Atlanta; that trains to and from the south were running regularly; that 600 Union prisoners had been removed to Andersonville.

It was largely trivial stuff, as Glass was aware. He wanted to get inside the fortifications and study their strength, their troop and gun emplacements in detail; but when he asked Hill for a pass permitting him to do so, he found the provost marshal difficult to handle. Under the stress of the times, Hill had taken to the bottle. Usually drunk, he was generally belligerent, ready to refuse, on reflex, anything the spy requested. Accordingly, wrote Wilbur Kurtz who studied Glass's papers some years later:

> The spy's reports are all a tissue of headquarters and street gossip—a lot of it, grapevine rumor. The desired data was just within that chain of huge forts, that followed, roughly, the mile and a half circle, with the Union depot as a center. From the immediate precincts of the great earthen walls with the plank revetment, the wooden gun-platforms, and the board shacks of the defenders, the spy was prohibited. True, he passed in and out of the earthen walls, but in only one instance . . . does he speak of a battery with four guns in it.

Not only were there several batteries containing more than four guns, but at this point in the battle for Atlanta, Confederate guns were generally heavier than those arrayed against them. Lieutenant Andrew Neal's artillery battalion was positioned "in a fort about 100 yards from the Ponder Home," he wrote to Ella.

> The Yankees have their line of Battle and several Batteries a short distance in front and on our right have approached so near our works by digging that we can keep out no pickets.
> Almost all the shells they throw into the City come screaming just above our heads. Generally they commence on this fort and throw around it shells and then elevate their guns and send the balance into the city. For a while we exchanged shots with them, but where Batteries are as well protected as ours and the Yankee batteries before us, about as much is made of artillery duels as the sledge hammer makes out of the anvil.

In off-duty hours Neal paid sorrowful visits to the city of his birth and found it sorely ravaged by the enemy bombardment. His own home had been struck twice, one shell passing through his brother's bedroom, the other through the parlor. Yet, "very few people think the enemy will get any nearer Atlanta," he assured his sister, "though they have ruined its value to us in great measure."

The Atlanta *Intelligencer*, viewing the situation more objectively from Macon, could afford to be more positive, promising its readers: "The Yankee forces will disappear before Atlanta before the end of August."

"Our position before Atlanta," Sherman wrote as of August 1, "was healthy, with ample supply of wood, water and provisions . . . the skirmish lines were held close up to the enemy, were covered by rifle trenches or logs, and kept up a continuous clatter of musketry. The main lines were held farther back, adapted to the shape of the ground, with muskets loaded and stacked for instant use. The field-batteries were in selected positions, covered by handsome parapets, and occasional shots gave life and animation to the scene."

The Federal breastworks approximately paralleled the

Confederate walls around Atlanta and the parapets extending down to East Point. The distance between the two lines varied, but was rarely more than two or three hundred yards. The area between had been cleared of trees and thickets, for the sake of visibility and for timber with which to shore up breastworks and branches with which to fashion abatis. Skirmishers of both sides probed the enemy's lines. Pickets stood secretive guard before the respective parapets. At night, flaring pine cones soared across this no man's land to illuminate the potential targets and discourage any sneak attacks.

"The troops had become habituated to the slow and steady progress of the siege," wrote Sherman, noting that they seemed as snug and comfortable as if at home. But he himself would never become habituated to slow progress. When, a few days later, he received reports of Stoneman's surrender near Macon and McCook's defeat at Newnan, his simmering impatience reached the boiling point. "I now became satisfied that cavalry could not, or would not, make a sufficient lodgment on the railroad below Atlanta, and that nothing would suffice for us but to reach it with the main army."

Seizure of the Macon railroad had now become, in Sherman's mind, "the vital objective of the campaign. Its possession by us, would in my judgment, result in the capture of Atlanta, and give us the fruits of victory. . . ." To this end, he moved Schofield from the extreme left of his line to the extreme right, and assigned him to this critical mission. To supplement Schofield's single corps of 12,000 men, he placed General John M. Palmer's corps of the Army of the Cumberland under General Schofield's orders.

Palmer balked at the assignment, claiming that he technically outranked Schofield. He refused to submit to orders from a junior. For all of an afternoon, both Thomas and Sherman tried to reason tactfully with Palmer. The matter ended with Palmer resigning from the army, and Sherman writing to him bitterly, "I regard the loss of time this afternoon as equal to the loss of two thousand men." Major General Jefferson C. Davis was given the command of Palmer's corps.

The delay had cost Sherman much more than two thousand men. For all practical purposes it cost him the entire mission.

By the time Schofield had crossed Utoy Creek and was ready to assault Hood's breastworks covering the East Point railroad, the Confederates were ready for him. General William Bate's division of Hardee's corps, comfortably entrenched and barricaded, watched Schofield's infantry struggle through thickets and brambles in two desperate attempts to reach their parapets— and picked them off almost at leisure, leaving 800 Union dead and wounded on the field. On August 6, Schofield was forced to withdraw and to report to Sherman "total failure" of the ill-starred effort.

To the same degree that Sherman was disheartened by the double failure of his cavalry under Stoneman and McCook, Hood had reason for renewed hope in his own Confederate cavalry under Generals Iverson and Wheeler. Dissuaded by Jefferson Davis from again attacking Sherman outside the city's fortifications, there was only one means left—a good chance— of dislodging the Union general from his stand before Atlanta. That was to sever Sherman's long and tenuous supply line stretching back to Chattanooga. To this end, with the President's approval, he sent Wheeler circling around the city with his 7,500 mounted troops, to cut Sherman's jugular vein, the Western & Atlantic Railroad.

In effect, as one historian expressed it, Wheeler "rode himself out of the war," not to rejoin the Army of Tennessee till late October. He would be heard from again—from time to time, and from different places—but over the storm he raised along the Chattanooga railway could be heard the whistle of the locomotives riding down over the tracks that Sherman's men repaired as fast as Wheeler could destroy them. Though Hood would later credit Wheeler with success, all that really resulted from this madcap ride was the loss to the Confederates of several thousand mounted troops that could have been better employed around Atlanta for reconnaissance.

Within a radius of a few miles from the center of Atlanta, Georgians were already feeling the adversities of enemy occupation. On South Utoy Creek, falling within Union lines as soon as Schofield made his abortive move against the East Point railroad, citizen Joseph Willis and his community of twenty-six

neighbors and relations clung to their sixteen-foot-square subterranean chamber, scarcely daring to open their doorway to the
fresh air. Blackberries grew within a few feet of the entrance,
and though they were well supplied with water and nonperishable staples, these were the only fresh foods they enjoyed
throughout these early weeks of long confinement.

East of Atlanta, Mary Gay's home, with its barns and servants' quarters, was once again partially occupied by Union
troops and officers, though she herself retained a portion of the
house to live in. Concern for the Confederate supplies and uniforms hidden in the ceiling of her parlor was only one source
of distress for Mary. "The haughty, insolent boast of the enemy
. . . that they would make quick work of the rebellion, and of the
complete subjugation of the South, had in no way a tendency to
mitigate anxiety or to encourage hope."

There was, however, one advantage to the enemy's proximity.
By a little coaxing, Mary obtained permission to read Northern
newspapers sent to the Union officers from New York, Cincinnati, Philadelphia, and Washington. It occurred to her that the
information they contained might be useful to her brother Tommy's superiors in the Confederate Army at Atlanta. But how to
get that information to them?

A solution came in the hands of a Federal private, bringing
her a letter from a relative some miles away. A cousin, the writer
said, was seriously ill. On an impulse, Mary showed the letter
to the Union provost marshal, requesting permission to visit the
patient as an act of mercy. He not only consented, but offered
to supply her with an escort through the Union lines.

Ostensibly dressing in her bedroom for the journey, Mary
clipped pertinent stories from the Northern papers, and sewed
them into the lining of her bustle. Their bulk was undetectable
in the caverns of that bell-like garment. With her maid Telitha
and the guard she visited the ailing relative, at which point the
escort left them. At the conclusion of the visit she and Telitha
made their way on foot toward Atlanta, evaded both Union and
Confederate pickets, and slipped into the city via the McDonough Road.

Who would know best the current military structure of Atlanta? Certainly Captain Lemuel P. Grant who had designed the
fortifications. She stopped at Mrs. Grant's, with whom her

mother had been friendly, and Mrs. Grant ordered one of her servants to guide Mary to the Confederate high command. Here, as officers discreetly turned their backs, Mary snipped the clippings from her undergarments and laid them on a table.

"The papers," she recalled, "seemed most acceptable."

On their way back to the Grants, "Telitha and I had not gone farther than the First Presbyterian Church . . . before a bombshell fell by that gate and burst into a thousand pieces, literally tearing the gate to bits." Atlanta, Mary decided, was no place to tarry. With no longer anything to hide, the two women boldly approached Confederate pickets on the outskirts of the city who advised them on the best way to circumvent the Union lines and return in safety to Decatur.

Among the newspaper clippings Mary Gay had left with the Confederate officers was a story in the *Cincinnati Journal* dated "August 1 (delayed)" reporting the fall of "Georgia's stronghold" to the Federal forces. The imaginative correspondent "saw the Star-Spangled Banner floating from the public buildings of Atlanta, and heard the heavy tread of our victorious soldiers through the sombre streets."

It made entertaining reading; but of greater interest were reports of growing discontent throughout the North with the progress of the war. Grant was stalled before Petersburg as Sherman was checked before Atlanta; peace negotiations held in Canada at Horace Greeley's instigation had collapsed; Lincoln had called for half a million more troops. All combined to dim the prospects of the President's reelection in November—heartening news to the Confederacy which looked now to Atlanta as the key to its survival.

The Sunday which ended that first week in August brought sudden, blessed quiet to Atlanta. The shelling ceased, and even the pickets seemed to observe a wary, unofficial truce. To Carrie Berry "it almost seems like Sunday of old . . . it is the first time I have been to church in a month." In a similar vein Samuel Richards noted in his diary, "We have been to church this morning for the first time in three weeks. . . . Our cruel foe has the grace to cease from shelling us on the Sabbath, at least he has not done so yet."

Richards took advantage of the calm to visit his book and

stationery store on Whitehall Street. On entering, he discovered he had had a visitor:

> I was puzzled at finding the stove tumbled down and moved forward six feet, but the rubbish around the flue in the wall told that a shell had "dropped in" but where it had made its entrance I could not discover until I went upstairs and there the mystery was explained. The shell had entered the roof and passing through five partitions of wood and plaster had pierced the side wall into the flue, and its force being expended it *dropped* in the flue to the store below and there exploded, doing the mischief before spoken of.

On the northern fortifications of Atlanta, Captain Key spent the morning reading *Titcomb's Letters to Young People, Single and Married*, a copy of which mysteriously "fell into my hands." Key found the book instructive and inspiring, and "a solution to the unhappy marriages that one sees daily. Young men and women who wish to make useful and happy husbands and wives should purchase 'Titcomb's Letters' and read them carefully." Having written which encomium, Key noted in conclusion: "This is the Sabbath and the Yanks have not fired a shell into the streets of Atlanta. This is contrary to their general course."

Lieutenant Andrew Neal, a little more convinced that Hood would hold Atlanta, was nonetheless content with a precaution he had taken. Since joining the Army of Tennessee he had carried with him the Marion Light Artillery battle flag, under which he had served in Florida and which, for sentimental reasons, he could not bear to let go—even though "by order of the general commanding, none but flags of large bodies of troops would be retained."

The silken banner had been made and presented to his company by the citizens of Marion, with "mantle and jewels" contributed by the women. The beautiful flagstaff had been carved and gilded by a Florida artisan. In Andrew's eyes it was more than priceless, it was sacred. But practicality finally outweighed sentiment. After carrying the flag and staff down the long highway of retreat from Dalton, Andrew wrapped the sacred spear and silken banner with protective clothing, and shipped the bundle to his father in Zebulon for sakekeeping.

If there was one who failed to appreciate that quiet sabbath at the front, it was William Tecumseh Sherman. Schofield's failure to break Atlanta's defenses and flank the city from the west had left him with no acceptable alternative. "The enemy hold us by an inferior force," he complained to Schofield, "we are more besieged than they."

While he would continue to press his earthworks closer to Atlanta's walls, leapfrogging yard by yard under cover of darkness, it was a tedious procedure for a man of action. And it promised nothing. The fortifications of the city were, he believed, impregnable.

Of those fortifications, more than ten miles in length and averaging one and a quarter miles from the center of the city, Sherman could see with his own eyes what Captain Lemuel P. Grant had seen when he had finished them the previous summer:

> As completed the earthen banks had a trench in front, which meant that all sorts of impediments to an enemy could be laid in the trench and the trench itself would make it difficult to scale the bank. The earth walls were revetted—that is, they were held in place by timbers from sawmills near Atlanta and from lumber from houses which stood in the way of the defenses. At intervals there were platforms constructed for gun emplacements.

What could not be seen or counted was the number of guns installed on those emplacements, or the deployment of troops and guns among the seventeen demiforts, or major points of resistance, connected by rifle pits to form an interlinking chain or wall around three quarters of the city. Sherman might well have agreed with the observation of Captain Conyngham that "We cannot with the least chance of success attempt to carry the enemy's fortifications by assault." Such an attempt would be apt to yield the same disastrous results experienced at Kennesaw.

Reporting by messenger to Thomas of "Slow progress here," he instructed that general to: "Telegraph to Chattanooga to have two 30-pounder Parrots sent down on the cars, with 1,000 shells and ammunition. Put them into your best position and knock down the buildings of the town." On the same Sunday, August 7, he wrote to General Halleck in Washington:

I do not deem it prudent to extend any more to the right, but will push forward daily by parallels, and make the inside of Atlanta too hot to be endured. I have sent back to Chattanooga for two thirty-pound Parrots, with which we can pick out almost any house in town. I am too impatient for a siege, and don't know but this is as good a place to fight it out on, as farther inland. One thing is certain, whether we get inside of Atlanta or not, it will be a used-up community when we are done with it.

It would take two days, at least, to bring the big guns down from Chattanooga. The Union general braced himself for the most difficult of all tasks in his campaign for Atlanta: waiting.

16

Red Day in August

It promised to be like any other day in August, humid and misty in the early morning, with the sun a bright red in the east.

Samuel Richards started for his bookstore wondering if any other "visitor," like the shell which had slithered down his flue, had broken in. Carrie Berry planned to clean house for her mother, then work on the stockings she was trying to finish before school opened. Major Charles Hubner arrived early at his telegraph office in the American Hotel, hoping for word from General Wheeler's cavalry now believed to be raiding Marietta. Solomon Luckie, the popular Negro barber, set out for his shop on Alabama Street.

All over Atlanta the familiar scenes, the trivial rituals of another wartime day beginning, were replayed—the principals as anonymous as the acts themselves. A housewife on North Pryor Street laid out the damp clothes for her morning's ironing. An officer billeted at a home on Forsyth Street took polite leave of his hostess in the front yard of the house. A young girl wended her way to the car shed to meet the morning train from Macon. A Confederate soldier trudged through the inner city with a sack of grain across his shoulders.

All became frozen in time with the sudden, chilling blast from Sherman's batteries. The first shells struck without warning. In seconds the sky became alive with screaming lead and twisting fire. Columns of smoke and dust soared upward from the trembling city as the buildings tumbled down. Sherman's big guns, on that fateful Tuesday, August 9, had arrived from Chattanooga.

The housewife, about to press her husband's shirts, dropped across her ironing board, horribly mangled, dead by the time her body was discovered. The departing soldier was mortally wounded by an exploding shell, along with his landlady's son. The girl on her way to the car shed dropped in her tracks in a pool of blood. Major Hubner looked up in time to see a blunt-nosed shell plunge through the center of his office to the floor below; it failed to explode and the major was unhurt. Solomon Luckie, the barber, was about to enter his shop when a bomb-shell hit the sidewalk, richocheted off a lamppost, and shattered his body with its fragments. Two bystanders carried him to the nearest hospital where he bled to death.

The city was briefly numb with shock. Citizens had grown used to dodging shells, but from this bombardment there was no escape. A family of six fled to their bombproof which, seconds later, suffered a direct hit. None could be identified. Wherever one happened to be, a citizen reported, one was surrounded by "an inferno of noise swollen at frequent intervals by the roar of a falling building. The very air was loathsome with the odor of burned powder, while a pall of dust and smoke overhung the city." Wallace P. Reed, the journalist, would never forget that sudden reign of horror and its dreadful toll of human life:

If any one day of the siege was worse than all the others, it was that red day in August, when all the fires of hell, and all the thunders of the universe seemed to be blazing and roaring over Atlanta. It was about the middle of the month, and everything had been comparatively quiet for a few days, when one fine morning, about breakfast time, a big siege gun belched forth a sheet of flame with a sullen boom from a Federal battery on the north side of the city. The Confederates had an immense gun on Peachtree Street, one so large and heavy that it had taken three days to drag it to its position. This monster lost no time in replying to its noisy challenger, and then the duel opened all along the lines on the north and west. Ten Confederate and eleven Federal batteries took part in the engagement. On Peachtree, where Kimball intersects, the big gun of the Confederates put in its best work, but only to draw a hot fire from the enemy. Shot and shell rained in every direction. Great volumes of sulphurous smoke rolled over the town, trailing down to the ground, and through this stifling gloom the sun glared down like a great red eye peering through a bronze colored sky.

An estimated 5,000 bombshells struck the city, leaving scarcely a block undamaged. The five hundred volunteer firemen led by chief Thomas Haney, raced from one blazing building to another in a futile fight against the almost universal holocaust. Though exempt from military duty, the firemen faced as much danger as troops in combat since the towering flames and smoke provided handy targets for the Union gunners who turned their two hundred cannon on the burning structures. While many of the firemen were injured, none, surprisingly, was killed.

To the younger people of the town the heightened siege had its elements of spectacle and thrill. Five-year-old Noble Williams, Dr. Ezekiel Calhoun's grandson, climbed to the top of the grape arbor, ignoring appeals to take refuge in the cellar, and watched the stricken houses crumble in the streets around him. On Peachtree Street, Lucy Hull swung on the garden gate, listened to the symphony of cannon, and watched the frantic soldiers and civilians hurry back and forth, "so weary, barefooted, wounded and dirty." Carrie Berry, sticking to knitting, was not especially perturbed. "We have had to stay in the cellar all day," she wrote in her diary, "the shells have been falling so thick around the house. Two have fallen in the garden, but none of us were hurt. Cousin Henry Beatty came in and wanted us to move, he thought that we were in danger, but we will try it a little longer."

Behind the Union breastworks, soldiers stoppered their ears against the blasting of their eleven batteries. They hailed each shell that whistled overhead as "A kiss for Jeff Davis!" or "There goes the Atlanta Express!" Posted signs that ordered them to "Keep down! Don't stand on the works!" gained due respect when one of their guns in the rear started firing short and dropping its bombshells in their trenches. Through cupped hands they shouted at the gunners, "She slobbers at the mouth —take her away!" And they also had reason to respect the mammoth Confederate gun on Peachtree Street, the "Big Bertha" of Atlanta, that shot-for-shot outweighed anything Sherman's guns could hurl into the city.

On the Confederate line confronting the Union batteries, Captain Key wrote somewhat contemptuously of the barrage, noting that, with little surcease,

> ... the Yanks have been throwing chunks of iron weighing twelve pounds around me, often passing within five steps of me. The balls of iron have splintered the trees and torn ghastly wounds in the houses nearby. The federals are at some of their tricks, either to demoralize the troops with artillery and then attack them with infantry, or to attract attention to this part of the line and then assault us at some other point. However, the rebels don't sleep. We are ready for them and invite them most cordially to come out and meet us.

Before the day was over, Captain Key, and other officers and men along the miles of fortifications, were reading General Hood's exhortation to his troops. They were told to hold the positions that they occupied "to the very last . . . the destiny of Atlanta hangs upon the issue."

Heavy as the destruction to Atlanta was, Sherman remained impatient. He reminded General Thomas that the city must be totally destroyed; "let us . . . make it a desolation." He bombarded Thomas with messages throughout the day: "I don't hear the 4½ -inch guns . . . keep them going. Time is too valuable to waste." And later, "Keep up a steady, persistent fire on Atlanta with the 4½ -inch guns and 20-pounder Parrots . . . ." The following day he needled the artillery with further orders:

> I hear Brannan's guns at Geary's battery, and hear the shells burst in Atlanta. Send word to the battery to work all night and

not limit themselves to 5-minute guns, but to fire slowly and steadily each gun as it is ready; also order the gun on Williams' front to be got ready and put to work with similar orders tonight. Howard will get his 20s near the same point . . . the intervening angle being cleared ground giving a fine field of fire. I think the 4½-inch gun on Williams' right can demolish the big engine house.

In counterpoint to the heavy-toned artillery duel, there was the sharp rifle fire of the infantry and constant skirmishing between the pickets. "The picket firing never ceases, day or night," wrote Union Major W. H. Chamberlain. "Sometimes it is lazy, scattered and weak, and again swelling to volleys like the beginning of a battle, and now and then being followed by the roar of artillery." Private Elisha Stockwell, ever concerned with physical discomfort, complained that Confederate skirmishers would not leave his regiment alone and "A big gun near town disturbed our sleep at night."

On the Confederate side General Samuel French also regarded this firing between pickets an intolerable nuisance. "When the siege began," he wrote, "I sent for my principal officers and told them all that I did not intend my camp should be unpleasant from rifle balls." His solution was to divert the artillery from its main task of shelling Sherman's breastworks, and train it on the enemy pickets. It worked. While the pickets were kept busy ducking cannon balls, with no time to engage in rifle fire, General French and his officers enjoyed eight hours of sound sleep a night.

John Bell Hood was outraged and indignant at the stepped-up bombing, and sent several messages, under flags of truce, to General Sherman. His armed forces, Hood pointed out, were entrenched a mile or more from the center of the city. There were no military gains to justify the shelling of noncombatants, many of them women and children, in that area. It violated all the rules of civilized warfare.

Sherman replied tersely that if there were women and children still in the city they had no business being there; that he regarded Atlanta as a principal Southern depot for the instruments of war; and that war itself, by definition, took no account of innocent lives or property. His intention was, and would remain, to make Atlanta (and all of the South, he indicated) unfit to live in and incapable of waging war.

Not all Union officers, or troops for that matter, shared their commander's intransigent stand. Brigadier General Jacob Cox, far to the right or south end of the Union line, felt sympathy for the civilians caught between the warring armies. He wrote with commiseration of their suffering and hardships, brought about in part by their unwillingness to leave their much loved homes and lands. His compassion had been further aroused when his army had taken a position close to Utoy Creek on the property of Joseph Willis. Cox peered into the entrance of what seemed to be a massive bombproof in the hillside near the miller's house:

> I never felt more pity than when . . . I looked down into the pit and saw there, in the gloom made visible by a candle burning while it was broad day above, women sitting on the floor of loose boards, resting against each other, haggard and wan, trying to sleep away the days of terror, while innocent-looking children, four or five years old, clustered around the air-hole, looking up with pale faces and great staring eyes as they heard the singing of the bullets that were flying thick above their sheltering place.

Since there was a lull in the fighting at that section of the line, and Joseph Willis had come forth to ask for food, Cox ordered crude tables prepared outside their shelter and summoned the earth dwellers from their temporary tomb to eat their fill. One by one all twenty-six emerged like woodchucks from their hole, women, children, white-haired men, blinking their eyes at the sudden glare of sunlight, staring with disbelief at the war-shattered countryside they had not seen for three weeks. They wolfed down army rations of hardtack, beef, and Yankee coffee with the avid hunger of the starving, then crawled back into their burrow to wait in blind faith for the war to end or leave this part of Georgia.

Atlanta was still young and supple. It recovered quickly from that first shock of bombardment, and accepted the new, more hazardous existence thrust upon it. General Hood noted with satisfaction that the people complained little, stuck to their homes with faith, and believed with him that Atlanta would never be conquered and would never yield.

The *Atlanta Intelligencer,* safely ensconced in Macon, could afford to take a light view of the ordeal in its mother city. "The enemy continues to perpetrate his practical jokes in the neighborhood of Atlanta. He amuses himself by shooting shot and shell over the entire surface of the city . . ." Even in the grim bombardment of August 9 the newspaper found sources of amusement. The Confederate soldier toting a sack of grain in downtown Atlanta had been struck but not seriously injured because "the shell went against the grain."

There reappeared on the streets a lovable, familiar figure, trailing the noxious fumes of his perpetual cigars. Dr. Charles Quintard, army chaplain and minister of St. Luke's Church, was back from a visit to Macon where he had been asked to preach to local congregations. With Bishop Henry C. Lay the doctor hastened to his Atlanta church, to check on the reported damage it had suffered. He found that one of the shells had pierced the wall and struck the prayer desk, and that the Bible lying on the desk had fallen upon the shell "so as apparently to smother it and prevent its exploding."

> Before leaving the church I sat in one of the seats for a few moments and thought of the dear friends who had assisted in the building of the church, and who had offered up the sacrifice of praise and thanksgiving in that place; of the Bishop General over whom I had said the burial service there; of the now scattered flock and the utter desolation of God's house.

His immediate mission in Atlanta concerned a talk he had had with General Hood the night before. Hood had told him, "Doctor, I have two objects in life. . . . One is to do all I can for my country. The other is to be ready and prepared for death whenever God shall call me." The general had asked to be confirmed, along with nine others, including two officers belonging to his staff.

The service was held in a room of the Windsor Smith house; the actual rites were performed by Bishop Lay. The crippled

general was unable to kneel, and supported himself on his
crutch and staff as he bowed his head to receive the laying on
of hands. "The praying was good, the service animated," wrote
the Bishop. "Shells exploded nearby all the time."

Conditions in Atlanta grew so unbearable for Mrs. Huff and
her children that she decided to return to her home on the
outskirts of the city, in territory that had now become a no-
man's land. Arriving in a rainstorm with her horse and buggy,
cows and mules, she found the farmhouse held by the enemy,
and moved on to the home of Mr. and Mrs. William White,
friends of the family living near Utoy Church. This too was
occupied by a Federal officer, who nonetheless invited her in
from the rain. Mrs. Huff preferred to sleep with her family in
the buggy, rather than share the shelter with an enemy. During
the early morning hours some picket firing alarmed the cows,
who broke loose and ran away.

There seemed no escape from the fighting. "Trying to get out
of the shell-infested danger zone," wrote Sarah Huff, "and failing in every effort, mother returned to the Railroad Street cot-
tage behind the Shearer home."

The expedition, though unsuccessful, provided Sarah with a
revealing glance at those of her former neighbors who remained
behind enemy lines. An elderly widow whom Sarah discreetly
did not identify, except to pronounce her "one of the most
aristocratic old ladies in that section," saw a Union soldier chasing one of her chickens, with an infantry captain standing by,
watching the operation with amusement. The rooster ran under
the porch, and the soldier started crawling after it. At this point
the white-haired lady of the house emerged.

"If you don't come out from there I shall kill you," she told
the soldier firmly.

The young man, half under, half out, gave the elderly matron
a derisive look, and started crawling forward. Whereon the old
lady picked up a loose beam from beneath the house, and
whacked him across the base of the skull. When the captain, who
had refused to intervene, approached the soldier, he pronounced
the man dead. Having rightfully defended her property in wartime, the old lady was not even arrested.

Between the opposing lines before Atlanta, though the artil-

lery of both sides held the center of the stage, the fighting continued between skirmishers and pickets. Each night the Federals tried to move a few yards closer to the city, by digging new
trenches forward of those they had previously occupied, while
Confederate sharpshooters—tossing out fireballs of kerosene-
soaked cotton to illuminate the field—tried to hold them where
they were. Throughout the daytime, there was little or no movement, only burning summer heat and thirst and boredom. Men
risked death to raise awnings of brush and branches over their
trenches to protect them from the sun's rays.

Had Andy Neal, that quiet morning of August 10, raised his
head for a glimpse of the city of his youth? Or, like the fictional
hero of a later war, reached from the rim of his trench for a
passing butterfly? No one would ever know more than that a
Union marksman put a bullet through his temple. Andy was
buried, as were other casualties at the front, approximately
where he fell. If he were conscious long enough to think of it,
he must have drawn consolation from the fact that the battle flag
of the Marion Light Artillery survived him, due to his own
forethought.

Private Elisha Stockwell of Sherman's command found himself caught in a war of little progress and unlimited frustration.
Covering a week's activity, he wrote:

> We moved a little farther to the right and nearer town, and built
> good breastworks. . . . We just got them done when we were
> marched out and saw another regiment take our place. . . . We
> went farther to the right and built another line facing an open
> field with head logs on top to protect our heads. . . . A few days
> later we advanced across that field and built another line. We
> carried those head logs across the field to the new line by moon-
> light. The sharpshooters made it disagreeable in the daytime.

Skirmishing between the lines often took the form of individual, gladiatorial combats, witnessed by the opposing troops.
Wrote a Northern military correspondent:

> Like another Troy, the enemy fought outside their walls and
> intrenchments, and many an amusing combat took place, particu-
> larly between the skirmishers. I have often seen a rebel and a

Federal soldier making right for the same rifle-pit, their friends on both sides loudly cheering them on. As they would not have time to fight, they reserved their fire until they got into the pit, when woe betide the laggard for the other was sure to pop him as soon as he got into cover. Sometimes they got in together, and then came the tug of war; for they fought for possession with their bayonets and closed fists. In some cases, however, they made a truce, and took joint possession of it.

Improvised truces took place as they had along the Chattahoochee River. Firing was suspended while the men could barter coffee for tobacco, whiskey for Union army rations, setting up regular trading posts between the lines. When it came time to separate the men had often become so friendly that they warned each other when the firing resumed. "Look out, Yank," a Southern rifleman would shout, "we're goin' to shoot!" A Union soldier would obligingly raise his cap, on bayonet point, above the earthworks to provide a convenient target.

Strict observance of these rules, or understandings, was a matter of high principle with both sides. When a Confederate major found his troops fraternizing with the enemy he not only ordered them back to their trenches but commanded that they open fire on the Federals. The troops stood obstinately silent; not a gun was raised nor a trigger pulled. Whereupon the infuriated major seized a rifle from a nearby private, shot and wounded a Union soldier who had not thought it necessary to seek cover.

The Confederates were outraged at this breach of faith. "Sorry, Yanks, we couldn't help it!" they shouted in apology. That night, according to a Northern newspaper correspondent, "these men deserted into our lines, assigning as a reason, that they could not with honor serve any longer in any army that thus violated private truces. . . ." Coming from a Union source, the story of desertions may be open to some doubt.

There was no letup in the shelling of Atlanta. If anything, it increased in intensity as the month wore on, with Sherman instructing Thomas to "Keep the big guns going and damage Atlanta all that is possible." If Thomas ran out of ammunition, as he once complained, more was rushed forward to him. Joseph Semmes wrote to his wife Eo that the shells were falling at the rate of one a minute near his commissary; while Samuel Richards complained that he got little sleep, the bombardment continuing from dusk to dawn. Little Carrie Berry kept a record of three busy days, beginning with:

> August, 14. Sure enough we had shells in abundance last night. We expected every one would come through and hurt some of us but to our joy nothing on the lot was hurt. They have been throwing them at us all day today but they have not been dangerous. Papa has been at work all day making the cellar safe. Now we feel like we could stay at home in safety. I dislike to stay in the cellar so close but our soldiers have to stay in ditches.

The next morning, however, Carrie had reason to be less complacent. After breakfast she and her sister Zulette had been standing in the area between the house and dining room when "a very large shell filled with balls fell by the garden gate and bursted. The pieces flew in every direction. Two pieces went in the dining room. It made a very large hole in the garden and threw dirt all over the yard." And on the following day, "We had shells all night," she wrote. "There was a large piece came through Mama's room directly after we went to bed and fell on the little bed and I expect if we had been sleeping there some of us would have been hurt."

Lieutenant Jeremiah Huff, having received an uncomplaining letter from his wife, had deduced between the lines the danger that his family was in. Having requested and obtained a furlough from his regiment in Virginia, he rode into the battle zone of northern Georgia, dismounted, and crept, on foot and by night, through the Federal lines before Atlanta.

Once inside the besieged city, he succeeded in getting a government wagon in which to take Sarah and the rest of his family to Tanner's Church, ten miles south of Atlanta. They spent the night in the church, while Jeremiah, of necessity, started back to his command in north Virginia. The following morning the Huffs took prearranged shelter with Jeremiah's brother-in-law, Miles Penn of Conyers, later moving farther east to the home of relatives in Social Circle. For the time being, at least, their participation in Atlanta's agony was over.

Samuel Richards and his brother Jabez also contemplated moving their business to Macon, having suspended publication of *The Soldier's Friend* as soon as the siege began. "I got off militia duty," Richards wrote, "and we packed up the books in the store drawers, boxes, but changed our minds about sending it off as we preferred going to Augusta if we move the stock at all and Jabez is going first to see if a store can be obtained there. . . . The future is very dark and uncertain, truly a *sealed book* in our finite minds."

Corporal Sam Watkins left the fortifications with his company commander, Lieutenant John Whitaker, to visit one of the hospitals within the city, evidently out of curiosity. His curiosity led to a grim impression of army hospitals everywhere throughout the battle zone:

> Great God! I get sick when I think of the agony, and suffering, and sickening stench and odor of dead and dying; of wounds and sloughing sores, caused by the deadly gangrene; of the groaning and wailing . . . in the rear of the building I saw a pile of arms and legs, rotting and decomposing; and although I saw thousands of horrifying scenes during the war. . . . I recollect nothing with more horror than that pile of legs and arms that had been cut off our soldiers.

The doctors of Atlanta and the Army surgeons were working night and day to ease pain and to save lives. Yet the fate of the wounded was, in many cases, worse than death. There was a scarcity of drugs and anesthetics; sanitation under those overcrowded, improvised, emergency conditions was imperfect from necessity; a wounded arm or leg could be more quickly and surely treated by amputation, generally without an anesthetic, rather than by time-consuming methods that might save the limb. And infection and gangrene were common concomitants of amputations as they were to many open wounds.

Watkins was surprised to find among the patients one familiar face, that of James Galbraith, the private who had shouted "God have mercy on my soul!" as Cheatham's division advanced against the enemy in the Battle of Atlanta. Sam had thought that the elderly conscript, seemingly shot in two, was dead, and jocularly told him so. Then he made the mistake of asking Jim if he was seriously wounded. In reply,

> He only pulled down the blanket, that was all. I get sick when I think of it. The lower part of his body was hanging to the upper part by a shred, and all of his entrails were lying on the cot beside him, the bile and other excrements exuding from them, and they full of maggots. I replaced the blanket as tenderly as I could, and said, "Galbraith, goodbye." I then kissed him on his lips and forehead, and left.

He never expected to see Galbraith again, and didn't. Nor did Watkins ever visit another hospital throughout the remainder of the war.

Care of the wounded behind Union lines above Atlanta was no less forbidding. While conditions at the improvised field hospitals resembled torture chambers, those in the converted houses near the battlefield were little better. Wrote Captain George W. Pepper who visited a medical station in a farmhouse behind General Howard's lines:

> Six surgeons are in attendance. They receive and operate upon each case upon the instant. A wound is dressed in from two to 15 minutes. Amputations are performed in a trice, chloroform being administered. Pools of blood upon the floor are mixed up with the mud that is tracked in. The house's family dining table makes a good dissecting bench. Drawers from a bureau are laid upon the floor, bottoms up, for a couch to be spread. In a bed in one small room lay three terribly wounded men, side by side, the family bedding saturated with their blood. A lieutenant lies in a corner, dead—died before his wound could be dressed. A private sits upon a table, naked to the hips, a musket ball having passed through his body, from side to side, three inches below the armpits—he talks, is very pale and ghastly, but will live. Another sits on a chair, his leg cut off below the knee with a shell, as clean as with a knife. A Kentucky captain, shot through the thigh, is seized with a spasm of pain while being taken from the ambulance into the house. He catches the sleeve of his coat near the shoulder with his teeth and bites, as would a mad dog.

On August 18 Union commander in chief Ulysses Grant declared a ban on the exchange of prisoners, asserting that it could only prolong the war. To Atlanta, with little provision for prisoners, this presented one more problem. Those who were captured by Confederate cavalry, or in skirmishes before the city, were shipped to Macon or in greater numbers to the new stockade at Andersonville—an oblong of horror containing 34,000 men on less than 30 acres, with little food available and only an unreliable, polluted stream for drinking water.

Men died by the hundreds from thirst and hunger and disease. Perhaps predictably, considering the temper of the times, the Daily *Intelligencer* showed little compassion for the victims. Reporting that "during one of the intensely hot days last week more than 300 sick and wounded Yankees died at Andersonville," the editor added, "We thank heaven for such blessings." Enlarging on this theme, the paper reported that "To bury them side by side would require a trench 600 feet long, 7 feet wide and five feet deep. It would require 120 men to dig the graves . . . 200 carpenters to make boxes . . . 25 wagons to haul them." The funeral cortege would probably contain "0000000000 mourners."

To one man in the Confederate fortifications, such figures would have poignant meaning. He was Sergeant Thomas McCauley, formerly of a New York cavalry company, who had escaped from Andersonville with three companions by digging a sixty-five-foot tunnel. Captured and returned to the prison, his hands and feet manacled to heavy cannonballs, he cut himself loose with a hidden file and escaped again. Recaptured, and manacled to six other prisoners, he once more managed to break his bonds. This time he obtained a Confederate uniform and tried to make his way to Sherman's lines before Atlanta.

Briefly, McCauley's luck ran out. He was apprehended as a Confederate deserter, given a rifle, and placed on the inner defenses of the city with the difficult charge of firing at his compatriots. He tried to "desert" by sneaking through the open, southern extremity of the city, but was caught and returned to his post and threatened with execution if he left it. He did leave it, this time by taking his life in his hands and walking directly up the Marietta road and into Sherman's forward lines. By a miracle, his incredible story was accepted by Union officers—and McCauley at long last trained his Confederate-issue rifle on Atlanta's breastworks.

Other characters of dubious loyalty were not so fortunate. James L. Dunning, superintendent of the Atlanta Machine Company, being from Connecticut, was forced to surrender his business to native Georgians and was jailed on suspicion of treason. William Markham, proprietor with Lewis Scofield of the Atlanta Rolling Mill, also a New Englander, was attacked on the streets by a knife wielding patriot but managed to make good his escape. A Confederate soldier claimed to have seen a copy of *Uncle Tom's Cabin* in a local bookstore, and organized a mob to tar and feather the proprietor and confiscate his stock. The innocent bookseller was saved when the invading mob could find no copy of the book; the story had apparently been a fabrication.

The Federal spy, Milton Glass, continued to roam with relative freedom through Atlanta, but found little of proven importance to relay to his Union bosses. He noticed that a large work force of blacks was engaged in strengthening the entrenchments between Atlanta and East Point, and that "four large pieces of artillery" had been sent to the latter junction—apparently to forestall any attempted attack upon the railroad.

Included with these accurate but insignificant reports were some extraordinary bits of misinformation that Glass had obtained, perhaps with intended deception, from an orderly at Confederate headquarters. One was that Hood was preparing to launch another attack against Sherman's armies outside the fortifications. The other, even less credible, was that General Robert E. Lee was on his way from Virginia with 32,000 men, either to take over or assist in the defense of the Gate City.

The last report was dated August 18. It was, apparently, the secret agent's swan song. In the tradition of spies everywhere, he simply disappeared; and also characteristically, he left no clues or traces. Wilbur Kurtz, who studied the spies' wartime activities, recounts an interview with Union Major John G. Dunbar of the 19th Indiana Infantry, who during the approach to Atlanta was walking through a dense woods when he

. . . came upon the swinging body of a man, hanging by a halter
from the limb of a tree. Just a man in civilian clothes, and nothing
to explain the whys and wherefores. The major had seen quite a
bit of stirring service during the four years of the war, but this
spectacle in the lonely woods near Atlanta had remained in his
memory ever since. Of course, the man was not likely J. Milton
Glass, but who is there to say that for him there was no halter and
no lonely wood, and no apparent reason for anything?

Battered with field artillery since the third week in July, under heavy siege since August 9, Atlanta showed no signs of
yielding. The railroad to East Point, forking to the Alabama
border on the west and to Macon on the east, continued to bring
supplies into the city. Cleburne's and Bate's divisions still held
the ramparts protecting that essential lifeline. Though Sherman
kept Schofield's army opposite East Point, as a threat to those
defenses, one direct assault had already proved disastrous. And
he dared not move Schofield farther south to flank the Confederate line. To do so would take the Army of the Ohio too far from
the bulk of Sherman's forces stationed north and northwest of
Atlanta.

There seemed only one immediate alternative. Hood, Sher-
man believed, had made a serious error in sending General
Wheeler on a raiding expedition in north Georgia. It left the
Confederate commander without adequate cavalry support.
And it gave Sherman an opportunity to use his own cavalry in
a second attempt to sever Hood's railway lines below Atlanta.
The first attempt had failed, but largely due to Wheeler's inter-
ference. With Wheeler gone, the field was clear.

He selected for the mission one of the few cavalry commanders to whom he accorded some chance of success, General Hugh
Judson Kilpatrick. "I know that Kilpatrick is a hell of a damned
fool," he told an aide, "but I want just that sort of man to
command the cavalry on this expedition."

He relayed his instructions to General Schofield, Kilpatrick's
superior commander. Young Kil was to take his mounted division on a wide sweep to the west; then cutting eastward, would
destroy the East Point-Alabama railroad in the neighborhood of
Fairburn and continue on to sever the Macon railway line near

Jonesboro. "Tell Kilpatrick he cannot tear up too much track nor twist too much iron," he instructed Schofield. "It may save this army the necessity of making a long hazardous flank march."

In short, "Kill Cavalry" was "not to fight, but *work.* "

Predictably, Kilpatrick did the opposite. Though following the route prescribed, he spent most of his time chasing every Confederate uniform in sight, returning with glowing accounts of his success. He had put the railroads out of commission "for at least ten days," he told General Sherman the moment that he got back.

The words were scarcely out of his mouth when Sherman detected the whistle of trains approaching Atlanta from the south, over tracks the Confederates had easily repaired. Confirmed for good in his low opinion of cavalry, Sherman ordered Kilpatrick's division to dismount and man the trenches —the ultimate rebuke.

What now were the possibilities, if any?

Sherman knew he could not hold out forever, here before Atlanta. An army in a state of stalemate was a dying army. Whatever its strength in guns and troops, that strength was sapped by inactivity and waste of supplies. Moreover, Sherman was concerned about his own supply line stretching back to Tennessee. Wheeler's cavalry had broken it at several points below Chattanooga. These breaks could be repaired, and were; but the constant threat required releasing more units from the front to guard the Federal rear.

He was convinced that Hood would never abandon Atlanta unless somehow forced to do so; and the Confederate army was snugly ensconced behind miles of forts and rifle pits and breast-works. The alternative, then? For Sherman to withdraw his army from before Atlanta, and admit defeat? Unthinkable, but —he could not batter his head forever against immovable walls.

That night, in the last week of August, he called his generals into conference, placing a map on the table before them, moving his armies over its surface like figures on a chessboard. It was long after midnight when the conference broke up, ending with an acceptance of the facts and risks and possible defeats that lay before them, without any latitude of choice.

That evening Sherman warned Halleck by telegraph, "for some time you will hear little of us. . . ." For he had a plan in which his generals had concurred—a plan of which Joe Johnston would say, on hearing of it three days later, "It is Sherman's one mistake of the whole summer."

"Atlanta Is Ours!"

August twenty-sixth dawned as a day of deliverance.

The guns were silent; no shells had fallen since the night before. As far to the north and west as eye could see the parallel trenches which had harbored the besieging troops were empty. No smoke rose from the bivouacs beyond; no flags or tents, no glint of morning sun on steel. What had been the breeding ground of death by day and terror by night was devoid of any sign of life.

Gingerly, in cautious disbelief, the citizens emerged from their "gopher holes" and cellars to look with wondering eyes on the smokeless skies and cratered, silent streets. It seemed too good to be true. The enemy had gone! Where or why was, for the moment, unimportant. After weeks of tension and anxiety, the siege had been lifted; Sherman had withdrawn his army, presumably back across the Chattahoochee. Elated citizens savored the truth that Atlanta was theirs for keeps, rid forever of fear and hunger, danger and despair.

At his battery on the defense line Captain Key was puzzled by the sudden cease-fire and disappearance of the bluecoats. He didn't trust the enemy, especially one he could not see. He decided to "get the feel of them," or send over some shells to see if the Union batteries replied. When there was no response, Key assumed the enemy had shifted their position. Hearing firing from the west, he turned his guns in that direction, on the chance of catching the retreating forces. He had no way of knowing what he hit, but recorded with some satisfaction that "These loud mouthed gun wagons made the night hideous with their bass voices, and no doubt caused many bluecoats to fall in the cold embrace of death."

The same probing by artillery went on all down the line. Sam Watkins' regiment was awakened that morning by its own guns banging away at unseen targets from the breastworks, "scaring us almost to death." Grabbing their arms the men rushed to their battle stations, only to learn that the sudden barrage was a "feeler" to determine whether or not the enemy was still entrenched before Atlanta.

This much was determined: the entire front north of the city had been emptied of the enemy overnight. Watkins, however, found the evidence inconclusive. "It was impossible to tell what had happened, because those 'feelers' or shells that we sent over did not come back and report to us. We'd always heard that cannon balls were blind, and I suppose they could not see to find their way back."

By Saturday morning, August 27, with the Union batteries still silent and no sign of enemy activity before Atlanta, Hood was convinced that Sherman had withdrawn his troops and that the siege was lifted. This conviction was corroborated when a refugee woman tottered into Confederate headquarters to report that she had just come from behind the Union lines. She had been in search of food and been told that there was none to spare. The troops were folding their tents and loading their wagons, preparing evidently to evacuate their camp.

Hood had other confirmation. He knew that many of Sherman's troops had finished their terms of enlistment and were being mustered out. He had heard from prisoners and deserters that the Federal armies were short of food and ammunition, due to Wheeler's raid upon the railroads. Wheeler's own reports had indicated great success; the Western & Atlantic railway, Sherman's lifeline, had been heavily damaged if not cut beyond repair. Hood agreed with the cautious statement of his chief of staff, General Francis Shoup. Declared Shoup, "the prevailing impression of the scout reports this far indicated that the enemy were falling back across the Chattahoochee."

Hood was more positive. "Sherman has been starved out," he declared. "We have won!"

Though few of its citizens had ever doubted that Atlanta would survive the siege, there was a great upswelling of relief and joy throughout the city. Families returned to their homes with pride in their battle-scarred roofs and cratered yards. Men in Confederate gray were apotheosized as heroes. Bands played "Dixie" in the streets. People told one another they had known it all along: Hood had "Hoodwinked" General Sherman and repelled his army. With Atlanta still the strongly beating heart of the Confederacy, the war's end was in sight. Lincoln would be defeated in November; Europe would see the writing on the wall; the South had truly "made a nation."

Special trains arrived that weekend from Macon and Decatur bringing gaily clad ladies and musicians to help the city celebrate. There would be victory balls, and surely Mayor Calhoun would proclaim a day of ceremonial thanksgiving. That no such organized events took place did not diminish the lighthearted festive spirit that prevailed. Though the rumble of guns could still be heard occasionally to the west and south, it was attributed to Confederate troops pursuing the departing Federals.

Once again the church bells pealed their notes of peace on earth and that Sunday the doors opened to the largest congregations since the siege had started almost forty days before. In attendance were many officers and soldiers—Captain Key wore a brand new uniform for the occasion—glad to be worshipping under roofs that offered shelter from the rain. The messages from the pulpit expressed universal thanks to the Almighty for His intervention and the town's deliverance.

The relief was all the greater since, during the latter days of siege, the problem of food in Atlanta was becoming grim. In addition to supplying his troops, General Hood was obliged to issue 1500 rations a day to some four thousand members of impoverished families who would starve without them. Wood, too, was in short supply for cooking or in anticipation of the coming, colder weather. Almost all available wood had been used by the army for shacks and barracks or shoring up fortifications; and were any wood available in the southern outskirts of the city, there were no means or able-bodied men to deliver it to those in need.

Though the specter of famine was not as inescapable as it had been at Vicksburg, Atlantans were reported as living off "Confederate fricassee," a potpourri of kitchen scraps, leftovers, odds and ends, or "Sherman hash," a similar concoction even more lacking in nutritional value and allegedly containing everything but the Union general's britches. A strange and sudden absence of pets throughout the city, especially dogs and cats, led to speculation as to whether this was due to the lethal shelling or to the compelling hunger of their owners.

Samuel Richards had some doubts about the city's permanent salvation. "It was rumored," he wrote in his diary, "that the Federals were retreating and it is now known that they have deserted their camps around the city and are going *some*where but what is their design it is hard to tell. I fear that we have not yet got rid of them finally, but they have some other plan in view to molest and injure us. But in the meantime we can rest in security for a while, safe from shells."

The Maxwell Berry family felt it was safe to leave the Jacobs' cellar and return to their own home on Fairlie Street; Cousin Henry Beatty had called to assure them that Sherman's troops had withdrawn to Tennessee. There was much to do in the way of cleaning and straightening up the house which, in just five days, had been coated inside and out with the grime and dust of war. But for Carrie, sweeping up and dusting, it was a "delightful day. I feel so glad to get home and have no shells around us."

She started sorting out her clothes, getting things ready for school; and was overjoyed when Miss Fannie Holmes, her teacher, called to make sure that she would be in class on opening day. Indeed she would. "I am tired of staying at home," she wrote in her diary—a human reaction since, for Carrie, home had been for many weeks the four walls of a cellar.

Sam Richards, irked by still having to stand guard duty in the city, found an afternoon free to walk out Marietta Street with Sallie "to see the devastation caused by the bombardment, and truly that part of the city is badly cut up." Mollie Smith also hiked with friends down the once embattled Marietta road, scarred and pitted by a thousand shells, to the Federal breastworks three miles beyond the city. In an abandoned Federal camp they came upon an interesting structure in which "strips of planks had been nailed, ladder-fashion, in the tall pine trees, from which, with the aid of a spy glass, the men could see all over the city."

Souvenir hunters by the score began to forage over the deserted battleground, picking up everything from bent forks and bullet-pocked canteens to Union caps and castoff weapons. An editor of the *Intelligencer* salvaged a shell to stand on his desk in Macon as a memento of the war days. He made sure that it had been deactivated, aware that a Confederate soldier had tested a similar trophy by tapping gently on its snout, and had been blown to bits.

General Samuel French inspected the enemy entrenchments with a more professional, if jaundiced, eye:

> I found everything in their works horrible filthy and alive with "dog flies" to such an extent that our horses could not be managed. The clothing, new and old, was covered with vermin. My servant boys carried some jackets home that had to be buried. . . . I found the brick furnace where they made "hot shot" to fire day and night at intervals to burn the city. At first little "niggers" got their fingers burned picking them up to sell to the ordnance department.

Captain Key also surveyed on horseback the abandoned works "where I found that bowls, chairs, and ammunition boxes as well as other kinds were strewn so thickly that it was difficult to ride through them. The scales have turned in favor of the South and the Abolitionists are moving to the rear toward their own homes. Thank heaven for this and for the gallant soldiery who so nobly have fought against overpowering numbers."

At that moment of Confederate confidence, General Sherman, a mile from Atlanta's vital lifeline in the south, spoke to George Thomas seated on a horse beside him.

"I have Atlanta as certain as if it were in my hand," he said.

It had been a reckless, daring plan that Sherman had initiated five days previously, after Kilpatrick's raid had failed to isolate Atlanta. He had forewarned General Halleck of his purpose: "Since July 28th Hood has not attempted to meet us outside his parapets. In order to possess and destroy effectually his communications, I may have to leave a corps at the railroad bridge, well entrenched, and cut loose with the rest to make a circle of desolation around Atlanta."

General Thomas regarded the move as "extra-hazardous" since it meant breaking away from their base of supplies, but Sherman dismissed the objection. His troops would carry ten days' rations, and could forage for the ripening corn when that ran out. On the evening of the 25th he sent General Slocum's corps back to the Chattahoochee River to guard the railroad bridge—he would need the railroad when and if he took Atlanta; then led the rest of his army in a wide sweep west and south— to attack the railroads well beyond the limits of the fixed Confederate defenses. With Wheeler's cavalry raiding north of Marietta, there was little chance of Confederate reconnaissance detecting the maneuver.

South of Utoy Creek, Sherman divided his army into two attacking columns. Schofield would strike the Macon railroad near the little town of Rough and Ready; Howard with a larger force would undertake to capture Jonesboro, with Thomas' army supporting him as needed. These missions accomplished, all three armies would march upon Atlanta from the south.

Not until August 30 did Hood realize what was happening. A portion of the Union Army—he was uncertain of its strength —was threatening his southern flank. The West Point railway had been cut, meaning that the more important Macon railroad was in danger. His scouts informed him that the Union forces, two or three corps at best, were headed toward Jonesboro. He must nip this enemy effort in the bud.

Summoning Hardee to his house on Whitehall Street, Hood instructed that general to take two corps, those of Lee and Cleburne, to Jonesboro and check the Union advance before it crossed the Flint River west of the Macon railroad. The fate of Atlanta, Hood told his corps commander, rested on his shoulders. Hardee would have at his disposal some 24,000 troops to

counter the two or three Union corps, say 17,000 men, now
threatening that point. The rest of Hood's forces, Stewart's
corps and the Georgia militia, would remain in the fortifications
to guard the city.

When Hardee had left, Hood paced the floor of the high-
ceilinged room, mopping his brow nervously. He wondered if
he had made the right move. Atlanta was his first concern; he
did not want to strip her of defensive troops. Hardee would have
to settle things quickly at Jonesboro, see that the town was well
protected, then hurry back. He sent off a message in pursuit of
Hardee:

"You must not fail to attack the enemy as soon as you can get
your troops up."

It was the last telegram he would send. The following morning Sherman's forces cut the wires.

Once again Atlanta heard, on August thirty-first, the rumble
of cannon, this time from the south. General Schofield's Union
army had arrived at Rough and Ready to find the tiny town
defended by Confederate breastworks manned by dismounted
cavalry. In one massive charge the Federals boiled over the
earthworks and paused only long enough to regroup before
marching to the village. Before they had taken full possession of
the town, they heard the whistle of an incoming locomotive, and
saw what would surely be the last train from Atlanta, racing
south. After it had passed, the troops investing Rough and
Ready began tearing up the rails.

"You must thank God," Joe Semmes wrote to Eo, "for preserving me from a most horrible death or most shocking
wounds." For his had been the passing train, carrying supplies
to Hardee's forces marching down to Jonesboro. The engine had
become uncoupled eight miles from its destination, "leaving no
force between the enemy and my train except a small number
of pickets . . . the enemy was pressing toward the railroad
. . . my capture was inevitable."

I prepared for the worst, sent off my most valuable and important public papers by passing horsemen, tore up others (and all
your dear letters which I treasure so much) and prepared piles of
brush and light wood to burn the train of 18 heavy loaded cars to

prevent the enemy from using the stores, as soon as they should get in sight. When they were within 400 yards of me a train appeared. I made the engineman couple my train to his and I was moved off just 15 minutes before the enemy struck the road in force.

Semmes reached Jonesboro under a "shower of shot and shell" to find the expected battle raging. He remained with his train, uninjured, though "men were killed and wounded all around it." Hardee had arrived late, about midafternoon, to find that Howard's forces had already crossed the Flint River (strangely the bridges had been left intact) and were massing a mile from town. Following instructions he attacked at once, not giving his troops time to recover from their forced march from Atlanta.

It was a slipshod, uncoordinated assault with poor communication between Lee and Hardee. As at Ezra Church, the different divisions attacked separately, without regard to timing, hurling themselves against the outnumbered but well-entrenched Federals. The slaughter was frightful. From 1500 to 2,000 Confederates fell before the steady Union musket fire, against 300 losses among Howard's men. General William B. Hazen, whose brigade bore the brunt of the attack, reported that "the dead and wounded were actually piled on top of one another."

"The attack was fierce," noted Union General Jacob Cox, "but neither in weight nor persistency did it seem to equal the former efforts of the Confederate infantry," while Hazen concluded, "They seem to know they are beaten and nothing they can do can alter the results." Lee himself was forced to pronounce the attack "a failure, with the loss to our corps of about 1,300 men. . . ."

Though a few individual units achieved brief success in piercing the Federal lines, the heart had gone out of many of the Southern troops. Some refused to march to the attack. One soldier serving with Cleburne's division shared the prevailing feeling that "all was against us. . . ."

The soldiers distrusted everything. They were broken down with their long days' hard marching—were almost dead with hunger and fatigue. Every one was taking his own course, and wishing and praying to be captured. Hard and senseless marching, with little sleep, half rations, and lice, had made their lives a misery. . . . It was too much for human endurance. Every private soldier knew that such things as this could not last. . . . There was no hope in the future for them.

At dusk, Lee and Cleburne withdrew their forces to the outskirts of Jonesboro, and prepared to dig in for the night.

In Atlanta, Hood received word that Schofield had cut the railway line at Rough and Ready. He concluded that Sherman was planning to attack Atlanta from the south. He had had no word from Hardee, since the telegraph wires had been cut, and presumed that Jonesboro was secure. He sent a courier to General Hardee. Lee's corps must return at once to help defend the city.

There was no quick way that Hardee could protest the move. The real danger, the Confederate general knew, was here—not back in Atlanta. He needed all the reinforcement he could get; but instead was being ordered to release an entire corps for duty elsewhere. So be it. That evening Lee's divisions started trudging back toward Atlanta by a roundabout route east of the Federal held railway—leaving Hardee and Cleburne to face, alone, six full-strength corps of Sherman's army.

Hood had guessed wrong. Sherman's immediate target was not Atlanta. As Lee's corps returned to that city, Sherman ordered Schofield down from Rough and Ready to join the massive assault on Hardee's isolated troops at Jonesboro. He timed his attack for shortly after noon, September 1, and meanwhile sent General Howard to tear up the railway tracks six miles below the town, thus cutting off Hardee's possible escape route.

That first September morning was one of fatalistic waiting for the trapped Confederates. The outlook was bleak, as Sam Watkins summarized:

> Stewart's corps was at Atlanta, Lee's corps was between Atlanta and Jonesboro, and Hardee's corps, then numbering not more than five thousand men—because the woods and roads were full of straggling soldiers, who were not in the fight—was face to face with the whole Yankee army, and he was compelled to flee, fight, or surrender. This was the position and condition of the grand

Army of Tennessee on this memorable occasion.

Little happened in the early morning hours except for occasional artillery bombardment from the Union lines. Most of the fire fell short, and the Confederates were wryly amused by the ricocheting cannon balls that bounced and rolled towards them harmlessly. But some proved deadly. A soldier tried to stop one with his foot and it carried his leg off. Another playfully attempted to catch one like a centerfielder, and was instantly killed. A companion of Watkins, Nathan Shephard, was struck by a ricocheting ball and hurled twenty feet, breaking his ribs and dislocating his shoulder.

By noon, when the troops tried to eat a hasty lunch, the firing had grown more accurate. Sam Watkins recorded:

We were sopping up gravy with some cold corn bread when the captain shouted, "Look out, Sam!" I just turned my head, and in turning the cannon ball knocked my hat off, and striking Lieutenant Whittaker full in the side of the head, carried away the whole of the skull part, leaving only the face. His brains fell in the plate from which we were sopping, and his head fell in my lap, deluging my face and clothes with his blood. Poor fellow. . . . His spirit went to his God that morning. . . . The cannon ball did not go twenty yards after accomplishing its work of death.

Discovering that Lee had disappeared, Sherman concentrated on surrounding Jonesboro and forcing Hardee to choose between annihilation and surrender. No need for a costly assault on Hardee's breastworks. He deployed his troops around three sides of the city awaiting only one corps under David S. Stanley, on its way from Rough and Ready, to close the eastern gap. When Stanley failed to arrive by late afternoon Sherman could afford to wait no longer. The attack was launched.

"It was a glorious battle!" wrote Major James Austin Connolly with Thomas' army. "Generals, Colonels, Majors, Captains and privates, all had to go forward together over that open field, facing and drawing nearer to death at every step we took, our horses crazy, frantic with the howling shells, the rattling of canister and the whistling of bullets, ourselves delirious with the wild excitement of the moment, and thinking only of getting over those breastworks—great volleys of canister shot sweeping through our lines making huge gaps.

"But the bluecoated boys filled the gaps and still rushed forward right into the jaws of death—we left hundreds of bleeding comrades behind us at every step, but not one instant did that line hesitate—it moved steadily forward to the enemy's work—over the works with a shout—over the cannon—over the Rebels, and then commenced stern work with the bayonet. . . ."

Confederate Captain Tom Key lost all but twelve men of his battery to "the overwhelming forces of the Yankees" who swept over the Southern lines regardless of murderous artillery fire. Key himself escaped capture to join another battery still operating further in the rear; he concluded, "The defense of the Confederates was noble, but they were too weak to contend against such numbers."

It was a costly victory for the Federals. In contrast to the previous day, when Hardee's losses heavily outweighed Sherman's, the casualty figures were approximately reversed. But even among the Union dead and dying in the closing moments of the battle, Major Connolly found himself "as happy as a mortal is ever permitted to be. . . .

> I could have lain down on that blood-stained grass, amid the dying and the dead and wept with excess of joy. I have no language to express the rapture one feels in the moment of victory, but I do know at such a moment one feels as if the joy were worth risking a hundred lives to attain it. Men at home will read of the battle . . . but they can never feel as we felt, standing there quivering with excitement, amid the smoke and blood, and fresh horrors and grand trophies of that battlefield. . . .

As Hardee drew his forces back into Jonesboro, behind hastily constructed earthworks, Sherman called off hostilities at dusk. He saw no need to press his advantage, at the cost of further casualties. He had Hardee cornered. A mass attack would "destroy our enemy" at dawn. But Hardee would not wait for that attack. Under cover of darkness he slipped out of the city by its unobstructed eastern flank and led his weary troops to Lovejoy Station six miles farther down the railway.

The following morning Sherman entered Jonesboro, the band playing "Hail, Columbia," to find the city a charnel house of horrors. Virtually nothing was left intact. The few large homes and churches offering even partial shelter had been converted into hospitals, but even these had been left unattended in the precipitate retreat. Piles of dead from both sides lay unburied on the city's fringes. In the sweltering heat of a nearby pine grove, parallel rows of trenches, four feet deep, were dug. Into these the bodies were piled like cordwood and covered with earth, with only a single, unidentifying wooden cross erected to mark the resting place of some four thousand unsung heroes.

In Atlanta, Hood learned that Hardee had failed to dislodge the Federal troops from the Macon railroad at Jonesboro. "The general attack," he wrote, "must have been rather feeble, as the loss incurred was only fourteen hundred (1400) in killed and wounded." Again he was measuring performance in terms of casualties suffered. He blamed Hardee for the loss of the Macon railroad which "necessitated the evacuation of Atlanta at the earliest hour possible," and sent word to Lee to reverse his march and link up with Hardee at Lovejoy Station

Meanwhile Hood gave orders to the ordnance department to prepare all trains to move supplies and ammunition from Atlanta. He himself with Stewart's corps and the Georgia Militia would proceed to Lovejoy Station because, as he reported, "the presence of thirty-four thousand (34,000) Federal prisoners at Andersonville rendered it absolutely incumbent to place the Army between Sherman and that point."

Just as Hood shifted the blame to Hardee for rendering Atlanta untenable, so he attributed the prisoners at Andersonville as his reason for withdrawing from the city. It was not retreat on his part, it was strategy—required by circumstance not of his creation. Had Hardee held the enemy at Jonesboro, he, Hood, would have advanced against Slocum north of the city, repossessed the Western & Atlantic railroad, and trapped the Federal commander just as he himself was trapped. It was a comforting bit of hindsight.

That first day of September, which had dawned in Atlanta as a day of high hopes, ended in a twilight of despair. People awoke to rumors that the Battle of Jonesboro had been a glorious Confederate victory. The Union troops had been repulsed in their last desperate effort to cripple the city from the south. Atlanta was still secure. The rather unusual troop movements in the streets suggested that Hood was planning to pursue the fleeing Federals and was readying the supply trains for that purpose.

Then came the trickle of deserters seeking refuge in the city, bringing stories of disaster on the southern front. Roving bands of stragglers and unfamiliar blacks appeared from nowhere, loitering along the streets like vultures hovering around a corpse. Wrote Wallace Reed:

> Throughout the day troops were moving in every direction and unusual bustle and activity prevailed. The citizens noticed that they were no longer halted and made to show their papers on the streets. Crowds of strange negroes also made their appearance but they acted with great caution, and spent most of their time in cellars and houses that had been abandoned by their owners. Something was up; but the citizens could not tell what was coming. They could not believe that the city was to be given up. Their idea was that the Confederate forces were being massed for another battle.

Samuel Richards continued the story in his diary:

> This was a day of terror and a night of dread. About noon came the tidings of a severe fight on the Macon RR and that our forces were worsted and the city was to be evacuated at once. Then began a scramble among the inhabitants thereof to get away— others to procure supplies of food for their families. If there had been any doubt of the fact that Atlanta was about to be given up it would have been removed when they saw the depots of Government grain and food thrown open and the contents distributed among the citizens free gratis by the sackful and the cartload. The RR cars and engines were all run up to one place in order to be fired just as the army left. Five locomotives and 85 cars, cousin Bill told me were to be burned. Mr. West told me that the militia were ordered to be on hand to go out with the army, so I thought I would resign, as I was not bound to go.

In the fortifications of Atlanta, Stewart's corps and the Georgia militia prepared to evacuate the city. It was an orderly but disheartening procedure. In the steaming heat the troops waited for the final order. "And before noon," wrote General Samuel French, "the order came. I became the rear guard. There is confusion in the city and some of the soldiers in the town are drunk. Common sense is wanted. The five heavy guns that I had ordered to be spiked by the rear guard at 11 P.M. were burned by order of the Chief of Ordnance at 5 P.M., a proclamation to the enemy in my front line that we were evacuating the place."

Major Charles W. Hubner of the telegraph squad ordered his men to pack up their equipment; they were leaving. He noticed that "the streets were filled with hurrying men, crying women, and children." There was little authority left in the city, no policing of the streets, although Brigadier General Ferguson had stationed his mounted troops on Marietta Street with the cavalier idea of resisting to the last man any Federal bluecoats that dared to enter his domain.

At dusk the Confederate troops began withdrawing through Atlanta, down the long length of Peachtree Street to the McDonough Road and on toward the south, weary of body and sick of heart. No bands played. No citizens crowded their windows to wish them Godspeed. Their tattered flags were furled, their bugles silent. These were truly Stephen Vicent Benét's "soldiers of retreat . . . beneath a fading star."

They had known nothing but retreat since leaving Dalton early in May. But at that time in the distant past each withdrawal was accompanied by hope sustained, for "Uncle Joe" knew what he was doing. They had been luring Sherman to that day of reckoning before Atlanta when the Union General, exhausted by a running battle of attrition, far from his base of supplies, would be overwhelmed and annihilated by a glorious Confederate army charging from the city's walls.

But that day had never come. Instead had come Johnston's removal, General Hood's devil-may-care recklessness, and four battles around Atlanta that had left twelve thousand of their dead in shallow graves around the city. As they trudged south through the dusk, the woebegone army chanted the ballad that best expressed the heartbreak and frustrations of the war:

We loved each other then, Lorena,
More than we ever dared tell;
But what we might have been, Lorena,
Had but our loving prospered well . . .

A hundred months have passed, Lorena,
Since last I held that hand in mine;
And felt the pulse beat fast, Lorena,
Tho' mine beat faster far than thine . . .

But then, 'tis past—the years are gone,
I'll not call up their shadowy forms;
I'll say to them, "Lost years, sleep on!
Sleep on! nor heed life's pelting storm."

That night the citizens of Atlanta were awakened from their troubled sleep by the most terrible bombardment that the city had as yet experienced, this time of Confederate creation. General Hood, irked that the ordnance train had not left Atlanta before the railroads had been severed—"contrary to my specific commands"—had ordered that nothing be left in the city to comfort or aid the enemy. All government stores, munitions, and immovable equipment, including the munitions train and locomotives, must be put to the torch or dynamited.

Mary Rawson, startled out of her sleep by the unearthly sound of the explosion rushed to her window to witness

a most beautiful spectacle. . . . The heavens were in a perfect glow while the atmosphere seemed full of flaming rockets, crash follows crash and the swift moving locomotives were rent in pieces and the never tiring metallic horse lay powerless while the sparks filled the air with innumerable spangles. The crashing had scarcely ceased when our attention was called in another direction by a bright light which proved to be the burning of some more Government provisions.

Nobody knew for certain, even Hood himself, precisely how many locomotives and cars of ammunition and supplies had gone up in flames and dynamite—perhaps ten locomotives and more than eighty cars. The military authorities had taken the precaution of clearing all buildings for a quarter of a mile around, and wisely so. The structures were later reported as "either torn to pieces or perforated with hundreds of holes by fragments of the shells."

The searing flames, the constant thunder of the explosions, were, according to Wallace Reed, "more terrible than the greatest battle ever fought." It was as if the entire city were in flames, doomed by a merciless, invading foe. Using his own figures for damage done, Reed chronicled the scene:

> The infernal din of the exploding shells sent a thrill of alarm through the city. Many believed at first that the Federals were coming in, and that a desperate battle was going on in the streets. It took five long hours to blow up the seventy carloads of ammunition. The flames shot up to a tremendous height, and the exploding missiles scattered their red hot fragments right and left. The very earth trembled as if in the throes of a mighty earthquake. The houses rocked like cradles, and on every hand was heard the shattering of window glass and the fall of plastering and loose bricks. Thousands of people flocked to high places and watched with breathless excitement the volcanic scene on the Georgia Railroad.

In nearby Decatur the effect was equally electric and alarming. It seemed like an earthquake or some natural disaster. "The angry, bellowing sound," wrote Mary Gay, "rises in deafening grandeur, and reverberates along the far-off valleys and distant hilltops. What is it? This mighty thunder that never ceases? The earth is ablaze—what can it be?"

Mary's half-brother, Tommy Stokes, was with them on sick leave from his regiment. Perhaps it was his shocked expression that supplied them with the answer they could not believe. Atlanta was being evacuated and laid waste in anticipation of the enemy's arrival.

"Dumbfounded we stood, trying to realize the crushing fact. Woman's heart could bear no more in silence, and a wail over departed hopes mingled with the angry sounds without.

"Impelled by a stern resolve, and a spirit like to that of martyred saints, our brother said:

" 'This is no place for me. I must go.' "

"As he walked away from his sobbing mother, through the

war illumined village, I never beheld mortal man so handsome, so heroically grand." Mary wondered if she would ever see Tommy again in this crumbling world.

Twenty miles to the south, in his camp two miles northwest of Jonesboro, Sherman waited for news from Slocum on the northern reaches of Atlanta. Hood would have heard of the Confederate defeat by now. Would he try to quit Atlanta without a battle? Or, knowing of the Union army's absence in the south, would the Confederates launch an attack on the isolated troops of General Slocum and try to regain the Chattanooga railroad—which might enable them to hang on to the city for a while, even, possibly, reverse the situation and put Sherman's troops on the defensive?

He sent a courier to Slocum, instructing the general to probe the enemy's defenses, see if the time was ripe to force an entry into the city. An hour later his keen ear caught the sound of an explosion, then another, until blast after blast echoed down the valley, interspersed with what sounded like sharp musket fire. He strode to the nearest farmhouse and summoned the owner to the door.

Had the farmer ever heard a sound like that before, from the direction of Atlanta?

Yes, the man told him. It sounded like that when there had been fighting around the city, several times in recent days.

What then? Had Slocum attacked? Or been attacked by Hood?

Sherman would wait, before jumping to conclusions. He instructed Thomas to hold up on further operations for the day. "Until we hear from Atlanta the exact truth. I do not care about your pushing your men against breastworks. Destroy the railroad well up to your lines; keep skirmishers well up, and hold your troops in hand for anything that may turn up. As soon as I know positively that our troops are in Atlanta I will determine what to do. . . ."

Riddled with sleeplessness he tossed pine cones into the fire to keep it flaming, listened to the sound of the explosions twenty-six miles to the north, and waited until dawn when he heard the "wild hallooing and joyous laughter" of the men awakened by a message just received and relayed by General

Thomas to the troops. The rejoicing told Sherman all he needed to know. It was early morning, but he could sleep now.

At the White House in Washington there had been little sleep for many nights for President Lincoln. For four weeks he had waited hopefully for word from General Sherman—ever since early August when, with the Union troops at Atlanta's gates, the Northern papers had falsely reported the downfall of that city. But Atlanta had endured, and in the political firmament the President's star had waned in the twilight of public disapproval. The people had wanted a victory; they had not got it. Nor had he—at a time when his future and that of the Union depended upon victory.

The last week in August he had composed a memorandum to the Congress. A brief message, for there was little he could add to salve the sting:

> This morning, as for some days past, it seems exceedingly probable that this administration will not be reelected.
>
> Then it will be my duty to so cooperate with the President-elect as to save the Union between the election and the inauguration; as he will have secured his election on such ground that he cannot save it afterward.

He was half asleep at his White House desk on Friday evening, September 2, when a knock on the door was followed by the entrance of his chief of staff. General Halleck handed the President a message just arrived from General Sherman. The first six words told him that a nation's fate had been decided.

"Atlanta is ours and fairly won."

Northern cities rocked to the booming of 100-gun salutes in celebration of the city's fall. Congress and the public agreed with the encomium of General Grant that Sherman "had accomplished the most gigantic undertaking given any general in the war." To Sherman's disgust, Democratic convention delegates proposed his name for the presidency ("if forced to choose, I would prefer the penitentiary," said he).

President Lincoln decreed a day of Thanksgiving for Atlanta's capture, meanwhile tendering his own and the nation's gratitude to:

. . . Major-General William T. Sherman and the gallant officers and men of his command before Atlanta, for the distinguished ability, courage and perseverance displayed in the campaign in Georgia, which, under Divine favor, has resulted in the capture of the City of Atlanta. The marches, battles and sieges, and other military operations that have signalized the campaign, must render it famous in the annals of war, and have entitled those who have participated therein to the applause and thanks of the nation.

18

The Dispossessed

The news spread over the heartland of the South like tolling bells from hollow, burned out steeples. In her diary, Mary Boykin Chesnut wrote:

> Atlanta is gone.
> Well, that agony is over.
> Like David, when the child was dead,
> I will get up from my knees,
> Will wash my face and comb my hair . . .
> The end has come,
> No doubt of the fact.
> Since Atlanta, I have felt as if
> All were dead within me,
> Forever.

Mary ran the sentences together; the content of her diary was not written as blank verse. But it might have been. In parts, it reads as if it should have been. So perhaps the license is allowable.

For the Federal troops of Major General Henry W. Slocum, the morning of September second would be long remembered.

Their camp illuminated by Atlanta's flames, the ashes of the exploding city coating their bedrolls with a powdery dust, the soldiers had been kept awake throughout the night. But they welcomed the dawn with a freshness of spirit that no slumber could provide. The noise, the flames, the booming explosions had told them that Atlanta, the Gate City of the South, the Pride of the Confederacy, was theirs at last. They had only to march in and claim the prize.

Reveille sounded, and after the quickest of breakfasts the corps was on its way, Brigadier General William Ward's division in the lead. "For us it was a glorious morning," wrote Major Stephen Pierson serving under Ward, "just how glorious those who were not marching with us cannot fully comprehend. . . ."

> It meant the end of the campaign of more than a hundred days of almost continuous fighting, upon each one of which, somewhere along those lines, could have been heard the sounds of war, the sharp crack of the rifle of the outpost, the rattle of the skirmish, or the roar of a full line of battle; the end of a campaign of more than a hundred miles of marching, maneuvering, struggling, scarcely one of which was made unopposed; the end of a campaign crowned with victory and honor for the one, closed by defeat, without dishonor, for the other. The end of a campaign fought to a finish by antagonists worthy of each other . . .

As they neared the city Pierson turned in the saddle to look back upon the regiment. "A fine and hardy lot of men they were; not an ounce of superfluous flesh upon any one of them; lean-visaged, bright-eyed, quick of step, power and vigor; joy and triumph all over them and their every movement. Schooled, trained, disciplined, hammered in the fiery College of War."

Atlantans, bleary-eyed after a night of sleeplessness beneath the fiery rain of exploding ammunition, awoke to a dawn of apprehension. The city was still enveloped in the acrid smell and lingering smoke through which the early sun shone bright red. "In the dread silence of that memorable morning," Wallace Reed observed, "ten thousand helpless people looked into each others' faces for some faint sign of hope and encouragement, but found none."

Remnants of Confederate cavalry were leaving in the wake of generals Hood and Stewart, who had slipped out of Atlanta the night before to join the rest of the army at Lovejoy Station. They, too, offered little comfort or encouragement. Sherman's troops, the cavalrymen said, were coming down the Marietta road, the soldiers drunk and uncontrollable, intent upon wreaking their vengeance on the population regardless of age or sex. Barely pausing to make this pronouncement they spurred their horses and fled the city.

Then came the hours of intolerable waiting. Children were herded into their houses behind closed and shuttered windows. War widows fingered kitchen knives and muskets and wondered if they would be able to use them, against the enemy or against themselves if dishonor threatened. Family silver was packed and stored in cellars and attics. Old men with muskets on their laps sat in their rockers on the porch in a feeble posture of defiance. Most of the slaves had disappeared, and the few who remained began to wonder who their masters were, and whether the Yankee devils might not be worse than their familiar owners.

Some housewives who had learned to remain indoors during this period of uncertainty, if not anarchy, were unaware that the city had been surrendered and the enemy was in possession. One woman, who saw two soldiers in nondescript jackets helping themselves to the produce of her garden, attempted unsuccessfully to order them off.

"You scamps!" she cried indignantly. "You're worse than the Yanks!"

"Madam," said one of the soldiers politely. "We are Yanks."

The ruined, smoldering center of the city was filled with bands of looters ransacking the shattered stores for anything remaining. They plundered the vacant buildings and abandoned homes, joined by a ragged crowd of men and women, even children, intent on getting their share of the dwindling wartime loot. "Every one has been trying to get all they could before the Federals come in the morning," Carrie Berry dutifully recorded. "They have been running with sacks of meal, salt, and tobacco. They did act ridiculous breaking open stores and robbing them."

Atlanta, hovering between two flags, was in a state of anarchy.

The city was without a government, without military or police protection. People of known Union sympathies looked forward to the approaching Federals, meanwhile apprehensive of the city's last extremes of violence. Mayor Calhoun, aware of his responsibilities but unsupported by the normal complement of government officials, had more reason to worry than anyone. Possibly, he thought, the Union troops could restore some order, but only if they were not angered by popular resistance.

He trudged up Marietta Street to consult with cavalry General Ferguson who had formed a line of defense across that roadway to resist the vanguard of the enemy's invasion forces. He requested Ferguson to withdraw his troops on the grounds that such resistance would not only be futile, but might incite the Federals to unintended violence and bring otherwise unwarranted reprisals and destruction to the city. Ferguson denied the request; his orders were to defend Atlanta to the last, and he would do so. But he later reconsidered, on what basis no one knew, and agreed that there should be no battle in the city. He was taking his brigade south to join the rest of Hood's army at Lovejoy Station.

When he was certain of Ferguson's departure with the reluctant cavalry, Calhoun undertook the most painful mission of his career, the formal surrender of Atlanta to save its people and what remained of property from violence. He led a mounted group of influential citizens, unarmed and carrying a white flag, up the Marietta road in search of General Sherman, uncertain of their reception, unaware of Sherman's whereabouts. Between houses reduced to splintered timber by the shells, over the torn-up roadway littered with debris, they made their way with difficulty.

"In a short time," Wallace Reed recorded, "the dismantled breastworks were reached. They were entirely deserted, and, with the exception of a spiked cannon here and there, no traces of recent occupation were left. A peaceful quiet brooded over the red redoubts and the empty trenches, and a bird, perched upon one of the big siege guns, looked inquisitively at the horsemen, and after a few prefatory flirts and twitters, poured forth a flood of silver notes—a song of welcome—a jubilee carol of peace."

Beyond the red clay fortresses, over the fragments of army wagons and caissons, with eyes averted from the skulls and bones that gleamed like so many white horrors in the fierce sunlight, the little band rode on. They passed the rifle-pits and entrenchments of the enemy. Not a human being, not a living thing, was in sight. Two, three, four miles, and not a sign of the enemy.

Finally they met a squad of United States infantry in widely spaced formation, gingerly creeping toward the city. The mayor asked the captain in charge where he might find General Sherman. He was told that Sherman was twenty miles to the south, near Jonesboro; that General Henry W. Slocum now at the Chattahoochee River bridge would be in command at Atlanta; and that Colonel John Coburn was his immediate subordinate. Calhoun talked with Coburn who now joined the group, and appealed for the safety of his citizens and their possessions. Coburn assured him:

"We do not come to make war upon non-combatants or on private property; both shall be protected and respected by us."

Coburn then asked the mayor what resisting forces still remained within Atlanta. Calhoun assured him he would meet with no resistance; that he could march in and possess the city any time he chose. The colonel asked for more binding assurance, in short a written surrender, to be addressed to division commander William Ward. Calhoun tore a page from his pocket notebook and drafted a note that would be bitterly enshrined in history:

> Atlanta, Ga., September 2, 1864
>
> Brigadier-General Ward,
> Comdg. Third Division, Twentieth Corps:
> Sir: The fortune of war has placed Atlanta in your hands. As mayor of the city I ask protection of non-combatants and private property.
>
> James M. Calhoun,
> Mayor of Atlanta.

There was no official reply; perhaps Calhoun did not expect one. But within the year he regretted not having insisted on some written assurance, at least from Colonel Coburn, regarding the latter's promise to protect civilians and their property. It had not seemed important at the time, but in July of the following year he wrote, "I will always regret my failure to give Gen'l Sherman notice of his promise of protection. . . ."

Shortly after noon the occupying forces began entering the city. Marietta Street was a ribbon of blue as far as the eye could see, as regiment after regiment stepped smartly to the tunes of "Yankee Doodle" and "Battle Hymn of the Republic." Atlantans witnessed this victory parade with mixed emotions. It marked for them the end of the war along with the months of unremitting tension. But what did these foreign vandals have in store for them? Some gently taunted the invaders, a few left their Confederate flags displayed, and one or two daring individuals whistled, "Dixie."

But there was no disorder, no resistance, and no violence. The bells of Wesley Chapel pealed and, with that signal, the Stars and Stripes were hoisted over the city hall. Wrote the Reverend G. S. Bradley, Union army chaplain, "As the Old Flag caught the breeze from the spire of the Court House, such a cheer went up as only a conquering army, flushed with victory, can give. Commencing in the Gate City, it rings out loud and long as it spreads from regiment to regiment . . . alas! in this hour of the Nation's rejoicing, thousands of happy hearthstones are made desolate and places that knew our brave boys shall know them no more."

While most of the troops were impressed and astonished by the damage their shells had wrought in the city, declaring that they did not see how any one could have lived through such wholesale destruction, some were moved by general compassion for the beleaguered occupants, as was army chaplain James Comfort Patten on reaching the fortifications of Atlanta. "Here," he noted, "I saw the most pitiful sight I have ever witnessed. A young looking woman was at work by the roadside skinning a cow that had been killed and a little girl some six or seven years old had a piece of the raw bloody meat in both hands devouring it with the eagerness of a starving dog. I could see the leaders in this thing starve, but the poor children . . ."

Soon army supply wagons started rolling through the city from the railroad in the north, and stores and depots sprang up in the vacant offices and ruined buildings. The soldiers were billeted around the town in tents, on the fair grounds, in the state square, in the vacant yards of private but abandoned houses. The officers looked over the better homes, debating which one they would choose for quarters. Some of the churches were used for storage depots and for stabling horses, though Father Thomas O'Reilly vigorously defended the Immaculate Conception Church from such abuse.

In general the blue-coated soldiers, from whom the worst had been expected, behaved pretty well. They took liberties with apple orchards, strawberry beds, grape arbors, and the like, and sometimes demanded food at fragrant kitchen windows. A Federal officer warned Mrs. Perkerson to keep her chickens out of sight; a large body of soldiers was coming that way. "And they did come," wrote Lizzie, just as the family was preparing Sunday dinner.

> . . . they took pretty well all the chickens, all the bee gums and pretty near all our cooking vessels. We were cooking dinner in the kitchen and they took dinner, pots and all. All we saved is what we snatched from them and brought into the house. They didn't come in. I suppose several of the officers being on the porch all the while restrained them some.

In her diary Carrie Berry noted for September 2: "About twelve o'clock there were a few federals came in. They were picketed. In about an hour the cavalry came dashing in. We were all frightened. We were afraid they were going to treat us badly. It was not long till the Infantry came in. They were orderly and behaved very well. I think I shall like the Yankees very well."

The next day, Carrie's composure showed no signs of being ruffled. "The soldiers have been coming in all day. I went up to Auntie's this morning and she said that she had a yankee officer to spend the night with her. We have not seen much of them. Only two of them have been here to beg something to eat." And on September 4: "Another long and lonesome Sunday. How I wish we could have Church and Sunday School. We have been looking at the soldiers all day. They have come in by the thousands. They were playing bands and they seemed to be rejoiced. It has not seemed like Sunday."

Sam Richards, initially hopeful, became disillusioned by the troops' behavior, noting:

The private homes were not molested by the soldiers and I was therefore very much surprised when I went down town to see armsful and baskets full of books and wallpaper going up the street in a continuous stream from our store and when I reached the store, the scene would have required the pencil of a Hogarth to portray. Yankees, men, women, children and niggers were crowded into the store each one scrambling to get something to carry away, regardless, apparently, whether it was anything they needed, and still more heedless of the fact that they were stealing!

Such a state of utter confusion and disorder as presented itself to my eyes then, I little dreamed of two hours before when I left it all quiet and, as I thought, safe. The soldiers in their mad hunt for tobacco had probably broken open the door and the rabble had then "Pitched in" thinking it was a "free fight." At first I was so dismayed that I almost resolved to let them finish it, but finally I got them out and stood guard until after dark when I left it to its chances until morning, as I was very sleepy.

Atlantans had not felt, as yet, the crunch of the oppressor's heel. They had heard and believed the worst of Sherman, that he was a tyrant born of Satan, but for the first few days Mary Rawson, among others, found the occupation "a relief. I had expected them to enter in disorder, exulting loudly in the success of their enterprise," Mary wrote, but added: "Atlanta was taken possession of quietly. . . ."

The city throbbed to the strains of martial music, Mary noted, and the streets were "filled with cavalry and infantry, pack mules and army wagons and cattle crowded promiscuously together. . . . The musicians all riding on white horses . . . broke into the old soul-stirring 'Hail Columbia'. . . . They then, after finishing the piece, slowly and silently marched through the city."

Mary's equanimity was short-lived. On the night of the second, a Union provost marshal and several other officers called at The Terraces to requisition the house as headquarters for General John W. Geary who would take over civil administration of the city. Mary's father, Edward Rawson, bluntly rejected the demand insisting that he could not be ejected with no other place in which to live. The officers finally settled for the adjacent schoolhouse, once inhabited by the Ladies College, and Mary was grieved "to see the beloved old playground in front of the school covered with tents and the beautiful little shade trees cut down . . . and the flowers trampled down by those who could not appreciate their beauty and their fragrance."

Joseph Semmes was with the Army of Tennessee south of Jonesboro, having survived, on the way thereto, a train wreck "which surpassed in horror the most frightful scenes of the battlefield." As to the fall of Atlanta, Semmes wrote to Eo that "it will, I fear, prolong the war at least a year. It may have a depressing effect on the people for a while, but I trust we will soon make another strong effort to regain lost ground." The Army of Tennessee was still intact, barring the way into southern Georgia. Sherman, Semmes believed, would rest on his laurels in Atlanta—for a while at least. The future looked dark, but not despairing.

Sherman himself had firm plans for the occupation of Atlanta and the future operations of his army, conforming to a degree with Semmes' appraisal. He had informed Washington, "I shall not push further on this raid, but in a day or two will move to Atlanta and give my men some rest. Since May 5th we have been in one constant battle or skirmish. . . . He planned, as he noted in a later communication, to "afford the army an opportunity to have a full month's rest, with every chance to organize, receive pay, replenish clothing, and prepare for a fine winter's campaign." The nature of this campaign, already forming in his mind, he was not ready to reveal.

On September 3, he telegraphed to General Slocum in Atlanta, "Move all stores forward from Allatoona and Marietta to Atlanta. Take possession of all good buildings for Government purposes, and see they are not used as quarters. Advise the people to quit now. There can be no trade or commerce now until the war is over. Let Union families go to the north with their effects, and secesh [secessionist] families move on. All cotton is tainted with treason, and no title in it will be respected." Southern produce, King Cotton especially, would become United States property and be shipped to Nashville, with the owners reimbursed when and if such goods were properly disposed of.

As for the occupation and administration of Atlanta, following its "complete reduction," a Special Field Order provided for the distribution of the troops. The Army of the Cumberland under General Thomas would occupy the city and its railroad connection with Chattanooga. The Army of the Tennessee under General Howard would hold the area between East Point and Atlanta. The Army of the Ohio under General Schofield would command the eastern section of the city and Decatur. The cavalry would control the outer suburbs such as Sandtown, Roswell, and other towns along the lines of communication.

Sherman himself arrived in the city on September 7. His entry was quiet and unostentatious. No guard of honor greeted him, no heralding salute of cannon, no drums or bugles. While the accompanying officers, a handful of them, wore their best regalia, were mounted on handsomely caparisoned prancing steeds, and seemed to relish this moment of glory, the beak-nosed general himself, mounted on a mottled mare, wore only "a gray flannel shirt, a faded old blue blouse and trousers that he had worn since long before Chattanooga."

He set up headquarters in the John Neal house on Washington Street, while General Thomas settled in the Greek Revival mansion of Austin Leyden on Peachtree Street a few blocks north. Schofield's quarters were a handsome house on the opposite corner, with those of General Slocum close by.

Resident families, even those imposed upon, were treated with a measure of respect. At the Braumuller home on Whitehall Street, young Oliver watched with apprehension as the Federals occupied the house next door. His father was in Tennessee on business and he regarded himself as surrogate head of the house. He had heard that they might be required to leave the city, "but our home contained many valuable things, such as paintings, rugs, and draperies, and mother decided to stay and protect them."

His fears were confirmed when an army wagon pulled up at their door and several soldiers entered the house. "Without saying good morning, by your leave, or anything, they began tearing boards off the walls. They were going to use the wood to build a camp, they said, and then told me to get out of the way . . . I was scared at the thought that we would be left without a roof, and I was so mad that I could hardly see."

His mother was "frantic," and young Oliver assured her that he would protest to the colonel in command. He ran to the officers' headquarters and burst breathless into the colonel's office.

"Hello, sonny," the colonel said. "What's your trouble?"

"Well, general," Oliver said, raising the officer several ranks, "I'm from the big house next door, and they're tearing it down over our heads. I didn't believe you gave them any such orders."

"No," said the colonel, "I didn't." He rose, reached for his pistol and called for the corporal of the guard. The three returned to the Braumuller house where the colonel demanded of one of the soldiers, "Let me see your authority to tear down this house."

The soldier handed him a piece of paper. The colonel looked at it, tore it up, and threw it at the man's face; then ordered his corporal to arrest the group. Turning to Mrs. Braumuller the colonel said:

"This won't happen again. I have my orders, of course, but they don't provide for tearing down houses over people's heads. If you have any more trouble just send for me." The Braumullers had no more trouble.

Lizzie Perkerson found the Yankees obnoxious once they began to build breastworks and set up camps in the vicinity. The Perkerson house, some three miles south of Atlanta, as well as the homes of neighbors, became sources of materials and provisions. As the work crews invaded the property Lizzie wrote that "they tore down the Ginn house, Screws, stables, crib, smoke house, the cook kitchen, the shop, garden and yard palings. I do reckon there was five hundred here, knocking, cursing, ripping and staving all day, swearing they would tear the house down from over us if we didn't get out of it." The family, of course, protested and, as Lizzie wrote:

> They gave us one man to guard us and he poked about and whispered and encouraged them until they got everything they wanted and then they gave us three men every day while they stayed here. They prevented them coming into the house. That was all the good they did us. And that was a great deal. The house was never plundered by them except the ones that came in first.

They were for a whole week picking up boards to build their camps and when they got done you never saw a place as nicely cleaned up as ours was. You couldn't have found a board or a piece of plank as large as your hand on the place.

What the average Union soldiers saw on entering Atlanta was in sharp contrast to Atlanta's vision, real or conjectured, of the Northerners. Newspaper correspondent David Conyngham with Sherman's army observed "strong proof of the military despotism of the Confederacy," writing that "we captured in the trenches feeble old men, with tottering steps, and mere striplings, who were too young to be taken from their mothers' leading strings. Everything had been made subservient to the army. It swallowed up the blood and wealth of the land, leaving its poor deluded dupes stripped of everything—of the enjoyments of life itself."

The people [Conyngham continued], after awakening from the first shock inspired by the terrible barbarities they heard of the Federal soldiers, seemed to welcome the new order of things. They were now protected, and could walk abroad in security. Gen. Slocum's administration of Atlanta was so impartial and rigidly enforced, that life and property there were as secure as in the city of New York.

Rufus Mead of Connecticut, with the vanguard of Federal troops arriving in Atlanta, also recorded his initial observations:

Our Regt. was the first that came into the city. . . . Our boys helped themselves to tobacco . . . of which there was any quantity, in fact that was about all that was left. Yesterday there was a guard put on so all pilfering is stopped and all the citizens say our soldiers are not half so bad as the Rebs were when they found they were going, and even citizens themselves went in for their share along with our boys as long as they could. . . . The destruction of property by the Rebs exceeds everything I ever saw in my life, and I thought I had seen something of that work before.

To those who had lived in and loved Atlanta, the desolation of the city and its bucolic setting was particularly painful. Young Noble Williams, who had roamed the meadows, swum the creeks, and climbed the inviting oaks and pines, found now that most of the trees had been felled by the troops for barricades, and those left standing were trimmed of their branches by the shells.

"The woods and fields," he wrote, "were strewn with the carcasses of dead and decaying animals, most of which had performed valuable service, but become disabled were shot or left to die of starvation, and the sickening stench of their dead bodies attracted numbers of buzzards which fattened on the dead and decaying remnants of war. Many hungry and half wild dogs made night hideous with their howling, and frightened the women and children greatly, as they could be seen at almost any hour daily running wildly about the streets, seemingly seeking whom they might devour."

In many cases, afflicted Southern families were treated with compassion by the occupying troops. When the home of the ailing Dr. Ezekiel N. Calhoun was approached by blue-coated Federals, Dr. Calhoun's grandson hid under his grandmother's bed and only the most ardent entreaties and promises of safety could bring him out. According to Noble Williams, "The Negroes working on the place had pictured the Yankees, as they called them, to him in the most glowing colors, as beastly and blood-thirsty monsters, whose delight it was to catch men, women and innocent children for no other purpose than to murder them."

The boy emerged only to see hundreds of faces peering through the fence, with no more sinister target in mind than the ripe grapes in the arbor. Soon temptation became too much, and the bluecoats swarmed over the fence and attacked the vines like "a flock of hungry bluebirds."—all except one, a young soldier who identified himself as Private Kellogg and courteously asked permission to gather a few grapes. Dr. Calhoun was without an attending physician at that time, his own doctor having fled the city in anticipation of its occupation, and Mrs. Calhoun asked the courtly private if he could persuade a Union surgeon to visit her husband.

The young man disappeared and returned with Dr. William C. Bennett, an eminent Northern surgeon, who found Dr. Calhoun afflicted with a serious tumor. An operation was necessary, and he called another Union surgeon to assist him. They worked far into the night by candlelight, until at dawn the operation was pronounced successful. The Federal officers packed up their hospital kits, presented no bill but only courteous good wishes, and departed.

But for most Atlantans the rude blow was yet to come. Sherman had given some warning in a paragraph consolidated in his general orders issued on September 4: "The city of Atlanta being exclusively required for warlike purposes, will be at once evacuated by all except the armies of the United States, and such civilians as may be retained."

Three days later he detailed his proposal in a letter delivered by messenger to General Hood at Lovejoy Station: "General: I have deemed it to be for the interest of the United States, that the citizens now residing in Atlanta shall remove; those who prefer, to go south, the rest to go north. . . . Atlanta is no place for families and non-combatants, and I have no desire to send them north if you will assist to convey them south."

There followed specifics of this proposal. For civilians choosing to go south, the Federal authorities would provide free transportation, for themselves and their possessions, as far as Rough and Ready. From that point on the Confederates were to take the refugees in hand. During the transfer at Rough and Ready each side would refrain from interference with, or hostile acts toward, the other. "Each might send a guard, say of one hundred men, to maintain order, and to limit the truce to ten days after a certain time appointed."

Hood replied the following day. He reluctantly agreed to the evacuation, "not considering that I have any alternative in the matter." He suggested only minor changes in the manner of its execution. Then, in the closing paragraphs of his reply, he gave vent to righteous indignation:

And now sir, permit me to say that the unprecedented measure you propose transcends, in studied and ingenious cruelty, all acts ever before brought to my attention in the dark history of this war. In the name of God I protest, and believe you will find yourself wrong in thus expelling from their homes and firesides the wives and children of a brave people.

"Cump" Sherman had expected this reaction. In an earlier letter informing General Halleck of this project he had written, "If the people raise a howl against my barbarity and cruelty, I will answer that war is war and not popularity seeking." To General Hood his reply was surprisingly eloquent and lengthy, and perhaps one reads between the lines a sense of indignation over the fate of the South, a land which he once loved and called his own. Some extracts from his letter to Hood deserve review:

... You yourself burned dwelling-houses along your parapet, and I have seen today fifty houses that you rendered uninhabitable because they stood in the way of your forts and men. You defended Atlanta on a line so close to town that every cannon-shot and many musket-shots from our line of investment, that overshot their mark, went into the habitations of women and children.

I say that it is a kindness to these families of Atlanta to remove them now, at once, from scenes that women and children should not be exposed to ... "brave people" should scorn to commit their wives and children to the rude barbarians who thus, as you say, violate the laws of war, as illustrated in the pages of its dark history.

In the name of common sense, I ask you not to appeal to a just God in such a sacrilegious manner. You who, in the midst of peace and prosperity, have plunged a nation into war—dark and cruel war—who dared and badgered us to battle, insulted our flag, seized our arsenals and forts ...

Talk thus to the marines, but not to me, who have seen these things, and who will this day make as much sacrifice for the peace and honor of the South as the best-born Southerner among you!

If we must be enemies, let us be men and fight it out as we propose to do, and not deal in such hypocritical appeals to God and humanity. God will judge us in due time, and he will pronounce whether it be more humane to fight with a town full of women and the families of a brave people at our back, or to remove them in time to places of safety among their own friends and people.

The people of Atlanta learned immediately of their fate. On September 8, Mayor Calhoun posted a "Notice" of plans for the compulsory evacuation, calling on all citizens to choose their destination, North or South, and register with his office as soon as possible, listing persons and possessions needing transportation.

There were some Union-minded families in Atlanta with an inclination to go north. No problem these. It was those who loved Atlanta with the Southerner's inherent love of land and place, and who had deeply rooted lives there, who were stunned by this decision. Mayor Calhoun and several councilmen appealed to Sherman in their behalf: certain families had sick to care for, others had no place to go or means to establish a new life elsewhere; southern Georgia, in fact the whole heartland of the South, was already overcrowded with war refugees. "We most earnestly and solemnly petition you to reconsider your order, or modify it, and suffer those unfortunate people to remain at home."

Sherman rejected the petition. But his denial was tinged with compassion for those driven from their land. Thirty years before, his youthtime idol, General Winfield Scott, had in similar fashion uprooted twenty-five thousand Cherokees from their homes in northern Georgia—sending them on the long "Trail of Tears" to exile and death in Oklahoma Territory. Could that memory have haunted Sherman? Was this another Trail of Tears that he was charting for the people of Atlanta? He told his petitioners, almost gently:

> . . . Now you must go and take with you the old and feeble, feed and nurse them and build for them in more quiet places, proper habitations to shield them against the weather until the mad passions of men cool down.

An armistice of ten days, starting on September 12, was concluded between Hood and Sherman to expedite the operation. They were the saddest ten days that the weary, wartorn city was to know. When families had been actually fighting for their homes, battling the flames that would destroy them, there was heart and spirit for the struggle, hope and purpose. But to be forced simply to give up everything and leave was like demanding that the human heart be emptied, senses numbed, all hope abandoned.

For those choosing to go north there were only minor problems. Sam Richards, with no real allegiance although antiwar in sentiment, had no trouble making up his mind. He wrote in his diary on September 9, "We have determined upon going to New York if we are sent off, as we want to get away from the war and the fighting if we can. . . . One unpleasant feature of present circumstances is the impudent airs the negroes put on, and their indifference to the wants of their former masters. Of course they are all free and the Yankee soldiers don't fail to assure them of that fact. . . . So our negro property has all vanished into air."

To obtain a pass to go north required several vouchers from Union citizens or soldiers testifying to the emigrant's loyalty to the United States. Richards' leanings throughout the war, although he had voted against secession, had been too ambiguous to make this easy. However, he went about selling his furniture and other personal possessions to raise money for the trip, and one of the purchasers, Captain George Ward Nichols, turned out to be an officer on General Sherman's staff. Through this cultivated contact he obtained a pass to Jeffersonville, Indiana; disposed of his stock of books; and on September 21 he, Sallie and their children, "started forth from our homes, exiles and wanderers upon the earth with no certain dwelling place . . . to return, perhaps never."

Others reacted to this enforced evacuation with varying degrees of outrage. "By this order," wrote Mary Gay, "and by others even more oppressive and diabolical, the Nero of the nineteenth century, alias William Tecumseh Sherman, was put upon record as the born leader of the most ruthless, Godless band ever organized in the name of patriotism—a band which, but for a few noble spirits who, by the power of mind over matter, exerted a restraining influence, would not have left a Southerner to tell the tale of its fiendishness."

Mary's first thought, typically, was for the blankets, uniforms, and clothing she had kept concealed for Tommy and his friends. Enforced evacuation might have one advantage. It might give her a chance to carry these possessions south, safe from enemy hands, disguised as family possessions. She and her maid Telitha reversed the procedure of five months before when she had hid the articles. Building a pyramid of chairs and tables with Telitha's help, Mary pried loose the boards of the ceiling, retrieved the uniforms and blankets, and packed them in innocent-looking sacks. They looked like nothing more than casual bedding or apparel.

But where were they to go, she and her mother and the servants? There was a family farm at Gordon, east of Macon, but that had been devastated by the war. And if they abandoned their home in Decatur, she had no doubt about its fate; it would "furnish material for a bonfire for Nero to fiddle by. . . ."

There was a spirit of intrigue in Mary Gay; she might have been a good Confederate spy. Now she had an idea. She would go through the pretense of evacuating her dependents and possessions to the transfer point at Rough and Ready. There she would place the precious Confederate wardrobe in safe hands for delivery to her brother; then return to Decatur and her home. If her return were challenged, she would solve that problem when she came to it. Meanwhile she would have fulfilled her sacred pledge to brother Tommy.

To get a pass to Rough and Ready she would need some Federal official to intercede in her behalf with General Schofield. Her calculating mind suggested Major Campbell who had won her friendship—or had she won his?—earlier that summer. He who had given her precious Yankee coffee as a token of esteem, would surely give her a recommendation to the general. Somehow, by methods not revealed, she got a message to Major Campbell and received a letter in reply:

Miss Gay—It was hard for me to reconcile my conscience to giving the enclosed recommendation to one whose sentiments I cannot approve, but if I have commited an error it is on the side of mercy, and I hope I'll be forgiven. Hereafter I hope you will not think of Yankees as all being bad, and beyond the pale of redemption.

Very respectfully,
J. W. Campbell.

Mary forwarded the recommendation to General Schofield, confident that her plan was shaping up with promise.

Mary Rawson's family was in a "vacillating condition." Most of the family, her grandparents, aunt, and cousins had decided to seek refuge with relatives and friends in southwestern Georgia. She, too, would prefer to remain in the heartland, but that would make her father subject to conscription since the Confederacy was calling upon young and old alike, and Mr. E. E. Rawson was neither able nor inclined to serve in the army. If he could sell his tobacco, he would have money to go north. But Sherman had put a stop to Southern trade. "Ill fated weed," wrote Mary, "though much loved and longed for by Yankee soldiery, you seem as ever to be only a source of trouble to those who possess and use you."

Through the intervention of a Federal Colonel Beckworth, Rawson applied several times to General Sherman for written permission to dispose of his tobacco, but without success. So "the days drifted by slowly and sadly with no certainty of our journey." Finally Rawson called on the general in person and secured the necessary papers. His tobacco was sold and, with resignation rather than elation, Mary and her parents prepared for an arduous journey northwest to Idaho.

The traveling papers had come just in time. Civil administrator General Geary had decided to take over The Terraces for himself and staff. As fast as the Rawson servants carried out furniture and packed the family's possessions, the booted soldiers tramped into and through the house like an invading army, carrying General Geary's trunks and cartons. Some, to Mary's wry amusement, were sweeping the lawn in preparation for setting up their tents.

O. L. Braumuller and his mother had also elected to go north hoping to join the boy's father in Nashville where he was still engaged in business. Mrs. Braumuller was intent on keeping her two pianos, since these could be more easily converted into cash than paintings, rugs, and other household articles. One fourth of a box car, however, was hardly large enough for two pianos.

Mrs. Braumuller made a sly deal with the Federals. If they would grant her an entire car for her pianos she would find it expedient to leave behind the rest of her possessions, some of them valuable rugs and paintings. The troops agreed. They even helped carry the pianos to the freight cars; then returned to the house to draw lots for the rest of Braumuller heirlooms left behind as a not-so-subtle bribe.

Some citizens and servants simply departed on their own, the civilians generally going south, their black retainers often going north or seeking employment or acceptance in the Union camps. The Perkerson's black servant, Dan, feeling the call of freedom, simply bowed politely to the family and said, "I now bid adieu to you and slavery," and, recorded Lizzie, "off he went." But unescorted travel through that still contentious country had its hazards. A friend of the Perkerson's, Dr. William Gilbert, rode off with his family toward South Carolina. He had barely left the city when, as Lizzie wrote, "he fell off his horse dead in the road. His family buried him by the road side and went on."

"Every one I see seems sad," wrote Carrie Berry in her diary. "The citizens think that it is the most cruel thing to drive us from our home but I think it would be so funny to move. Papa says he don't know where on earth to go." Maxwell Berry had heard, however, that men might be allowed to remain in the city if employed in an essential industry. As a building contractor he thought he might qualify and did. As he started for business the next morning, the whole Berry family was infected with a spirit of industry, in keeping with their image of determined, useful residents. The house was scrubbed and cleaned, clothes and bedding were washed and aired and ironed, the yard was tended and the pony groomed. Carrie never paused to rest between her multiple duties, until she was able to record that evening: "I think I will sleep right sound tonight if the mosquitoes don't bite me too much."

Colonel Willard Warner, of Sherman's staff, had partial charge of the evacuation. "The fact is," he wrote, "that not more than half the people of Atlanta obeyed the order, and no force was used to compel obedience. I was detailed by the general to attend to the delivery of the people to General Hood at Rough and Ready. . . . The inhabitants had choice of transportation by rail or wagons—Colonel Le Duc, of General Geary's command . . . sending as many wagons to each house as was were asked for. I had a train of cars standing on the track in Atlanta every day from 8 A.M. to 3 P.M. and the people were allowed to put on what they chose. The only limit to the amount of goods to be taken was Hood's ability to transport from Rough and Ready."

The family of L. C. Butler, Atlanta newsboy, also remained in the city, "having no where to go." They decided, wrote Butler, to take the chance of "being killed or burned out again, and in the providence of God, we fared much better than many who refugeed. My mother cooked for the Yankee band, and made our board, and I will say that these soldiers treated her with the utmost respect and consideration. Only one time did one of them speak in any way disrespectfully to my mother, and then a superior officer gave him such a rebuke that he was glad to slip away."

Newspaper correspondent David Conyngham accompanied a trainload of those moving south, and noticed that they "seemed to enjoy the thing."

The cars taking them down were loaded with a miscellaneous cargo. In some were crowded together tottering old age and maidens in their youthful bloom. The former fretted very much at being thus rudely torn away, root and branch, from the soil on which they grew, and in which they hoped soon to rest their weary hearts. As for their young companions, they seemed to treat the thing as a kind of sentimental journey. I fully understood this when we reached the rebel quarters, when I saw with what a warm greeting the rebel officers and soldiers received them. Some even carried their enthusiasm so far as to welcome them with warm kisses and embraces. In addition, the wagons were crowded with a heterogeneous medley of poodle dogs, tabby cats, asthmatic pianos, household furniture, cross old maids, squalling wondering children, all of which, huddling together, made anything but a pleasant travelling party, which I accompanied.

On the first day of the evacuation, sixty-seven groups left the city, listed among them: "Mrs. G. W. Adair . . . 2 adults, 4 children, 2 servants, 53 packages, and 2 horses, carriage, cow and calf." By the time the operation was officially concluded, 1,651 citizens had departed with 8,842 pieces of baggage, and assorted horses, cattle, carriages and wagons. In the already overcrowded city—with its thousands of occupying troops, its hordes of refugees and stragglers—the exodus hardly seemed to make a dent.

The Rawsons were among the last to go, with a wagon for their possessions and an ambulance for Mary and her family. It was a heartbreaking experience for Mary to leave the only home that she had ever known, the black mammy who had raised her, the garden on which she had lavished tender care. Heartbreaking, too, to leave behind the familiar school house on the hill, the comforting grove of oaks, the landmarks which reminded her that "the dearest spot on earth" was this small corner of Atlanta.

When, she wondered, would she see it again, if ever? "When, oh when?" As the wagon train wound north in an appropriately setting sun, Mary soliloquized:

Dear, dear Atlanta! City of hills, with your bright blue sky, southern constellations, innumerable bright flowers and birds and clear sparkling water. . . . May your spires never be brought low!

19

Ordeal by Fire

"I think Atlanta can be recovered; that Sherman's army can be driven out of Georgia, perhaps utterly destroyed."

So President Jefferson Davis wrote to Herschel Johnson, friend of Governor Brown, in words intended for the governor's consideration. For the key to Atlanta's recovery, the President implied, rested in Brown's hands. If Georgia would call to arms the hundreds of men so far exempt from military duty, if Brown could raise 10,000 more militia to serve with the Confederacy, then the enemy could be repelled and Atlanta restored to its former position of symbol and citadel of Confederate resistance.

Brown's indirect reply was devastating. Declaring that the emergency in Georgia was over, he withdrew the state troops from Hood's command and granted them furloughs to harvest their crops and look after their personal affairs.

There was worse to come—a period in which Georgia, it was thought, might make a separate peace with the United States. Two prominent state citizens made not-so-secret calls on General Sherman, carrying papers of negotiation; while Sherman wrote President Lincoln that he was anticipating a visit from Brown and Alexander Stephens ("a Union man at heart") with

similar peace proposals. If so, he would welcome their decision
to end this state's rebellion "begun in error and perpetuated in
pride," and allow Georgia to "save herself from the devastation
of war preparing for her."

The peace talks never got beyond these vague preliminaries;
and Sherman settled down to his original intention for Atlanta.
While he had told his troops that the capture of the Gate City
"completed the grand task which has been assigned to us by our
government," he himself had further plans. First was to make
Atlanta an efficient, compact Union fortress. Much as he admired Hood's abandoned fortifications, they were not for him.
Too long, requiring too large a garrison. He instructed his chief
of engineers, Colonel Orlando M. Poe, to contract the line and
build shorter trenches capable of being held by 7,000 troops. He
wanted the rest of his army free for future operations.

Atlanta was swamped in a sea of blue. The "Devil Yank
Devils"—as Mary Gay's Telitha called them to their faces—took
over the city like a restless tide. The sidewalks came alive again
with mushrooming bars and sutlers' stores and tenpin alleys.
The streets that radiated from the Five Points in the city's center teemed with unshaven men in tattered uniforms, black-
visored caps, and stout black brogans. They were sloppy, dirty,
and unmilitary-looking, and they could not care less. Theirs was
the heady wine of triumph; and after three months of campaigning, according to Adjutant Fenwick Hedley of the 32nd Illinois
Infantry,

> . . . they gave way to a protracted jubilee. The brass and martial
> bands, which had been silent all the way from Chattanooga to
> Atlanta [whenever they broke that silence, Sherman would bel-
> low, "Send that damn band to the rear!"] now played their most
> exultant airs; and the men vied with the instruments in making
> noise expressive of great joy. All were happy and smiling, from
> the commander-in-chief to the humblest private in the ranks, and
> even the bray of the half-starved government mule seemed mellow
> and melodious, as it added to the din.

As the officers settled in the better residential buildings, the
troops dismantled whole or partially damaged houses to build
shacks and barracks for themselves or to supply with fuel and

flooring the tent cities mushrooming around the town. Since supplies were slow in coming down from Chattanooga, foraging parties roamed the countryside for food and fodder, fruits and vegetables, and whatever the farms and neighboring plantations could provide. There were occasional attacks on the city's outposts by Confederate cavalry, but these provided more excitement and diversion than material damage.

Apart from the scrubby attractions of Humbug Square and the bars and brothels on the south side of the city, there was pitifully little entertainment in the town. Western Indians in the army were persuaded to perform their war and tribal dances in the streets. At one point Private Charlie Benton of Slocum's corps watched "a couple of trick mules who tossed the unsophisticated who could be induced to ride them . . . while at still another place a rude ten-pin alley had been constructed. The pins were termed 'Rebels,' and the balls used were some unexploded shells which our artillery had thrown into the city." The Athenaeum had been undamaged by the siege, and, as Benton wrote:

> . . . this was soon taken possession of. Some of the company had possibly been connected with theaters before, but now they were all stars of the first magnitude, though the actresses were conspicuous by their absence. The "strong man" nightly tossed the cannon balls, catching them on the back of his neck, and allowed a rock to be broken on his breast by a sledge hammer in the hands of "t'other strong feller," and with the help of the soloist, the impromptu comedy, and the inevitable minstrels, the time was filled, and a not over-critical audience was delighted.

Sherman himself condoned and even encouraged concerts for the benefit of Southern refugees and widows and civilians in distress. Colonel William G. Le Duc, quartermaster with Slocum's corps, became so active an entrepreneur that he earned the gratitude of many Atlanta widows and orphans whom he helped with money earned through his theatrical productions.

One of his talent discoveries was Mrs. Rebecca S. Welch, whose husband and son had been killed in the war and who was living at the time in the Adair home on Peters Street. Mrs. Welch, described as "an accomplished pianist with a beautiful and well-trained voice," had been left with four children to care for, and Colonel Le Duc suggested she give concerts to help support them. He arranged with the celebrated band of the 32nd Massachusetts Volunteers to perform with her, a formidable combination of accompanists. As the Colonel recorded:

> I fixed up the theater, the Athenaeum on Alabama Street, which had suffered from a shell or two through the roof during the bombardment. The programs I had printed on the little army printing press, which I used for printing general orders.
>
> This concert came off in good form. General Sherman and other officers attended, the house was full, with not even standing room left. The frightened little woman trembled at first, but the soldiers applauded and she finally got through triumphantly.

Flushed with his protégée's success, Colonel Le Duc became Atlanta's temporary impresario, and kept the Athenaeum running for seventeen successive days of SRO performances. He lowered the tone of the performances somewhat, with, among other presentations, a "laughable pantomime" called "The Cobbler's Frolic." This also featured Mrs. Welch as well as one of her daughters. Admission was a dollar for a gentleman or lady, and considering that a Union private's pay was thirteen dollars a month, a surprising number of soldiers helped to pack the auditorium. At the end of the brief "season," Rebecca Welch found herself richer by two thousand dollars.

Mary Gay, traveling with the last of the evacuees to Rough and Ready, finally reached her destination, the point of exchange where Federal transportation ended and Southern authority took over. She told the story of her mission to the Confederate officer of the day. He did not believe her. She invited him to inspect the sacks of army material she had smuggled with her on the train. He slit one open with his knife, saw the familiar gray of uniforms, coats, and blankets, and promptly went in search of transportation to General Geary's camp where Mary's half-brother, Tommy Stokes, was bivouacked.

While Mary waited in a dismal rain, she studied this curious twilight zone where homeless civilians and prisoners of war were caught between two mighty armies. It seemed as if:

The entire Southern population of Atlanta, with but an occasional exception . . . were dumped out upon the cold ground without shelter and without any of the comforts of home, with an autumnal mist or drizzle slowly but surely saturating every article of clothing upon them; and pulmonary diseases in all stages admonishing them of the dangers of such exposure. Aged grandmothers tottering upon the verge of the grave and tender maidens in the first bloom of young womanhood, the little babes not three days old in the arms of sick mothers, driven from their homes, were all out upon the cold charity of the world. . . .

As she watched, another train of evacuees rolled in, and from it stepped "a queenly girl, tall and lithe in figure, willowy in motion . . . the embodiment of feminine grace, Grecian beauty, and nobility of manner . . . a typical Southern girl who glorified in that honor." Impulsively the statuesque, aristocratic woman fell to her knees and kissed the earth of her native South—an act so moving to an attendant Union officer that he asked Mary if she knew the lady's name and could possibly introduce them. If so, "I would offer her the devotion of my life." Mary declined to play the role of cupid.

Shortly she was with her half brother, Lieutenant Stokes, in Geary's camp, and the sacks of Confederate supplies were gratefully received. That night she slept in a tent with a buffalo robe and overcoat for bedding, and Tommy awoke her at dawn for roll call. Why she should be at roll call was a question quickly answered. As Geary's regiment lined up, row upon orderly row, an order went down the ranks, a signal was given, and eight hundred men gave three lusty cheers for Mary Gay, heroine of the Army of Tennessee.

It was perhaps the most moving experience of Mary's life, excepting only her farewell to Tommy. "He took me in his arms and kissed me once, twice, thrice . . . I felt intuitively I should never look upon his face again." She never would.

While the Confederate army at Jonesboro licked its wounds, smarting from defeat, John Bell Hood surveyed the wreckage of his dreams. He had lost more than the city he had vowed to hold. Destroyed with the Atlanta commissary depots and the ordnance trains were the army's total reserves of powder and ammunition, hand guns and siege guns, badly needed foodstuffs and supplies—all through the "gross neglect" of the quartermaster who had failed to follow "positive instructions." Hood asked Richmond to replace the man, as "I am reliably informed that he is too much addicted to drink of late to attend to his duties."

Something much more had been lost, as well. The army's morale which had briefly revived, Hood felt, when the men had their backs against Atlanta's walls had dropped sharply with this last retreat that had left that Southern citadel behind them. He refused to dwell on the actual loss of men since mid-July when he had assumed command and the army had been close to peak strength.

In point of fact, the Atlanta campaign from Dalton to Jonesboro had cost both sides close to 40,000 men apiece, from death, disabling injuries, illness, and desertions. The figures were perhaps a little lower for the Federals than for the Southerners, and Sherman could better absorb the losses. Hood's current strength at Jonesboro, infantry, cavalry and artillery, was roughly 39,000 men—compared with the approximately 80,000 that Joe Johnston had commanded in late June. This discounted Wheeler's cavalry which was still marauding somewhat ineffectually northwest of Atlanta.

Hood had been puzzled when Sherman had failed to attack his forces during the Confederate withdrawal from Atlanta. He was puzzled now, as well as relieved, when the bulk of Sherman's army left Jonesboro for Atlanta without pressing the offensive. Perhaps there was some weakness in the Federal command that he should take advantage of. Possibly even the loss of Atlanta was reversible. On September 6, he wrote to President Davis: "According to all human calculations, we should have saved Atlanta had the officers and men of the army done what was expected of them. It has been God's will for it to be otherwise. I am of good heart, and feel we shall yet succeed."

He began telegraphing Bragg for reinforcements, using as an argument the threat to Georgia posed by Sherman's forces in Atlanta. "The enemy will not content himself with Atlanta, but will continue offensive movements. . . . To prevent this country from being overrun, reinforcements are absolutely necessary . . . never, in my opinion, were our liberties in such danger.

ATLANTA
TO
LOVEJOY'S STATION

AUGUST AND SEPTEMBER
1864

CONFEDERATE MOVEMENTS
UNION MOVEMENTS

APPROX. 5 MILES

TRM

(1) WEEKS OF HEAVY SHELLING FAIL TO BREAK THE SPIRIT OF THE ATLANTANS. SHERMAN TURNS TO OTHER METHODS. AUG. 25, 1864

(2) LEAVING A FORCE TO HOLD THE CHATTAHOOCHEE R. BRIDGE SHERMAN DESERTS HIS LINES AROUND ATLANTA AND SHIFTS HIS ENTIRE ARMY TO THE SOUTHWEST TO SEVER ALL SUPPLY LINES. THEN HE WOULD ATTACK THE CITY FROM THE SOUTH. AUG. 26, 1864

(3) LEARNING THIS, HOOD RUSHES HARDEE SOUTH TO STOP THE UNION ADVANCE AT JONESBORO. AUG. 30, 1864

(4) SCHOFIELD SIEZES ROUGH-AND-READY AND SEVERS COMMUNICATIONS FROM THE SOUTH. AUG. 31, 1864

(5) HARDEE'S ATTACK ON THE ENTRENCHED FEDERALS AT THE FLINT R. FAILS WITH HEAVY LOSSES. AUG. 31, 1864

(6) ASSUMING JONESBORO TO BE SECURE, HOOD ORDERS S.D. LEE TO RETURN TO THE DEFENSE OF ATLANTA, BUT, LATER, INFORMED OF HARDEE'S DEFEAT, REVERSES THE ORDER AND LEE MARCHES BACK TO JONESBORO. SEPT. 1, 1864

(7) THE SECOND BATTLE FOR JONESBORO RESULTS IN A COSTLY UNION VICTORY. DURING THE NIGHT, HARDEE SLIPS OUT TO STRONG POSITIONS AT LOVEJOY'S STATION. SEPT. 1, 1864

(8) BLAMING HARDEE, HOOD DECIDES TO EVACUATE ALL TROOPS AND SUPPLIES FROM ATLANTA. HOOD THEN MARCHES BY CIRCUITOUS ROUTE TO LOVEJOY'S. SEPT. 1-3, 1864

(9) ATLANTA'S MAYOR CALHOUN SURRENDERS ATLANTA TO SHERMAN'S SUBORDINATE — SEPT. 2, 1864 — SHERMAN SETS UP MILITARY RULE IN ATLANTA AND VICINITY, PROHIBITS TRADE, AND ORDERS COMPULSORY EVACUATION OF ALL CITIZENS. SEPT. 3-8, 1864

CHATTAHOOCHEE
SANDY CR.
Lick Skillet
Decatur
ATLANTA
EZRA CHURCH
HOWARD
SCHOFIELD
UNION
THOMAS
HARDEE
UTOY CHURCH
MT. GILEAD CHURCH
UNION
East Point
MT. ZION CHURCH
Red Oak
SCHOFIELD
Rough and Ready
ELAM CHURCH
HARDEE
LEE TO LOVEJOY'S
HOOD TO LOVEJOY'S
HOOD
Fairburn
BETHLEHEM CHURCH
THOMAS
HOWARD
SCHOFIELD
FLINT
Jonesboro
LEE TO ATLANTA
HARDEE
HOOD
HARDEE
Lovejoy's Station

What can you do for us?" Though he blamed Hardee, to a large degree, for his predicament, he asked Hardee to use his influence with President Davis. Hardee did; adding his plea for more men and supplies.

No reinforcements were forthcoming. Bragg and Davis advised Hood that all resources had been exhausted. Though reluctantly accepting this, Hood would not accept a "stand-still policy." Before the Federal army could refresh and strengthen itself at Atlanta, he would, he resolved, try Sherman's recent tactic in reverse—circle around the city and cut the vital railway line to Chattanooga, thus forcing the Federal general to abandon the Gate City.

Atlanta would be his again. The tide of war would be reversed.

With this in view, Hood started, in late September, to shift his army to the left or west, taking up a position between the West Point railroad and the Chattahoochee River with his right flank anchored at Palmetto. To that town came Jefferson Davis on September 25, to appraise the situation and address the troops. He was greeted with cries of "Give us back Joe Johnston!" which Hood considered an "uncourteous reception to His Excellency." In meetings between the President and general, Hood explained his plan for taking the offensive and attacking Sherman's rear, asserting, "Sherman is weaker now than he will be in the future, and I as strong as I can expect to be."

When Davis agreed in principle to the offensive, Hood set forth a couple of prerequisites. One was the removal of Federal prisoners from Andersonville threatening his own rear; the other was the removal of General Hardee whom Hood held responsible for the defeats around Atlanta. The President agreed to both.

Dropping Hardee was no blow to that general; he had already threatened to resign. Davis handled the matter skillfully by creating a new over-all department of the West under General Beauregard, and placing Hardee in command of the department of South Carolina, Georgia, and Florida. Hardee was out of the fighting for now, but not for long.

By the end of September Hood was ready to make his move. Railroads leading south from Atlanta were extensively damaged

or destroyed to hamper a Federal attack from that direction, and
on the 28th Hood started his westward advance across the Chattahoochee River. He sent word to Wheeler to rejoin the army
as soon as possible, and left a cavalry regiment under General
Iverson below Atlanta to keep an eye on Sherman.

By October 1 the Army of Tennessee was headed for Lost
Mountain starting to follow, in reverse, the route of the campaign for Atlanta from Kennesaw to Ringgold Gap—reentering
that forlorn and desolate chain of battlefields of which one
Southern journalist wrote: "So startling is the utter silence that
even when a wild bird carols a note you look around surprised
that amid such loneliness any living thing should be happy."

Sherman was fully aware of Hood's intentions, and was
amazed at how gratuitously this information had been handed
to him. President Davis, in his public speeches at Palmetto and
mid-Georgia towns had declared that "we will flank Sherman
out of Atlanta, tear up the railroad and cut off his supplies, and
make Atlanta a perfect Moscow of defeat.... With his communications all cut off, and our army in the rear, he will be powerless."

An idle boast? Sherman was not so sure. Governor Brown had
aided the Union cause by granting an extended furlough to the
Georgia militia to enable them to harvest autumn crops, an act
which President Davis regarded as little short of treason. Hood's
army, however, remained a formidable threat to Sherman's hold
upon Atlanta; and as long as the Gate City stood, it remained
the key to Georgia's and the Southland's future. Sherman meant
to keep it; to do so, "it was absolutely necessary to keep General
Hood's infantry off our main route of communication and supply." On October 5 he started in pursuit.

Leaving General Slocum to protect Atlanta, and sending
General Thomas' army up to Tennessee to guard the important
railroad junctions of Nashville and Chattanooga, he led the bulk
of his remaining forces back across the Chattahoochee, the Rubicon of Georgia, and established headquarters near the former
battlefield of Kennesaw. From the crest of that mountain on
October 5 he watched, through his field glass, the explosion of
one of the fiercer and more gallant battles of the war, where
Brigadier General John M. Corse defended a major Union depot

at Allatoona against attack by General Samuel French's Confederate division.

Corse, a slightly built West Point dropout of twenty-eight, had less than 2,000 men to protect supplies that included nine thousand head of beef and a million rations of hardtack—vitally important to the Union army. French, with more than 3,000 men and heavy guns positioned to shell Allatoona, demanded that Corse surrender to avoid "a needless effusion of blood." Corse replied that he preferred the needless effusion "whenever it is convenient for you."

From early morning till midafternoon, French's artillery smothered the fortified town with shells. Four successive infantry attacks, furious but inconclusive, took a heavy toll of the defenders. The hard-pressed Corse, himself wounded, propped his own dead against the breastworks to give the appearance of adequate numbers. With not enough men left to man the batteries, the wounded were laid beside the guns with lanyards tied to their wrists. As long as they lived, they could tug the lanyards to discharge the cannon.

From his perch on Kennesaw Mountain, Sherman signalled Corse to "Hold on! We are coming!" Corse held on—so gallantly that the evangelist Philip Paul Bliss was inspired to compose the popular hymn, " 'Hold the fort, for I am coming,' Jesus signals still!" As French's division made its final charge, the rebel yell echoing above the rifle fire, the prostrate Federal wounded tugged their lanyards, and the Union guns exploded in a sheet of flame. It was as if, wrote one observer, the attackers had been "jerked inside out." The Confederates stumbled back in panic, leaving 800 dead and wounded on the field. The "effusion of blood" had cost the Federals more than a third of their numbers, but Hood's first serious attempt to isolate Atlanta had been thwarted.

Undismayed, Hood pushed farther north, with Sherman on his heels. He attacked the railroad at numerous points between Resaca and Tunnel Hill, briefly recaptured Dalton, and destroyed another fifteen miles of track. His intention had been to draw Sherman as far as possible from Atlanta, then surprise and destroy the Union forces with a turnabout offensive—as soon as he felt his army ready for a full-scale battle.

Wheeler had finally rejoined the army, but Wheeler's cavalry was only a fraction of its former strength. Beauregard had promised Hood that Bedford Forrest with 4,500 mounted troops in Tennessee would arrive shortly, but so far no sign of Forrest. Nor had the Army of Tennessee regained the fighting spirit and will to win that it had had before Atlanta.

Accordingly, the Confederate commander revised his original plan (though he preferred to call this revision a "further development of so-far successful maneuvering"). He would strike north into Tennessee, destroy or rout George Thomas' army at Nashville or wherever he encountered it, then march into Kentucky and Ohio. Or perhaps swing east and attack Grant's rear in Virginia. Or perhaps reinforce Robert E. Lee in the glorious defense of Richmond.

It was a grandiose project, full of wonderful alternatives, any one of which might save the Confederacy at this moment of great crisis. Off Hood went into Alabama, reaching Gadsden on October 20, and trying to make up his mind just where to cross the Tennessee River and link up with Bedford Forrest. It would take him weeks to make up his mind. Meanwhile he was leaving Georgia and Atlanta's future and the fate of the Deep South for good. And taking with him, down into a deep abyss, the still magnificent Army of Tennessee, one of the proudest names in Southern history.

As early as October 10 Sherman was wearying of this cat-and-mouse game. Hood was a nuisance, and an incalculable one, but he would not waste his army on this hare-brained chase. Thomas could take care of Hood if the latter ever got as far as Tennessee. Meanwhile, "Let Hood go north, and I'll go south," was his decision. It meant abandoning Atlanta and the Chattanooga Railroad but as he telegraphed to Grant, "I would infinitely prefer to make a wreck of the road and of Atlanta . . . and with my effective army move through Georgia, smashing things to the sea."

Joining Sherman's staff that fall was a young lawyer of New England ancestry, Major Henry Hitchcock, whose family responsibilities had kept him from volunteering up to now. Along with another of Sherman's aides, Major George Ward Nichols, Hitchcock kept a staccato diary of events, supplemented by copies of letters to his wife, in which he recorded:

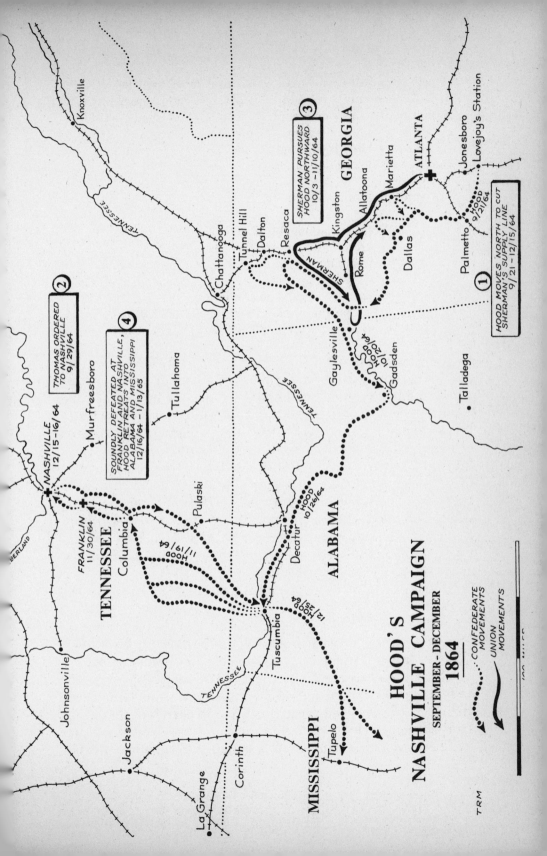

HOOD'S
NASHVILLE CAMPAIGN
SEPTEMBER–DECEMBER
1864

CONFEDERATE MOVEMENTS

UNION MOVEMENTS

100 MILES

T R M

KNOXVILLE

GEORGIA

③ SHERMAN PURSUES HOOD NORTHWARD 10/3 – 11/10/64

ATLANTA

Lovejoy's Station

Jonesboro

Palmetto

HOOD 9/21/64

① HOOD MOVES NORTH TO CUT SHERMAN'S SUPPLY LINE 9/21 – 12/15/64

Marietta

Allatoona

SHERMAN

Kingston

Rome

Dallas

Resaca

Dalton

Tunnel Hill

Chattanooga

Gaylesville

Gadsden

HOOD 10/20/64

Talladega

② THOMAS ORDERED TO NASHVILLE 9/29/64

④ SOUNDLY DEFEATED AT FRANKLIN AND NASHVILLE, HOOD RETREATED INTO ALABAMA AND MISSISSIPPI 12/16/64 – 1/13/65

NASHVILLE 12/15–16/64

Murfreesboro

Tullahoma

TENNESSEE

Pulaski

Columbia

FRANKLIN 11/30/64

HOOD 11/19/64

Decatur

HOOD 10/26/64

ALABAMA

Tuscumbia

HOOD 12/13/35/64

Johnsonville

CUMBERLAND

Jackson

Corinth

La Grange

MISSISSIPPI

Tupelo

When Gen. Sherman gives up Atlanta it will not be worth much to the Johnnies. Within a few days, probably three or four, *we* shall move—*not* northward, no matter what Hood does. He told me this evening his plans, adding, "It's a big game, but I can do it—I know I can do it." And you may be sure of one thing, that what he says he can do, he *can*.

To General Grant, Sherman offered further explanation:

It will be a physical impossibility to protect the [rail] roads now that Hood, Forrest, Wheeler and the whole batch of devils are turned loose without home or habitation. . . . Until we can repopulate Georgia, it is useless for us to occupy it; but the utter destruction of their roads, houses and people will cripple their military resources. . . . I propose we strike out for Macon, Milledgeville and Savannah. I can make this march and make Georgia howl.

Who first inspired Sherman's march through Georgia to the sea is hard to pinpoint. It was the sort of war of attrition that Grant might have suggested and was now conducting in Virginia. Lincoln later credited the idea principally to Sherman. But little matter. That week, Sherman established a new base at Kingston, there to provision his army for a march, raid, campaign—call it what you will—that would be the climax of his whole military lifetime up to now.

In Richmond, Mary Boykin Chesnut, keeping her finger as always on the pulse of transpiring events, noted, regarding Hood's withdrawal from Georgia. "We have but two armies, and Sherman is between them now." She did not presume to prophesy particulars, but concluded:

"We are going to be wiped off the face of the earth."

Atlanta had felt the sting of Hood's raids in the north, and as always it was the private citizen who suffered most. With food supplies from Chattanooga interrupted, meat becoming scarce and hardtack serving as a substitute, garrisoning troops engaged in foraging with all the fervor of a military mission. Organized raiding parties roamed the countryside in search of meat and fruit and vegetables. One Connecticut private, writing that he had never eaten so many sweet potatoes in his life, recorded a raid undertaken by several brigades, accompanied by artillery, cavalry and 500 wagons:

> They went about 25 miles, were gone 4 days & brought back every wagon full of corn or sweet potatoes, as well as any number of sheeps, calves, pigs, fowls, etc. . . . [And on another day] Our Regt wagon went too and brought back a calf, goose, 2 chickens, 2 pumpkins & a bushel of sweet potatoes for our mess of three. . . .It may seem barbarous to you to rob henroosts but Hood cut off our R. R. communications and forced us to forage and . . . all is fair in war, you know

Thomas Maguire's Promised Land Plantation was a typical target of such incursions. On October 19 Maguire noted in his diary: "This day devoted to hiding out wheat, two boxes in the farmer field, 80 bushels. Little hands pulling fodder of syrup-cane in the patches. Will put out some barrels of syrup this day making preparation for the evil time coming should it come." Later, "With sheep and cattle out of the way, we are ready to stand trial with the Yankees . . . may be here today or tomor-row."

Five days later the dreaded "tomorrow" came. "At 10½ o'-clock some 30 Yankees rode up. Took Phillip's wagon and two horses, all our meal and flour, one keg of syrup and several articles from the house that I do not know of, one bu. grain, the last we had. They stayed some 15 or 20 minutes and put back over the river. They also took John E's saddlebags and a large tin cup." The next day, "Hands gathering up corn and some trifling folks at it too, but this is war time and maybe worse is coming, but we must try and bear it as best we can." And later, "What will become of us, God only knows."

Nearer Atlanta, nothing edible was safe. Grandma Perkerson, who had kept a wooden paddle handy for whacking Confederate soldiers trespassing on the Perkerson estate, now used her mus-cle against Yankee foragers. According to Lizzie, "she gave one of them very good licks. He was taking wheat out of the wheat house and the paddling stick was close by and she just put it to him." The chastisement was not evidently a complete deterrent, for Lizzie added: "They took pretty well all the grain grandma had."

At the Berry Home on Fairlie Street, November 8, it was Zuie's birthday. Carrie noted in her diary only that her little sister was getting "pretty smart." Beyond this, the day was marred: "We lost our last hog this morning early. Soldiers took him out of the pen. Me and Buddie went around to hunt for him and every where we inquired they would say that they saw two soldiers driving him off to kill him. We will have to live on bread."

Carrie sensed the growing uncertainty that seemed to hang above the city like a dismal pall. What was going on between the generals Hood and Sherman? Was Atlanta soon to be reoccupied by the Confederates and "made safe for all of us again?" What would happen to the former slaves who, theoretically free, were roaming the city without occupation or design? "The black wimmen are running around trying to get up north," wrote Carrie, "for fear that the rebels will come and take them."

With Mr. Berry gainfully employed in repairing houses damaged by the siege, the family felt more secure but "stuck tight to the house." Missing school, which never opened after Atlanta fell, Carrie had spent her time cleaning, ironing, and sewing; hemmed a skirt for Zuie, made an apron for her mother, and dutifully attended to her diary. As a reward, her father made her a pair of shoes, since little or nothing could be purchased in Atlanta. Except for the theft of their pig, the family had not been greatly inconvenienced or alarmed—until a few days after Zuie's birthday, when Carrie noted in her diary for November 12:

> We were fritened almost to death last night. Some mean mean soldiers set several houses on fire in different parts of the town. I could not go to sleep for fear that they would set our house on fire. We all dred the next few days to come for they said that they would set the last house on fire if they had to leave this place.

In a sense, the spark that started the conflagration was Abraham Lincoln's reelection, news of which reached the city on November 10. To some, it signalled the doom of the Confederacy. To Sherman it meant the time was right for his great march to the sea, for now the South would be more demoralized than ever and less apt to resist.

His destination—long in his mind but still kept secret from the troops and many of his generals—was Savannah, 295 miles southeast of the Gate City. Grant had suggested Augusta or Charleston, but Sherman argued that "the possession of the Savannah River is more fatal to Southern independence. They may stand the fall of Richmond, but not all of Georgia."

He would make a wasteland of the richest part of Georgia, and burn the very heart of the Confederated States. He would "demonstrate to the world, both foreign and domestic, that we have a power which Davis cannot resist . . . there are thousands of people abroad and in the south who reason thus: If the North can march an army right through the South, it is proof positive that the North can prevail. . . ."

But first, Atlanta itself must be destroyed. With Hood far north and west in Alabama, there was no longer any need to hold this fortress as a base. Sherman's men could live off the land, and forage as they went. On Sherman's return from Kingston to Atlanta, the Western & Atlantic tracks were torn up, just in case, and the bridge across the Chattahoochee River burned; while in Atlanta Sherman's chief of engineers Colonel Orlando Poe circulated through the city, marking buildings destined for destruction. A young Boston architect, Colonel Charles F. Morse, followed in Poe's footsteps, planting explosives and kerosene-soaked flammables in designated buildings.

Morse had destroyed one house as an "experiment," or test rehearsal, for the massive demolition being planned. Most likely it was this experiment that triggered the early fires Carrie Berry noted in her diary. More than twenty houses were burned the night of November 11, apparently by soldiers who, aware of the coming holocaust, were intent on doing a little looting in advance. As a result, patrols were doubled and General Slocum offered a handsome reward for any soldier caught in an act of arson.

Slocum's orders from Sherman, effective November 12, were to "commence the work of destruction at once, but don't use fire until the last moment." The ingenious Colonel Poe invented a type of battering ram consisting of an iron rail, suspended from a crane, that could be pulled back in a high arc and released—crashing against a brick facade and turning it into dust-enveloped rubble. Like a primeval dinosaur it moved from block to block, battering down the more solid brick or concrete buildings. All surviving this behemoth would be burned, along with those of wood construction.

The cataclysm which began November 12 increased in fury over four volcanic days of flame, smoke, and exploding dynamite, compared with the burning of Moscow or the last days of Pompeii. Wrote Carrie Berry, in her diary:

> Sun. Nov. 13. The federal soldiers have been coming to day and burning houses and I have ben looking at them come in nearly all day.
> Mon. Nov. 14. They came burning Atlanta to day. We all dred it because they say that they will burn the last house before they stop. We will dred it.
> Tues. Nov. 15. This has been a dreadful day. Things have ben burning all around us. We dread to night because we do not know what moment that they will set our house on fire. We have had a gard a little while after dinner and we feel a little more protected.

Soldiers returning from their campaign against Hood, marching through Atlanta to their points of rendezvous saw "Clouds of heavy smoke rise and hang like a pall over the doomed city." Major Ward Nichols of Sherman's staff could think only of Atlanta as he first had seen it when roses bloomed in the gardens of fine houses on the shaded streets, and church bells calling the devout to worship were the only sounds on Sundays such as this. He concluded sadly that, "The heart was burning out of beautiful Atlanta."

Captain George W. Pepper, marching with Logan's corps toward selected bivouacs on the east and south sides of the city, was awed by the scene around him:

> Clouds of smoke, as we passed through, were bursting from several princely mansions. Every house of importance was burned on Whitehall street. Railroad depots, rebel factories, foundries

and mills were destroyed. This is the penalty of rebellion. Heaven and earth both agree in decreeing a terrible punishment to those perdidious [sic] wretches who concocted this wasting and desolating war.

One spot, however, Pepper found unscathed: "The cemetery, lovely city of the dead."

"Leave nothing standing," Sherman had said, referring, however, to buildings of business, commercial, or military value. Private dwellings were supposedly exempt, and sentries had been posted before churches to prevent their being damaged; soldiers had been forced to use the streets instead of sidewalks, to discourage arson and looting. But such precautions were largely futile; the holocaust could not be checked. Showers of sparks ignited private homes and spread the fire through residential areas. Pillaging became widespread as soldiers and civilians risked the flames to dart into the burning buildings in search of loot.

The reporter David Conyngham observed that "Drug stores, dry goods stores, hotels, negro marts, theaters, and grog shops were all now feeding the fiery element. Wornout wagons and camp equipage were piled up in the depot, and added to the fury of the flames . . . men plunged into the houses, broke windows and doors with their muskets, dragging out armfuls of clothes, tobacco, and whiskey, which was more welcome than all the rest. The men dressed themselves in new clothes, and then flung the rest into the fire."

A few important buildings were saved by resourcefulness and courage. The Medical College, formerly used as a hospital, was empty and marked for the torch. Dr. Peter Paul Noel D'Alvigny, the only Confederate surgeon remaining in the city, resolved to save it. Enlisting the aid of his staff and civilian volunteers, he placed them in cots on the upper floors and coached them in their roles.

As Federal soldiers began to ignite the tinder piled at the entrance to the college, Dr. D'Alvigny pleaded that he had patients inside, in too critical a condition to be moved. Impossible, the troopers said; the building had been abandoned. D'Alvigny led them to the upper floors where the well-rehearsed actors groaned and writhed in agony. Sobered by this sight, the soldiers helped Dr. D'Alvigny extinguish the flames already started and the building was saved, though the doctor himself was severely burned in the attempt.

Father Thomas O'Reilly of the Church of the Immaculate Conception, whose good works were known even to the enemy, appealed directly to General Slocum to spare his church, and succeeded in saving four others as well. There were enough good Catholics in the Union forces to support the priest; and when a renegade soldier was caught trying to fire Mayor Calhoun's house, which might have endangered O'Reilly's church, he was summarily shot. Since most of the sacrosanct churches were near the city hall, that building also escaped all but minor damage.

All the armories and arsenals, machine shops, laboratories, car shed, depot, mills and foundries, were burned. It was not enough that the buildings should be razed. Nothing within was left intact. In the machine shop, tools and machinery were smashed or twisted out of shape. In the ruins of the car shed, the flanges of surviving wheels were broken. Sheet metals were rendered useless; pumps and boilers were destroyed. Some equipment, such as fire engines, was shipped North.

On November 15 the inferno reached peak intensity. "Oh what a night we had," wrote Carrie Berry on the morning following. "They came burning the store house and about night it looked like the whole town was on fire. We all set up all night. If we had not sat up our house would have been burnt up for the fire was very near and the soldiers were going around setting houses on fire where they were not watched. They behaved very badly. They all left town about one o'clock this evening and we were glad when they left for no body knows what we have suffered since they came in."

After sunset, Henry Hitchcock witnessed the finale from heights above the city:

> At night, the grandest and most awful scene . . . immense and raging fires, lighting up whole heavens—probably, says Sherman, visible at Griffin, fifty miles off. First bursts of smoke, dense, black volumes, then tongues of flame, then huge waves of fire roll up

into the sky; presently the skeletons of great warehouses stand out in relief against and amidst sheets of roaring, blazing, furious flames—then the angry waves roll less high, and are of deeper color, then sink and cease, and only the fierce glow from the bare and blackened walls, etc. Now and then are heavy explosions, and as one fire sinks another rises, further along the horizon . . . a line of fire and smoke, lurid, angry, dreadful to look upon.

It was only fitting that this Wagnerian finale should be orchestrated. After dark a prize band of the Massachusetts Infantry, bivouacked in the city square, began serenading the city with its brass and cymbals. David Conyngham saw scores of soldiers gathered around the band, "cheering and singing and fairly revelling in the excitement and novelty of the situation." To the citizens of Atlanta, Colonel Underwood thought, the musicians must have appeared like "so many Neroes fiddling with delight at the burning of Rome. It seemed like a demoniacal triumph over the fate of the city that had so long defied Sherman's armies."

Underwood would never forget those final hours of Atlanta's agony:

No darkness—in place of it a great glare of light from acres of burning buildings. This strange light, and the roaring of the flames that licked up everything habitable, the intermittent explosions of powder, stored ammo. and projectiles, streams of fire that shot up here and there from heaps of cotton bales and oil factories, the crash of falling buildings, and the change, as if by a turn of the kaleidoscope, of strong walls and proud structures into heaps of desolation; all this made a dreadful picture of the havoc of war, and of its unrelenting horrors.

That night in the spirit of "the show must go on," but more in Nero's tradition than Broadway's, the band gave a concert in the Athenaeum—a building also marked for the torch but spared for this performance. Noted one member of the audience, "the flaming red light from the approaching fire which flooded the building, the roar of the flames and the noises of the intermittent explosions added scenic effects which were not down in the bill, and will never be forgotten." Major Hitchcock, also in the audience, agreed. "Always will the Miserere in *Trovatore* carry me back to this night's scenes and sounds."

Understandably, the performance started and ended early; and as soon as concluded, the untiring band, one of the finest in the army, assembled in front of Sherman's quarters on Washington Street to serenade their general. The musicians shifted from the classical cadences of Verdi to themes in which the gathering hordes of soldiers could join vocally, "John Brown's Body Lies a-Mould'ring in the Grave". . . . Other bands in bivouacs around the city, other voices, picked up and made the song a mighty paean to the flames, "We'll hang Jeff Davis to a Sour Apple Tree." . . . Late into the night, while Atlanta crashed and burned, the bands played and the soldiers sang—till dawn bleached out the flickering flames. Sherman's aide, Ward Nichols, thought he had never heard anything "so grand, so solemn, so inspiring."

At dawn on the 16th while the city still glowed beneath a pall of smoke from the ashes of its fires, Sherman assembled his 62,000 troops along Decatur Street and the McDonough road. He had divided his army into two wings, the right commanded by General Howard, the left by General Slocum, assigning himself to Slocum's column. Commissary General Amos Beckwith had supplied the troops with 1,200,000 rations, about twenty days' supply, and a herd of beef cattle would accompany the army on the hoof. To supplement these provisions Sherman had decreed: "The army will forage liberally on the march."

After telegraphing to Thomas that he was on his way and leaving to him the defense of northern Georgia and eastern Tennessee, a dot of whiskey was issued to the troops, and Sherman gave the signal to advance. Bugles relayed the order down the line, and the two long columns, bayonets gleaming in the morning sun, started moving south and east, followed by their white-topped wagons. To the beat of the march the troops raised their voices in a mighty chorus:

> Mine eyes have seen the glory of the coming of the Lord;
> He is trampling out the vintage where the grapes
>   of wrath are stored . . .

Sherman observed that never before had he heard the Battle Hymn of the Republic "with its chorus of 'Glory, glory hallelujah!' done with more spirit, or in better harmony of time and place."

20

Grapes of Wrath

Sherman was roaring to the sea. Jubilo! Jubilee! Nothing could stop his "dashing Yankee boys" or dull the knife-edge of their spirits.

As yet they did not know their destination, but who cared? They hooted and looted and sang as they marched; ate prodigiously of everything in sight; slept on sweet-scented pine boughs underneath the stars. It was a traveling picnic, a six-day carnival, with everything free and prizes spread along the roadside for the taking. There had never been anything, in this or any other war, to match it.

Yet for all its seeming lack of restraint, the march was a masterpiece of organization and carefully calculated self-sufficiency. Even without the two corps sent to Tennessee with General Thomas, to keep Hood's Confederates in check, it was a mighty army: 55,000 infantry, 5,300 cavalry, 2,000 mounted artillerists attending the caissons of some 65 guns. Woven into its columns were 600 ambulances and 2,500 canvas covered wagons drawn by 15,000 mules. In its wake trod 5,000 head of cattle to keep the troops supplied with beef. While the troops might forage the countryside for other foods, the army was a fully self-contained community, dependent on no supply line, no communication with the outside world, no base behind it or in front of it.

The route had been carefully prescribed. The army moved in four separate columns, to leave in doubt its destination. Mobile? Augusta? Charleston or Savannah? The two columns of the left wing under Henry Slocum, accompanied by General Sherman, followed roughly parallel courses southeast from Atlanta, heading toward Covington and Milledgeville. The two columns of the right wing, commanded by Oliver Howard, moved almost due south toward Macon, to swerve east and join with Slocum's divisions in the neighborhood of Sandersville. Thus deployed, the army cut a swath sixty miles in width, five miles in length.

Ahead of the army rode Kilpatrick's cavalry, snaking back and forth between the heads of the four columns, scouting for Joe Wheeler's troops which Hood had sent from Tennessee to harass the Federals in Georgia. Wheeler was there all right, but never there for long. He settled for gnatlike bites at Sherman's flanks, then generally vanished when "Kill" Kilpatrick's cavalry appeared. Sherman gave Wheeler little thought. A nuisance, no more. "Wheeler is whipped if boldly attacked by half his number," he observed. Later he would say of "Fighting Joe's" dragoons and of mounted troops in general: "My marching columns of infantry don't pay the cavalry any attention. They just walk right through it."

From the start, Sherman recorded in his memoirs, all the elements united to bode success for the adventure. "The day was extremely beautiful, clear sunlight with bracing air, and an unusual feeling of exhilaration seemed to pervade all minds—a feeling of something to come, vague and undefined, still full of venture and intense interest." On leaving Atlanta he had paused near the hill where McPherson had been slain, one of the saddest moments of the campaign, and looked back on the smoldering city. He etched that sight into his memory. For in a sense he was not leaving Atlanta but taking the precedent of its destruction with him. Just as Atlanta had fallen, and much of Southern morale with it, so all of Georgia must be devastated to bring to full fruition what had started here. All the towns and villages in his path were small Atlantas; he would make a similar example of them.

In Special Field Order No. 120 issued on November 9 the

General had stated the organization, the route, the chain of command, the pace to be observed ("about fifteen miles per day"), and above all the rules and regulations governing the march. The army would forage liberally, with each brigade maintaining its own raiding party led by "discreet officers." The soldiers were forbidden to enter private homes, threaten or abuse the occupants, but could gather cattle, poultry, grains and vegetables as needed by the army; could appropriate horses, mules, and wagons "freely and without limit; discriminating, however, between the rich, who are usually hostile, and the poor and industrious, usually neutral or friendly."

In short, the army would rely for food upon the foragers, who could range at any distance from the line of march. As to another objective,

> To corps commanders alone is intrusted the power to destroy mills, houses, cotton-gins, etc.; and for them this general principle is laid down: In districts and neighborhoods where the army is unmolested, no destruction of such property should be permitted; but should guerrillas or bushwhackers molest our march, or should the inhabitants burn bridges, obstruct roads, or otherwise manifest local hostility, then army commanders should order and enforce a devastation more or less relentless, according to the measure of such hostility.

More than any other factor, however, the character of the venture hinged, as it always does, upon the character of the participants. Of 218 regiments making up the army, all but 33 originated in the West and were imbued with the backwoods frontier qualities of independence and resourcefulness. They welcomed the order to stick to the fields and leave the roads to the wagon trains. They scorned to sleep in tents, but made their beds of pine boughs on the open ground. They took what they wanted from the countryside, and everything was fair game. They were a devil-may-care lot, arrogant, irreverent. Sherman, who had once inspired awe, was now hailed up and down the line with shouts of "Ho, there, Uncle Billy!" As the general noted with some anxiety, they might be hard to discipline.

The foraging parties, generally composed of 50 men from

each brigade and accompanied by carts and wagons, sometimes even by artillery, were the envy of the army. Known as "Sherman's bummers" they started out at dawn, often traveling far afield, to return at dusk with carloads of corn and vegetables, trains of mules and sheep and cattle, the soldiers often dressed in rich bizarre attire acquired from some plantation owner, with live chickens hanging from their belts and smoked hams aloft on their bayonets. Sometimes their clothing smelled suspiciously of smoke and singed wool and their boots were caked with ashes.

No farm, plantation, or hamlet in their rangy path was overlooked. Thomas Maguire's experience on his Promised Land Plantation near Stone Mountain was as typical as any. Maguire noted on November 15, "Smoke considerable at Atlanta . . . we are now waiting for the worst to come." The worst came on the following day, as the owner of the Promised Land recorded:

Up last night nearly all night. News that Yankees were coming this way after burning Atlanta, Decatur, and some houses at Stone Mountain. Hid out box tools, horse, buggy and other things . . . A little after ten Slocum's corps came and camped all around the house. At every side hogs and sheep are being shot down and skinned to regale the Yankee palates . . . Slept in the woods all night.

Nov. 17.—Still in the woods. Slept but little, was dodging about in the woods trying to see the Yankees from our hiding place. Yankees all gone about 11 o'clock. Came home to find . . . great destruction of property. Gin house and screw burned, stables and barn all in ashes, fencing burned and destruction visible all around. The carriage and big wagon burned up, corn and potatoes gone, horse and steers gone, sheep, chickens and geese, also syrup boiler damaged, one barrel of syrup burned, saddles and bridles the same . . . corn cribs, gin house still burning and the straw piles, also three bales of cotton burned and others cut open to make beds for the soldiers . . . the gin thrash and fan burned, the castings and other parts of machinery in ruins; the destruction of Jerusalem on a small scale.

In the wake of this destruction came a curious phenomenon. The following day Maguire noticed hordes of civilians, seemingly natives and distant neighbors, swarming over his property

—to glean what they could from what the Yankee foragers had overlooked. It was an ugly pattern. Frequently Wheeler's Confederate cavalry, fleeing before Sherman's troops, would be the first to raid a planter's or a farmer's stores. Then came the Yankee foragers to do a more thorough job. And finally the victim's neighbors or the local tramps who regarded their fellow, more unfortunate Southerners as fair game in these times of stress.

Worst of all were the stragglers—soldiers who dropped behind the line of march to join the foraging parties as unlicensed delegates. Their ranks were often swelled by hobo soldiers and deserters, belonging to no military unit, subject to no regulations. It was they who broke into private homes, stole what they wanted, then burned the house out of malice or to cover up their vandalism. It was impossible to control them; the march could not be hampered by sending policing units to the rear. Many stragglers suffered the fate of being captured by Confederate cavalry. "Serves 'em right," said Sherman grimly. "I hope the rebels shoot 'em."

Henry Hitchcock, recently enlisted and still new to army life, viewed these proceedings through civilian eyes and with civilian conscience. He was troubled by them. "If one stopped to think over all the losses or estimated all the real anxiety caused by the *simple march* of an army like this, it would be sad enough," he wrote. But the officers seemed to be tolerant of this unlicensed mayhem. Although guards were sometimes posted before private homes to watch for unwarranted violations, they often looked the other way. Reluctantly Hitchcock concluded, "I am bound to say I think Sherman lacking in enforcing discipline."

While the foraging parties deviated from the line of march like the offshoots of the Gulf Stream, some towns, such as Covington, were directly en route and marked for temporary occupation. At the Burge Plantation, Dolly Burge heard that the Yanks were on the way and thought, "Oh, God, the time of trial has come." Telling her frightened slaves to hide, Dolly ran to the gate to claim protection for her property:

> But like demons they rush in. My yards are full. To my smoke-house, my dairy, pantry, kitchen and cellar, like famished wolves

they come, breaking locks and whatever is in their way. The thousand pounds of meat in my smokehouse is gone in a twink-ling, my flour, my lard, butter, eggs, pickles of various kinds . . . jars and jugs are all gone. My 18 fat turkeys, my hens, chickens and fowls, my young pigs, are shot down in my yard and hunted as if they were rebels themselves. Utterly powerless, I ran out and appealed to the guard.

"I cannot help you, Madam; it is orders."

As I stood there, from my lot I saw driven, first, my dear old buggy horse . . . then came my brood mare, with her three-year-old colt, my two-year-old mule and her last little baby colt. There they go! There go my mules, my sheep, and, worse than all, my boys [slaves] . . . forced from home at the point of a bayonet.

Not often were slaves abducted by force, although Sherman's orders provided that "Negroes who are able-bodied and can be of service to the several columns may be taken." These reached a quota of 6,800, employed as cooks and wranglers, camp attend-ants, and a work force assigned to clear the road of felled trees and obstructions raised by Southern sympathizers to delay the army's progress. Their former owners scathingly referred to them as "Sherman's reinforcements," hoping that the stolen blacks, or those who willingly joined the Yankees for their free-dom's sake, might prove to be a liability.

They threatened to be, if not a liability, at least a problem. As the army progressed through central Georgia thousands of blacks, deserting the plantations, followed or flanked the col-umns in an endless jubilee. Though their numbers and faces changed with the geography, as many as 25,000 might be counted at a given time. They hailed "Marse Sherman" as the new Messiah, a red-bearded Moses come to carry them down freedom's road. They clung to his stirrups and caressed his horse; they begged to carry the soldiers' haversacks and rifles; the women frequently offered more intimate services. Mothers hid their babies in the army wagons, hoping thus to have them carried to the Promised Land. Sherman finally enlisted a black country minister to help to discourage this horde of followers; he had not the wherewithal to feed and clothe them.

Still, as he noted in his memoirs, Sherman was moved and gratified by this reception from the blacks of Georgia. Whereas white people watched the passage of his army with ill-concealed hatred, "the negroes were simply frantic with joy."

> Whenever they heard my name, they clustered about my horse, shouted and prayed in their peculiar style, which had a natural eloquence that would have moved a stone. I have witnessed hundreds, if not thousands, of such scenes; and can now see a poor girl, in the very ecstasy of Methodist "shout," hugging the banner of one of the regiments, and jumping up to the "feet of Jesus."

Though the pace of the marchers had been set at fifteen miles a day, it was slowed to a leisurely ten, to allow time for the thorough destruction of the railroads in their path: the Georgia, the Macon, and the Georgia Central. "Cump" Sherman personally supervised what had become, to him, almost an obsession. The rails, he instructed his troops, must be twisted and not merely bent. Bent rails could be straightened. Twisted rails required a rolling mill to put them back in shape. And sometimes as a playful flourish, the bent rails were formed into the letters "U S" and left on the roadbed as a taunting sign of Union power.

Sherman had vowed to make Georgia howl, and Georgia howled. The Georgia press referred to Sherman as "a thousand fiends in one," and predicted that the demoniac general was marching to his doom. "God has put a hook in Sherman's nose," a minister told his congregation, "and is leading him to destruction." Few editors saw Sherman's march for what it was, a punishing offensive against Georgia and the South. Rather, it was a flight from the dread specter of his adversary, General Hood and his inescapable Confederates. The Union leader was retreating to the Gulf where he would be, according to a popular pun, "engulfed." The *Macon Telegraph* confirmed this view. "Sooner or later his crimes will find their Nemesis. . . . The desolator of our homes, the destroyer of our property, the Attila of the west, seeks sanctuary. His shrine is the sea." Significantly, the paper did not specify what sea.

From higher quarters came the call for impossible resistance. Governor Brown cancelled all furloughs he had previously and unwisely granted the militia; and now tried desperately to augment the militia by recruiting young boys from the military schools, and by releasing convicts from the penitentiary on their promise to enlist. Beauregard hastened to Georgia to exhort its citizens to "Arise for the defense of your native soil! Rally around your patriotic Governor and gallant soldiers. Obstruct and destroy all the roads in Sherman's front, flank, and rear, and his army will soon starve in your midst." Howell Cobb, militia general, put Negroes to work at blocking roads and laying land mines, or torpedoes, in the army's path.

Traveling incommunicado, Sherman neither saw these published threats, nor suffered any consequence from them. Stopping at a mansion ten miles short of Milledgeville, he discovered a wooden chest with the name "Howell Cobb" inscribed upon it, and realized he was at one of the Georgia patriot's plantations. "Of course, we confiscated his property," the general wrote. "I sent word back to General Davis to explain whose plantation it was and instructed him to spare nothing."

With every mile the momentum and enthusiasm of the march increased. The foragers spared little, and the troops had more than they could eat or use—more cattle, more mules and wagons, so many horses that General Kilpatrick ordered five hundred of them shot in one community, leaving their carcasses strewn around a local planter's mansion. The owner protested he would have to move; he was left with no means of removing the dead horses and he could not live amid the stench.

The foraging parties became less discriminate and more abandoned in their looting. Sometimes slaves directed them to hidden family treasures, caches of silver, jewels, sentimental heirlooms such as Revolutionary swords and regimentals. Private William Sharpe of Slocum's Twentieth Corps saw the foragers arrive with "anything that had wheels, drawn by anything that could pull," and return with their conveyances piled high with baby carriages, musical instruments, four-poster beds, and "every imaginable thing under the sun a lot of good soldiers would take it in their heads to bring away." Atop one load was "a man in an antique two-story stovepipe hat, a Revolutionary shad-belly coat, and black velvet knee-breeches, who pressed to his lips a six-foot stage-coach horn and blew it as if his name was Gabriel. . . ."

Their ultimate goal, as well as their route and progress, remained secret. Even President Lincoln, asked about Sherman's destination, said complacently, "I know what hole he went in at, but I can't tell you what hole he will come out of." This lack of news gave scope for vicious rumors, most of them from Southern sources, many from Atlanta. In that city, it was said, Sherman had not only burned buildings but their imprisoned occupants as well. Blacks had been slaughtered, babies bayoneted in their cribs, women raped, Confederate prisoners had had their throats cut. And these atrocities were being perpetrated now all over Georgia by Sherman's rampant host of robbers, arsonists, and rapists.

Actually, there were few, if any, atrocities as such. Southern womanhood was respected, though Georgia belles were verbally chastised for encouraging their men to fight in the Confederate army. Foragers or stragglers found in overt violation of the rules were threatened with shooting on sight, and a number of suspects were court-martialed. Sherman himself might call on local leaders to convince them of his good intentions: Only those communities offering resistance, burning bridges or taking pot shots at his troops, would suffer punishment. Sometimes he met with plucky indignation, sometimes his smooth diplomacy won friends. An odd response was often, "Why not leave Georgia be, and go after the rebels in South Carolina. They seceded first; they started the whole thing."

There were strange contradictions in the troops' behavior. Though cautioned against expending bullets, they shot every dog in sight in the belief that hounds had been used to capture escaped prisoners as well as runaway slaves. Yet the ranks swarmed with pets: raccoons, lambs, opossums, cats, small donkeys, scores of gamecocks—the latter pitted against one another in campfire cockfights. The troops were harsh toward adult Southerners but sentimental about children. More than one orphaned child, abandoned by a fleeing and impoverished family, was adopted by the army, fed and clothed, and carried on the shoulders of the marching troops to care and safety.

Similarly, while the Western regiments especially held no brief for emancipation, and scoffed at the thought of using blacks for anything but menial labor, they had a kindly feeling for these hapless souls intoxicated by the heady wine of freedom. At one point the marchers noticed on their right an aged shoeless black, bent by years of servitude, who raised a battered hat in tribute to his liberators. Down the ranks went the order, "Eyes right!" Heads turned sharply, officers drew their swords and saluted as they passed. Moved to tears by the gesture, the old man shuffled into line behind the column. Asked where he thought he was going, he said reverently, "Anywhere you-all is going."

Right on schedule, November 22, Slocum's two columns reached the Confederate capital of Milledgeville, and Sherman entered the town to "a grand reception, colors dipped, cheers, music." Up to that moment the state legislature had been in caucus, voting on Governor Brown's bill to extend the draft age and framing appeals to noncombatants to bushwhack the invading army. Hearing of Sherman's arrival, the patriotic governor led the legislature's flight to Macon. The troops took over the capitol building, held a mock session in which they voted Georgia back into the Union and appointed committees to kick Joe Brown and Jefferson Davis in their respective derrières. "I was not present at these frolics," Sherman wrote, "but heard of them at the time and enjoyed the joke."

This buffoonery was not the only incident in the capture of the capital. "A full detail of enormities committed," said the Milledgeville *Confederate Union*, "would fill a volume," and some of the details were unfit to print. Troops and horses were quartered in the city's churches where the men poured syrup into the organs "to make the music sweeter." The capitol building was ransacked, factories, depots, arsenals destroyed, along with the penitentiary from which the convicts had been just released to fight with the militia.

Because of Confederate press reports which were seen for the first time in Milledgeville and which lied atrociously about the army's "criminal" behavior, there was more vicious vandalism here than hitherto. One citizen, Peterson Thweatt, complained of the wreck of his home in a letter to Alexander Stephens:

All our provisions, crockery, silver, bed clothing, our own clothing, &c &c were taken or destroyed. Our parlor furniture given away to negroes, and most of what we had, what they left, was what was returned to us by our own or other negroes. Our nurse was taken and has never been heard from since. My wife and children lived on Potatoes for several days, and the negroes fed them from the leavings of the Yankees. . . .

Milledgeville was tacitly regarded as a halfway point. Halfway to where was still uncertain, but the Gulf was out. Augusta seemed unlikely. Charleston or Savannah seemed the best bets. In any event, "Here begins Act Two," wrote Major Hitchcock in his journal, adding the description: "Life in open air, riding daily, and tent life, very jolly." It was, in the Major's eyes, "the perfection of campaigning," offering full opportunity for "independent and vigorous enjoyment."

The men were slightly more unruly after their Milledgeville rampage. Still, they sang jubilantly as they marched, twisted rails, foraged liberally, set fire to the roadside fences to illuminate their way by night. In the evenings the bands serenaded one another, and the soldiers chorused the perennial favorite, "John Brown's Body," and "When This Cruel War Is Over," and a hymn that had suddenly gained popularity and seemed to fit the circumstances, "This Far the Lord Has Led Me On."

Hitchcock turned his mind and pen to the scene, writing on November 29, "Afternoon perfectly lovely and tonight beautiful starlight: atmosphere dense and smoke from campfires hangs low."

> Have been out of tent since writing last sentence and strolled around camp to fix scene in mind. Worth remembering. Dark outlines of pine trees all around. Clear beautiful starlight above— atmosphere hazy with smoke. In rear of our line of tents, large "fly" tent for mess. . . . At distance glow campfires from which even this late (10:30 P.M.) come through still night air sounds of voices—soldiers calling, laughing, faint shouts, etc.; while, from without, the light in our tent shines through its white canvas walls.

All four columns loosely converged at Sandersville, southeast of Milledgeville, and proceeded toward the peninsula lying between the Savannah and Ogeechee rivers. Here tall stands of pine flanked sandy roads, and the plantations became more pala-tial. Though ricefields replaced the avenues of corn, there was still plenty of forage—for which Sherman could thank Jefferson Davis' edict that Georgia planters should substitute food crops for cotton. The yams were so big, the soldiers claimed, that they could sit on one end while roasting the other end over their fires. "Never," wrote Major Hitchcock, "was an army so bountifully supplied."

Advance cavalry units had hoped to liberate Union prisoners held in the Confederate stockade at Millen. But the prisoners had been removed, and the army saw only bleak evidence of the dreadful life they had endured. Their plight was confirmed when several emaciated soldiers who had escaped from Ander-sonville Prison told of the horrors of that infamous stockade. The army clamored for revenge. Sherman ordered the destruc-tion of all transportation and commercial facilities at Millen, adding, "Let it be more devilish than can be dreamed of."

The troops, however, did not stop at quasi-military targets. They made an example of the Greek Revival mansion of the William Jones plantation where, with Jones in the Confederate army, his wife was mourning the untimely death of twins. The raiders ravaged the plantation, set fire to the house, and dug for silver believed hidden in the yard. All they dug up were the bodies of the twins. Sherman called on Mrs. Jones to apologize and ordered that provisions be delivered to the mother from the army mess.

But as Hitchcock noted at the time, the general's attitude toward these injured Southerners was hardening. Jefferson Davis, not he, had brought this destruction on his people. If they were outraged, let them vent their wrath on those who had led them into this rebellion. Meanwhile, if Sherman could drive them to despair, he was being merciful. That much sooner would the war be ended.

Major Hitchcock had begun to share this point of view. Though admitting that "It is a terrible thing to consume and destroy the sustenance of thousands of people, and most sad . . . to see the terror and grief of these women and children," he added:

Evidently it is a material element in this campaign to produce among the *people of Georgia* a thorough conviction of the personal misery which attends war, and of the utter helplessness and inability of their "rulers," State or Confederate, to protect them. And I am bound to say that I believe more and more that only by this means can the war be ended—and that *by this means it can.*

Sherman had anticipated Confederate resistance at a number of likely points: Milledgeville, Millen, and several fords and bridges over the Ogeechee River on his right. For this, among other reasons, Howard's corps followed a path south of the Ogeechee, ready to flank any stand that the Confederates might make, while Kilpatrick's cavalry continued to zigzag ahead of the army to keep Wheeler's cavalry off balance. Rarely did Wheeler have time or opportunity to make a solid stand. Barricades hastily erected near Waynesboro were stormed and broken by Kilpatrick's cavalry with 500 Confederate horsemen killed or wounded, the rest retreating in confusion.

After Millen there was no doubt that their destination was Savannah. Here it was known that General Hardee, now commanding this department of the South, lay in waiting with from 10,000 to 15,000 Confederate troops and orders from Davis to make "every effort" to obstruct the Federal advance. Sherman regarded Hardee as an able successor to Joe Johnston, schooled in the latter's strategy of retreat and ambush practiced in the campaign for Atlanta. Danger from Hardee increased as Sherman moved down the peninsula between the Savannah and Ogeechee rivers. But armed resistance failed to materialize, though expected, at the hamlet of Ogeechee Church where the Confederates had erected breastworks across Sherman's route, then fled at the threat of being flanked by Howard's corps across the river.

One form of hostile action was evinced, however, when a young lieutenant of cavalry was found lying on the roadway, his horse killed and his leg blown off by a sunken "torpedo" or land mine buried in the sand. Sherman's low boiling point was lowered further by the incident. Torpedoes might be sanctioned before breastworks threatened with assault. Planted in the open highway they were barbarous murder. He ordered a group of rebel prisoners brought to the front, armed them with picks and shovels, and made them precede the army in close formation, "so as to explode their own torpedoes, or to discover and dig them up." Though the use of prisoners as any form of screen was generally frowned upon, even the moderate Major Hitchcock condoned the action as an answer to what he scathingly called "Southern chivalry."

The otherwise unobstructed march slowed down as it approached Savannah. Scouts reported that General Hardee had retreated to the city with his troops intact and well entrenched; that Savannah was, in fact, as strongly fortified as Vicksburg formerly had been.

For the first time the question of supplies arose. With the army halted before Savannah, perhaps facing a prolonged siege, it was imperative that Sherman make contact with the South Atlantic squadron blockading the coast from Charleston to Ossabaw Sound. He could not take the city unless he were certain of the fleet's support. He presumed the Navy knew of his position, but the secrecy on which he had insisted worked now to his disadvantage.

On Decembser 8, eight miles from Savannah, three scouts from Howard's corps were dispatched in a canoe, to drift past Fort McAllister near the mouth of the Ogeechee River and to convey to the fleet the news of Sherman's arrival, his position, and the army's need for food and clothing. Two days later they had not been heard from. Some blacks in the neighborhood reported seeing rockets fired out at sea, but what they signified nobody knew.

Meanwhile, on the road to Savannah, Sherman trained his field glass on the city, saw the familiar Southern parapets bristling with abatis, gun barrels shining from the rifle pits. As if in calculated warning a puff of smoke rose from one of Hardee's batteries. The General watched the dark speck of the cannonball approaching. He and a strolling negro were directly in its path. He called to the other to duck and leaped to the side of the road, barely escaping the missile which decapitated the unheeding black.

Plainly Hardee's batteries were on their toes, his forces well prepared. Sherman would not risk a frontal attack, in spite of his superior numbers. Nor could he afford a prolonged siege such as was forced upon him at Atlanta. Then he had had supply lines feeding him ammunition and provisions from the north. Here he was isolated, with the army on its own. The only alternative was to flank the city by following the Ogeechee River which flowed into Ossabaw Sound. There he could join with the fleet and effectively surround Savannah, forcing Hardee to face starvation or surrender.

Only one obstacle blocked this route: Fort McAllister, built at the start of the war, since strengthened, and now garrisoned by 230 men under Major G. W. Anderson. Well gunned and strongly constructed as it was, it would have to be taken by his infantry. He picked for the job the men of his own division which had served with him at Shiloh, greenhorns then but veterans now. He placed them, on December 13, under the command of General William B. Hazen, who had also fought with him at Shiloh, telling Hazen that the success of the whole campaign depended on the capture of the fort. Then he climbed with his staff to the roof of a nearby rice mill to observe the action.

At precisely 4 P.M. Hazen's forces were seen emerging from a woods and onto a plain extending to the fort—a single column in parade formation, bayonets fixed, twenty regimental colors flowing in a perfect line. No one broke step, no shot was fired, as they pressed toward the fort. "My old division," Sherman murmured. "I knew they'd do it!" This was the moment of truth on which he had staked his reputation and the future of his army.

The fort exploded in flame and thunder. The earth beneath the rice mill trembled. When the smoke had cleared the entire division had disappeared. An aide next to Sherman whispered, "No, by God!" The General lowered his glasses in stunned disbelief. He could watch no more. A whole division, his own division, wiped out in a single blast!

Then, like a shimmering mirage, the picture changed. A freak of topography had tricked the viewers. Just at the moment of the blast the troops had reached a shallow depression in the field which dropped them briefly out of sight and out of range. Now they swarmed over the rim of the hollow and raced toward the

fort, their sharpshooters picking off the gunners on the breastworks, the infantry seemingly immune from bullets. In seconds
they were beneath the trajectory of the cannon, climbing the
parapets like flies.

Sherman breathed a sigh of deep relief. Still shaken, he allowed his gaze to shift from the fort to the river just beyond. His
eyes caught sight of the Stars and Stripes flying from a warship
on the river—his first contact with the outside world in thirty
days. An officer on the vessel's bridge wigwagged the question:

"Who are you?"

His signal officer sent the reply: "General Sherman."

The ship's flags posed the cardinal question. "Is Fort McAllister taken?"

"Not yet, but it will be in a minute."

Sherman's confidence was not misplaced. In hardly more than
a minute Fort McAllister came alive with Union troops. They
swarmed atop the parapets, dancing, waving flags, and shooting
off their muskets. With almost a quarter of his garrison lost,
Anderson had readily surrendered. Hazen signalled to General
Sherman, "Take a good big drink . . . the fort is ours!" Then,
with Southern-type courtesy, Hazen invited his defeated adversary to have dinner with him. Major Anderson accepted.
Though not included in the dinner invitation, the victorious
division celebrated with a banquet of its own: "Oyster soup,
oysters on the half shell, fried oysters, raisins, coffee, and roast
oysters." No doubt about it, they had reached the sea.

Sherman's first act on pausing before Savannah showed a rare
consideration for his troops. They had had no word from home
for many weeks. Sherman ordered that all mail, held on order
at Atlanta, be delivered at top speed. With the first batch came
a message for him from the President, intended for delivery at
whatever destination Sherman's march should take him. Lincoln's words: "God bless you and the army under your command. Since cutting loose from Atlanta, my prayers and those
of the nation have been for your success."

His success, however, was not quite complete. Hardee still
occupied Savannah in an obstinate, defiant fashion, while a message from Grant suggested that Sherman forego capturing the

city and proceed "with all dispatch" to join Grant in the siege of Richmond. Sherman was irate at the idea, "for I had set my heart on the capture of Savannah." He was aware how much his conquest of Atlanta had demoralized the South; how his march to the sea had all but climaxed his campaign in Georgia. He needed Savannah not perhaps for military reasons but to tidy up the job.

He could not turn down his commanding general but he answered Grant evasively, citing his achievements on the march through Georgia and his plans to take Savannah. Sherman had the city, with 25,000 civilians and 15,000 troops (his estimate), surrounded—virtually. Only one little used wagon road was open to South Carolina; it hardly seemed worth the risk of sending a part of his force to occupy it. He would bring up his siege guns, ring the city, and force Hardee to surrender. "With Savannah in our possession we can punish South Carolina, as she deserves, and as thousands of people in Georgia hope that we will do." Then he would hasten up the coast, by land and sea, to join Grant's forces pressing against Richmond.

Time became a factor now. He could not keep Grant waiting long. Under a flag of truce Sherman sent a courier to Hardee, demanding the surrender of Savannah. The city was surrounded, its supply lines cut. If Hardee resisted, Savannah would face the same intense bombardment, the same ultimate destruction, as was vented on Atlanta.

Hardee, with little more than 9,000 troops against Sherman's 62,000, tersely rejected the demand, adding significantly that he still had means of getting adequate supplies.

That "unused" wagon road again! Sherman decided to request that General John G. Foster of the Union Army, conveniently stationed at Port Royal, send troops to obstruct the road. He proceeded up the marshy coast on Admiral Dahlgren's flagship *Harvest Moon* to call on Foster. Caught by low tide, the ship became ingloriously stranded in the mud. As Sherman nervously paced the deck and ran his fingers through his ruddy hair, General Hardee led his entire army out of Savannah, up the wagon road, to the safety of South Carolina.

Sherman's troops entered the city on December 21. Though Hardee's escape was disappointing, the Confederates had left behind abundant stores of cotton, guns, and ammunition. Timing his message to reach Washington on December 25, the general telegraphed to President Lincoln:

> I beg to present you as a Christmas gift, the city of Savannah, with one hundred and fifty guns and plenty of ammunition, also about twenty-five thousand bales of cotton.

Then he settled down to study the many dispatches now delivered to him from Atlanta, bringing him up to date on events of which he had been uninformed since leaving that city in the middle of November. He read from Southern press reports that his army had suffered a terrific beating, had been "harassed, defeated, starved, and had fled for safety to the coast." He also discovered that in spite of all his secrecy there had been a leak of information in Atlanta where his entire field orders on leaving that city had been published. "It is impossible to carry on a war with a free press," he growled.

More to his satisfaction were Grant's reports on the outcome of Hood's pursuit of Federal forces in east Tennessee . . .

John Bell Hood, finally crossing the river from Alabama into Tennessee in late November, was a long way from Atlanta. But out of sight was not out of mind—he smarted from the shame of his defeats around Atlanta. He could not recover that city now, with three hundred miles of distance intervening. But he might recover his lost prestige, with glory after all, by defeating Thomas and Schofield, ranged against him now in Tennessee. This might force Sherman to leave Georgia, or enable Hood to go to the aid of Robert E. Lee and share in the defense of Richmond.

The Army of Tennessee was in far from the best condition. Thousands were shoeless and ill-clothed for that bitter winter. But their numbers were still formidable: three corps under Davis, Stewart, and Cheatham, totalling almost 32,000 men. Although Wheeler had been returned to Georgia to gnaw on Sherman's flanks, Hood had been joined by 8,000 cavalry under the wily Nathan Bedford Forrest. Hood set his sights on Nashville, one of the most strongly fortified cities to the north, where Thomas was entrenched.

At Franklin, Tennessee, on November 30, the Confederates

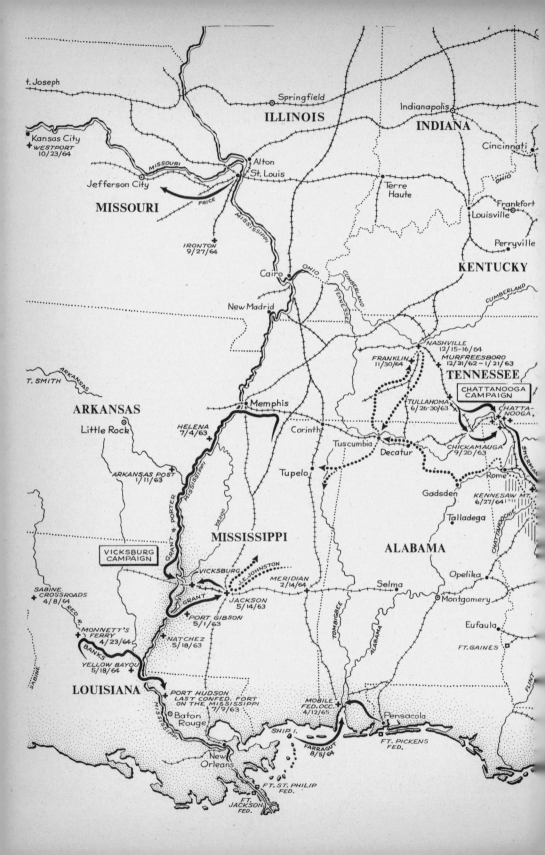

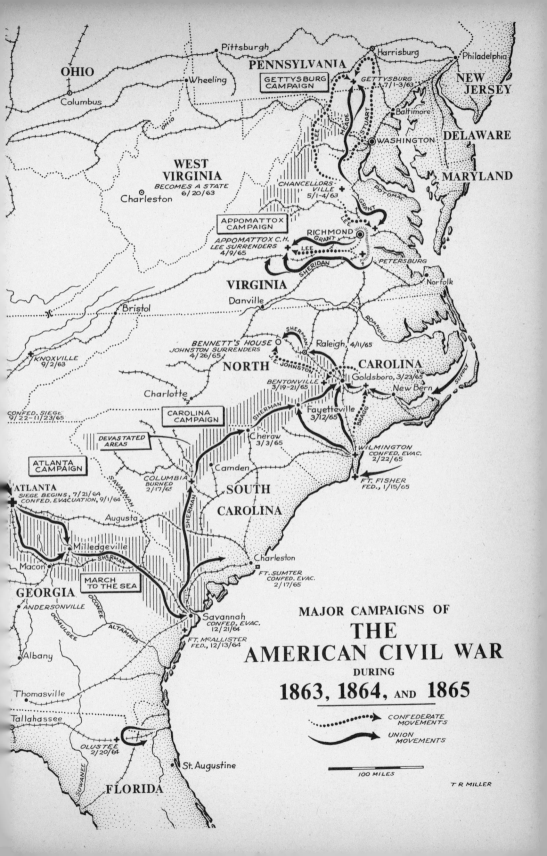

OHIO
Pittsburgh
PENNSYLVANIA
Harrisburg
Philadelphia
Wheeling
GETTYSBURG 7/1-3/63
Columbus
GETTYSBURG CAMPAIGN
STUART
NEW JERSEY
Baltimore
MEADE
LEE
DELAWARE
WEST VIRGINIA
BECOMES A STATE 6/20/63
Charleston
WASHINGTON
CHANCELLORS-VILLE 5/1-4/63
POTOMAC
MARYLAND
GRANT
APPOMATTOX CAMPAIGN
RICHMOND GRANT
LEE
APPOMATTOX C.H. LEE SURRENDERS 4/9/65
LEE
PETERSBURG
SHERIDAN
VIRGINIA
Danville
Norfolk
Bristol
ROANOKE
SHERMAN
BENNETT'S HOUSE JOHNSTON SURRENDERS 4/26/65
Raleigh 4/11/65
KNOXVILLE 9/2/63
J.E. JOHNSTON
NORTH
CAROLINA
Goldsboro, 3/23/65
SUPPLY
Charlotte
BENTONVILLE 3/19-21/65
New Bern
CAROLINA CAMPAIGN
SHERMAN
Fayetteville 3/12/65
BRAGG
CONFED. SIEGE 9/22-11/23/65
DEVASTATED AREAS
Cheraw 3/3/65
WILMINGTON CONFED. EVAC. 2/22/65
ATLANTA CAMPAIGN
Camden
FT. FISHER FED., 1/15/65
COLUMBIA BURNED 2/17/65
SOUTH CAROLINA
ATLANTA SIEGE BEGINS, 7/21/64 CONFED. EVACUATION, 9/1/64
SAVANNAH
SHERMAN
Augusta
Milledgeville
Charleston
SHERMAN
FT. SUMTER CONFED. EVAC. 2/17/65
Macon
MARCH TO THE SEA
GEORGIA
ANDERSONVILLE
MAJOR CAMPAIGNS OF
THE AMERICAN CIVIL WAR
DURING
1863, 1864, AND 1865
OCONEE
OCMULGEE
ALTAMAHA
Savannah CONFED. EVAC. 12/21/64
FT. McALLISTER FED., 12/13/64
Albany
Thomasville
Tallahassee
SUWANEE
CONFEDERATE MOVEMENTS
UNION MOVEMENTS
OLUSTEE 2/20/64
St. Augustine
100 MILES
FLORIDA
T R MILLER

were blocked by General Schofield's strongly entrenched forces. Disregarding the reluctance of his officers, Hood ordered most of his army forward in a mass assault. It was the General's last great hour of display, a spectacle never again to be equalled in the war. In perfect formation, eighteen brigades, with banners whipping in the breeze, advanced to the music of their regimental bands. Artillery and musket fire mowed them down like shucked corn. Those remaining climbed over their dead to reach the breastworks where fierce hand-to-hand fighting left few survivors. According to one comment, "It was more a slaughter than a battle." By the time both armies withdrew in darkness, Hood had lost 6,300 men, with a disproportionate number killed. Five Generals had died, including the irreplaceable Pat Cleburne. The Army of Tennessee was all but crippled.

Undeterred by this catastrophe, and assuring his troops that they had gained a "victory," Hood pressed on toward Nashville where Thomas' Army of the Cumberland awaited him. Commander in Chief U. S. Grant was worried about the aging Thomas and thought of replacing him with Logan. Would the slow-moving, fifty-eight-year-old general come out from behind his breastworks and fight? Thomas did. The first day, December 15, in a furious assault, he almost swamped Hood's tattered army. On the following day the Confederate general met his Waterloo. His flank crumbled from the Federal offensive, "and in a few moments," Hood confessed, "our entire line was broken . . . ."

Hood, too, was broken. In a few weeks he relinquished his command. The once indomitable Army of Tennessee, glorious under Joseph Johnston, retreated across the frozen land, its dispirited soldiers chanting in the sleet and snow:

> And now I'm going southward
> For my heart is full of woe,
> I'm going back to Georgia,
> To find my 'Uncle Joe.'

Headquartered at the home of Charles Green, wealthy English merchant of Savannah, Sherman took stock of his campaign in Georgia, from Atlanta to the sea.

As his final reports to Grant and Halleck would reveal, his troops had inflicted damage amounting to $100,000,000—$80,000,000 of which could be considered "simple waste and destruction." More than 200 miles of railroad had been wrecked, bridges and trestles burned, telegraph wires downed. Some 1,500 "first rate mules" had been appropriated from their owners to replace the overworked, underfed animals with which the army had set out. The number of horses stolen was incalculable, perhaps 60,000, so many that Sherman had had "great numbers" shot because he felt it was bad for morale to have his army riding when it ought to be on foot. Besides, the wholesale slaughter deprived the enemy of valuable mounts.

The 5,000 head of cattle he had started with had not been touched; the number had been doubled. And the quality as well had been improved as underweight or sickly steers were traded off for better animals. The army had consumed great quantities of turkeys, chickens, pigs, sheep, cattle, corn, oats, rice, potatoes. Most of what it couldn't eat, it had destroyed—along with barns, bins, presses, wagons, farming and industrial tools. Arsenals, factories, warehouses, mills, and business houses had gone up in smoke. In short, all means of production had been crippled, all produce or equipment that could be used by Hood in Tennessee, or by Robert E. Lee in Virginia, had been demolished.

Except for minor losses in Kilpatrick's cavalry, there had been no serious casualties until the storming of Fort McAllister which had cost the army only ninety men in dead and wounded. And virtually no desertions. The army was stronger, healthier, and happier than any army since the war began; adequately clothed and more than adequately fed. Morale was as high as weeks of lording it over the enemy and living off his land could make it. And in Sherman's eyes, the army's multiple rewards had been well earned.

So, on January 8, was issued Sherman's Special Order No. 6. It hailed General Thomas' victory over Hood at Nashville and linked the Army of Tennessee's defeat to the capture of Savannah—two distant but related conquests that had sealed the fate of the Confederacy. With a knife plunged into the heart of Atlanta, its twin blades slicing alternately north and south, the Confederate States of America had been split in half, a wound no miracle could heal. In Sherman's words, "So complete a success in military operations, extending over half a continent, is an achievement that entitles it to a place in the military history of the world."

Thus, continued Sherman's Order No. 6, the army that had defeated Hood in Tennessee and that which had marched with Sherman to the sea were alike entitled "to inscribe on its colors, at pleasure, the word 'Nashville' or 'Savannah.' " They had marched in two directions to the same goal, the destruction of the South. Greater, however, than the sum of all its parts was the initial army that had marched from Ringgold Gap in early May, with another more important name inscribed forever on its shield: 'Atlanta.'

21

Unconquered and Unconquerable Hearts

At first there was just that eerie sound . . .

It seemed [wrote Sarah Huff] to start a long way off and came to us from the northeast or the direction of Peachtree Creek. Mother said it sounded to her like the moaning of doves. But no doves or other birds were heard, even when the springtime came. The bluebirds were missed for three years. No, it was not the sound of doves, but the distant baying of dogs, dangerous dogs.

The memory of Sherman's "mad dogs" in blue uniforms was still rife when wild dogs, in canine flesh, took over the wrecked city of Atlanta. Abandoned by their fleeing masters they roamed the hollow streets in vicious packs, threatening everything that moved including their own kind, and feeding off the carcasses of thousands of dead animals that lay within the city limits. But the cats—that was a different story. "Man's best friend had reverted to wolflike tendencies," wrote Sarah Huff. "But Tabby, who had been inconstant ever, welcomed us back home."

The Huffs, who were among the first to return to the ruined

city, found their home only partially destroyed. A Scottish neighbor, George Edwards, had raised a British flag over the house in the hope of protecting it from arsonists and vandals. Even so, the Huffs were obliged to live in the old log kitchen until the main house could be repaired; and as soon as a fire was lit in the stove "in came the cats. Cats of all sizes, cats of all colors, white, gray, yellow, spotted and black . . . ready to devour the scanty food before anybody could scare them away from the pot, the skillet or the half canteen in tin plates on the table."

Yet anything living was welcome in that charred husk of a city, surrounded by a landscape like the surface of the moon. The Perkersons still clung to their once prosperous and well-provisioned farm on the southeastern limits. The house had suffered only minor damage, but all outbuildings had been burned. They were left, wrote Lizzie, with "one hog, two old Yankee mules, and ten dogs." The family was dressed in little more than rags because "The Yankees broke our loom all to pieces and burned it." But Lizzie and her mother foraged around and found another loom, and now, "if we can get any wool carded we will make some clothes yet."

Writing on the back of an army hospital muster roll, which was the only paper she could find, Lizzie informed her brother Angus, fighting in Virginia:

> We are cut off from the world as yet. Atlanta is a perfect mass of ruins. All the public buildings are gone except the City Hall. Whitehall street swept completely. Cousin Dan . . . says he hasn't the shape of a house on the place, although he is coming back just as quick as he can get a place to go into. All the citizens are pushing back.

No city during the war, or previously in America, had been so thoroughly annihilated as Atlanta. Yet the people, as Lizzie said, were "pushing back," grimly resolved to pick up the loose threads of their broken lives. They came, the formerly dispossessed, with little more than what they carried on their backs or in dilapidated wagons pulled by blind, decrepit army mules who were also castoffs of the war—bringing their kitchenware, bedding, one or two cherished family heirlooms, and nearly useless

Confederate dollars worth 4½ cents if there was anything to buy. Like the settlers of the Western frontier towns now rising on the Plains, they had little going for them but the will to survive until they could salvage enough materials to build a shelter from the weather—then a home, then a city.

The sight that met their eyes was one of utter desolation: streets all but obliterated, pocked with bomb craters threatening to swallow the unwary; charred, skeletonlike chimneys marking where homes and buildings once had stood; piles of tin roofing and loose bricks, some of these reconstructed into wretched shelters from which peered the frightened, hungry eyes of homeless Negro children. Three thousand corpses of dead animals spread a stench of death and decay above the ruins, while on the surrounding red hills still rose, in stark relief, the stout clay fortifications built to make Atlanta unassailable.

On top of all were the hordes of bushwhackers and deserters from both armies, some calling themselves Confederate scouts, who sought to pick the rubble clean of anything of sustenance or value. Residents of surrounding neighborhoods were not above participating in this ghoulish quest, as Carrie Berry noted on November 17: "Some Confederates came in here today and the town is full of country people seeing what they could find. We have been picking up some things." And on the following day, "We children have been plundering about today seeing what we could find. Mama has been trying to straiten up for the house was torn up so bad."

Only a few days after Sherman's troops had left, the family had "begun to feel at home," wrote Carrie in her diary, "but it does not look like Atlanta." She went to the park to see if she could gather up some hickory nuts, but did not get many, because two thirds of the trees had been destroyed; and she also helped her sister bury their pet guinea pig, cause of death unknown. On November 22 Carried noted, "It is just a week to day since the federals were burning. Papa and Mama say that they feel very poor. We have not got anything but our little house. It is still very cold. . . . We all feel very lonesome."

Mary Gay, who had ridden back to her home from Rough and Ready behind an army surplus mule, found that she was "hungry, very hungry," but was more concerned with the welfare of her ailing mother. "In vain did I look around for relief. There was nothing left in the country to eat. Yea, a crow flying over it would have failed to discover a morsel with which to appease its hunger. . . . Every larder was empty, and those with thousands and tens of thousands of dollars were as poor as the poorest, and as hungry, too." Confederate money, Confederate bonds, were all but worthless; no one had any gold or silver. Those who still possessed their slaves found these an added burden, since they had to be fed and clothed.

Mary had heard that a trading post had opened in Atlanta "for the purpose of bartering provisions for munitions of war. . . . Minie balls were particularly desirable." She and Telitha, baskets in each hand, set out to comb the battlefields. It was the end of November, bitterly cold, with a sharp wind blasting through the stripped and unprotecting trees. But they moved fast and purposefully toward the site of the old Confederate arsenal, whose wreckage provided a mine of ice-encrusted bullets, pieces of lead, and minie balls. Feet almost frozen, hands cracked and bleeding, they filled their baskets and trudged back to the city.

Presaging the words of Winston Churchill by almost a century, Mary recorded her emotions on this journey: "Lead! Blood! Tears! O how suggestive! Lead, blood, and tears, mingled and comingled. In vain did I try to dash the tears away." But there was relief in the tears they shed, and both were composed when they reached the city, finding no streets to follow but directed to the "commissary" by kindly strangers.

A wounded ex-soldier in faded gray uniform sized up the two blood-stained, tearful women, and asked what they wanted for their lead. Mary requested a few essential staples with possibly a little meal. The man weighed the lead in a back room and returned with the baskets filled with sugar, coffee, flour, meal, lard and meat.

"Sir, I did not expect so much," said Mary frankly.

"You have not yet received what is due you," said the man in gray. Kind words, but charged with bitter irony in the light of subsequent events.

With no doctors or medical supplies available, the specter of sickness and epidemic haunted citizens remaining or returning. Lizzie Perkerson wrote to her brother Angus fighting with the Confederates in Virginia:

They all fear that I am taking fever now, but I hope not. I feel very badly, but I have gone through enough to make a stouter person than me feel badly. I hadn't undressed to go to bed until last night. There has been a great deal of sickness in this country since the army came here. But I don't think strange of it. The whole country is full of dead horses and mules, and the ditches full of stagnant water.

Lizzie summed up her situation in a closing paragraph to Angus: "We are making our calculations to live rather hard next year. But if we can live at all, I am not afraid that we will perish."

By "we" it is fair to believe that Lizzie was thinking of the South and the Confederacy. For the women of Atlanta were the guardians of more than memories; they were the keepers of the flame. As one perceptive Southerner, Robert S. Henry, wrote, " . . . it was among the women of the South that the spirit of resistance flamed highest." Now, at this moment of extreme trial, it flamed higher still; and William Tecumseh Sherman, marching through Georgia, complained that the mothers, wives, and sisters of the Confederacy offered more open defiance to his plundering troops than did the gray-clad cavalry nipping at his heels.

In Atlanta they showed the same defiance to adversity. With most of their men away at war, they would get by somehow, and rebuild the city with their bare hands if they had to.

Ten days after Sherman left Atlanta sinking in an "ocean of flame," Georgia's Howell Cobb, general of militia, made plans to reoccupy the city. He appointed Colonel Luther J. Glenn commander of the reestablished military post, and by the following week Glenn had invested the city with a semblance of authority. A provost marshal, Captain L. T. Todd, was appointed and a commissary depot reestablished for the purpose, at this stage, of distributing wheat and other grains. Farmers around the city were urged to bring whatever produce remained from the fall harvest after Sherman's troops had disappeared.

To offset the shortage of wood for fuel, almost all trees in the city and environs having been demolished, enterprising youngsters like Atlanta newsboy L. C. Butler gathered charcoal and seared lumber from the burned-out buildings to be peddled to returning natives.

That same week Georgia's Governor Brown assigned General W. P. Howard of the state militia to survey the ruined city, appraise the damage, and report to him. Howard estimated that of 3,800 houses in the corporate limits, only 400 remained. In the greater city area, some 4,500 homes had been destroyed, or roughly ninety percent.

Every hotel but one had been consumed, all educational institutions, and all public buildings, save the damaged city hall. "The car shed, the depots, machine shops, foundries, rolling mills, merchant mills, laboratory, armory, etc., all burned. . . . All business houses, except those on Alabama Street, were burned. . . . The suburbs present to the eye one vast, naked ruined, deserted camp. . . . "

Had he arrived with some militia ten days earlier, Howard told the governor, he could have saved a million dollars worth of property left behind by fleeing troops and citizens and subsequently looted and stolen in "incalculable amounts. Bushwhackers, robbers and deserters, and citizens from the surrounding country for a distance of fifty miles have engaged in this dirty work."

But, concluded Howard, "the crowning act of all their wickedness and villainy was committed by our ungodly foe in removing the dead from the vaults in the cemetery, and robbing the coffins of the silver name plates and tippings, and depositing their own dead in the vaults."

The general sounded one note of hope. While the Federal troops had destroyed all machinery and tools, boilers, engines, pipes and switches—seemingly everything tangible of use— "yet a vast deal of valuable material remains in the ruins. Three-fourths of the bricks are good and will be suitable for rebuilding if placed under shelter before freezing weather." Among machinery put out of commission, particularly in the railroad shops was a quantity of brass and copper that could be melted down and used again. In Atlanta's ashes lay the seeds of future life.

As November turned to December, the city's heart began to beat again. Mayor James M. Calhoun returned to resume his

duties, along with most of the city council, armed with a treasury reserve of $1.64. Municipal elections were held—though
hardly more than a formality—and a newspaper correspondent
found that "Col. L. J. Glenn, the efficient commandant of the
post is considered the right man in the right place. He is courteous to all, yet rigidly attentive to the interests of the government
and people."

A start had been made, a nucleus created. Er Lawshe, formerly one of Atlanta's leading merchants, came back to look for
a place in which to set up business. Finding none, he arranged
for a single-story wooden building to be towed to Whitehall
Street, where he opened its doors for the sale of almost anything
available, from hats costing hundreds of Confederate dollars to
a bushel of wheat costing fifty. In time, Lawshe's makeshift
establishment would be replaced by a three-story building of
good Atlanta brick.

Other businesses were resurrected in humble form through
individual initiative. A bar was opened on Decatur Street where
proprietor Whit Anderson "services his customers with dignity
and grace." A drink of poor whiskey cost $5, good whiskey $10.
Sid Holland's grocery store started up on Peachtree Street, and
Johnson Birdwell's salt factory began operating. A post office
opened on Decatur Street, with Bob Yancey's barber shop starting up next door. The railroads no longer ran, of course, but tie
by tie and rail by rail they were being rebuilt on the north and
south approaches to Atlanta.

In mid-December Jared Whitaker returned from Macon with
the *Daily Intelligencer* to resume publication in a battered shoe
factory on Alabama Street. The newspaper was, of necessity,
reduced to tabloid size, and the editor asked petulantly why
surviving journals in other cities "do not send us their paper.
With our railroad torn up and the telegraph wires down, we
have but little chance to hear what is going on in the outside
world . . . this deprivation is particularly unpleasant."

There was plenty to record, however, on the state of things
at hand. "Twenty-five years ago the present site of Atlanta was
a forest, which but a few years previous to that time was the
abode of the red man. Then a great system of railroads was
developed . . . to what is now the Gate City of the South.

"War came, and Atlanta was still a progressive city. Until the spring of the present year population and wealth literally poured into it. As a commercial depot it was in advance of any city in adjoining states. As a financial mart it rivaled the most progressive cities of the South, and, as a military post, it became second to none, save Richmond, in importance.

"To the enemy it became a prize, coveted as much as Richmond. Almost superhuman efforts were made to capture and possess it."

And now:

> Today, as you approach Atlanta from either side, you no longer find it hidden from view by the dense forest of trees which a few months ago obstructed the eye of the traveler. For miles around scarcely a tree is standing, and within a few miles of the city, fire and ax have destroyed habitations and laid waste fields. As you reach the city limits, you see the awful effects of one vast conflagration. A city destroyed by fire! . . . But so much for the past and present of Atlanta. Let us now look to its future.

During December there was evidence that people were heading the *Intelligencer*'s call to "put their own shoulders to the wheel" and raise Atlanta "out of the slough into which she has been cast." In increasing numbers the older citizens returned and "the general watchword," noted one correspondent, "is repair and rebuild." Maxwell Berry, contractor for some of the finer structures in the former city, now aided in repairing the few salvageable homes; while scores of jerry-built wooden shacks, adequate for shelter, began rising along Peachtree Street. George W. Adair opened an office for the sale and exchange of real estate, and "Cousin John" Thrasher who had built the first sawmill in Atlanta twenty years before reappeared on the streets as a symbol of the city's pioneer determination.

Many returned to spend Christmas in their shattered homes or in the homes of friends. There was little to celebrate, that holiday season, and few amenities with which to rejoice. For those wishing to enjoy good coffee, suggested the *Southern Confederacy*, tongue in cheek, let them "take bark, three parts, three old cigar stumps and a quantity of water, mix well, and boil 15 minutes in a dirty coffee pot." The resultant brew would match the best available, the paper guaranteed.

At Thomas Maguire's Promised Land Plantation, as the holidays approached, Maguire "whipped three negroes after dinner . . . so much for stealing. I hope this will be the last for some time." A few days later he found that "Little or no preparation for Christmas is being made." And on December 25, "Not much fuss this morning by the little ones about Christmas. Not like it used to be in other years."

At the Burge plantation in Covington, stripped of most of its precious household possessions by Sherman's bummers, Dolly Burge, that Christmas, made a sorrowful notation in her diary: "December 25, 1864. . . . Sadai jumped out of bed very early this morning to feel her stocking. . . . She ould not believe but that there would be something in it. Finding nothing, she crept back into bed. . . ."

Nor in Atlanta was Christmas as it used to be, with nothing to be exchanged but wishes for a better year to come. One church, however, opened for the holy day, the First Baptist where the Reverend Henry C. Hornady delivered the first post-destruction Christmas sermon in the city, a message of not-so-visionary hope for Peace on Earth.

Day by day, hour by hour it seemed, the Confederacy was shrinking, its spirit broken by defeat, its armies riddled by desertions. And in the first four months of 1865 the saddest war in American history drew to its conclusion.

As Washington talked of reconstruction and both sides groped for a negotiated peace, an intransigent Jefferson Davis named Robert E. Lee commender in chief of the Confederate armies. The appointment meant little, came too late. Lee remained with the Army of Northern Virginia holding a taut line around Petersburg and Richmond which, however, eroded and raveled week by week under relentless Union pressure.

After a month's rest in Savannah, William Tecumseh Sherman and his 60,000 dashing Yankees headed north, leaving the seacoast to the Union Navy for subjection. Burning Columbia, South Carolina, the unopposed column captured Fayatteville and headed for Goldsboro in North Carolina, with the dread cry of " 'ware Sherman!" heralding its progress and columns of black smoke rising in its wake.

Davis and Lee brought "Little Joe" Johnston back into the war, replacing John Bell Hood as commander of the Army of Tennessee—an army reduced by death and desertions to a pitiful 18,000 men. Johnston joined forces with Hardee and stood up to Sherman for the last time at Bentonville, North Carolina, outnumbered by almost four to one. A three-day battle that started well for the Confederates ended in disaster.

Lee's over-extended line before Richmond snapped and broke, and President Davis fled the capital, calling on the South to resist with "unconquered and unconquerable hearts." It was almost all the South had left, and it was not enough. When Lee surrendered to Grant at Appomattox ("in awed stillness . . . as if it were the passing of the dead"), Johnston was left alone with the battered, once-glorious Army of Tennessee. With extraordinary consideration and compassion, Sherman offered his long-time foe surrender terms so generous that Washington demanded more severity before approving them. After that there were just a few loose pockets to clean up, Kirby Smith in the Trans-Mississippi, Bedford Forrest in the West.

By the end of May, 1865, the war was over.

One million ninety-five thousand dead.

Ten thousand skirmishes and battles fought.

From six to nine billion dollars squandered (though who could tell how much for sure?).

And what had it all accomplished? A disunited country never to be quite the same again; a way of life, for better or worse, destroyed; seeds of hatred sown that would require generations to suppress.

With the resilience of a youthful nation, Americans turned from the past and looked toward the future, to their manifest destiny in the great expanding West. But Atlanta looked to the future on its own soil, fertilized by blood and ashes, waiting for the spring rains.

On a warm, moist evening of early June, 1865, young John Townsend Trowbridge, Boston writer, arrived in Atlanta with an unfinished manuscript in his carpetbag. Its tentative title: *A*

Picture of the Desolated States and the Work of Restoration. He found Atlanta's streets unlighted, the mud ankle deep, the hotels full; but he managed to find lodgings in a tavern overrun by "capering rats" who made off with his stockings while he slept. The next morning he set out to make a survey of the city:

> Everywhere were ruins and rubbish, mud and mortar and misery. The burned streets were rapidly rebuilding; but meanwhile, hundreds of inhabitants, white and black, rendered homeless by the destruction of the city, were living in wretched hovels, which made the suburbs look like a fantastic encampment of gypsies or Indians. Some of the Negro huts were covered entirely with ragged fragments of tin roofing from the burned government and railroad buildings. Others were constructed partly of these irregular blackened patches, and partly of old boards, with roofs of huge warped, slouching shreds of tin, kept from blowing away by stones placed on top.

One returning refugee assured the Boston writer that extraordinary progress had been made that spring. "When I came back in May," he said, "the city was nothing but bricks and ruins. It didn't seem it could ever be cleared. But in six weeks new blocks began to spring up, till now you see more stores actually in operation than we ever had before."

Yet Trowbridge, arriving from a land untouched by war, observed the disconsolate rows of shanties used as stores, and in between, the plight of families crowded into huts "which a respectable farmer would hardly consider good enough for swine." Speculators charged enormous rents for scarcely habitable lean-tos, and encouraged the returnees who had lost their homes to build on land where they could live, rent free, for twelve months, after which the property reverted to the broker.

Blacks and whites stood on a common footing: destitution. Families who had lost all other property in the war had sent their slaves into hiding in advance of Sherman's army. Now these were returning to share in the paucity of their owners, needing to be clothed and fed. Freedom was not their principal concern; Sherman had promised them that; he had not promised anything beyond that, such as mere survival.

There was talk in Richmond of recruiting blacks to fight for the Confederacy, a move proposed and bitterly opposed before the Atlanta campaign started. Now it made sense; Davis and Robert E. Lee approved; and several black regiments were forming to join in a last-ditch fight for the old South.

In addition, thousands of blacks were passing through the city headed for plantations on the Mississippi. Many got no farther than Atlanta, wives and children abandoned by their hardier menfolk to seek shelter in the ruins and subsist on charity. Smallpox was prevalent and observed no color line. "Half the black children will be dead within a year," one refugee assured John Trowbridge.

A young Confederate officer, Edward Young Clarke, chose this point in history to commence what he insisted "may generously be considered the first history of Atlanta ever attempted." From one point of view, he selected his beginning well—a time when Atlanta was rising like a phoenix from its ashes, to become in time one of the great cities of the nation and the capital of Georgia. He devoted much of his chronicle to that summer of 1865, when the metropolis was recovering from

> . . . a calamity as terrible as was ever experienced by an American city, even in the Revolutionary times of 1776. The desolation was utter; but marvelous as had been its career up to its capture, the resurrection of Atlanta from its ashes, by a people moneyless as well as homeless, with thousands of widows and homeless thrown upon their care, is more marvelous still in the rapidity with which the city not only recovered its former proportions, but sped far ahead of them.

Clarke gave credit where credit was deserved. "To the return of the old population, with their olden characteristics, intensified by an almost total loss of property, is chiefly due the restoration to former prosperity with a rapidity rarely, if ever, paralleled in American history."

They returned, the old-new pioneers, with what Jefferson Davis had appealed for—unconquered and unconquerable hearts. John Neal came back, having given two sons to the cause (James had been killed in the three-day conflict at Kingston, North Carolina, in late March, one of the last battles of the war).

Neal brought with him the Marion Battalion battle flag which Andrew had sent him for safekeeping. Sherman's bummers had discovered the silken banner where Andy's sister had secreted it, and had made off with the gilt point of the spear. But the flag itself was preserved.

Perhaps because of painful memories of what the war had cost him, Neal did not reoccupy his former home on Washington Street, since desecrated by serving as Sherman's personal headquarters in Atlanta. He leased it for use as a hotel, and built a new house on Pryor and Mitchell streets where he lived out the rest of his days in service to the city. Five years later the original house became the first home of Oglethorpe College.

As Franklin Garrett notes, "Few of the returnees lost time in vain regret over their property losses. The ruin by which they were confronted spurred them to action. Indeed, survival required action." Even the elderly of the old regime like Judge John Collier, unaccustomed to manual labor up to now, learned to mix brick and mortar for the reconstruction of businesses and homes. Collier's commercial building on Whitehall Street had been reduced to rubble in November. Now, with the aid of his two sons, the judge rebuilt the structure, with an office in which to resume his practice of law.

Samuel P. Richards, the bookseller, who the previous September had considered his exiled family "wanderers upon the face of the earth . . . to return, perhaps never," was back in August to set up shop again, writing in his diary for August 10:

> We are once more in Atlanta! Altho' we cannot say with the MacGregor "my foot is on my native heath"—we can say our feet are in accustomed dust. We arrived safely last evening and found Jabe [Richards' brother and partner] awaiting us at the —*depot*, I was going to say—but alas! that is no more. The ruthless hand of Sherman's vandal host has left nothing of that but the debris of its materials. Our quarters are now in the upper room from the window of which just one year ago, I used to watch the shells as they came hurtling and whizzing towards us. This afternoon Jabe and I walked to town, and a dirty ruin it is, but still, busy life is resuming its sway over its desolate streets and any number of stores of all kinds are springing up as if by magic in every part of the burnt district, and enormous rents are asked and obtained for

very indifferent store-houses. I guess we shall have to start in the
"Peters St." house, which is rather too much retired tho' for a
store.

Dr. Henry Hornady, having reactivated his Baptist Church,
opened the first postwar school in its basement for the boys and
girls of parents and guardians in Atlanta. The *Intelligencer* regarded the school as one that "the youth of both sexes . . . now
running wild . . . absolutely require—a school where they can
be taught all that the necessities of the times demand for the
rising generation . . . that they may be prepared to play their
part in the time which will soon come."

Lizzie Perkerson, who had so resented the Yankee occupying
forces in the summer of 1864—suggesting by letter to her
brother Angus that if he ever met up with a certain Captain
Williams in Sherman's forces he should punch him in the mouth
—ended up by marrying a Yankee, Sumner Butler of New York.
After Butler's death, however, Lizzie returned to Atlanta and
the home where she was born, living to a venerable ninety-seven
years, to see the city become the towering, shining symbol of a
New South.

Others, too, lived out their lives in the burgeoning metropolis:
the Huffs, the Hulls, the brothers Calhoun, the Braumullers
(having returned after vowing they never would), the family of
Carrie Berry who became Mrs. William Crumley of Atlanta.
Edward E. Rawson, Mary's father, returned to rebuild his store
on Whitehall Street; Jonathan Norcross promoted yet another
railway entering Atlanta from the east, the Air Line Railroad;
while Lemuel P. Grant, builder of the fortifications, retired a
wealthy man and left a portion of his holding to the city as
"Grant Park."

On his Promised Land Plantation, Thomas Maguire still complained of the "vile Yankees" who had left him "nothing we can
call our own . . . I will try to put up with my loss as best I can."
In his journal he expressed the postwar quandary of the Georgia
planter in that summer of 1865:

What is to become of us as a people? I fear we will have bad
times, but some think otherwise, and some think we will be

treated kindly by the Yankee government, but I am not of this opinion. I have no faith in the Yankees, nor in their love for us. They have treated me so badly I can never forget their meanness and dishonesty—as a people I look upon them as rogues and swindlers.

For his blacks who had run away or been taken by Sherman's troops as they rampaged to the sea, he felt a mixture of compassion and self-pity. Their departure "will be a disadvantage to me and a great misfortune to them. . . . The race, I think will be exterminated in a few years."

Though Southern rural life changed greatly in the interval before the next great war in 1918, "I doubt," wrote Julian Street in that year, "that there is in the entire South a place where it has changed less than on the Burge Plantation near Covington, Georgia." The widow Burge, Dolly Sumner Lunt, remained in the old, white, comfortable house, surrounded by its oaks and cotton fields, with her second husband, the Reverend William J. Parks. Her daughter Sadai also married a minister and inherited the home and the tradition of Southern fortitude and gracious living that it represented.

Mary Gay, seemingly paler and more fragile than a year before, saw and heard, down the long corridor of years to come, "the quiet closing, one by one, of doors." There was not a pittance of sympathy for the small brunette who had lost a beloved half brother, Tommy Stokes, and then her mother, not to mention her faithful servant Toby.

But she had been too friendly with the Yankees. Neighbors had seen her enjoying and serving "Lincoln coffee" to the occupying troops. She had used her feminine wiles and her Yankee connections to travel behind enemy lines, often bearing bundles of suspicious nature. And her home had been spared much of the damage inflicted upon others. In the overheated passions of the times, in a less basically civilized community, Mary, an "obvious collaborator," might have suffered a much sterner fate than ostracism. As it was, the neighbors left her pointedly alone, and she in turn rarely left the vacant house. She had no friends, no lovers, only occasional visits from her widowed sister, Missouri, to relieve the loneliness of her declining years.

With Tommy gone, she never wanted to betray the trust he had imposed upon her, saw no reason to explain that her overt chumminess with the enemy had been a means of preserving and carrying provisions to the Army of Tennessee. She who had been roundly cheered by an entire regiment of that immortal army needed no further reassurance of her loyalty, her service to the Cause. What others thought mattered little now. Nothing mattered very much; and in this deserted house with little more than memories for company, Mary spent the waning years in finishing her diary and in writing poetry for her own diversion.

The stern, self-righteous women of Decatur never softened their opinion of her, never lifted the pressure of their contempt. And Mary, for her part, never crumbled under persecution, any more than she had yielded to the trials of a cruel war she had helped to fight. Growing bent, old, and crippled she survived well into another century, dying at ninety years of age.

That was in 1918; and once again the lights were going out all over the world, not, said Sir Edward Grey, to "be lit again in our lifetime."

One might have said the same on seeing the flames die over Atlanta in the fall of 1864. And been wrong. For the lights were already being lit again, never to be extinguished in the nation's lifetime.

Bibliography

Abernethy, Byron R. (ed.), *Captain Elisha Stockwell Jr. Sees the Civil War.* Norman, University of Oklahoma Press, 1958.

Allen, Ivan, *Atlanta from the Ashes.* Atlanta, Ruralist Press, 1928.

Ambrose, Stephen E., *William T. Sherman: a Re-appraisal.* American History Illustrated, January 1967.

Archer, William P., *History of the Siege and Battle of Atlanta.* Knoxville, Moncrief Co., 1941.

Austin, J. P., *The Blue and the Gray.* Atlanta, Franklin Publishing Co., 1899.

Battery, Robert, personal papers and letters for 1864. Manuscripts, property of Special Collections Department, Robert W. Woodruff Library, Emory University, Atlanta, Ga.

Beers, Fannie A., *Memories.* Philadelphia, Lippincott, 1889.

Bell, Piromis H., *The Calico House.* Atlanta Historical Bulletin, Vol. I, No. 6, January 1932.

Benton, Charles E., *As Seen from the Ranks.* New York, Putnam, 1902.

Berry, Carrie, diary, August-December, 1864. Typescript in possession of Atlanta Historical Society, Atlanta, Ga.

Blay, John S., *The Civil War.* New York, Crown, 1958.

Bryan, T. Conn, *Confederate Georgia.* Athens, University of Georgia Press, 1953.

Buchanan, Lamont, *A Pictorial History of the Confederacy.* New York, Crown, 1951.

Buck, Irving A., *Cleburne and His Command.* Jackson, Tenn., McCowat-Mercer Press, 1959.

Burge, Dolly L., *The Diary of Dolly Lunt Burge* (James J. Robertson, ed.). Athens, University of Georgia Press, 1962.

Calhoun, James M., *Affidavit as to Facts in Regard to Surrender of Atlanta, September 2, 1864.* Typescript, property of Atlanta Historical Society, Atlanta, Ga.

Calhoun, Patrick H., *Reminiscences.* Atlanta Historical Bulletin, Vol. I, No. 6, January 1932.

Cate, Wirt A., *Two Soldiers: The Campaign Diaries of Thomas J. Key and Robert J. Campbell.* Chapel Hill, University of North Carolina Press, 1938.

Catton, Bruce, *A Stillness at Appomattox.* New York, Doubleday, 1954.

Catton, Bruce, *This Hallowed Ground.* New York, Doubleday, 1955.

Chesnut, Mary Boykin, *A Diary from Dixie.* Boston, Houghton Mifflin, 1949.

Civil War Times, "The Campaign for Atlanta!" Gettysburg, Historical Times Inc., 1964.

Clarke, Edward Y., *Illustrated History of Atlanta* (facsimile reprint of 1879 edition). Covington, Ga., Cherokee Publishing Co., 1971.

Coleman, Kenneth, *Georgia History in Outline.* Athens, University of Georgia Press, 1960.

Commager, Henry S., *The Blue and the Gray* (Vols. I & II). Indianapolis, Bobbs-Merrill, 1950.

Connelly, Thomas L., *Autumn of Glory.* Baton Rouge, Louisiana State University Press, 1971.

Conyngham, David P., *Sherman's March Through Georgia.* New York, Sheldon & Co., 1865.

Cooper, Walter G., *Official History of Fulton County.* Atlanta, Historical Commission, 1934.

Cox, Jacob D., *Atlanta.* New York, Scribner's, 1882.

Cox, Jacob D., *Military Reminiscences of The Civil War.* New York, Scribner's, 1900.

Crane, Sarah Clayton, personal reminiscences, 1861–1864. Typescript in possession of Atlanta Historical Society, Atlanta, Ga.

Crew, James R., letters to his wife, 1864. Typescripts in the possession of the Atlanta Historical Society, Atlanta, Ga.

Crew, Mrs. James R., extracts from diary kept during 1865. Typescript in possession of the Atlanta Historical Society, Atlanta, Ga.

Cumming, Kate, *Gleanings from the Southland.* Birmingham, Roberts & Son, 1895.

Daily Intelligencer, Atlanta. News reports and editorial comments from selected issues published during 1856–1864.

Dodge, Grenville M., *The Battle of Atlanta and Other Campaigns*. Council Bluffs, Iowa Monarch Printing Co., 1911.

Dubose, John W., *General Wheeler and the Army of Tennessee*. New York, Neale Publishing Co., 1912.

Dufour, Charles L., *Nine Men in Gray*. New York, Doubleday, 1963.

Dwight, Henry O., "How We Fight at Atlanta." *Harper's New Monthly Magazine*, xxix, 1864.

Dyer, John P., *The Gallant Hood*. Indianapolis, Bobbs-Merrill, 1950.

Forsyth, Annie, *How the Forsyth Family Refugeed from Atlanta*. 1864. Manuscript in the possession of the Atlanta Historical Society, Atlanta, Ga.

Freeman, Douglas S., *Lee's Lieutenants*, Vol. iii. New York, Scribner's, 1944.

Fremantle, Arthur J. L., *Three Months in the Southern States*. New York, John Bradburn, 1864.

French, Samuel G., "Two Wars." Nashville, *Confederate Veteran*, 1901.

Gay, Mary A. H., *Life in Dixie During the War*. Atlanta, Foote & Davies, 1894.

Garrett, Franklin M., *Atlanta and Environs*, Vol. i. Atlanta, University of Georgia Press, 1969.

Gibson, John M., *Those 163 Days*. New York, Coward-McCann, 1961.

Gorgas, Josiah, *Civil War Diary*. University, Ala., University of Alabama Press, 1947.

Govan, E. G., and Livingood, J. W., *A Different Valor*. Indianapolis, Bobbs-Merrill, 1956.

Grant, Lemuel P., papers and plans for the fortification of Atlanta, 1863–1864. Documents in the possession of the Atlanta Historical Society, Atlanta, Ga.

Grant, Roland, "Memoir of John Chipman Gray." Boston, *Proceedings of the Massachusetts Historical Society*, xlix, 1915–1916.

Grant, Ulysses S., *Personal Memoirs*, Vol. ii. New York, Webster & Co., 1886.

Hagan, John W., *Confederate Letters of John W. Hagan*. Athens, University of Georgia Press, 1954.

Harrison, John M. (ed.), *The Promised Land: A Glimpse of Ante-Bellum Georgia Taken from the Farm Journal of Thomas Maguire*, 1860–1865. Typescript in the possession of the Atlanta Historical Society, Atlanta, Ga.

Hedley, Fenwick Y., *Marching Through Georgia*. Chicago, Henneberry & Co., 1890.

Hill, Louise B., *Joseph E. Brown and the Confederacy*. Chapel Hill, University of North Carolina Press, 1939.

Hitchcock, Henry, *Marching with Sherman*. New Haven, Yale University Press, 1927.

Hoehling, Adolph A., *Last Train from Atlanta*. New York, Thomas Yoseloff, 1958.

Holleran, Cecil J., *Know Your Georgia*. Atlanta, Tupper & Love, 1951.

Hood, John B., *Advance and Retreat*. Bloomington, Indiana University Press, 1969.

Hornady, John R., *Atlanta: Yesterday, Today, and Tomorrow*. Atlanta, Index Printing Co., 1922.

Hubner, Charles W., *Reminiscences of the Sixties*. Excerpts from unpublished autobiography in possession of Atlanta Historical Society, Atlanta, Ga.

Huff, Sarah, *My 80 Years in Atlanta*. Atlanta, privately printed, 1937.

Johnson, R. U., and Buel, C. C. (ed.), *Battles and Leaders of the Civil War*. New York, Century Co., 1884–1888.

Johnston, Joseph E., *Narrative of Military Operations*. Bloomington, Indiana University Press, 1959.

Jones, Katharine M., *Heroines of Dixie*. Indianapolis, Bobbs-Merrill, 1955.

Kemble, Frances A., *Journal of a Residence on a Georgia Plantation*. New York, Harper, 1863.

Kurtz, Annie Pye (ed.), *Atlanta and the Old South*. Atlanta, American Lithograph Co., 1969.

Kurtz, Wilbur G., "Atlanta in the Summer of 1864." Dinkler Hotels, *Inn Dixie Magazine*, January, 1936.

Kurtz, Wilbur G., "A Federal Spy in Atlanta." *Atlanta Historical Bulletin*, Vol. x, No. 38, Dec. 1957.

Kurtz, Wilbur G., "Embattled Atlanta." *Atlanta Constitution*, July 20, 1930.

Leech, Margaret, *Reveille in Washington 1860–1865*. New York, Harper, 1941.

Lewis, Lloyd, *Sherman: Fighting Prophet*. New York, Harcourt, Brace, 1932.

Long, E. B., *The Civil War Day by Day*. New York, Doubleday, 1971.

Lowry, Edward G., "I Have Discovered . . ." *Saturday Evening Post*, June 19, 1920.

Lunt, Dolly S., *A Woman's Wartime Journal*. New York, Century, 1918.

Martin, Thomas H., *Atlanta and Its Builders*. Atlanta, Century Memorial Publishing Co., 1902.

Massey, Kate, "A Picture of Atlanta in the Late Sixties." *Atlanta Historical Bulletin*, Vol. v, No. 20, January 1940.

McCallie, Elizabeth H., "Atlanta in the 1850's." *Atlanta Historical Bulletin*, Vol. VIII, No. 33, October 1948.

McCallie, Elizabeth H., *The Atlanta Campaign*. Atlanta, privately printed, 1939.

McCullar, Bernice, *This Is Your Georgia*. Montgomery, Ala., Viewpoint Publications, 1968.

McMurry, Richard M., "Kennesaw Mountain." Gettysburg, *American History Illustrated*, January, 1970.

Memoirs of Georgia, Vol. I. Atlanta, Southern Historical Association, 1895.

Miers, Earl S., *The General Who Marched to Hell*. New York, Knopf, 1951.

Milhollen, H. D. and Kaplan, M., *Divided We Fought*. New York, Macmillan, 1952.

Morison, S. E. and Commager, H. S., *The Growth of the American Republic*, Vol. I. New York, Oxford University Press, 1962.

Myers, Robert M., *The Children of Pride*. New Haven, Yale University Press, 1972.

Neal, Andrew Jackson, personal letters, 1861–1864. Manuscript in the possession of Special Collections Department, Robert W. Woodruff Library, Emory University, Atlanta, Ga.

Nichols, George W., *The Story of the Great March*. New York, Harper, 1865.

Pepper, George W., *Personal Recollections of Sherman's Campaigns in Georgia and the Carolinas*. Zanesville, Ohio, Hugh Dunne, 1866.

Perkerson, Medora F., *White Columns in Georgia*. New York, Crown, 1952.

Phillips, Ulrich B. (ed.), "The Correspondence of Robert Toombs, Alexander Stephens, and Howell Cobb." Washington, *American Historical Association Annual Report*, 1911, Vol. II, 1913.

Pioneer Citizens Society, *History of Atlanta*. Atlanta, Byrd Printing Co., 1902.

Pratt, Fletcher, *Eleven Generals: Studies in American Command*. New York, William Sloane, 1949.

Pratt, Fletcher, *Ordeal by Fire*. New York, Smith and Haas, 1935.

Rawson, Mary, personal papers for 1864 in possession of the Atlanta Historical Society, Atlanta, Ga.

Reed, Wallace, *History of Atlanta, Georgia*. Syracuse, N. Y., D. Mason & Co., 1889.

Richards, Samuel P., diary. Typescript in possession of the Atlanta Historical Society, Atlanta, Ga.

Secrist, Philip L., *Atlanta 1864: A Study of the Effect of War on Civilian*

Activities. Manuscript in the possession of the Atlanta Historical Society, Atlanta, Ga.

Shavin, Norman, *The Atlanta Century.* Atlanta, Capricorn Corp., 1965.

Sherman, William T., *Memoirs* (Vols. i & ii). New York, Appleton, 1875. Second Edition, Revised and Corrected, Appleton, 1913.

Sibley, Celestine, *Peachtree Street, U.S.A.* New York, Doubleday, 1963.

Simmons, Henry E., *A Concise Encyclopedia of the Civil War.* New York, Crown, 1965.

Small, Sam W., *My Story of Atlanta.* Atlanta, Constitution Press, 1926.

Smith, George G., "Reminiscent Sketches." Published in pages of the *Atlanta Journal* during June, 1932.

Southern Confederacy, Atlanta. News reports and editorial comments from selected issues published during 1863–1864.

Stern, P. Van Doren, *Soldier Life in the Union and Confederate Armies.* New York, Crown, 1961.

Strode, Hudson, *Jefferson Davis, Tragic Hero.* New York, Harcourt, Brace & World, 1964.

Sullivan, James R., *Chickamauga and Chattanooga Battlefields.* Washington, Government Printing Office,1956.

Trowbridge, John T., *The Desolate South, 1865–1866.* New York, Duell, Sloan and Pearce, 1956.

U. S. Department of the Interior, *Kennesaw Mountain National Battlefield Park and the Atlanta Campaign.* Washington, Government Printing Office, 1961.

U. S. War Department, *The War of the Rebellion; A Compilation of the Official Records of the Union and Confederate Armies.* Washington, Government Printing Office, 1880–1901.

Upson, Theodore F., *With Sherman to the Sea.* Baton Rouge, Louisiana State University Press, 1943.

Vandiver, Frank E., *Their Tattered Flags.* New York, Harper & Row, 1970.

Watkins, Sam R., *Co. Aytch.* Nashville, Cumberland Presbyterian Publishing House, 1882.

White, George, *Statistics of the State of Georgia.* Savannah, W. Thomas Williams, 1849.

Wiley, Bell I., *Embattled Confederates.* New York, Bonanza Books, 1964.

Wiley, Bell I., *The Life of Johnny Reb.* Indianapolis, Bobbs-Merrill, 1943.

Wiley, Bell I., *The Life of Billy Yank.* Indianapolis, Bobbs-Merrill, 1951.

Wiley, Bell I., *They Who Fought Here.* New York, Bonanza Books, 1959.

Williford, William B., *Peachtree Street, Atlanta.* Athens, University of Georgia Press, 1962.

Federal Forces in the Campaign for Atlanta, May, 1864

Major-General William T. Sherman, Commander

ARMY OF THE CUMBERLAND

Major-General George H. Thomas, commanding

FOURTH ARMY CORPS

1. Major-General Oliver O. Howard, commanding
2. Major-General David S. Stanley, commanding

First Division
    1. Major-General D. S. Stanley, commanding
    2. Brigadier-General Nathan Kimball, commanding

Second Division
    1. Major-General John Newton, commanding
    2. Brigadier-General George D. Wagner, commanding

Third Division
    Brigadier-General Thomas J. Wood, commanding

FOURTEENTH ARMY CORPS

1. Major-General John M. Palmer, commanding
2. Brevet Major-General Jefferson C. Davis, commanding

First Division
 1. Brigadier-General Richard W. Johnson, commanding
 2. Brigadier-General John H. King, commanding
Second Division
 1. Brigadier-General Jefferson C. Davis, commanding
 2. Brigadier-General James D. Morgan, commanding
Third Division
 Brigadier-General Absolam Baird, commanding

TWENTIETH ARMY CORPS

1. Major-General Joseph Hooker, commanding
2. Major-General Henry W. Slocum, commanding

First Division
 Brigadier-General Alpheus S. Williams, commanding
Second Division
 Brigadier-General John W. Geary, commanding
Third Division
 1. Major-General Daniel Butterfield, commanding
 2. Brigadier-General William T. Ward, commanding

CAVALRY

Brigadier-General W. L. Elliott, Chief of Cavalry

First Division
 Colonel Edward M. McCook, commanding
Second Division
 Brigadier-General Kenner Garrard, commanding

ARMY OF THE TENNESSEE

1. Major-General James B. McPherson, commanding
2. Major-General Oliver O. Howard, commanding

FIFTEENTH ARMY CORPS

Major-General John A. Logan, commanding

First Division
 1. Brigadier-General Peter J. Osterhaus, commanding
 2. Brigadier-General Charles R. Woods, commanding

Second Division
1. Brigadier-General Morgan L. Smith, commanding
2. Brigadier-General J. A. J. Lightburn, commanding
3. Brigadier-General William B. Hazen, commanding

Third Division
Brigadier-General John E. Smith, commanding

Fourth Division
Brigadier-General William Harrow, commanding

SIXTEENTH ARMY CORPS

Major-General Grenville M. Dodge, commanding

Second Division
1. Brigadier-General Thomas W. Sweeny, commanding
2. Brigadier-General John M. Corse, commanding

Fourth Division
1. Brigadier-General James C. Veatch, commanding
2. Brigadier-General John W. Fuller, commanding

SEVENTEENTH ARMY CORPS

Major-General Frank P. Blair, Jr., commanding

Third Division
Brigadier-General Mortimer D. Leggett, commanding

Fourth Division
1. Brigadier-General Walter Q. Gresham, commanding
2. Brigadier-General Giles A. Smith, commanding

ARMY OF THE OHIO
TWENTY-THIRD ARMY CORPS

Major-General John M. Schofield, commanding

First Division
Brigadier-General Alvin P. Hovey, commanding

Second Division
1. Brigadier-General Henry M. Judah, commanding
2. Brigadier-General Milo S. Hascall, commanding

Third Division
Brigadier-General Jacob D. Cox, commanding

CAVALRY, ARMY OF THE OHIO

Major-General George Stoneman, commanding

> *First Division*
>   Colonel Israel T. Garrard, commanding
>   Principal Cavalry Commanders
>   Major-General George Stoneman
>   Brigadier-General Judson Kilpatrick
>   Brigadier-General Kenner Garrard
>   Brigadier-General Edward M. McCook
Estimated strength of Union army, May, 1864–100,000

Confederate Forces in the Campaign for Atlanta, May, 1864

General Joseph E. Johnston, Commander

ARMY OF TENNESSEE

Lieutenant-General William J. Hardee's Corps
  Major-General Benjamin F. Cheatham's Division
    Brigades: Maney's, Stahl's, Wright's, Vaughn's.
  Major-General W. H. T. Walker's Division
    Brigades: Mercer's, Jackson's, Gist's, Stevens'.
  Major-General Pat R. Cleburne's Division
    Brigades: Polk's, Loring's, Govan's, Granbury's.
  Major-General W. B. Bate's Division
    Brigades: Tyler's, Lewis', Finley's.

Lieutenant-General John B. Hood's Corps
  Major-General Thomas C. Hindman's Division
    Brigades: Deas', Manigault's, Tucker's, Walthall's.

Major-General C. L. Stevenson's Division
Brigades: Brown's, Cummings', Reynolds', Pettus'.
Major-General A. P. Stewart's Division
Brigades: Stovall's, Clayton's, Gibson's, Baker's.

Major-General Joseph Wheeler's Cavalry Corps
Major-General William T. Martin's Division
Brigades: Allen's, Iverson's.
Brigadier-General J. H. Kelley's Division
Brigades: Anderson's, Dibbrell's, Hannon's.
Brigadier-General W. T. C. Hume's Division
Brigades: Ashbys, Harrison's, Williams'.

ARTILLERY, Brigadier-General F. A. Shoup, commanding
Attached to Hardee's Corps under Col. M. Smith
Battalions" Haxton's, Hotchkiss', Martin's, Cobb's.
Attached to Hood's Corps under Col. B. F. Beckham
Battalions" Courtney's, Eldridge's, Johnston's.
Attached to Wheeler's Corps
Five batteries under Lt.-Col. F. W. Robertson
Reserve battalions (eight batteries): Williams', Palmer's Waddell's.

ENGINEER Troops under Major J. W. Green

Lieutenant-General Leonidas Polk's Corps (Army of Mississippi)
Major-General William W. Loring's Division
Brigades: Adam's, Featherstone's, Scott's
Major-General Samuel G. French's Division
Brigades: Ector's, Cockrell's, Sears's
Major-General Ed. C. Walthall's Division
Brigades: Quarles', Canty's, Reynolds'
Brigadier-General William H. Jackson's Cavalry Division
Brigades: Armstrong's, Ross's, Ferguson's.
Artillery brigades: Storr's, Myrick's, Preston's, Waitie's.

First Division Georgia Militia, Major General Gustavus W. Smith (after June 1)

Estimated strength of Confederate Army, May, 1864 - 64,000

Index

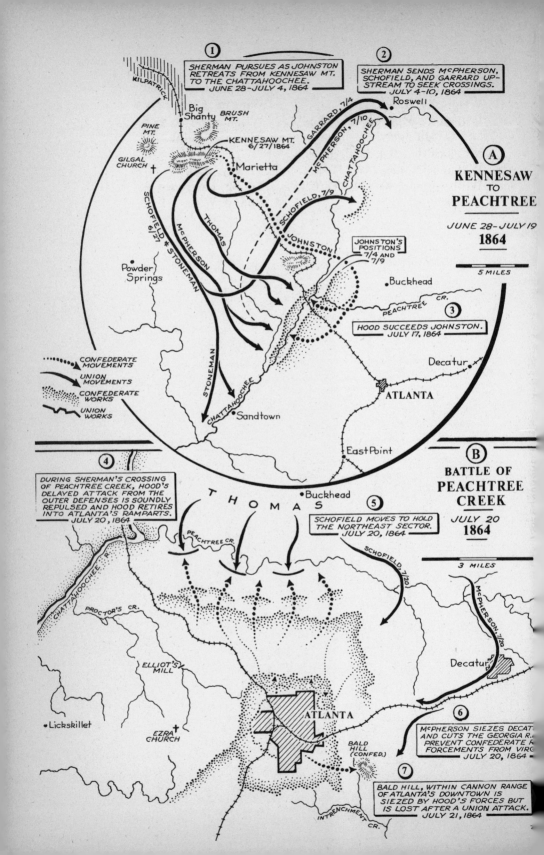

① SHERMAN PURSUES AS JOHNSTON RETREATS FROM KENNESAW MT. TO THE CHATTAHOOCHEE. *JUNE 28–JULY 4, 1864*

② SHERMAN SENDS McPHERSON, SCHOFIELD, AND GARRARD UPSTREAM TO SEEK CROSSINGS. *JULY 4–10, 1864*

Ⓐ KENNESAW TO PEACHTREE

JUNE 28–JULY 19 **1864**

5 MILES

KILPATRICK

PINE MT.

Big Shanty

BRUSH MT.

GARRARD, 7/4

Roswell

KENNESAW MT. 6/27/1864

GILGAL CHURCH ✝

McPHERSON, 7/10

CHATTAHOOCHEE

Marietta

SCHOFIELD, 7/9

SCHOFIELD 6/27

McPHERSON

THOMAS

JOHNSTON

JOHNSTON'S POSITIONS 7/4 AND 7/9

Powder Springs

STONEMAN

•Buckhead

PEACHTREE CR.

③ HOOD SUCCEEDS JOHNSTON. *JULY 17, 1864*

CONFEDERATE MOVEMENTS

UNION MOVEMENTS

CONFEDERATE WORKS

UNION WORKS

STONEMAN

Decatur•

CHATTAHOOCHEE

ATLANTA

•Sandtown

•EastPoint

④ DURING SHERMAN'S CROSSING OF PEACHTREE CREEK, HOOD'S DELAYED ATTACK FROM THE OUTER DEFENSES IS SOUNDLY REPULSED AND HOOD RETIRES INTO ATLANTA'S RAMPARTS. *JULY 20, 1864*

Ⓑ BATTLE OF PEACHTREE CREEK

JULY 20 **1864**

T H O M A S

•Buckhead

⑤ SCHOFIELD MOVES TO HOLD THE NORTHEAST SECTOR. *JULY 20, 1864*

3 MILES

PEACHTREE CR.

SCHOFIELD 7/20

CHATTAHOOCHEE R.

PROCTOR'S CR.

McPHERSON 7/20

ELLIOT'S MILL

Decatur

•Lickskillet

EZRA CHURCH ✝

ATLANTA

⑥ McPHERSON SIEZES DECAT[UR] AND CUTS THE GEORGIA R. [TO] PREVENT CONFEDERATE R[EIN]FORCEMENTS FROM VIRG[INIA] *JULY 20, 1864*

BALD HILL (CONFED.)

⑦ BALD HILL, WITHIN CANNON RANGE OF ATLANTA'S DOWNTOWN IS SIEZED BY HOOD'S FORCES BUT IS LOST AFTER A UNION ATTACK. *JULY 21, 1864*

INTRENCHMENT CR.

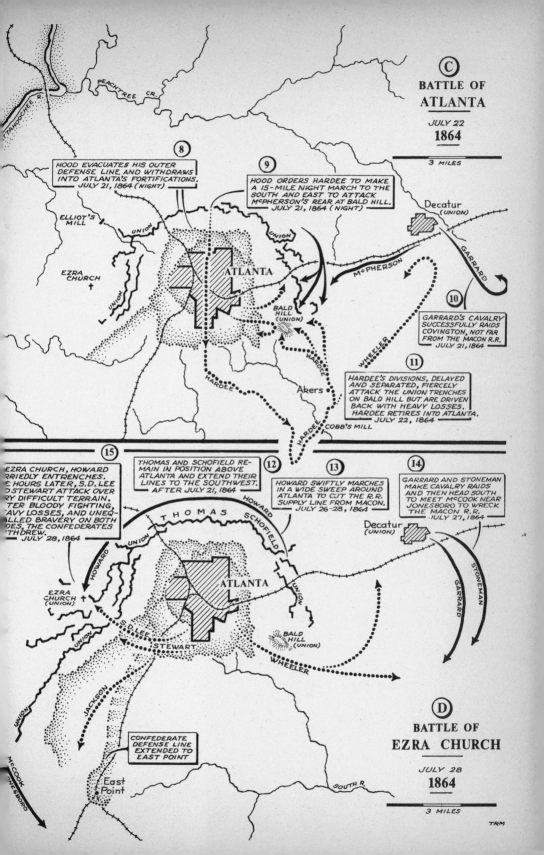

© BATTLE OF ATLANTA

JULY 22 1864

3 MILES

8 HOOD EVACUATES HIS OUTER DEFENSE LINE AND WITHDRAWS INTO ATLANTA'S FORTIFICATIONS. JULY 21, 1864 (NIGHT)

9 HOOD ORDERS HARDEE TO MAKE A 15-MILE NIGHT MARCH TO THE SOUTH AND EAST TO ATTACK McPHERSON'S REAR AT BALD HILL. JULY 21, 1864 (NIGHT)

10 GARRARD'S CAVALRY SUCCESSFULLY RAIDS COVINGTON, NOT FAR FROM THE MACON R.R. JULY 21, 1864

11 HARDEE'S DIVISIONS, DELAYED AND SEPARATED, FIERCELY ATTACK THE UNION TRENCHES ON BALD HILL BUT ARE DRIVEN BACK WITH HEAVY LOSSES. HARDEE RETIRES INTO ATLANTA. JULY 22, 1864

Decatur (UNION)

ELLIOT'S MILL

EZRA CHURCH †

ATLANTA

BALD HILL (UNION)

McPHERSON

GARRARD

WHEELER

HARDEE

Akers

Cobb's MILL

---

15 ...EZRA CHURCH, HOWARD ...RRIEDLY ENTRENCHES. ...HOURS LATER, S.D. LEE ...STEWART ATTACK OVER ...RY DIFFICULT TERRAIN. ...TER BLOODY FIGHTING, ...AVY LOSSES, AND UNEQ...LLED BRAVERY ON BOTH ...DES, THE CONFEDERATES ...THDREW. JULY 28, 1864

12 THOMAS AND SCHOFIELD REMAIN IN POSITION ABOVE ATLANTA AND EXTEND THEIR LINES TO THE SOUTHWEST. AFTER JULY 21, 1864

13 HOWARD SWIFTLY MARCHES IN A WIDE SWEEP AROUND ATLANTA TO CUT THE R.R. SUPPLY LINE FROM MACON. JULY 26-28, 1864

14 GARRARD AND STONEMAN MAKE CAVALRY RAIDS AND THEN HEAD SOUTH TO MEET McCOOK NEAR JONESBORO TO WRECK THE MACON R.R. JULY 27, 1864

THOMAS

SCHOFIELD

HOWARD

Decatur (UNION)

STONEMAN

GARRARD

EZRA CHURCH (UNION) †

ATLANTA

BALD HILL (UNION)

S.D. LEE

STEWART

WHEELER

JACKSON

CONFEDERATE DEFENSE LINE EXTENDED TO EAST POINT

East Point

McCOOK JONESBORO

SOUTH R.

Ⓓ BATTLE OF EZRA CHURCH

JULY 28 1864

3 MILES

TRM

PEACHTREE CR.

CHATTAHOOCHEE R.

UNION